Corporate Strategy and Business Planning

FRAMEWORKS

Each book in the Frameworks series is a comprehensive and concise introduction to the subject. The books are well structured and provide a step-by-step guide to essential principles. They develop a basic framework of understanding to underpin further study of core business, financial and legal subjects in the higher education curriculum.

FRAMEWORKS

Corporate Strategy and Business Planning

Roger Bennett

BA, MSc(Econ), DPhil
London Guildhall University

FINANCIAL TIMES
PITMAN PUBLISHING

FINANCIAL TIMES
MANAGEMENT

LONDON · SAN FRANCISCO
KUALA LUMPUR · JOHANNESBURG

*Financial Times Management delivers the knowledge,
skills and understanding that enable students,
managers and organisations to achieve their ambitions,
whatever their needs, wherever they are.*

London Office:
128 Long Acre, London WC2E 9AN
Tel: +44 (0)171 447 2000
Fax: +44 (0)171 240 5771
Website: www.ftmanagement.com

A Division of Financial Times Professional Limited

First published in Great Britain 1996

© Pearson Professional Limited 1996

ISBN 0 273 63416 X

British Library Cataloguing in Publication Data
A CIP catalogue record for this book can be obtained from the British Library.

10 9 8 7 6 5 4 3 2 1

Printed and bound in Great Britain by Bell and Bain Ltd, Glasgow

The Publishers' policy is to use paper manufactured from sustainable forests.

CONTENTS

NOTE: a reference in the text such as see **12** refers to numbered section 12 in that particular chapter; a reference such as see 7.**23** refers to section 23 of chapter 7.

PREFACE

Strategic management is a difficult and, at the time of writing, contentious subject with a voluminous literature and much disagreement among writers and practitioners active in the field. This book attempts to unravel the complexities of current debates on strategic processes and seeks to present and explain the concepts, techniques, frameworks and methodologies of strategic management and business planning in a useful, straightforward and understandable way. It gives the reader all the essential information needed to identify central issues in strategic management and planning and hence be able to make up his or her own mind on the best approaches to strategic problems.

The book adopts a systematic approach to the subject, outlining the 'conventional wisdom' on strategic management while recognising that the entire kaleidoscope of commercial activity has altered in recent years. It should be helpful to undergraduates completing business and/or management studies degrees, students of the major professional bodies which offer examinations in strategic management, and others who require a general survey of the subject prior to tackling the more difficult journal articles and textbooks in the area. The historical roots of strategic management are discussed; not because the propositions advanced by early writers on strategic matters are superior or necessarily correct, but because they offer concrete ideas against which alternative approaches may be assessed. Thereafter the text examines various functional strategies and planning techniques.

I am grateful to Rosalind Bailey for word-processing the manuscript, to Adrienne Crossley for research assistance, to Prentice-Hall Ltd for permission to reproduce Figure 1.1 in Chapter 1 from Igor Ansoff's book *Implementing Strategic Management*, to the professional bodies listed in Appendix 3 for their kind permission to reproduce questions on strategic management from recent examination papers, to the Ford Motor Company for permission to reproduce its mission and values statement, and to Pitman Publishing for their efficient processing of the book.

Roger Bennett

Part One

BUSINESS STRATEGY

1

THE NATURE OF STRATEGIC MANAGEMENT

1. Business strategy

Business strategy may be defined as the totality of management decisions that determine the purpose and direction of the enterprise and hence its fundamental goals, activities, and the policies it selects in order to attain its objectives. The strategies adopted will determine the internal character of the organisation, how it relates to the outside world, the range of its products, the markets in which it operates, and its intentions for the future. Strategic decisions are the most important that senior management has to take, as they commit extensive resources and have substantial consequences for the life of the organisation. Decisions made at the strategic level set precedents for lower echelons and cascade down to affect functional, divisional and departmental operations. Examples of strategic decisions include:

- matters relating to diversification, acquisitions and divestments;
- competitive strategies (see p.66) intended to maximise the firm's competitive strengths, minimise its weaknesses and establish competitive advantage in the market place;
- measures for increasing the efficiencies and effectiveness of various business functions (marketing, manufacturing, finance, etc.);
- whether to operate at the top or bottom end of the market;
- how the business is to be financed (equity versus loan capital for example);
- fundamental organisational structures and legal forms, e.g. the pattern of divisionalisation, establishment of subsidiary companies, etc.;
- whether to franchise retail outlets;
- how many workers to employ and the technology to be used in production;
- quality levels and the means for assuring that quality targets are met;
- whether to recognise trade unions and how, in general terms, employees are to be treated.

2. Levels of strategy

The determination of strategies necessitates planning (see 15.1); the specification of objectives (see 2.1); and the deployment of people, financial and physical capital to achieve those objectives. Planning usually involves the preparation of forecasts of future events and environments.

Large businesses typically devise strategies at three levels: company, division/subsidiary, and function. Company (corporate) level strategies integrate and co-ordinate all the firm's activities and are the responsibility of senior management. They define the very nature of the business, the lines of activity in which the enterprise is to be engaged, the overall allocation of physical, human and financial resources, and the firm's general long-term goals. Divisional strategies dovetail the operations of divisions or other subsidiary units into the corporate plans that result from corporate strategies. To the extent that divisions and subsidiaries are effectively self-contained businesses they need to develop competitive strategies (see 3.31) specifically relevant to their particular lines of work, to determine product offers and to utilise divisional resources. The creation of strategic business units (see 7.23) is one way of organising divisional/subsidiary strategy formulation processes.

Functional strategies are concerned with specific operational areas such as marketing, human resources and finance. Strategies relevant to each of the major business functions are considered separately in later chapters.

3. Problems of definition and vocabulary

Strategy, as it has been outlined, is a proposed series of actions intended to beat the competition. It unifies the various decisions of the organisation and determines, logically and coherently, the direction it is to follow. Unfortunately many people use the words 'strategies', 'plans', 'policies', and 'objectives' interchangeably, and what is actually meant by each of them can be unclear – especially the question of whether strategy is the means whereby an enterprise achieves an end (i.e. an attainment of the company's mission – see 2.2), or whether strategy is an end in itself. Hence, we often come across statements such as:

'our strategy is to achieve a five per cent market share within the next three years'
'our policy is to achieve a five per cent ... etc.'
'our aim is to achieve a five per cent ... etc.'
'we plan to achieve a five per cent ... etc.'

The individuals uttering these statements mean the same thing (namely the desire to increase market share) but express themselves differently. This can create enormous confusion when discussing 'strategy', which itself has several dimensions (actions, perspectives, intentions and other matters discussed in subsequent sections). In this book the word *strategy* is used to describe the direction that an organisation chooses to follow in order to fulfill its mission. Thus, a corporate strategy is (i) a broad programme for realising the requirements specified in the company's mission statement, and (ii) a sort of route map to guide the enterprise towards its desired destination.

Policies

A 'policy' is a set of ground rules and criteria to be applied when taking decisions relating to a particular function or activity. Thus, the existence of a policy establishes boundaries that restrict the scope and nature of decisions concerning a specific issue. Examples of policies are:

- internal promotion;
- only recruiting new people who possess certain levels of academic qualification;
- advertising in print rather than broadcast media;
- requiring at least three quotations for all purchases exceeding a particular value;
- not settling suppliers' invoices until the month following delivery.

Advantages to having policies are that problems arising within the area covered by a policy do not have to be analysed each and every time they appear (decisions are simply applied in accordance with company policy); precedents are established; and delegation becomes easier. Managements develop policy guidelines to facilitate the co-ordination of diverse operations and to ensure that all decisions are compatible with the overall aims of the organisation. Coherent policies avoid confusion and lead to consistency of action in the area concerned.

Objectives

Strategies frequently (but not always) lead to the specification of 'objectives'. An objective is a statement of something a business needs to accomplish in order to succeed. The more concrete are the company's strategies the easier it is to determine objectives, since the strategies selected impose constraints on policies and generally define the lines of activity the firm will pursue. Typically, objectives relate to such matters as financial returns, rates of growth, market shares, introduction of new products, efficiency improvements, cost cutting programmes, removal of competitors and so on. Objective setting is discussed more fully in Chapter 2.

Plans

Whereas strategies define the general path a business is to follow, plans state precisely how it intends its strategies to be realised. Strategy concerns ideas, creativity and grand conceptions; plans involve mundane and instrumental measures for the efficient allocation of human, material, financial and other resources within the firm. Planning can occur at strategic, divisional, functional and operational levels, and is examined in depth in Chapters 15 and 16.

4. Strategy and tactics

Tactics comprise the practical methods for implementing strategic decisions. Responsibility for tactics often lies with executives who are not themselves concerned with strategy determination. Examples of tactical management are decisions concerning:

- selection of distributors;
- use of outside consultants rather than internal staff to oversee projects;
- choice of advertising agent;
- whether to purchase or lease company vehicles, or have them on contract hire with a repurchase option;
- whether to operate an overdraft rather than (say) business development loans.

Note how a business with sound and effective strategies has a good chance of succeeding in the longer period even if it makes tactical errors. The converse is not true however.

5. Why study strategic management?

It is is sometimes suggested that because the determination of strategy is a top management function and that since, of necessity, few executives climb to very senior positions then there is little point in teaching strategic management at the university/college level or including it in the syllabuses of professional bodies which examine in the business studies field. Also, it is alleged, people who attain senior strategy making positions normally do so only after ten or fifteen years of work experience following the completion of their initial qualification. Hence, it is inappropriate to teach concepts and methods that students will not be able to apply until many years in the future.

The arguments for learning about strategic management at the beginning of a business career are powerful and numerous, and include the following:

(*i*) An appreciation of strategic management enables the student to relate his or her knowledge of particular business functions (marketing, finance, etc.) to a wider conceptual framework that embraces all aspects of a firm's activities.
(*ii*) The significance of day-to-day business operations is better understood by people who can connect the attainment of specific targets with the broader needs of the organisation. Students become able to 'see the wood from the trees' and to analyse corporate issues in an orderly and logical manner. Complex problems are dealt with methodically.
(*iii*) Creative thinking is encouraged.
(*iv*) A knowledge of the elements of strategic management means that a junior manager can contribute useful ideas to discussions concerning higher-level corporate problems.
(*v*) The study of strategic management develops the individual's analytical abilities, conceptual skills, sensitivity to the wider business environment, understanding of conventional (and not so conventional) management theories, decision-making potential, and awareness of the importance of people in facilitating the introduction of change.
(*vi*) Arguably the purpose of business education is to equip students with knowledge and competencies that will be used throughout their careers, not just during the early stages.
(*vii*) There are many interconnections between strategic management and the study of organisational behaviour, financial planning and control, employee

relations, and other core management disciplines. Strategic management is a holistic subject, uniting diverse functions. Techniques learned in other subjects are brought together.

Individuals who have learned about strategic management possess an overall awareness of how a business operates from top to bottom, and how its basic policies are determined. This is an invaluable attribute for anyone about to start a career in business management.

Paradigms in strategic management

Dictionary definitions of the word 'paradigm' equate it to an 'example' or 'model'. In the academic context, however, a paradigm is a conceptual scheme that lies at the heart of a field of study, representing basic assumptions about the nature of the discipline. The word paradigm has passed into common usage in academic management studies and is increasingly used – loosely – to describe any basic principle or concept underlying a major business decision or system. Paradigms have emerged in the field of corporate strategy in relation to views on how an organisation should be structured, the sorts of people it recruits, methods for taking management decisions, and many other areas. Paradigms represent core assumptions about the central nature of a subject, and as such affect:

- how information is interpreted;
- attitudes towards what is regarded as 'proper';
- the procedures through which decisions are taken.

As an academic subject develops (through fresh empirical research, reinterpretation of existing ideas, critical analysis of old data, investigations of anomalies that cannot be related to established theory and so on) fresh paradigms emerge. Note however that it can be extremely difficult to change an existing paradigm. New paradigms require fundamental changes in how people think about the subject, and it is not surprising, therefore, that they are frequently resisted by existing writers and thinkers in the field. Old paradigms will have been discussed, refined, clarified and extended for many years, and those committed to them have much to lose if they are abandoned. Only when it is quite obvious that a paradigm is hopelessly wrong and/or inadequate for current circumstances will it be abandoned. And even then the old paradigm might be modified and resuscitated in a new format. Thereafter, various approaches compete with others in terms of their capacity to explain phenomena and to clear up problems that other approaches cannot handle.

6. The contentious nature of strategic management

The collapse over the years of so many businesses that invested heavily in sophisticated strategy formulation and business planning procedures has led in some quarters to cynicism about the entire subject of strategic management. Note particularly how in all major industrial countries the list of the top 100 companies is liable to rapid and drastic alteration. Profitable business, arguably, is about beating current trends, spotting imminent changes in consumer sentiment, responding to environments, and certainly not about adhering to predetermined strategies. Today's commercial world is so uncertain and turbulent that it is unrealistic – so critics of corporate strategy allege – to expect the realisation of any medium to long term plan. Companies need not only to adapt to change; they should actively look for and wherever possible create change. Hence, the only credible corporate strategy is the decision not to have a strategy! Further problems and disadvantages associated with devising and adhering to corporate strategies are discussed in **11**. If strategic management is genuinely worthwhile then firms engaging in it should outperform others. Long-term revenues, net profits, earnings per share and sales volumes of these businesses should be higher than for companies that eschew strategic management.

There is no shortage of research studies attempting to establish whether this is actually the case, but the results of these investigations are inconclusive and sometimes contradictory. However, it is certainly the case that many companies that have not bothered to devise formal strategies have done better than the average for their respective industries. Problems with empirical investigation in the field of strategic management include the following:

(a) How to measure performance. The success or failure of a company can be assessed in terms of numerous variables: short-term financial profits, long-term growth in the value of assets, market share, return on capital employed, dividend distribution, etc. Which of these are relevant to particular businesses will differ over time and between industry sectors.

(b) Published company financial accounts upon which studies are based might not reveal the true positions of the companies concerned. Clever accounting is routinely used to minimise businesses' tax obligations. The book values of declared profits might not be accurate (reflecting tax considerations more than genuine worth) while data on market share and several other potentially salient factors is confidential to the firm. Estimates of the values of these variables are subject to significant error.

(c) Inaccurate responses to questions. Managements are rarely prepared to admit that their business's performances are unsatisfactory, regardless of whether they engage in corporate planning. Replies to questionnaires distributed among companies must be treated with extreme caution. Also, questionnaire respondents are likely to overemphasise the sophistication of their firms' planning procedures, as this may be deemed to reflect favourably on the calibre of the company's management overall. Responses may be unreliable, casual and the result of widely differing perceptions of what strategic management involves.

(d) Sample sizes used in surveys are necessarily limited, and may not be representative of the industry being observed.

(e) Bias among researchers, who may be setting out to 'prove' a conclusion they have already decided to make.

(f) Definition of planning and measurement of the extent of planning activities. The very word 'strategy' means different things to managers in disparate companies so that evaluating whether a business engages in 'much' or 'little' corporate strategy formulation is highly subjective. And even if a company has explicit procedures for determining strategy, the people administering them could themselves be fools.

(g) The existence or otherwise of a corporate strategy is but one of numerous variables affecting a firm's success or failure, all of which are subject to constant change. Observed performance (good or bad) depends on a myriad of interconnecting factors, making it difficult to trace out cause and effect. Presence or absence of a distinct corporate strategy within an organisation that performs well or badly does not necessarily mean that one causes the other.

ORIGINS AND DEVELOPMENT OF STRATEGIC MANAGEMENT

7. Military parallels

The Concise Oxford Dictionary defines 'strategy' in militaristic terms. Strategy, it asserts, is 'the imposition upon an enemy of a place and time and conditions for fighting preferred by oneself' and the parallels between military and business strategy are easy to observe. A business, like an army, has to determine a direction in which to travel and a plan for deploying its resources in the most effective way. It has enemies (rival firms), objectives, operates within a hostile competitive environment, and needs to defeat its adversaries.

Military strategists distinguish between the overall deployment of resources in order to secure the most favourable advantage (and hence ultimately to win a war) and the specific manoeuvres (tactics) needed to win particular battles. The latter relate to operational schemes for implementing the strategy selected. Tactics are more flexible than strategies, involve fewer resources, and can be reversed more easily.

Lessons from military strategy

Business has much to learn from military strategy, and many business issues have military parallels, for example:

- what are the factors that create strategic advantage in various environmental conditions?
- why do adversaries with inferior resources sometimes win wars?
- what degree of resource superiority is needed to guarantee success in a competitive situation?
- when should potential enemies be appeased rather than confronted?

Companies confront all these questions when dealing with rival businesses. Note moreover how the principles of military organisation: functional specialisation, chains of command, line and staff systems, unity of command, etc., are used in the management of many businesses enterprises (see the M&E volume, *Organisational Behaviour*, for an explanation of these concepts). Several contemporary theories of leadership and motivation have roots in military experience.

Among the specific lessons to be learned from military strategy are the needs:

- to outsmart the enemy and always be aware of the latter's continuing attempts to mislead its opponents;
- to gather intelligence;
- to motivate by leadership and example;
- to concentrate forces against the enemy's weakest point, and to strike when the enemy is off-guard and its forces dispersed;
- constantly to assess one's own strengths and weaknesses and those of the opposition;
- to recognise the critical importance of psychological factors (morale, commitment to attaining objectives, spreading fear and uncertainty among rivals, surprise attacks, doing the unexpected, deceiving the enemy into thinking that its forces are inferior, etc.);
- to set realistic objectives and not overstretch resources;
- to have fallback options as circumstances change;
- not to repeat losing strategies.

It is important to note that military strategy is itself a problematic subject, and military strategists themselves hold numerous opposing and contradictory viewpoints. Were military strategy not problematic, then the application of a single set of strategic principles would have guaranteed success in every war throughout the centuries. In fact, fighting conditions, personnel, alliances and military technologies vary from war to war and battle to battle, so that learning from past mistakes and the willingness to adopt fresh outlooks is just as important in military situations as in business. Generals have to identify the unique characteristics of each scenario and decide the most appropriate strategy for that particular environment.

8. The origins of long-term planning

It is unlikely that nineteenth century businesses engaged in corporate planning and strategy formulation as we know it today. Most firms were owned by families, and external environments (by current standards) were stable. As companies grew in size, however, they became hierarchical and bureaucratic; and technologies changed radically – causing businesses to attempt to forecast the future in order to plan and control their activities. The emergence in the 1920s and 1930s of large corporations using mass production, mechanisation, and the extensive division of labour created complex problems of organisation and management; notably the needs to co-ordinate individual and departmental decisions and to establish formal systems for gathering and processing internal and external business information. Budgetary control mechanisms were developed, and longer planning horizons adopted. Cost accounting became a highly valued business function.

The era of long-term planning

Following the Second World War, western countries experienced unprecedentedly high rates of economic growth and levels of employment and economic prosperity. Markets expanded; further growth was seemingly assured. Hence the problems confronting successful businesses concerned how best to invest long-term in capital equipment, how to increase output without upsetting existing administrative systems, and how to control risk and integrate operations. Long-term planning became popular among progressive enterprises. Plans were typically based on five-year sales forecasts and included objectives for capital investment, labour recruitment, intended increases in market share, etc. Note the emergence of the (then) fresh academic discipline of 'marketing' over the early post-Second World War years: sales could be manipulated, it was believed, by the application of appropriate marketing mixes, selling methods and promotional techniques. Much attention was devoted to the refinement of statistical forecasting processes.

9. Corporate strategy and strategic management

Western business environments altered dramatically during the 1960s and early 1970s: financial capital markets became more sophisticated; it was easier than ever for businesses to borrow large amounts of money; new technologies appeared; and overall business environments became liable to sudden and dramatic change. There was widespread introduction of completely new products, many of which resulted from the computing and information technology revolutions occurring at the time. Firms diversified into unfamiliar product areas. Mergers and acquisitions were numerous, and the need to manage a 'portfolio' of products emerged.

Long-term planning could not cope with these new realities. Corporate long-term planning had been appropriate perhaps for stable environments not subject to unpredictable and ferocious competition or to extensive social, political or technological change, but not for a fast-moving business world. Hence the more general concept of 'corporate strategy' was developed, embracing business planning, risk analysis, investment appraisal, statistical forecasting, acquisition and divestment, and the attempted integration of marketing with all other functions of the firm. Corporate strategy extended long-range planning to include a consideration of the options facing a business. It did not assume that past trends would continue into the future or that the firm was irrevocably committed to particular products, industry sectors or types of work.

Strategic management

Unfortunately the corporate strategy formulation and planning mechanisms established by many large businesses began to fail. International competition had intensified, western economic growth rates slowed down; new production methods based on robotics, lean production and computer integrated manufacture totally altered the business scene. Companies found it necessary to reduce their workforces by drastic amounts, to acquire and develop new skills, and generally to adopt a more flexible approach.

New firms entered previously stable markets; competitors discovered fresh ways to gain a winning edge. The entire competitive infrastructures of industries altered. Successful businesses no longer followed established rules, procedures or norms of behaviour, but rather would constantly seek to reverse the status quo and find entirely new ways of making money. It followed that strategies had to relate to fast changing environments; to recognise the inevitability of change and to develop techniques for harnessing its consequences. This more general and flexible approach became known as 'strategic management'. Its aim was to deploy all the resources of a company in an efficient and rationally determined manner in the context of turbulent environments, and hence to optimise the long-term performance of the firm. One author's account of historical evolution of strategic management is reproduced in Figure 1.1.

The main elements of strategic management include

- analysis of environments;
- planning and forecasting;
- formulation and implementation of corporate and functional strategies;
- performance monitoring and control;
- resource allocation at the company level;
- organisation design;
- management auditing and the establishment of competitive benchmarks (see 16.2);
- setting objectives;
- balancing the interests of stakeholders in the firm (see 3.3).

10. Benefits of having strategies

The increasing complexity of today's business world can make it extremely difficult to assess the opportunities open to a company, so that a realistic appraisal of its strategic position is extremely useful, to say the least. Specific advantages to having strategies include the following:

(a) Co-ordination of divisions, subsidiaries, and other component parts of the organisation is made easier. The existence of a strategy provides a focal point towards which all the firm's energies may be directed.

(b) Strategy formulation forces management to think through the possible future actions of major competitors and hence to prepare reactions to changes in competitors' behaviour.

(c) Strategies provide the business with definite criteria against which to evaluate performance.

(d) The process of formulating a strategy forces the company to analyse its position and hence identify and remedy internal weaknesses.

(e) External threats and opportunities will be identified.

(f) The company can decide in advance how it will respond to predictable changes in customer tastes and spending patterns.

(g) Speculation about possible future events and circumstances may cause the firm to discover ways of influencing the future for its own benefit.

(h) Important decisions are taken only after considering all the facts, not in chaotic short-run crisis situations.

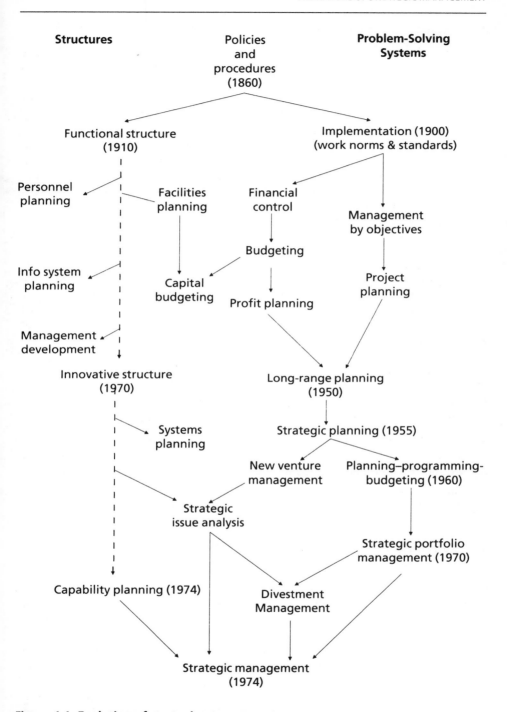

Figure 1.1 Evolution of strategic management
(reproduced from *Implementing Strategic Management* by H.I. Ansoff, by permission of the publisher Prentice Hall International)

(i) Long-term investments will be properly evaluated.

A firm with a coherent strategy should be able to deploy its resources more effectively and monitor the efficiency of its working methods and rate of growth against predetermined norms.

A not uncommon situation is that firms fail to consider strategy issues seriously until they are forced to do so following some catastrophic event (e.g. loss of a crucial contract, collapse of an expensive project, inability to match a leading competitor's prices or quality levels) which dramatically exposes the inadequacy of their strategic planning systems. Such businesses then rush to establish strategies, discovering too late the gravity of their situations and the fact that different senior managers and departments see the firm's base objectives in entirely different ways.

11. The case for not having strategies

Some businesses do not bother formulating strategies, preferring instead to respond to situations, opportunistically, as they arise. Several (valid) reasons might be advanced for this: inaccuracy of forecasts, sudden and unforeseeable changes in laws, regulations and technical and market environments, the costs and inconveniences of long-range planning, and so on. Further reasons for not having clearly formulated strategies might include:

(a) recognition of the realities of environmental turbulence and of the impossibility of planning for unforeseeable environmental change;

(b) the needs to react instantly to competitors' actions and to seize fresh opportunities as they arise;

(c) the likelihood that the circumstances pertaining to an important strategic decision are likely to be unique. Thus, there is no precedent to follow and consequently a significant probability that the decision will be wrong. Incorrect strategic decisions could result in squandering large amounts of resources. Arguably therefore it is better simply to await change and respond to it as its consequences unfold.

12. Evaluation of strategies

High profits, expanding sales, etc., do not necessarily mean that a strategy has been successful, as special factors could have caused the good results (unexpected collapse of a competitor, a sudden upsurge in demand, etc.). Equally, a strategy that fails does not have to be a bad strategy: poor performance may in some circumstances have been even worse had the strategy adopted not been pursued! The problem in the former case is that the experience of success can lead to complacency, followed by the collapse of the business as soon as the short-run influences behind the favourable outcomes begin to change.

When asked to judge the usefulness of a physical object – a machine, a cutting instrument, or a piece of office equipment for example – most people instinctively think first about its suitability for fulfilling the purpose for which it was originally intended. They ask 'What function is the item supposed to perform?' and then 'How well does it complete that function?' A road map for instance is expected to show all the alternative routes available, the presence of major obstacles (road-works, rivers, unfinished bypasses and so on), essential features of the local landscape (forests, lakes, estuaries), etc.

Business strategies and tactics should be looked at in a similar manner; they need to be instrumental and utilitarian – not works of art, and never works of fiction. Strategies should be clear, concise and coherent, and the SMART test should be satisfied, i.e. that each strategy needs to be: Specific, Measurable, Agreed, Realizable and Time-related. In assessing the usefulness of a particular strategy, management should ask itself whether:

- the firm's resources and potential are being fully and efficiently utilised;
- everyone concerned with the strategy has the same perception of what it involves and is working towards a common goal;
- the tactics needed to implement the strategy are obvious from the strategy statement;
- the strategy implies guidelines and criteria against which the company's future performance can be appraised;
- reasonable assumptions have been made about (i) the market, (ii) techno-logical and legal environments affecting the firm and (iii) the firm's ability to operate in the future as efficiently as it has in the past;
- all the possible side effects of pursuing the strategy have been considered;
- targets emerging from the strategy are realizable. There is little point in setting ridiculously optimistic objectives since this only leads to cynicism and disillusionment when they are not achieved;
- the strategy is concrete, with clear and precise specifications of the re-sources and activities needed for implementation. The resources neces-sary to achieve strategic objectives should be compared with those actually available and a statement prepared on how deficiencies will be made up.

Progress test 1

1. Define business strategy.

2. List the three levels of strategy.

3. What is a 'policy'?

4. List six examples of tactical management.

5. What are the reasons for studying strategic mangement?

6. Give six examples of problems associated with empirical investigation in the field of management.

7. List some of the reasons that have been advanced for not having business strategies.

8. What criteria might be used to evaluate the calibres of a firm's strategies?

2

OBJECTIVES

1. Nature of objectives

Objectives are statements of what management wants to achieve. The clearer the statement of a company's objectives, the more obvious are the policies necessary for their attainment. All businesses have at least two common objectives: to break even, and in the longer term to offer to owners a reasonable rate of return. Thereafter, however, different firms typically possess differing base objectives. Some seek maximisation of immediate financial returns, others want to build for the future and are willing to sacrifice short-term profits in exchange for long-term security. A firm might expand its sales through price cutting, heavy advertising, special offers and other promotions in order to dominate a market, albeit at the expense of a lower return on capital employed. In contrast, some businesses will only operate if unit returns are high, constantly switching from one market to another without ever gaining significant market share. One firm may choose low profits with almost guaranteed survival; another might aim for high returns and accept a high risk of collapse. Within these contexts, particular objectives are selected and targets set for various functional activities, preferably expressed in quantitative terms.

Objectives can be strategic, tactical or operational. Primary (strategic) object-ives might include:

- attaining a prespecified overall rate of return on capital employed within the business;
- increasing shareholders' earnings per share to a certain level:
- becoming the market leader in a particular field;
- reducing the firm's dependence on borrowed capital;
- improving industrial relations within the enterprise.

Examples of tactical objectives are as follows:

- acquiring a subsidiary in a particular country within a specific period;
- extending the firm's range of products to include a certain number of new models;
- introducing a new technology to a manufacturing process;
- revising the organisation structure of one of the firm's divisions.

Short-term and/or operational objectives might involve:

- the volume of sales over the next few quarters;

- market shares of various market segments;
- cost cutting programmes;
- plant utilisation;
- cash inflows;
- expansion of working capital;
- improvements in credit control (reducing the average period needed to collect a debt for example).

All objectives need to result from management's perceptions of the enterprise's fundamental purpose, i.e. the statement of its mission.

MISSION STATEMENTS

2. What a mission statement is

A mission statement is a declaration of an organisation's fundamental purpose: why it exists, how it sees itself, what it wishes to do, its beliefs and its long-term aspirations. Thus it is a statement of intent, combined perhaps with an outline of the basic ground rules that management has determined will govern the firm's behaviour. Normally a mission statement will define the company's core business(es) and its strategic aims and objectives – but without going into detail. Accordingly, the statement has a dual purpose: to provide guidance on how the business will operate on a day-to-day basis, and to map out its desired future situation.

The statement needs to be broad in order to accommodate (i) necessary changes in strategies resulting from altered circumstances and the emergence of fresh opportunities, and (ii) the requirements of interested parties such as shareholders, employees, functional departments, outside regulatory bodies, etc.

3. Why have a mission statement?

The discipline of preparing a mission statement compels management to clarify basic issues affecting the organisation, relate the firm's strengths and weaknesses to its competitive environment, identify external constraints, and develop a central focus for all the company's activities. Advocates of mission statements argue that only through careful analysis of a business's mission may effective strategies be devised: the more concrete the mission statement the more obvious are the strategies needed to satisfy the firm's mission. Also the possession of a mission statement affirms the organisation's long-term commitment to essential values and activities, and generates an aura of confidence and credibility to the outside world. Other advantages to having a mission statement are that it:

(a) encourages top management to adopt a 'strategic vision' derived from a coherent philosophy concerning what the business is about, where it is headed and what it needs to do to get where it wants to be;

(b) acts as a 'corporate constitution' against which the firm's behaviour (including acts with ethical and social implications) may be evaluated;

(c) presents the firm and its employees with the challenge of attaining the mission, hence facilitating the implementation of change;

(d) enables total company resources to be allocated according to the priorities explicit or implicit in the organisation's mission.

Once management has decided what the organisation exists to do it can then devise appropriate strategies and plans and is in a position to detail the corporate skills needed to attain key objectives.

4. Formulating a mission statement

To draft a mission statement the firm needs to determine each of the following issues:

(a) the scope of the business's operations and the markets it wishes to cover (geographical, customer type, mail order versus retail outlet, etc);

(b) desired market share and whether the firm intends leading or following its competitors;

(c) the degree of excellence to which the business aspires, including product quality levels, extent of customer care, staff development, etc.;

(d) whether the organisation will seek consciously to be a good employer and neighbour (and spend the money necessary for this), will not pollute the environment, and will always act in a socially responsible manner;

(e) whether the business is to operate at the top or bottom ends of its markets;

(f) the frequency with which new products and variations on existing models will be introduced;

(g) how the firm perceives the balance between the requirements of customers (price and quality policies), shareholders (dividend and profit retention policies) and employees (wages and working conditions).

A realistic and sober assessment of the organisation's competencies and capacities is required, bearing in mind:

(a) the age and calibre of the firm's plant and equipment;

(b) constraints on the feasibilities of major objectives;

(c) the successes and failures of other businesses with similar goals;

(d) how quickly the firm's environmental circumstances might change (missions are long-term commitments and should not be frequently revised, though they must never be allowed to become irrelevant or outdated).

Other factors to take into account are:

(a) the business's history and traditions (e.g. a firm with an established reputation for high quality – albeit expensive – output would not benefit from entering the bottom end of a market even if that segment offered extremely profitable opportunities);

(b) its strengths and competencies and;

(c) the extent of its resources. These include financial resources (such as cash reserves), the skills of employees, productive capacity and efficiency, control over inputs and access to channels of distribution.

Who should draft the statement?

The first draft of the document might be formulated by a single person (e.g. the chief executive or owner of the firm) and distributed for comment prior to general release, or by a committee specially convened for the purpose. Advantages to having just one or two people draft the mission statement are that:

(a) there is fast decision taking, without any need for tedious and quarrelsome committee meetings;

(b) very senior management should possess the maturity and experience necessary to prepare the statement;

(c) it is usually easier for one person to choose an appropriate wording for the paragraphs that make up a mission statement than for statements to be collectively worded by a committee. Where committees are used it is common for the committee secretary actually to write the document; so why not have the initial draft prepared by a single person in the first place?

The benefits of having a committee draft the statement are that a wider breadth of knowledge will be applied to the process, issues can be examined in depth, and all interested parties can become involved. These factors should encourage acceptance of committee decisions, for which committee members are collectively responsible. Individuals must argue their case before colleagues and arbitrary or extreme decisions are less likely. Against these potential advantages are the possibilities that participants may be short of time and not really interested in strategy issues, and might not be competent to discuss relevant matters. Also a single committee member might so confuse essentially straightforward issues that missions and strategies are never actually determined.

Whichever approach is adopted, the main steps in formulating a mission statement are as follows:

(*i*) establish current managerial attitudes and opinions regarding the company's objectives;
(*ii*) identify and assess the desirability of the external images projected by the organisation;
(*iii*) define the core businesses of the firm;
(*iv*) list the critical factors likely to determine whether the company succeeds or fails, and the barriers to success that will be experienced in various operational areas.

5. Contents of a mission statement

A mission statement should outline the firm's strategies at the highest level of generality, succinctly summing up the purpose and major intentions (to customers, shareholders, suppliers and employees) of the enterprise. The mission statement of a particular firm might contain much technical, product, market and other information and extend to several pages. Equally it may occupy a single short paragraph and emphasise just a couple of key concepts. Examples of extracts from a few actual mission statements are given below.

(a) Our mission is to be the worldwide leader in automotive and auto-related products and services as well as in newer industries such as aerospace, communications and financial services.

(b) This business will produce and sell low-cost, functional lighting systems to UK television studios and will install these whenever required.

(c) This company seeks to be the market leader in the passenger car entertainment business and will achieve this through the frequent introduction of new models of high-quality, top-end-of-the-market car radios, speakers, cassette players and related equipment.

(d) Our mission is to search for oil and produce, refine and market petroleum and petroleum products throughout the world (multi-national oil company).

(e) Our mission is to be a major factor in the worldwide movement of information (US telephone company).

(f) Our purpose is to search continuously for fresh opportunities for developing measurement control technology and constantly to improve the quality of and reliability of our products.

Everyone who works for the enterprise should support its mission. In practice, however, different managers may interpret a business's mission in entirely different ways. Thus it is essential that the mission statement be precise, explicit, neither too broad nor too narrow, and written in language that all interested employees can understand.

Sometimes a mission statement is combined with a statement of a firm's values and general guiding principles. Figure 2.1 is an excellent example of how this may be achieved.

6. Problems with mission statements

Among the many problems associated with mission statements the following are especially important:

(a) Mission statements can be so vague as to be meaningless. Imprecision invites conflicting interpretations and lack of understanding.

(b) Practical operational benefits resulting from mission statements may be difficult to identify.

(c) Departmental boundaries and interests often inhibit the adoption by all individuals and sections of a uniform view on the firm's basic goals and values.

(d) Staff changes, poor vertical communications within organisations and disinterest among employees frequently result in the majority of a firm's workers

MISSION

Ford Motor Company is a worldwide leader in automotive and automotive-related products and services as well as in newer industries such as aerospace, communications, and financial services. Our mission is to improve continually our products and services to meet our customers' needs, allowing us to prosper as a business and to provide a reasonable return for our stockholders, the owners of our business.

VALUES

How we accomplish our mission is as important as the mission itself. Fundamental to success for the Company are these basic values:

People — Our people are the source of our strength. They provide our corporate intelligence and determine our reputation and vitality. Involvement and teamwork are our core human values.

Products — Our products are the end result of our efforts, and they should be the best in serving customers worldwide. As our products are viewed, so are we viewed.

Profits — Profits are the ultimate measure of how efficiently we provide customers with the best products for their needs. Profits are required to survive and grow.

GUIDING PRINCIPLES

Quality comes first — To achieve customer satisfaction, the quality of our products and services must be our number one priority.

Customers are the focus of everything we do — Our work must be done with our customers in mind, providing better products and services than our competition.

Continuous improvement is essential to our success — We must strive for excellence in everything we do: in our products, in their safety and value — and in our services, our human relations, our competitiveness, and our profitability.

Employee involvement is our way of life — We are a team. We must treat each other with trust and respect.

Dealers and suppliers are our partners — The Company must maintain mutually beneficial relationships with dealers, suppliers, and our other business associates.

Integrity is never compromised — The conduct of our Company worldwide must be pursued in a manner that is socially responsible and commands respect for its integrity and for its positive contributions to society. Our doors are open to men and women alike without discrimination and without regard to ethnic origin or personal beliefs.

Figure 2.1 The Ford mission/values statement
(reproduced with the permission of the Ford Motor Company)

not even knowing that the company has a mission statement, let alone its contents.

(e) Companies with well-publicised mission statements sometimes take and implement decisions that are inconsistent with the contents of the statement, and in so doing bring the entire concept into disrepute. Individuals and departments might pursue their own interests independently, losing sight of the need to relate decisions to the organisation's overall mission.

(f) The common pursuit of a clearly defined mission by all employees might inhibit their creativity and responsiveness to changing environments.

(g) Arguably, today's business world is altering so rapidly and extensively that no statement of mission can be relevant for more than a very short period, so why bother drafting a mission statement? In a ferociously competitive situation the need to take decisions at odds with a company's mission might be inevitable. Blind adherence to a pre-existing mission could guarantee failure.

(h) Mission statements need to be followed up by the development of strategies and plans for their implementation. Failure to devise action plans means the effort devoted to formulating the mission will have been wasted, and can lead to cynicism and disillusion.

Too often the language of mission statements comprises hackneyed cliches assembled with little genuine concern for their relevance to the business in question. Indeed, books are available containing sample words and phrases to include in impressive looking statements. These words and phrases appear again and again in the missions of various enterprises. Examples include:

- people are our greatest asset;
- dedication to excellence and customer care;
- steadfast maintenance of values;
- thrust, imagination, innovatory potential, internationalist perspectives, building on progress, creatively harnessing change, respecting the contributions of others, inspirational pursuit of objectives, etc.

These slogans decorate a company's staff handbooks and promotional literature, but make little difference to how the business is actually managed. Note moreover how some of the world's most elaborate mission statements have been published by companies engaged in ethically dubious (even fraudulent) practices.

STRATEGIC OBJECTIVES

In a famous article 'Marketing Myopia' published in 1960 in the *Harvard Business Review*, Theodore Levitt suggested that all firms should begin their search for meaningful corporate objectives by asking themselves three fundamental questions:

What business are we in?
What business do we want to be in?
What do we have to do to get to where we want to be?

Careful analysis of the answers to these questions can help a firm formulate corporate objectives in a sensible way.

(a) What business are we in? Is a motor vehicle manufacturer in the engineering business (focusing therefore on the production of engines and car bodies); or is it in the general transport business and thus needs to be interested in all forms of transport (air, sea, electrically powered vehicles and so on) regardless of purely technical considerations? Should a stationery firm regard itself as in the paper business, or in business communication (including graphic design, photo-copying machines, electronic mail equipment, etc.) as a whole?

Failure to define a company's range of interests sufficiently widely makes it vulnerable to predatory competitors and to the adverse effects of technical change, since the obsolescence of a product or process or an alteration in a competitor's prices or product line may create enormous difficulties for the supplying firm.

(b) What business do we want to be in? Firms need to examine the profitabilities of various markets, market segments and product lines. They should ask, 'What else can we do to improve our performance?'

(c) What do we have to do to get where we want to be? This might involve product repositioning (see 9.4), structural reorganisation, new investment, and/or a change in the capital structure of the firm (see 10.2).

7. Objectives and goals

Some writers distinguish between 'objectives' and 'goals', saying that whereas objectives are quantifiable and time-related, goals are general open-ended statements of desired outcomes without quantification or specification of the periods in which they are to be achieved. Usually however the two terms are used interchangeably. Examples of quantifiable objectives are sales and market share increases, rates of return on investments and capital employed, growth of total assets, capacity utilisation levels, etc. Non-quantifiable objectives/goals might include:

- concern for employee welfare;
- putting the customer first;
- being the technological leader in the field;
- quality consciousness;
- being environmentally friendly;
- contributing to the welfare of society as a whole.

Quantifiable objectives should be SMART (i.e. Specific, Measurable, Agreed with those who must attain them, Realistic and Time-related). All objectives, quantifiable or otherwise, need to be understandable and communicated to everyone involved in their implementation, reasonable, and within the resource capability of the firm. Further desirable characteristics of an objective are that it should be compatible with other objectives at higher and/or lower levels, and sufficiently flexible to enable rapid adjustment as circumstances change. Also:

(a) Objectives should be consistent. For example, the maximisation of short-term returns usually implies the frequent switching from one market or line of activity to another and would not be consistent with an objective of attaining long-term security and steady growth.

(b) Objectives should follow a hierarchy, with the most general at the top and the most detailed and specific at the bottom (see **9**).

(c) Each objective should be accompanied by statements of:

(*i*) who is responsible for its attainment;
(*ii*) when the objective is to be achieved;
(*iii*) how the objective is to be accomplished, including a specification of the resources necessary and where and how they will be acquired.

(d) All objectives should relate directly and identifiably to the mission of the enterprise.

Objective setting should be an on-going process. Once a particular target has been achieved its effects and implications should be evaluated and new and more demanding objectives imposed. This will systematically stretch the firm's capabilities and lead to continuously improving performance in the longer run. However, targets should not be increased arbitrarily and/or in too short a period.

Acting under heavy political pressure from its local government authority a continental European water company set itself the objective of restricting its annual price increase to a maximum of three quarters of the year end rate of inflation. Senior managerial remunerations were tied to the attainment of this and other key objectives. The aims of the exercise were to curb rises in local water rates, reward cost-saving, and improve the morale of managerial personnel. What actually happened was that costs were slashed to insupportably low levels (resulting in a significant reduction in the quality of service) so as to increase managers' bonuses; managerial salaries soared (provoking extensive public criticism in the local community) and numerous allegations of false accounting began to emerge. The adverse effects of the wrongful cost cutting surfaced in subsequent years, with consequent increases in costs. Eventually the region had the highest water rates in the country.

Strategic objectives are determined by a company's board of directors in accordance with pre-established corporate strategies and the mission of the firm. Note how the objectives actually set within a business often emerge from the interplay of a number of divergent influences, corresponding to the interests of the various stakeholders (see **3.3**) in the enterprise. Stakeholders' bargaining power, access to information, knowledge of issues and interest in outcomes will help determine the weights attached to the preferred objectives of each group. Divisional and departmental managers set lower-level objectives, typically relating to operational areas and/or business functions.

8. Why have company objectives

Specification of objectives has a number of benefits:

- activities are jointly directed towards the attainment of common goals;
- criteria are established for the effective utilisation of existing resources;
- resource deficiencies are identified;
- objectives provide guidelines for the preparation of human resource plans and budgetary controls;
- individual managers' roles and task expectations are clarified.

Further advantages to having corporate objectives are that they should infuse a sense of direction among senior employees, facilitate the co-ordination of diverse activities and establish benchmarks against which actual performance may be appraised. Hence they act as motivators, guides to action, and a device for exercising managerial control. Behaviour within a company that has clearly defined objectives should be predictable, as everyone in the organisation ought to be working towards the same ends. Note moreover that every business has objectives even if these are not stated in explicit terms. Formal specification of objectives provides a means for measuring progress towards the achievement of aims – however vaguely these are defined.

Problems with setting corporate objectives are that:

- competitors may hear of them and initiate activities designed to prevent their accomplishment;
- they might impose rigidities on the firm's operations and inhibit its ability to respond immediately to changes in market trends;
- objectives can interact and multiply, resulting perhaps in managers' inabilities to cope with numerous objective-related activities.

MANAGEMENT BY OBJECTIVES

9. Hierarchy of objectives

Strategic objectives are broadly defined and connected with the long-term profitability and survival of the firm. They might be changed from time to time, but should not be altered too frequently. Hence they are normally defined over longer periods (time horizons for strategic objectives are usually measured in years rather than months or quarters) and are more comprehensive than objectives set at lower levels. Overall strategic objectives may be likened to grid references on a map, representing specific targets for where the company should be positioned at particular moments. The firm's strategies, conversely, give the directions in which the business should move in order to reach the grid references.

Strategic objectives have 'trickle-down' effects in that they predetermine the characters of lower-level objectives for divisions, subsidiaries, functions, etc. The procedure whereby managers and their subordinates jointly agree the latter's individual goals is known as the system of management by objectives (MBO).

10. Nature of MBO

The concept of MBO is not new: in Britain it has been formally applied in military administration since 1914 – and informally since long before then. MBO imposes disciplined and logical approaches to decision taking. It forces managers to consider carefully the nature of their objectives, the factors affecting attainment of objectives, possible barriers, and all the alternatives available. It is at once a method of performance appraisal and a technique of organisational planning and control. Corporate objectives are segmented into divisional and departmental targets and then into objectives for individual employees. Superiors and subordinates meet and jointly agree subordinates' job specifications and goals, preferably in quantitative terms. MBO supposedly motivates employees through involving them in the determination of objectives, and should help them develop their individual careers. Subordinates who exceed their targets will experience a sense of satisfaction in their achievements. Causes of success can be isolated, analysed, and applied elsewhere. Further advantages to MBO are as follows:

(a) Management is forced to clarify its aims and to state the criteria used in their formulation. Superiors and subordinates are obliged to communicate.

(b) Employers are compelled to consider their roles and how best to achieve their targets.

(c) MBO can be related to training and management development programmes.

(d) Subordinates' personal achievements are recognised.

(e) Performance is appraised against quantified targets, not subjective criteria.

(f) There is forced coordination of activities, between departments, between junior and senior management, and between short and long term goals.

The problems with MBO are listed below:

(a) Devising MBO programmes is extremely time consuming. A system whereby managers simply impose targets on subordinates without consultation might be more efficient.

(b) Targets might become out of date immediately following their determination.

(c) Certain targets cannot be specified numerically (advisory work for instance).

(d) Possible overemphasis on the achievement of immediate short-term goals at the expense of longer-term objectives.

(e) Difficulties created through subordinates not being given the resources or authority necessary for completion of tasks allocated to them.

Progress test 2

1. Give three examples of strategic objectives and three examples of tactical objectives.

2. What is a mission statement?

3. What factors should a company take into account when formulating its mission statement?

4. According to Theodore Levitt, all businesses need to ask themselves three fundamental questions. What are they?

5. Some writers distinguish between 'objectives' and 'goals'. What is the difference?

6. What are SMART objectives?

7. What are the advantages of management by objectives (MBO)?

3

STRATEGY FORMULATION

1. The strategy formulation process

Strategies can be formulated once the business has determined its mission (see 2.2). The first step in the process is to conduct a situation analysis to establish where the company is; the markets it is serving; its internal strengths and weaknesses and the environmental threats and opportunities that it confronts. This will involve a SWOT analysis (see 5.4), environmental scanning (see 5.13), and a management audit (see 5.1). Situation analysis assesses the conditions in each of the firm's major environments at a particular moment in time and the company's capacity to meet its objectives. It requires forecasting (see Chapter 4), the analysis of available data, and specification of the assumptions about missing information. Hopefully the analysis will indicate the direction in which the company needs to move (the markets in which it ought to be operating, whether it needs to diversify its product range, etc.) and what precisely it has to do to get to its desired destination. Then plans can be devised and implemented and the consequences observed. The results might cause the firm's management to look again at the feasibilities of its core objectives, the adequacy of its resources and the relevance of current operational activities in relation to the attainment of the company's mission.

2. Influences on strategy

A variety of factors can influence the selection of strategies, as shown in Figure 3.1. Some of the most important elements of these factors are as follows.

(a) The market situation. Small firms in markets dominated by one or two giant companies may have little scope to pursue any strategy other than simply following industry norms (on pricing or types of advertising for example) imposed by market leaders. Competitive strategy in general is discussed in 3.31.

(b) Product characteristics. Design is a key strategic variable for some businesses, whereas for firms supplying basic and relatively homogeneous products (cement, timber or raw materials for example) design need not be a major consideration. Advertising strategies (see 9.15) are crucial for firms with highly differentiated product offers; research and technical development is critical in high-tech industries.

(c) Protection of intellectual property. Fears concerning possible counterfeiting

29

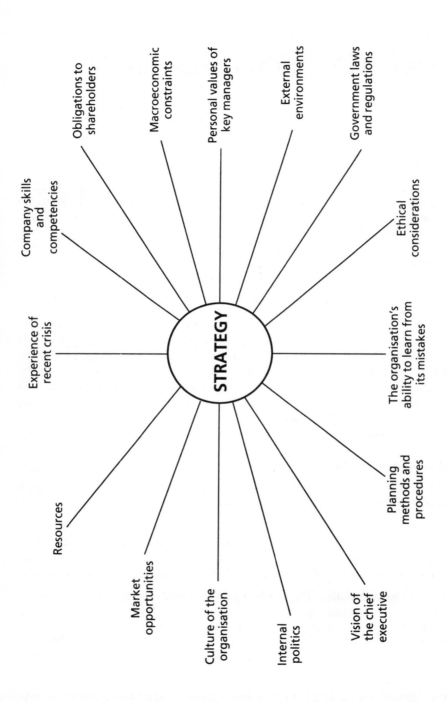

Figure 3.1 Influences on strategy

in foreign countries could cause a firm to produce all output domestically rather than engage in licensing, joint ventures or franchise deals.

(d) Access to materials and other inputs and to distribution channels. Barriers to the acquisition of inputs and/or outlets for the sale of the firm's products might result in acquisitions or mergers with other companies.

(e) The diversity of the firm's activities. Large businesses with complex and wide-ranging operations are perhaps more in need of detailed and carefully co-ordinated strategies than are small firms with a single unsophisticated product. Strategies may be just as important for a small enterprise as for a multinational corporation, but their extents and contents are likely to differ.

London Underground Ltd is a government financed organisation responsible for operating (but not extending) the tube network in the UK's capital city. It invests several hundreds of millions of pounds each year. Limits on annual investment are imposed by the government. The company needs to maintain existing rolling stock, stations, escalators, etc., and periodically to modernise equipment and systems. Experience has demonstrated that it usually pays to 'over-invest' in new projects, because any resulting short-term excess capacity will almost certainly be fully utilised (sometimes overstretched) in the longer period. Decisions on how to allocate London Underground's (generally inadequate) resources are extensively publicised and can have far-reaching political repercussions. Safety is a major issue in all investment decisions and very-long-term time horizons (50 or 60 years in many cases) have to be applied. Note however that political time horizons rarely extend beyond the next general election. This creates difficulties for the formulation of strategy. For example, the Kings Cross fire (which resulted in many deaths) led to a concentration of resources on station refurbishment, but government concerns about inflation in South East England resulted in restrictions on the rate of fare increases. Then the government insisted that large sums be spent on improving London Underground's public relations and corporate image. Note moreover how the nature and extent of the competition facing London Underground are themselves determined by government policies *vis-à-vis* bus and overground rail fares, parking restrictions in London, road improvement programmes, etc. This again makes it difficult to decide in which main areas London Underground needs to invest. It follows that the formulation and implementation of proactive business-orientated strategies are problematic – to say the least. The company's strategies are necessarily drafted in the most general of terms (eg. 'cutting costs', 'improving customer satisfaction' and similar vaguely defined objectives), leaving London Underground with little choice but to react to external influences, as they arise, in as sensible a way as possible.

(f) The number and characteristics of the stakeholders in the enterprise. This is discussed below.

An overview of the entire strategic process is given in Figure 3.2.

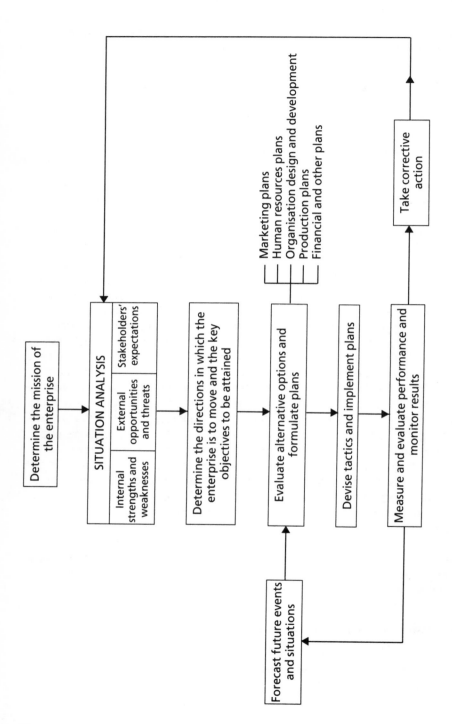

Figure 3.2 The strategic process

3. Stakeholders

Stakeholders are people or groups with a vested interest in the behaviour of a company. Examples are shareholders, various categories of employee, customers, creditors, unions and possibly local and national government. Stakeholders may or may not hold formal authority although each will have invested something in the organisation, whether this be work, finance or other resources. Accordingly, every stakeholder will expect a reward from the enterprise and normally will wish to influence how this is determined. Each major stakeholder is likely to desire a unique set of benefits from the company. Customers want low prices, high quality products and extensive guarantees and after-sales service; suppliers are concerned with allowable delivery periods, prompt settlement of invoices, etc.; employees want high wages and security of employment; shareholders demand good dividends and share price appreciation, and so on. Figure 3.3 shows the expectations of some of the major stakeholders in a typical firm.

Stakeholder theory

According to stakeholder theory, the fact that stakeholders exist and exert powerful influences on a business means that management's primary task is to balance the returns to various stakeholder groups. It follows that managers need to be politicians and diplomats. They must establish good relations with each group, develop persuasive skills, create alliances, represent one faction to others, etc. Management has to:

(a) identify the stakeholders in the organisation;

(b) determine the minimum return each stakeholder is willing to accept;

(c) seek to influence stakeholders' perceptions of the organisation (e.g. by persuading shareholders that a high dividend is not in a company's best long-term interest or convincing workers that a high wage settlement is simply not possible during the current year);

(d) identify key individuals in specific stakeholder groups and establish good relations with these people;

(e) assess the strength of each stakeholder's influence on the company's behaviour;

(f) evaluate various stakeholders' attitudes towards the business's mission, strategies, activities and, where appropriate, the need to implement change;

(g) specify which stakeholders support management's current policies and intentions and those which are against, and possible coalitions of opposing groups of stakeholders;

(h) assess what will be necessary to 'win over' antagonistic stakeholders. Note how it may be possible to increase the influence of stakeholders who are on management's side and reduce the power of others.

Shareholders are obviously one of the dominant stakeholders in a firm. If a

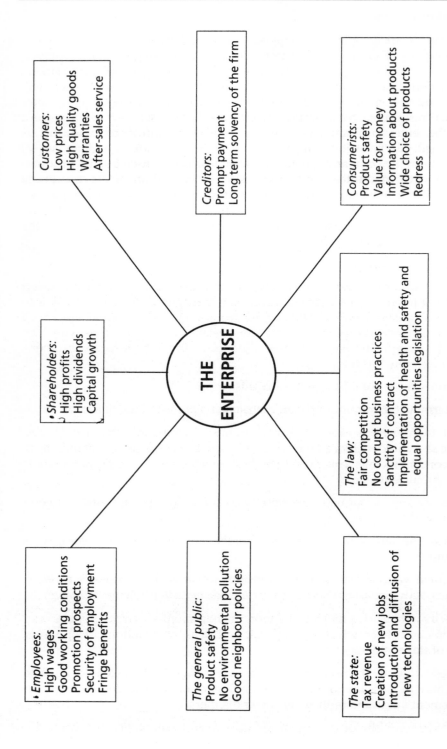

Figure 3.3 Stakeholders' expectations

majority of a company's shares are concentrated into the hands of just one or two shareholders then the views of these people will exert a major influence on the direction of the business. Wide diffusion of shareholding, conversely, usually means that individual shareholders have little impact on strategy, unless a financial crisis causes them to act *en bloc*.

Reorganisation of the National Health Service *via* the combination of a number of pairs of teaching hospitals occurred throughout Britain in the 1980s. The integration of one such pair under a single Health Authority in London presented the latter's managers with many possibilities for rationalising activities and cutting costs. Accordingly, management proposed the merger under one roof of the obstetrics departments of the two hospitals, for the following reasons:

(a) The space saved in the hospital housing the department that would have to move might enable the cancellation of an expensive lease on one of its outbuildings (occupants of which could be transferred to the space currently occupied by the obstetrics department).

(b) Total maintenance costs could be halved.

(c) Neither department had modern facilities, and these could be installed in one (but not two) of the hospitals. Operating theatres, waiting rooms, laundry equipment, delivery rooms, sanitation services, ultrasound investigatory machines and office accommodation all needed urgent attention. Cost savings consequent to amalgamation of the two departments had the potential to generate the funds necessary to meet these expenditures.

Ferocious opposition to the proposed merger arose from the threatened department's various stakeholders:

(a) Nurses complained that they would have to be rehoused. (The building housing the obstetric department also contained the Nurses Home.)

(b) Patients (predominantly pregnant women) were concerned about having to travel long distances for ante-natal treatment.

(c) Politicians in the area served by the department facing closure were unhappy because the local birth rate was predicted to increase, hence creating many disaffected female voters unable to obtain nearby obstetric appointments.

(d) Midwives pointed out that successful combination of the two departments would necessitate a reduction in patients' average length of stay in hospital, thus requiring more home visits by midwives with a consequent increase in their already very heavy workloads.

(e) Social workers were appalled at the prospect of some patients being discharged from hospital compulsorily before they felt fit to leave merely in order to keep the average length of stay in hospital below the planned level.

(f) Doctors declared that they had no confidence in the Area Health Authority actually using the money saved in consequence of the merger to improve facilities.

Consultant obstetricians in particular were annoyed by the intended reduction in patient choice and the inevitable decline in the extent of medical student teaching.

Also some members of the Board of Governors of the Area Health Authority were worried about the constantly escalating estimates of the administrative costs of implementing the merger. A special committee was set up to consider these issues, the outcome being a decision to go ahead with the merger — but only at a scale much more extensive (and costly) than anything originally envisaged.

4. Incrementalism

This is the proposition that strategies do not result from conscious once-and-for-all decisions and/or a grand master plan, but rather are formulated step-by-step via an interactive process of experimentation, probing the future, learning from experience and then 'adding-on' to existing policies. Strategy formulation proceeds cautiously and gradually, but the process is not 'illogical'. Indeed it might be the best approach to adopt in certain circumstances. Effective strategy making, so proponents of the incremental approach assert, is that which manages most efficiently this logical incrementalism. The need for incrementalism results from the complexity of the contemporary business environment and of modern management control processes, and hence the difficulty of constructing strategies based on all possible future scenarios. It is conservative and utilitarian, building on experience and continually testing the effects of small changes prior to formulating fresh strategic plans. Core activities are defended and maintained, seeking always to consolidate a sound financial base. The approach is rational in that it recognises the problematic nature of the strategy-making process and the reality of turbulent environmental change. Note moreover that the continuous reassessment and testing of current strategies helps the firm 'fine-tune' its operations and to gather useful management information. Also incrementalism might fit in with an organisation's internal politics (see 6.15) better than alternative approaches, and may assist a firm become a 'learning organisation' (see 6.13).
Criticisms of incrementalism are that:

- it can lead to narrow thinking and stifle creativity and innovation;
- it is backward looking and overly reliant on past events and experiences;
- strategy making becomes hesitant and uncertain, and the consequent strategies might not be fully understood by everyone in the organisation;
- although incrementalism might appear to develop from conscious strategic decisions, in reality it may result from political in-fighting within the organisation, compromises, and 'muddling through'.

5. Strategic vision

Conscious strategies are formed deliberately and systematically, often following set procedures and conforming to a predetermined model. Once strategic decisions are taken, actions are implemented. Sometimes however, a company's strategies emerge intuitively from the flow of its operations. Such strategies tend to be opportunistic and reactive, responding to current events and crises.

Emergent strategies develop naturally and, hopefully, should be totally relevant to current events and operations. The people who determine such strategies 'learn by doing' and tailor their decisions to the needs of the present situation.

The basic dispute is whether the best strategies emerge from systematic and detailed procedures; or from vision, opportunism and the ability to respond to events. In some businesses, the choice of strategy is heavily influenced by the views and preferences of the chief executive (who might also be the owner or a large shareholder in the firm), regardless of market opportunities and the capabilities of the enterprise. Here the approach to strategy is highly subjective and decisions may depend more on emotion than on balanced and rational criteria. Strategies are broad and innovatory, and the business can respond quickly to current events. It is undoubtedly true that many successful businesses are guided by the intuition and experience of one or a few senior executives. Equally, large numbers of companies have failed in consequence of their reliance on such an approach.

The work of Henry Mintzberg

According to Henry Mintzberg, all business strategies have at least some elements that evolve gradually over time. Otherwise, Mintzberg argues, executives seek (i) to 'manage stability', i.e. they formulate coherent plans and implement them vigorously, and (ii) to identify patterns and breaks in trends (Mintzberg 1993). Further approaches to strategy formulation identified by Mintzberg are 'entrepreneurialism', whereby all the company's strategies are determined and driven by a single strong leader, and the 'cognitive' approach which focuses on the thinking and reasoning processes that strategists apply to their work.

6. Role of the board of directors

Strategic decisions are normally taken by a business's most senior level of management, which in a limited company is the board of directors elected by shareholders to protect their interests. An efficient size for the board of a large company would appear to be somewhere between eight and twelve. If the board is too small each director will carry too heavy a workload, and the board will lack the range of skills and experience that a larger board could provide. A board with too many directors will be equally ineffective. Decision making will be slow; there might be too much debate and not enough action, experiences may overlap and efforts will be duplicated.

Part-time and full-time directors

Frequently, boards contain part-time (non-executive) as well as full-time directors. Full-time directors will be in charge of specific functions (accounts, marketing, production, etc.) and will work for the firm as executives in addition to taking strategic decisions in board meetings. Daily involvement with the firm's operations and staff gives full-time directors intimate knowledge of the organisation's structure and performance. However, because they depend on the firm for their jobs they might not be truly objective when assessing long-term company prospects. Regular contact with employees in their own functional departments could lead full-time directors to resist necessary reorganisations which cause redundancies or otherwise adversely affect their staff.

Part-time directors may not have the detailed knowledge of the company that full-timers possess, but they may be more impartial and objective when considering the company's affairs. Often, part-timers bring specific skills to the board. Part-timers might, for example, be specialist consultants, tax accountants or lawyers. Sometimes, firms themselves place representatives on the boards of other companies. It is not unusual to find major suppliers, customers, or creditors occupying seats on the board. Part-time directors have only limited time to devote to the affairs of the companies they assist. Also, a part-timer may lack positive commitment to the organisation, its aims and objectives.

The role of the board of directors is to take major decisions, not discuss technical or routine operational difficulties (which can be dealt with in committees outside the board). Thus the board will be concerned with such matters as:

- obtaining loans;
- choosing capital structures;
- discussing proposed large-scale expenditures;
- assessing risks of default by major customers (a large bad debt can bankrupt a firm);
- defining departmental structures and responsibilities;
- selecting senior managers (who are not directors);
- mergers and takeovers;
- joint ventures with other businesses.

Directors may or may not be shareholders in the firm, and this might affect their perceptions of the correct strategies for the organisation. Other factors potentially influencing directors when making strategic decisions include:

- their experience, background, skill and competence;
- personal relationships within the board;
- contacts with and the influences of middle managers;
- whether systematic procedures are applied to the strategy formulation process;
- management style and the extent of employee participation in management decisions;
- directors' personal characteristics: age, social class, etc.;
- peer group pressure and the social values of the wider society;
- how long they have served on the board.

7. Supervisory boards

In Germany, Belgium and The Netherlands there exist legal requirements compelling large companies to have two-tier boards of directors. The lower tier is an 'Executive Board', comprising managerial employees of the firm and responsible for day-to-day operational management. Above this is a 'Supervisory Board', which takes strategic decisions in relation to the overall direction of the enterprise. By law, employee representatives must sit on the Supervisory Boards of companies in these countries. The functions of Supervisory Boards include:

(a) the appointment and dismissal of executive managers and the determination of their remunerations;

(b) deciding the overall direction of the enterprise (its products, markets, major new investments, etc.);

(c) matters concerning mergers and takeovers and how the company is to be financed.

Two-tier boards were first used in Germany in the 1860s, when the German banks began making large financial investments in industry and demanded representation at board room level in order to protect their interests. The advantages claimed for having a separate Supervisory Board are that:

(a) general policy making is undertaken objectively and independently without interference from executives with vested interests in outcomes;

(b) interpersonal rivalries among lower-level managers can be ignored;

(c) employee interests may be considered in the absence of line managers who control workers;

(d) tough decisions that adversely affect senior line managers can be taken more easily.

Problems with Supervisory Boards are that:

(a) the people who determine basic strategy might be remote from the day-to-day realities of executive management;

(b) decision making is slowed down by the need to go through two separate boards for decisions on certain issues;

(c) confusions could arise between Executive and Supervisory Boards, with the decisions of each not being properly understood by the other.

8. Worker directors on supervisory boards

The essential argument for having worker directors is that since many employees devote much of their working lives to a particular firm, they are entitled, through elected representatives, to some say in how the firm is run. Against this is the fact that firms are owned by entrepreneurs and/or shareholders who put their personal capital at risk. Owners of firms may resent the imposition of worker directors who, in part, will control the owners' assets without having been elected by the owners themselves. Advantages to having worker directors on Supervisory Boards include the following:

(a) The knowledge and experience of employee representatives can be directly applied to strategic decisions without employee representatives having to argue with line managers.

(b) Matters concerning human relations are automatically elevated to the highest level of decision making within the organisation. Note that since the Supervisory Board appoints and dismisses senior managers then the latter will be highly sensitive to worker director's views, and to human relations issues generally.

(c) Arguably, the presence of employee representatives on a Supervisory Board facilitates the financial stability of the company, because worker directors' concerns for employees' continuity of employment invariably cause them to argue in favour of profit retention and the accumulation of reserves to guard against temporary economic downturns. Also, employee representatives will oppose any merger or takeover that could result in redundancies.

Problems facing worker directors are as follows:

(a) Worker directors may be patronised but effectively ignored.

(b) Reluctance of other board members to disclose confidential information to employees' representatives, in case it is passed on to union negotiators.

(c) To the extent that a worker director can influence the board's decisions, he or she will be presenting arguments as an individual and not as an employee representative as happens with collective bargaining: there is no question of negotiation occurring during board meetings.

(d) Boards of directors have to deal with a wide variety of issues, not just employee relations. Board members other than worker directors will have been selected for their knowledge of and ability to contribute to these wider discussions. Worker directors who have no experience of practical management but who wish nevertheless to express opinions on all matters could impede effective decision-making.

(e) Worker directors may not be able to relate their immediate workplace concerns with the need to adopt an overall perspective on the enterprise. Can worker directors realistically be expected to think strategically?

Nevertheless, the presence of worker directors confronts the board with new and different interpretations of issues. Also the presence on the board of employee representatives underlines senior management's commitment to employee welfare, and a climate of mutual confidence and co-operation between management and labour may emerge.

9. The chief executive

In a company the chief executive is the managing director, who may or may not also hold the chair of the board (sometimes the chair-person is a part-time non-executive director). The responsibilities of the chief executive are to:

(*i*) protect and further the interests of shareholders;
(*ii*) lead the business;
(*iii*) monitor and control the activities of lower-level managers;
(*iv*) prepare plans for submission to the board;
(*v*) deal with major customers and suppliers;
(*vi*) supervise the implementation of policies determined by the board;
(*vii*) attend to problems as they emerge;

(*viii*) co-ordinate the day-to-day operations of the firm;

(*ix*) act as a figurehead and spokesperson for the company.

Evaluation of senior managers

Directors and other senior managers are typically evaluated against the overall financial performance of the business (measured in terms of return on capital employed, share price, market share, etc.) and on their abilities as individuals to establish a strategic direction for the enterprise. Evaluation criteria might involve qualities of leadership, employee and investor relations, teambuilding, and the successful management of specific projects.

STRATEGIC ALTERNATIVES

Fundamental strategic options commonly open to firms are whether to grow or remain at a constant scale of operations, whether to integrate with other enterprises vertically (e.g. by merging with or taking over suppliers or distributors) or horizontally (via associations with firms at the same stage in the chain of production or distribution – mergers among retailers for instance), and whether to get rid of ('divest') certain divisions, subsidiaries or operations.

10. Growth strategies

Growth can be internal ('organic') and self-generated, or achieved externally via takeovers and mergers. Organic growth might involve the firm developing new products and markets, hiring more labour, or undertaking additional functions. It enables a firm to capitalise on its experience and core skills, to use its pre-existing technical knowledge and to utilise its physical capacity to the maximum extent. The company does as much as is possible for itself 'in-house'. Organic growth may be inevitable if no outside takeover opportunities are available, although if they are they might offer a vastly superior means for acquiring additional competence and/or entering unfamiliar markets. The organic growth option is only possible when a company has the financial resources to pay for the expansion (either from retained earnings, share issue or additional borrowing). Also, it requires employees who are capable of handling the growth process (see **12**) and a planned and coherent growth strategy. Organic growth gives the firm total control over the expansion process, which can proceed steadily using known and trusted employees (rather than people who come with an acquisition). There need be no duplication of activities in head office and acquired subsidiaries, and overall planning is facilitated. Operations, equipment, location of premises, etc., can be tailored to the precise requirements of the organisation rather than having to be taken as given, as occurs when a subsidiary is purchased. However, growth might take a long period, and the existing staff might not be up to the task. Financing organic growth might be difficult as it absorbs internally generated profits (at the expense of dividends to shareholders) or necessitates borrowing long-term funds.

The international subsidiaries of Penguin Books are classic examples of expansion *via* organic growth. Initially, each operation comprised a simple sales office with a basic marketing facility. As business improved, larger organisations were formed to take over the work of local distribution agents and themselves to determine marketing methods previously selected by head office in London. These subsidiaries would warehouse stock and import from the rest of the company. Eventually full-scale publishing operations were created, operating as equal partners in the worldwide organisation. Currently there are four main subsidiaries (in the USA, Canada, Australia and New Zealand) plus smaller operations in South Africa, India and Italy. Organic growth means that local profits are ploughed back into foreign subsidiaries, enabling them to develop a critical mass within the local market. And having substantial businesses in several nations allows Penguin to offset less successful operations in one country against expanding markets elsewhere. Foreign subsidiaries themselves acquire other publishing firms in appropriate circumstances (especially in the United States). Frequently Penguin will purchase hardback publishing companies, thus acquiring copyright on the latter's hardback book titles in order to be able to bring out paperback editions under the Penguin cover (or that of one of its other imprints) in subsequent years. Since 1970 Penguin has belonged to the Pearson Publishing group, currently accounting for 45 per cent of the group's sales and half its total profits.

Source: Adapted from *Royal Mail International Portfolio*, Issue 12, April 1994.

Horizontal and vertical integration

Vertical integration means mergers or takeovers among firms in the same industry but at different stages in the chain of production or distribution, e.g. by taking over distributors or suppliers of raw materials. It can enable the linking up of technically related processes, and removes the profit margins and transactions costs associated with contracts between different companies. The firm might obtain total control over sources of supply, sales outlets, etc., and may acquire the ability to deprive competitors of low cost inputs or convenient distribution systems.

Horizontal integration, conversely, is the combination of firms operating in the same industry and at the same stage of the production/distribution chain. Growth through horizontal integration has the following advantages:

(a) It enables a firm with a mediocre performance record to improve its market position.

(b) Economies of scale might become available (e.g. bulk purchasing discounts, integration of production processes, extensive application of the division of labour, etc.).

(c) The business develops a 'critical mass' which could improve its competitive position.

(d) Opportunities for diversification (see **13**) might arise from the process.

The problem with both vertical and horizontal integration is that the business is locked into a specific market which, if it collapses, leaves the company in a perilous position.

11. Reasons for growth

Numerous factors can encourage a business to expand: buoyant markets, rising consumer incomes, easy access to finance, low interest rates, receipt of extremely large orders and/or winning a lucrative public sector contract, to name but a few. Growth may lead to economies of scope (see 5.6) and experience curve benefits (see 3.28). It can be seductively attractive, indicating past success and promoting an exciting, thrusting atmosphere within the organisation. Further reasons for expansion might include:

- development of new products;
- possibilities for modifying existing products to enable the firm to enter fresh markets;
- discovery of export marketing opportunities;
- the need to secure control over supply sources or retail outlets.

12. Expansion problems

Many companies are best advised to remain at their existing size, because expansion can create administrative, operational and financial difficulties that reduce overall profitability and which ultimately might cause a business to fail. Existing smooth-running administrative systems might be disrupted. Industrial relations problems may emerge in a larger firm. Additional supplies of raw materials have to be purchased – perhaps for cash – and extra labour must be hired and paid immediately. However revenue from increased sales will not be received until some time in the future. Further potential problems are as follows:

(a) New customers may demand more credit, hence creating cash flow deficits in the short term The cost of debt collecting increases, and more bad debts are incurred.

(b) General administrative costs increase. There is extra clerical work, photocopying, more meetings, extra internal memoranda, etc.

(c) Stockholding costs rise dramatically (warehousing, stock issue procedures, pilferage, etc.).

(d) Expansion indicates to competitors that the firm is doing well. This may induce competitors to enter the market.

(e) New premises, plant and equipment and recently hired labour might not be fully utilised, so that (expensive) surplus capacity begins to appear.

An expanding business needs therefore continuously to monitor the effects of growth on profitability and periodically to measure key efficiency ratios.

Italian earth-moving equipment manufacturer FAI Spa found itself a victim of its own success when, following the development and launch of a new compact excavator, the company's rapid growth caused it to occupy an uncomfortable position between, on the one hand, the giant low-cost multinationals that enjoyed huge economies of scale and extensive business support services, and on the other, small and flexible firms able to 'make to order' and serve specialist niche markets. FAI is a well-established company (founded in 1914) which began to expand rapidly in 1979 — quadrupling sales by 1984 and, by 1990, recording a 17-fold increase on the 1978 sales figure. The firm had introduced just the right products at just the right time. It faced little competition for its articulated loader, was the first company in Italy to develop a four-wheel-drive hole-digging machine, and had become the undisputed leader in the Italian compact excavator market: its new model was ideal for work in the narrow streets and tight spaces characteristic of Italian towns and cities.

FAI's success did not go unnoticed, and competition from the UK multinational JCB, from France's Case Poclain and the US-based Caterpillar Tractor began to intensify. These firms have extensive financial and technological resources and much experience of 'seeing-off' smaller firms seeking to challenge their dominant position. Rapid expansion led to FAI purchasing (rather than manufacturing in-house) 65 per cent of its components. Stocks of components and of finished items rose alarmingly, the situation being worsened by the fact that the firm was not fully computerised so that existing manual inventory control and production planning systems became overwhelmed. Insufficient attention was devoted to marketing. FAI was a family business with a strong technical/production orientation and an organisation structure to suit. The sales department comprised three area divisions, plus an international division for foreign sales. Marketing was left to agents and distributors: the company itself did not advertise or otherwise promote its products. As sales rose it became apparent that an entirely fresh approach to marketing was necessary.

In order to address these problems FAI made a number of new managerial appointments, began the process of organisational restructuring and (importantly) entered a joint venture with Komatsu, a Japanese earth-moving equipment manufacturer anxious to enter the European market. Under the agreement each company could use the other's distribution network, and FAI obtained technical and R & D support. Cash for new capital investment and plant modernisation was obtained by a share issue to one US and two Italian banks.

Source: Adapted from Landreth, O. L., *European Corporate Strategy: Heading for 2000*, Macmillan 1992.

13. Diversification

A basic strategic decision is whether a firm should concentrate on the activities it performs (or could perform) best, to the exclusion of other lines of work; or whether it should diversify into different fields. Diversification can involve the supply of completely new products, entering fresh market segments (possibly using modified versions of existing brands), or imitating the products of other firms (subject of course to patent restrictions). Note how the latter practice can itself generate the inspiration and know-how necessary to develop completely new items. Implementation of a diversification strategy may occur via mergers and acquisitions through redeploying existing resources, or by raising external finance to pay for organic growth (see **10**).

Reasons for diversification include the following:

- Attempts to strengthen a hold on a market by controlling diverse activities connected with it, e.g. a paper manufacturer diversifying into carton making, wallpaper production, gift wrapping manufacture, etc. This is an example of 'concentric' diversification, i.e. diversification involving a common technological base and market outlets. Similar marketing methods will (normally) apply to the firm's diverse outputs.
- Loss of a traditional product or market.
- Large seasonal variations in demand for a firm's existing product.
- Overdependence on a handful of customers.
- Successful research and technical development activities resulting in new products and applications.
- Existing products reaching the ends of their life-cycles.
- Increased competition within existing markets.
- Possible synergies (see 3.**21**).
- Desires to expand the capital base of the firm.
- Potential for the joint marketing of a wide range of goods.
- Spare capacity within the firm that can be utilised via the supply of fresh products.

14. Diversification versus specialisation

The advantages to diversification are that:

(a) risks are spread over a number of disparate activities;

(b) lucrative opportunities can be exploited as they emerge so that the firm's profit earning potential is extended;

(c) profits earned in certain areas of a diversified company can be used to reinforce activities elsewhere.

However, diversification necessarily makes a company more complex and difficult to manage, and may lead to numerous operating difficulties. Invariably it requires significant changes to the firm's current organisation structure. 'Pure' diversification, i.e. that which extends the firm's activities to unrelated and unfamiliar products, is especially problematic and expensive, requiring the rapid acquisition of know-how and the deployment of large amounts of resources. New production and marketing methods have to be learned, and fresh relationships with third parties (input suppliers, agents, specialist consultancies, etc.) established. Further problems with diversification are as follows:

(a) Genuine opportunities for diversification might not be available.

(b) Faulty mechanisms for researching fresh market and/or product opportunities can lead to disastrous investment decisions that could ruin the firm.

(c) Diversification might result in the firm locking up large amounts of capital in particular technologies or administrative or distribution systems from which it cannot subsequently withdraw. Paradoxically therefore, diversification could reduce a business's flexibility and ability to cope with change.

Advantages to specialisation are that:

(a) it develops great expertise in a particular area;

(b) product specialisation can mean improved use of labour and equipment, the development of a strong corporate image based on a single product line, and a big reduction of stocks;

(c) the firm can maintain a position at the leading edge of the technology of its chosen field;

(d) large volumes of similar items will be supplied, leading perhaps to economies of scale, experience curve effects (see 3.**28**), better customer care and a higher level of product quality;

(e) it limits the range of problems that management has to confront, i.e. problems will relate to just one line of activity rather than diverse multi-market multi-product operations.

Difficulties with specialisation include the following:

(a) Outdated techniques and attitudes might be passed on from one generation of employees to the next.

(b) The strategy assumes that the firm can continue its current activities without hindrance and at peak efficiency, i.e. that no discernible threats from competitors, poor industrial relations, interruptions in supplies, or impending technological developments, exist or are likely to in the future. This might be a wholly inappropriate assumption.

(c) There is a presupposition that the more a management and employees know about something the better at it they become, which is not necessarily true.

(d) The firm could became inward looking and resistant to change. Managers might be uncritical and accept without question the prevailing status quo.

Empirical studies

Numerous empirical studies have investigated whether diversification leads to higher profitability, with conflicting conclusion. The main difficulties with empirical research in this area include the following:

(a) Studies commonly rely on intuitive research methods (interviews with chief executives, anecdotes, quotations from well-known business leaders, etc.) and not from rigorous and critical examination of statistical evidence.

(b) The extent of a firm's diversification is a matter of degree at a particular moment in time. It is likely to change from year to year, making quantitative analysis extremely difficult.

(c) Diversification is but one of a large number of factors potentially affecting a firm's profitability. It cannot be easily disentangled from other determinants of failure or success.

(d) Firms of varying levels of diversification move up and down the profitability league table with alarming speed. Companies presented by researchers as perfect models of how a business should be managed are liable to go into liquidation within a very short period from the publication of the research. All that can be said is that diversification works for some enterprises at certain times and in certain situations.

15. Acquisition strategy

Acquisitions may be in the field in which the purchaser already operates, or in an unrelated area. In the latter case the management of the acquiring company needs to be capable of handling activities and problems in lines of work not previously experienced. Acquisition strategy is critically important for a number of reasons:

(a) Failed acquisitions can ruin the entire company.

(b) The cost to the purchaser is invariably higher than the pre-bid valuation of the target, consequent to the purchaser's belief that the acquisition will improve overall group profitability.

(c) Rumours of an attempted takeover affect the current market prices of shares in the predator company as well as the takeover target.

(d) Takeovers have numerous human relations implications. A major acquisition will lead to changes in the duties and responsibilities of significant numbers of employees of both the acquired and purchasing businesses. Managers and other personnel have to adjust their perspectives and working methods.

(e) Senior management might become totally preoccupied with the implementation of an acquisition, resulting in the neglect of other duties.

(f) The publicity surrounding a takeover can enhance or greatly damage a company's image.

Motives for acquisitions include:

(a) removal of competitors;

(b) reduction of the likelihood of company failure through spreading risks over a wider range of activities;

(c) the desire to acquire businesses already trading in certain markets and/or possessing certain specialist employees and equipment;

(d) obtaining patents, licences and other intellectual property;

(e) economies of scale possibly made available through more extensive operations;

(f) acquisition of land, buildings, and other fixed assets that can be profitably sold off;

(g) the ability to control supplies of raw materials;

(h) expert use of resources, e.g. if one firm possesses large amounts of land and buildings and the other is exceptionally skilled in property management;

(i) desire to become involved with new technologies and management methods, particularly in high risk industries;

(j) the potential ability of a larger organisation to influence local and national government;

(k) tax considerations, e.g. the carryover of past trading losses into the merged business;

(l) additional financial and other resources, including greater capacity to undertake research;

(m) fullest use of production capacity and idle cash, and an increase in the ability to borrow funds.

16. Selecting acquisition targets

A number of factors need to be taken into account when choosing takeover targets, such as the following:

(a) The target's long-term prospects. A company experiencing short-run financial problems will pay poor dividends and in consequence the market price of its shares will fall. Yet the business might be fundamentally sound and thus represent a lucrative takeover opportunity.

(b) The calibre of the target's management team, and whether existing management will recommend shareholders to accept or reject a takeover bid.

(c) The number of shareholders in the target company. A business with just a few dominant shareholders who are anxious to sell their shares will be easy to take over, and vice versa.

(d) Share price of the target.

(e) The value of the target company's property and other assets (including its brands, goodwill and trademarks).

17. Valuation of takeover targets

Public companies with freely traded shares have a market value given by the current share price. However the market share price quoted could be an unreliable indicator of the true worth of the business. Random market fluctuations can distort market values, and the company may have lucrative investment plans and projects not known to the general public. Also, a company that has recently raised additional capital through share issue may have done so at low prices in order to attract investors. Thus it is necessary to have a close look at the target's actual assets. Unfortunately, balance sheet figures do not necessarily provide accurate valuations of the objective worth of company's assets. Balance sheets are prepared according to standard accounting conventions in relation to depreciation rates, historical costs versus market values, stock valuations, the treatment of intangibles (ownership of intellectual property), etc. In valuing a company it is necessary therefore to prepare what is in effect a 'Doomsday Book' of all the company's assets, liabilities, and current and intended activities.

Tax losses can crucially affect the takeover value of the business, since current trading losses can normally be carried forward and offset against future profits – provided these profits relate to the same trade. This is not the case, however, if the nature of the business changes substantially following the takeover. Past trading losses can represent a considerable 'hidden asset' within a target firm.

18. Problems with acquisitions

The acquiring company has to accept the basic characteristics of the acquired firm as they stand. In other words the latter's location, contractual commitments, physical conditions, etc. are predetermined, in contrast with a completely new start-up whereby the business selects the most convenient site, erects purpose-built premises, and so on. Further problems with takeovers are as follows:

(a) Market conditions might suddenly change following a costly acquisition.

(b) New competitors may emerge (attracted perhaps by the publicity surrounding the initial merger or takeover).

(c) Resignations of key employees in the acquired business might occur.

(d) Control difficulties created by having to manage a large and diverse organisation could arise. Note especially the need to collect, analyse and interpret enormous amounts of management information data.

(e) The activities, working methods and organisation structures of the amalgamating firms may turn out to be fundamentally incompatible. Note that it is not necessarily the case that an acquired firm has to be integrated into the parent's organisation system. Indeed it may be far better to leave the acquisition as an autonomous profit earning unit.

(f) Even if the smaller of the merging businesses is more efficient than the larger, it may have little or no influence on decisions taken by the amalgamated company after the merger.

(g) A firm which takes over another and which pays for it in cash may subsequently become extremely short of liquid assets, whereas a company paying for another business in shares (e.g. two shares of the bidding company in return for one share in the target of the attempted turnover) could experience share dilution (i.e. reductions in earnings per share), to the annoyance of existing shareholders.

(h) Senior managers in one of the firms taken over might not be worth

49

employing in the larger company hence involving the new business in dismissals and consequent employee compensation claims.

(i) Increased size can lead to diseconomies of scale rather than improved efficiency: bureaucracy increases and internal communications become difficult.

Conditions for success

Successful implementation of an acquisition strategy requires the following:

(a) Clear specification of acquisition objectives.

(b) Establishment of meaningful criteria for the choice of the firm(s) to be acquired.

(c) Development of sound search procedures for finding suitable target businesses. This will involve the screening of candidate firms: analysis and investigation of targets; propositioning and negotiation with the managements of suitable companies. Note that the search should not be restricted to businesses that happen to be for sale; reluctant takeover targets should also be considered.

(d) Careful planning of the entire process, using expert outside assistance where appropriate. The characteristics, products, management styles, finances and business systems of target firms all need to be examined.

19. Strategies for avoiding being taken over

Strategies available to companies with freely traded share capitals that wish to avoid being taken over are as follows.

1. Making the company unattractive as a takeover target

The problem here is that such actions will themselves damage the company in the longer term. Nevertheless, desperate managements do sometimes resort to this tactic. Specific devices include the following:

(a) Locking the firm into long-term supply and customer contracts which the target knows will not appeal to the predator business.

(b) Borrowing extensively and then rearranging the company's finances so as to be able, in effect, to use the money to pay higher dividends to current shareholders. Share prices will rise temporarily and, if the takeover goes through, the predator will be left with a large burden of high interest debt.

(c) Selling land, buildings and other fixed assets and using the proceeds to pay higher dividends to existing shareholders. Increased dividends might temporarily raise the market price of the company's shares, thus making it more expensive for a predator to buy a majority interest. The method is particularly appropriate if the motivation behind the attempted acquisition is the predator's desire to obtain the fixed assets of the target firm.

2. Direct action

Directors of the target company might circularise shareholders and advise them not to accept the outsider's bid. If the predator has offered to pay for target company shares using shares in the predator's company the target's circular may argue that acceptance would be against shareholders' interests, because dividends on the predator's shares could deteriorate following the acquisition. This would be due to (i) share dilution (see 10.5), and (ii) declining overall profitability caused by the predator's inability to manage the target firm properly (through lack of experience of the industry, inadequate technical knowledge, limited access to financial resources, etc.).

The existing management will enumerate its achievements – especially the company's long-run growth, its commanding positions in various markets, its success in developing new products and so on – and will explain future prospects under the existing management in an attractive manner. Other direct measures to prevent a takeover include the following:

(a) Encouraging a friendly outside business – quite unconnected with the predator – to purchase a large number of shares in the target company, thus making it more difficult for the predator to acquire a controlling interest. Such friendly outsiders are sometimes referred to as 'White Knight' companies.

The deal may involve an exchange of shares in the White Knight for shares in the target, or a straight cash offer to the target's shareholders – vigorously endorsed by the existing management. Equally the target might issue a large block of freshly created shares direct to the White Knight, provided this is permissible under the target's articles of association. Inevitably, however, share dilution will result in the latter situation, and current shareholders might object to this occurring.

(b) Merging with another company which is more acceptable to the existing management. Of course, the predator might then attempt to take over the entire newly merged conglomeration, but this will be more difficult in consequence of the increased expenditure needed to buy a majority stake in the larger business. This practice is referred to as 'defensive merger'.

3. Issue of 'A' shares

Non-voting 'A' shares are unattractive to investors (since their prices do not rise during takeover attempts) and thus can only be issued cheaply. And even then there could be few purchasers. Nevertheless, 'A' shares sold at a discount do enable managements to raise additional equity with no possibility of their losing control. Note that the large institutional investors will not normally consider purchasing 'A' shares, which further reduces their marketability.

Resistance to a takeover typically requires the engagement of specialist advisers: lawyers, public relations experts, merchant banks, etc. Factors affecting whether a takeover bid will succeed include the attitudes of the shareholders in both companies, national rules on competition and the administration of attempted takeovers, and – in countries where this is relevant – decisions of the firms' Works

Councils The latter are compulsory in certain nations. They comprise equal numbers of management and employee representatives and are legally required to discuss major company plans, including intended acquisitions, large-scale physical investments and divestments. The attitudes of worker directors on company boards are also crucial.

One of the most bitterly contested takeovers battles of the last quarter century was the attempt by the Hanson Trust to purchase the Imperial Group in 1985/86. Imperial had announced its intention to merge with United Biscuits, amid a blaze of publicity which, it could be argued, triggered Hanson's interest and caused it to conclude that Imperial was grossly undervalued and as such an extremely attractive takeover proposition. Imperial had a widely diversified portfolio of products, ranging from tobacco, food and alcoholic drinks, through to convenience snacks, hotels and restaurants. However its financial performance was poor compared to rival businesses. United Biscuit's results were better, but nothing out of the ordinary. Nevertheless, the merged company (UB shareholders were to receive five shares in Imperial for every four existing UB shares) would have much to offer, with sales exceeding £6 billion annually and a wealth of internationally famous brand names.

Hanson's bid was announced on 6 December 1985, immediately following the publication of its previous year's highly successful financial results. The offer document alleged incompetence on the part of Imperial's management, overpayment for acquisitions and the sale of Imperial's assests at too low a price. It outlined Hanson's impressive record of increasing the profitabilities of its acquisitions and stated that, although Imperial would be broken up into decentralised units, there were no plans to shut down or sell off any of Imperial's current operations.

Imperial's immediate response was to issue press releases claiming, *inter-alia*, that:

- the bid was totally inadequate and had no commercial logic;
- Hanson had no skills in the field of consumer products;
- shareholders would be deprived of votes because the offer involved part payment in (non-voting) convertible debentures;
- Hanson was deliberately misleading shareholders *vis-à-vis* Imperial's management record.

Next Imperial looked for a white knight but could not find a suitable candidate. Hanson then improved its offer, only to be confronted by a superior offer for Imperial by United Biscuits, the firm with which Imperial was initially intending to merge! Hanson desisted from increasing its offer any further, believing that UB was bluffing and could not possibly raise the cash needed to finance the bid. Simultaneously Hanson issued a document alleging that:

- UB's management had no experience of major acquisitions;
- the market price of UB shares would collapse;
- both Imperial and UB lacked 'discipline at the top', had managements with little sense of purpose, were bureaucratic, and lacked credibility.

Imperial now published advertisements stating that the Hanson Trust could not possibly sustain its past rate of expansion, would carry an enormous amount of debt after the takeover, and that Hanson's offer was of 'questionable value'. In response Hanson issued writs against Imperial, each of its directors and its advertising agency claiming damages for malicious falsehood and defamation. At the same time it launched yet another advertising campaign aimed at Imperial shareholders.

20. Financing acquisitions

Takeovers can be paid for using cash; shares or debentures in the predator company; or a mixture of these.

Payment in securities

The main advantage to target shareholders of being paid in securities rather than in cash is that no capital gains tax is payable on securities, whereas acceptance of cash represents a taxable 'disposable income' for capital gains purposes. The securities offered could include ordinary or preference shares, fixed interest stock, or convertibles (see 10.5).

This type of bid can be 'underwritten' through the predator arranging for a third party (a merchant bank for example) to guarantee that it will buy at a certain minimum price the shares distributed to target shareholders. In consequence, those who accept the predator's offer are assured they can quickly convert the shares into cash (albeit at an underwritten price somewhat below their face value). The third party financier charges the predator a fee for this facility.

To enhance the appeal of a 'shares for shares' offer the predator needs to convince target shareholders that shares in the predator company have genuine value, particularly if the offer is not underwritten in the manner previously described. This will be difficult if the predator's dividend payment record is poor, and/or the predator has few tangible assets. Convertibles, straight debentures, or a cash plus preference shares offer might carry greater credibility in these circumstances, especially if the share capital of the resulting larger business will be severely diluted in consequence of the acquisition.

Payment in cash

Predators that do not possess the cash needed to pay for intended acquisitions must borrow the necessary funds. Sometimes the loan is secured, in effect, against the assets of the target business. Such acquisitions are commonly referred to as 'leverage buyouts'.

Theoretically, a tiny business could purchase a huge corporation in this way. However, the predator firm will have to convince the third party lender of its competence and determination to see the deal through, of its integrity, and of its overall managerial experience and ability. What happens if the takeover fails and the borrowing predator collapses without repaying the money? The assets against which the loan were provisionally secured will not be available, and the predator's own assets may be insufficient to cover the loan!

The leverage buyout and the junk bond

Security offered for these purposes may be in the form of debenture stock issued against the predator's (currently inadequate) assets. Such debentures are often called 'junk bonds' because at the time they are issued they are not backed by assets sufficient to cover the loan. The term 'junk bond' is now a generic. It is used to describe any loan stock secured against dubious or intangible assets. Indeed, junk bonds have sometimes been secured against other junk bonds!

In fact, attempted leverage buyouts can make a profit even if the bids are unsuccessful. Suppose for example that the predator launches a hostile takeover bid and buys up (say) 20 per cent of the target's voting share capital. Assume that the bid is opposed by the target's board of directors, and that current major shareholders do their best to resist the takeover. The predator might now offer to sell its 20 per cent stake in the company back to these shareholders, but at a significantly higher price – in return for a promise by the predator to abandon the attempted takeover. Big profits have been made in this way. It is sometimes referred to as 'greenmail'.

Reluctant bids

All a predator requires is a 51 per cent stake in a target firm. For quoted companies, however, Stock Exchange rules require that once a bidder has acquired a 30 per cent shareholding he or she must offer to buy all remaining shares in the company at a price not lower than the highest price paid during the previous 12 months. Bids which result from this requirement are sometimes called 'reluctant bids'.

21. Synergy

A major reason for embarking on company mergers and acquisitions is the pursuit of synergy within the newly combined organisation. Synergy occurs when two or more activities or processes complement each other to the extent that, when undertaken in unison, the total output is significantly greater than when they are done individually. The idea is neatly summarised by the phrase 'making two plus two equal five'.

Synergy can occur between people, between sections of a firm, or even between separate businesses, for the following reasons:

(a) Group members may spur each other on towards the achievement of a common objective.

(b) Collective effort can stimulate innovation, effort and efficiency and generally bolster group morale.

(c) There is cross-fertilisation of ideas. Individual knowledge, talents and experience are combined.

(d) Management competencies can be carried forward from one group of activities to another.

Examples of synergy occur where:

(a) advertising and public relations undertaken for one product will benefit others;

(b) the results of research into one area of operations may be profitably used elsewhere;

(c) spare capacity can be reduced by the integration of production processes;

(d) the same distribution channel can be used for marketing several products;

(e) it is cheaper and more efficient to undertake two activities together rather than one after another;

(f) large discounts are available for bulk purchases;

(g) brand identities reinforce each other.

Joint activities by two or more businesses might:

(a) develop products and markets more quickly and inexpensively;

(b) improve the organisation's overall cash flow position through using money generated in some areas to finance others that are currently short of cash;

(c) enhance the collective corporate image of the firms involved.

Consequences of synergy include possibilities for lower selling prices, improved market share, higher returns on research and technical development, increased profitability and a greater return on capital employed.

DIVESTMENT AND TURNAROUND STRATEGIES

22. Divestment

This involves the sale or closure of operating units (usually subsidiaries or divisions) in order to rationalise activities, concentrate resources in particular areas, or downsize the organisation (though note how downsizing can occur via reductions in the size of the labour force rather than shutting down whole units). Reasons for divestment include:

(a) financial losses attributable to specific operations;

(b) the decision to focus all the firm's attention on its core businesses, at the expense of peripheral activities. This might result from perceptions that resources will be better used if they are concentrated in particular areas and/or that management is not able to control a widely diversified enterprise;

(c) the need to raise large amounts of cash at short notice;

(d) government insistence that a firm be broken up in order not to contravene state monopoly legislation;

(e) predicted technological changes that will cause products to become outdated;

(f) collapse of a market;

(g) failure of a merger or acquisition;

(h) a division absorbing more of the firm's resources than management is willing to provide.

Note how the selection of a unit for divestment offers management a convenient scapegoat that can be blamed for all the company's past problems.

Divestment strategies require careful attention to human resource planning within the organisation (redundancy consultations, redeployment, etc.), public relations, and the manners in which assets are discarded.

23. Management buy-outs (MBOs)

Rationalisation of a company may result in it discarding duplicated services or divisions which, although they are profitable, do not fit in with the enterprise's overall corporate plan. The term 'management buy-out' is used to describe the situation that occurs when a business's existing owners completely withdraw from involvement in its management and arrange for its assets to be taken over by a new team, consisting primarily of employees of the firm – though perhaps with a new chief executive. Accordingly the parent firm offers the surplus assets for sale (typically at a lower price than otherwise would be the case) to a management team drawn mainly from the current staff. This team approaches external financiers who, very often, are pleased to advance the necessary funds because management buy-outs carry less risk than conventional investments. The business is already operational. It has markets, established products, customers, goodwill, a sound organisation, skilled and experienced workers, and a well developed distribution system. The new firm's opportunities for future development and improved efficiency can be clearly identified, and since its staff depend on the continuing existence of the business for their livelihoods they will want the buy-out to prosper.

Banks and venture capital companies sometimes offer special loan packages for management buy-outs. Note however that MBOs do not normally require managers to buy the division or subsidiary entirely from their own pockets; indeed, this is impossible in cases where the assets are worth tens of millions of pounds. Nevertheless, the managers involved are expected to make substantial personal financial investments in the new enterprise in order to demonstrate their commitment to the venture.

Several operational benefits accrue to MBOs.

(a) Management is free to introduce generous performance-related incentive systems. The achievement of stiff targets can be rewarded with salary levels beyond the reach of employees of a larger firm.

(b) Inefficiencies previously tolerated will be ruthlessly exposed. Those who manage the business now have a direct personal investment in the success of its operations.

(c) The new firm can concentrate exclusively on what it does best, without concern for peripheral parent company activities.

(d) Lenders might provide the specialist top management expertise (via a non-executive seat on the board for example) that could be lacking in the MBO team.

24. Problems with MBOs

Over-optimism is perhaps the major difficulty confronting an MBO. Growth potential is overestimated; excessive new investment occurs. Other problems include the following:

(a) Determining a purchase price for the new business. A common way of dealing with this is to put the subsidiary or division up for sale and then offer its existing management the opportunity to match the highest bid.

(b) Deciding suitable selling prices for the MBO's product(s) once its inputs, assembly, manufacturing, distribution and ancillary services are its own responsibility and not that of the parent company. Previously, certain costs would have been shared with other divisions or subsidiaries.

(c) Since a substantial part of an MBO's initial capital typically consists of loan finance it will face heavy interest charges during early trading. MBOs are thus exceptionally vulnerable to unanticipated interest rate increases. Thus, MBOs are rarely suitable for highly geared, rapidly growing operations with high and expanding demands for working capital.

(d) Possible weaknesses in the management team. Technical ability relevant to the management of a division may not be sufficient to master the strategic complexities of running a complete business.

(e) Inherited plant and equipment might need early replacement, draining the MBO of cash. Not surprisingly, MBOs are less common in capital intensive industries than in industries where few fixed assets are required.

(f) Conflicts of interest and employee unrest may develop as early hopes are not realised.

25. Management buy-ins

With a management buy-out, control and administration of the company remain with the existing management. This differs from the management buy-in, which involves bringing in an outside team of managers to participate in the day-to-day running of the firm. Frequently the equity needed to persuade existing management to accept the buy-in is provided by a venture capital company. This finance will only be available to a management team that possesses a successful track record in firms similar to the one it is seeking to enter, and which seems able to strike a satisfactory working relationship with the company's existing administration. Businesses that are underperforming for want of a stronger and more experienced management are prime targets for buy-in attempts. Problems associated with management buy-ins include the following:

(a) Potential disagreements and conflicts between the current management and the outside team.

(b) The buy-in management team's lack of detailed knowledge of the company's day-to-day operations.

(c) Resentments by junior employees of the buy-in firm against the imposition by outsiders of new and unfamiliar working methods.

Also, companies seeking buy-in capital might not reveal the true extent of their problems, and then expect entrant managers instantly to cure intractible long-standing difficulties.

A large UK holding company decided that its non-ferrous components subsidiary did not fit in with its long-term corporate strategy. Numerous external components suppliers were able to offer comparable quality levels and price, and the subsidiary's sales to external customers over the previous 12 months had halved. However, the subsidiary continued to have value: worldwide demand for its products was increasing; new technologies could be introduced quickly and at low cost; and the unit had a strong management team. The holding company did not want simply to close its subsidiary as it had expensive lease obligations. Accordingly, a management buy-out was arranged, involving:

- the parent lending a substantial sum to the new business at market interest rates to enable it to purchase stock. Repayments were made on a monthly basis;
- a share issue organised by the holding company's bank.

The buy-out was a great success. It inherited 'blue chip' customers and reliable suppliers from its previous owner and soon established a diverse customer base.

---

26. Turnaround strategies

An ailing business, if it is to survive, must implement strategies and policies designed to restructure the organisation, move the company towards fresh objectives and thereafter consolidate the company's new position relative to other firms. The aim is not only to halt the decline, but also to generate the means for a substantial recovery. Initially however, crisis management is required.

Crisis management

A business in difficulties needs an organisation system quite different to that appropriate for a prosperous and expanding firm. Rigid and narrowly defined accountability structures, instant decision taking and strict cost control are required.

The firm should draw up an emergency cash flow projection indicating priority payments and which creditors can in the short term be ignored. Slow moving stocks should be sold at a discount in order to raise cash; surplus plant and equipment should be offered for sale at knock-down prices. The aim is to complete current orders at minimum cost yet leave the firm able to clear its debts. Additional orders should not be accepted if there is little or no chance of the work being finished. Credit sales cannot normally be allowed. Debtors should be informed of the firm's problems and asked to pay their bills, perhaps at a discount for immediate settlement. If credit orders have already been accepted it may be better to cancel these and compensate the customer than to go ahead with the work.

Sources of financial difficulty must be investigated. Is the firm overtrading? Are there bottlenecks in flows of production? How frequent are interruptions in supplies? Has the firm purchased technically complicated equipment that its staff are unable to use? A cost cutting programme must be initiated. All capital expenditure plans should be frozen and all budgets put onto a zero-base allocation system (see 18.16). Essential new assets should be hired and not purchased.

The European food business is changing at a faster rate today than at any time in its recorded history. This results from intense competition following the completion of the single European market, radical changes in the technology of food processing, and the widespread consumption of convenience foods. Major rationalisations of food manufacturers are occurring. Hand crafted foodstuffs are giving way to mass production, with a handful of key players dominating the pan-European market. Campbell Biscuits (a subsidiary of Campbell Soup) seemed in the early 1990s to be falling victim to these forces: with profitability, investment and product development in decline. The catalyst for change came with the failure of one of Campbell Biscuit's (CB's) foreign subsidiaries, leading to heavy financial losses and the imminent prospect of collapse. A rescue plan was put together within 60 days, calling for:

- replacement of existing diverse production units with a few state-of-the art manufacturing plants;
- creation of a 'lean' organisation structure backed up by the latest decision support systems;
- elimination of a number of senior management positions;
- an extensive cost cutting programme and a reduction in overheads of at least 15 per cent.

The firm's administrative, procurement and logistics activities were centralised; a single manager was appointed to take control of all production units worldwide (outranking plant managers in individual countries); the number of outside suppliers to the company was halved. Five brands were consolidated into one pan-European product with a single form of packaging (replacing 12 previous package designs), and just one advertising agency was appointed to replace the five that had been used in the past. A standardised pan-European advertising and PR campaign was then implemented, with identical TV and press advertisements being used in all European countries.

Profits rose by 55 per cent and share price by 70 per cent over the two years following the changes. CB attributes this success to the fact that change was introduced quickly (much of the work was completed within 60 days) and dramatically – many long-serving CB managers chose to leave the company as it was restructured.

Source: Adapted from Moerk, E.S., 'Managing Change in Manufacturing Organisations', in Foster, T.R.V. (ed.) *Winning Ways for Business in Europe*, Kogan Page 1993.

Sale and leaseback

Failing businesses that own their premises can inject capital through 'sale and leaseback' arrangements. The firm sells its land and buildings for a capital sum equal to just below their market value, but makes the transaction contingent on the purchaser formally agreeing to lease the land and buildings back to the selling firm for a certain period at a predetermined rent. Such a deal has costs – there are legal expenses and valuation fees, capital gains tax (possibly) on the disposal, the rent charged may be relatively high, and the firm loses its security of tenure.

Predicting failure

Crisis management deals with immediate short-run problems. Thereafter, it is necessary to establish a firm foundation for long-term survival, which means the identification and removal of the fundamental difficulties causing the lack of success. These might involve ineffectual management, poor strategy formulation procedures, lack of financial control, inefficient management information systems, etc. The need for a turnaround strategy may become evident from decreasing profitability, declining sales and/or market share, increased borrowing, a fall in the rate of return on capital employed, or a worsening of other key performance indicators. Further signs of trouble could include:

- major disagreements among senior managers regarding the direction of the enterprise;
- management succession problems;
- a range of products, activities and ventures that is far too diverse to be controlled efficiently, implying the needs for divestment and concentration on core businesses.

PORTFOLIO ANALYSIS

27. Nature of product portfolio analysis

Firms with a range of products need criteria for determining which products should receive most resources and which should be abandoned. Typically a multi-product business will possess three types of product: 'safe' products which generate a steady cash inflow; 'developing' products which are increasing their market shares in expanding markets; and 'declining' products which contribute little to company profits, say because they are at the ends of their life cycles or in consequence of fresh competition from other firms. Thus a multi-product company should aim for a balanced portfolio of products in order to ensure (i) a continuous inflow of cash, (ii) that new products are available to take over from those in decline, and (iii) that all the company's activities are not exceptionally risky.

One of the earliest analyses of the issue was by the Boston Consulting Group, which classified products according to two variables: the product's share of its total market, and the rate of the market's growth. The best products, obviously, were those with high market shares of buoyant markets experiencing high rates of growth, and the firm's strategy should be directed, therefore, to promoting these. Figure 3.4 illustrates the so-called 'Boston grid'.

The Boston grid

Each of the firm's products is allocated to an appropriate position in one of the four quadrants.

Cash cows are products with high market shares and thus are assumed to earn the cash needed for new investment in other lines of work.

Problem children (also referred to as 'question marks') are not generating cash because of low market share, but have potential and are in high growth market sectors. Investment in these products can yield rich dividends.

Stars have high market share in a buoyant market. They generate cash but may require further investment to maintain their market positions.

Dogs do not earn any cash; indeed their continuing existence might actually absorb money.

According to BCG, cash cows should be maintained but not receive significant investment. The cash received should be spent mainly on stars, with the balance being devoted to *selected* problem children. Typically, stars become cash cows as the growth rates of their markets decline, although some may end up as dogs.

Market share is measured in relation to that of the firm's largest competitor.

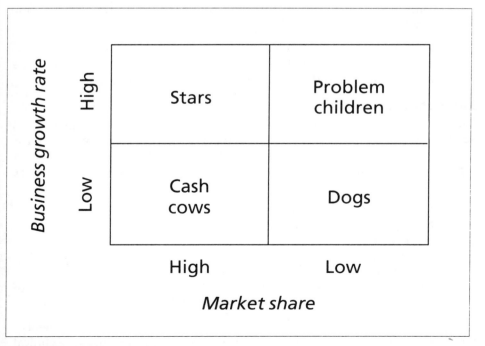

Figure 3.4 The Boston grid

Thus, if the firm in question has 60 per cent of the market and its biggest competitor has 30 per cent then its relative market share is 2. This is supposed to indicate a company's relative competitive position. High market share is assumed to result in high profitability and consequent generation of large amounts of cash.

Business growth rate means the rate of expansion of the market. For a national market this measure was provided by the rate of growth of domestic product of the country concerned. Otherwise industry growth rate or some other relevant proxy is used. The higher the business growth rate then, *ipso facto*, the easier it is for a firm to develop its activities and to succeed in the market.

Break-points between 'high' and 'low' categories for market share and business growth rate are selected subjectively and are, of course, somewhat arbitrary. For business growth rate, the average GDP of western countries might be used to define the boundary between high and low. The Boston Consulting Group suggested a value of 1.5 for the boundary between high and low relative market share.

28. Origins of the Boston grid

The Boston grid emerged from previous studies that purported to demonstrate the extent of 'experience curve effects' (see below) and, in consequence, rests on the fundamental assumptions that:

- increasing market share leads to higher profitability;
- the firm should always attempt to maximise its market shares in markets that are expanding most rapidly;
- businesses possessing a variety of products will be more successful than companies which concentrate on a single line of work, because this facilitates the transfer of learning between activities and gives the firm a balanced mix of products with different cash flow characteristics.

Experience curve effects

These are cost reductions and efficiency increases attained in consequence of a business acquiring experience of certain types of project, function or activity. These effects differ from economies of scale in that they result from longer experience rather than a greater volume of output. Costs decline in consequence of:

- the acquisition of know-how;
- the substitution of capital for labour;
- lower stockholding;
- higher labour productivity;
- better design of equipment and processes;
- specialisation of tasks (which naturally increases the experiences of individuals undertaking narrowly specified duties).

Also, greater experience of a particular technology facilitates the development of expertise in ancillary fields which can form a springboard for further technical advances.

Experience curve effects are said to represent a barrier to the entry of new firms to an industry, because entrant companies without experience face higher costs than established businesses.

The phenomenon of the experience effect was first documented in World War II in relation to the production of aircraft. It seemed that the fourth plane produced of a new model required just 80 per cent of the labour of the second plane; the eighth plane needed 80 per cent of the labour of the fourth; while the hundredth plane absorbed 80 per cent of the labour of the fiftieth. Studies conducted by the Boston Consulting Group in the 1970s concluded that, in general, unit production costs fall by at least 20 per cent whenever a business's output doubles (although this finding has been hotly disputed by subsequent researchers), suggesting that increasing the market share should be a primary strategic objective.

Anticipated experience curve effects can influence a firm's decisions on pricing, in that its management might *assume* that a low price will lead to high volume production that itself generates learning which contributes to increased efficiency. Thus profitability should rise and market share expand. Quantification of expected experience curve effects is especially important for the pricing of completely new products never previously manufactured.

Problems with this theory are:

(a) If it were generally true then firms operating in particular industries for the longest periods might be expected to exhibit the biggest market shares and/or levels of profitability, and there is little empirical evidence to back up this assertion.

(b) Economies of scale can vastly outweigh experience curve considerations.

(c) Technical change frequently causes a firm's past experience to be irrelevant.

(d) Acquisition of extensive experience in one line of work may be at the expense of diversification, causing the business to become overspecialised and less flexible than its rivals with consequent efficiency losses.

(e) Flexible manufacturing (see 13.7) enables firms to produce small batches of output custom made for particular market niches quickly and cheaply.

(f) In practice, experience curve effects seem to have been most significant in manufacturing (rather than service) companies, the production processes of which have a high labour content (notably within assembly industries). As robotics and computer assisted manufacture become increasingly important in these businesses the influence of 'experience' might decline.

29. Subsequent developments

A number of organisations developed the Boston Consulting Group (BCG) approach. Among the most important was the General Electric Company's 'Business Screen' method which uses the variables 'market attractiveness' and 'organisational strength' to categorise products. Market attractiveness depends on size, growth rate, profitability and competitive intensity of the market and on

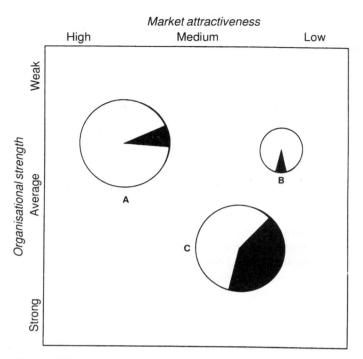

Figure 3.5

how easily it can be served. Organisational strength involves the quality of the firm's product, the firm's efficiency and the effectiveness of its marketing.

Consider for example a company with three products, A, B, and C as shown in Figure 3.5. The areas of the circles indicate the relative sizes of the markets for each product, while the wedges in each circle show the firm's share of that particular market. It can be seen that although the market for product A is large and highly attractive, the company is weak in its ability to serve this potentially lucrative segment, implying the need for further investment in this field.

Product B should probably be discarded, while product C presents a 'question mark' about how to proceed. There is a large market for product C, the firm can supply it easily, and the company already has a large market share. But the market for C is stagnant and profit margins are low.

Despite their popularity as an analytical device, the use of product portfolio models has the potential to create tremendous problems for companies. Consider for example, the case of an international computer software company which in 1992 completed a comprehensive review of its competitive strengths relevant to the attractiveness of the markets in which it operated, concluding that the firm's resources were spread far too thinly to enable it to maximise its potential in any one market. Hence it canvassed in-company views on how its competitive position could be improved and sought the opinions of key customers, suppliers and industry experts on the calibre of the firm's performance. 'Stars' and 'cash cows' were identified and, in the context of these findings, appropriate investment decisions were taken. The result was a disaster. Promotion of the company's 'star' products led to lower unit profits, because increases in their market shares could be obtained only at greatly reduced price/cost margins. A number of innovatory products were abandoned as it was felt that the company's competitive position in supplying these items was inadequate, thus allowing rival firms to dominate these important new product areas. Faced with a financial crisis the firm's management met to reconsider the usefulness of the original portfolio analysis. It emerged that individual managers possessed disparate and sometimes contradictory views concerning what exactly was meant by 'competitive position'; that it had been naively assumed that the release of resources from one area would *automatically* improve performance elsewhere; and that few of the long-term implications of withdrawing particular products had been considered!

30. Advantages and problems of portfolio analysis

Portfolio analysis became a widely used tool of analysis for multi-product companies in the 1970s and early 1980s. Doubts concerning its effectiveness began to emerge however, and today it is less widely employed. Portfolio analysis is a useful aid to decision making that compels management to analyse its present situation. It is a simple, logical and convenient device for taking a bird's eye view of the firm's activities, for varying the marketing mix applied to specific products, for corporate planning, departmental structuring of the firm, and for deciding which individuals shall assume responsibility for which products (managing a rapidly developing product requires skills different to those needed merely to maintain a stable situation). It is conceptually straightforward and easy to use. Graphical presentation enables the rapid communication of the results of the exercise. Management is compelled to think carefully about each of the firm's products, to set objectives and to allocate resources in a rationally determined way. Hence it facilitates strategy formulation and the budgeting process.

The technique has been criticised, however, for being simplistic and for encouraging managements to ignore complex yet crucially important environmental variables. Further problems are:

(a) Market growth and market share are not necessarily associated with cash flow and profitability.

(b) Skilful management might turn around the fortunes of a product which a portfolio analysis might suggest be discarded. Categorisation of products as cash cows or dogs can lead to self-fulfilling prophesies. Resources might be withdrawn from products that in fact have reasonably bright prospects.

(c) Strategies implied by the analysis may not be technically feasible or might be too expensive to implement.

(d) Portfolio analysis can give the impression of scientific rigour, when in fact the entire analysis is based on subjective value judgements.

(e) It is not always clear which particular market a product is actually serving.

Measurement of market share and industry growth rate can be meaningless in such circumstances.

(f) The analysis has little quantitative rigour.

(g) Empirical evidence to back up the fundamental propositions of the analysis is sparse. There are very many important examples of firms experiencing *declines* in profitability as market share has expanded.

(h) Human aspects of organisation and management are ignored.

(i) The analysis is only relevant for firms with a number of diversified products sold in different markets.

(j) Objective circumstances prevent a firm altering its product range.

(k) Market attractiveness can change suddenly, unpredictably and in consequence of factors beyond the company's control.

(l) Its application can become ritualistic rather than providing a genuinely useful analytical framework.

(m) Numerous factors contribute to 'organisational strength' and 'market attractiveness'. Selection of which to consider is necessarily arbitrary to some degree.

The analysis is static rather than dynamic, representing a 'snapshot' of a situation at a particular moment. It *describes* a firm's situation rather than telling management what it can do. In particular it has nothing to say about the *risks* associated with various options. Note how a market that happens to be expanding at a rapid rate today might be stagnant in the near future, and that high growth, high risk and environmental turbulence are frequently inter-related.

COMPETITIVE STRATEGY

31. The work of M.E. Porter

The theory of competitive strategy results largely from the work of M.E. Porter, who defines competitive strategy as 'the art of relating a company to the economic environment within which it exists'. According to Porter, five major factors determine this environment, namely:

- the ease with which competitors can enter the industry;
- the bargaining power of customers;
- the bargaining power of suppliers;
- the ease with which substitute products can be introduced;
- the extent of competition among existing firms.

Ease of entry
New firms will find it difficult to enter the industry where:

(a) economies of large-scale production (i.e. unit cost reductions as output increases) exist so that entrants must enter the industry on a large scale and hence assume great risk in order to gain a foothold in the market;

(b) there is much product differentiation through branding, differing designs and different product make-ups in various market segments, hence requiring potential entrants to spend large sums on advertising and sales promotion;

(c) expensive capital equipment is needed before starting production;

(d) entrants have limited access to existing distribution channels and thus need to invest heavily in establishing their own retail outlets, dealership networks, etc.;

(e) government policy restricts entry to the industry through, for example, quality regulations, licensing arrangements, and so on;

(f) miscellaneous factors create cost advantages for existing firms: experience of the industry, favourable locations, easy access to raw materials and similar benefits.

Bargaining power of buyers

The bargaining power of a purchasing firm depends on (i) the number of buyers and the sizes of their orders, (ii) customers' knowledge of the product and competitors' prices, and (iii) how easily buyers can switch from one source of supply to others.

Bargaining power of suppliers ✱

Suppliers have more power if there are few of them and if the item supplied is unique. Sometimes the client firm is 'locked into' the supplies of a certain business. This occurs where the client has designed its own production system to accommodate the special features of a certain input, so that high costs must be incurred to change the source of supply.

Availability of substitutes

Firms producing an item for which many readily available substitutes exist lose their ability to raise prices by significant amounts, since to do so would certainly cause them to lose trade.

The extent of competition

Firms can charge higher prices in industries where businesses avoid competing with each other. In such industries, companies set similar prices, and steer clear of competitive advertising.

Porter suggests the following general principles of inter-firm competition:

(a) Rivalry between firms increases as the market shares of existing firms become more equal. Severe competition is unlikely in 'market-leader, market-follower' situations.

(b) Competition intensifies as the rate of expansion of the total market slows down.

(c) Since goods which are perishable or difficult to store must be sold quickly, industries supplying such products will experience intense competition.

(d) Firms will compete most aggressively when they have much to lose from the activities of competing businesses (e.g. because of extremely large investments in plant and equipment).

(e) Competition becomes fierce when competing products acquire more and more similar characteristics, and is greatest in industries supplying homogeneous products.

A firm's competitive position depends on its market share, product quality, brand and corporate identities, distribution arrangements, and on its ability to expand or contract its operations at short notice.

Successful strategies, Porter argues, must involve at least one of the following elements:

(a) Cost leadership, e.g. through economies of scale or especially efficient product methods.

(b) Product differentiation, i.e. making the firm's output appear somehow different and superior to that of competitors.

(c) Supplying a particular market segment, i.e. finding a profitable niche in the market not yet serviced by competing firms.

How any one of these desirable characteristics can be achieved depends on the industry concerned: particularly on its age and the number of competing units. Thus, businesses in young industries might seek product differentiation, whereas for firms in mature industries the need to reduce costs may be seen as paramount.

A firm with many competitors might attempt to buy out as many other firms as possible in order to expand operations and hence achieve economies of scale. Conversely, businesses in declining industries may choose to divest subsidiaries and unprofitable divisions in order to focus all their efforts on small (but nevertheless profitable) market segments.

32. Criticisms of the theory of competitive strategy

Problems with the theory of competitive strategy include the following:

(a) Although it is sensible for a firm to have a competitive strategy, the environment in which it is applied will be constantly changing. Competing firms learn from each other's mistakes and emulate rivals' successes. It follows that it is perhaps more important to possess a well-developed framework for generating fresh ideas regarding suitable strategies as circumstances alter, particularly as competitors respond to the company's strategic actions. It is not possible to know today what tomorrow's competitive strategy should contain.

(b) Implementation of a competitive strategy might involve spending large amounts of money purely on the assumption that if the money is not spent then a rival firm might behave in a certain way. Yet there is no guarantee that the rival will behave in that manner if the resources are not in fact committed.

(c) Competitive strategy relies on speculation about competing companies' intentions, abilities and commitments to particular markets, not on hard evidence.

(d) Sometimes, firms have no formal strategies in the early years of their operations; yet managers take important decisions that commit resources in various ways. This process establishes a de-facto competitive strategy that eventually becomes the formal strategy statement of the firm. In the meantime however the entire competitive environment may have altered so that the enterprise is pursuing competitive strategy no longer appropriate to its needs.

(e) Effective competitive strategies are consistent yet flexible: they should not be altered immediately problems appear, yet need to be changed quickly whenever significant environmental change does occur. But where exactly should the line between continuity and responsiveness be drawn? There is no a priori method for determining this matter. Porter's model implies that firms should choose a specific strategy route. Yet businesses that simply react to current events can be more flexible, responsive to change and profitable than firms with distinct (and perhaps rigid) strategies.

(f) Businesses often change the 'industry' in which they operate. The criteria defining a particular industry sector are likely to alter (e.g. through technical innovation), and as the firm finds itself in new competitive environments so its competitive strategies will need to change. Industry structures are dynamic, so that the basic unit of analysis is constantly shifting.

(g) The model describes situations at a particular moment in time (rather like a snapshot of the early part of a horse race), but its ability to predict outcomes is questionable.

(h) Companies that score highly in terms of Porter's model (i.e. which face few rivals, substitute products, threats from new entrants, etc.) often fail, and vice-versa. Many organisational and efficiency factors determine whether a firm is successful.

33. Sources of competitive advantage

Competitive strategy means the development of those elements of the firm's overall activities that relate to beating the competition in the field. Firms obtain a competitive edge via their possession of particular assets, abilities or characteristics. Examples of factors possibly contributing to a business's competitive advantage include:

- ownership of patents, brands, know-how or other intellectual property;
- superior product offer, novel product design features, high quality output and/or excellent customer care facilities;
- economies of scale, efficient organisation and/or the possession of modern machinery, equipment or premises;
- effective distribution systems, ability to service niche markets, an attractive corporate image, good public relations and customer loyalty to the firm's brands;

- abilities to alter the firm's organisation structure quickly and to introduce new models at short notice;
- easy access to financial capital or high levels of financial reserves;
- well-qualified and highly motivated employees;
- ownership of raw materials or other input suppliers and of distribution outlets;
- superior R&D facilities;
- access to low cost labour.

Some businesses choose to develop just one source of competitive advantage, and allocate company resources accordingly. More commonly however, firms identify a combination of areas in which they need to excel and address these as a whole.

34. Critical success factors

Formulation of a competitive strategy involves a careful analysis of the strengths and weaknesses of the firm in question and of its rivals, identification of key success factors in the markets in which the business is to operate, and the precise definition of consumer attributes, demands, attitudes and behaviour. 'Critical success factors' are the variables that determine whether a company can beat its rivals in the market concerned. Some common critical success factors are:

- fast and reliable delivery;
- product quality and customer care;
- the ease with which a product can be modified, has appealing features, fulfils a clear need and has multiple uses;
- the rate of expansion of the market and whether it is concentrated in accessible areas;
- brand images and the location of products in their life cycles.

A firm's competitive edge could emerge from intangible rather than non-quantifiable factors, such as:

- senior managers' intuitive grasp of which strategic issues are most important;
- a chief executive's desire to achieve excellence, regardless of any other consideration;
- creativity in the strategy formulation process, leading to imaginative new ideas.

Other variables that might help a firm gain a competitive edge might include the provision of (i) lengthy credit periods (ii) low-cost installation, maintenance and repair of equipment; or (iii) technical advice.

35. Competitor analysis

It is useful for a firm's management to know something about each of its rival's strengths and weaknesses, costs, culture and management style, organisation system, strategies, mission and objectives, major markets, size, sales, production

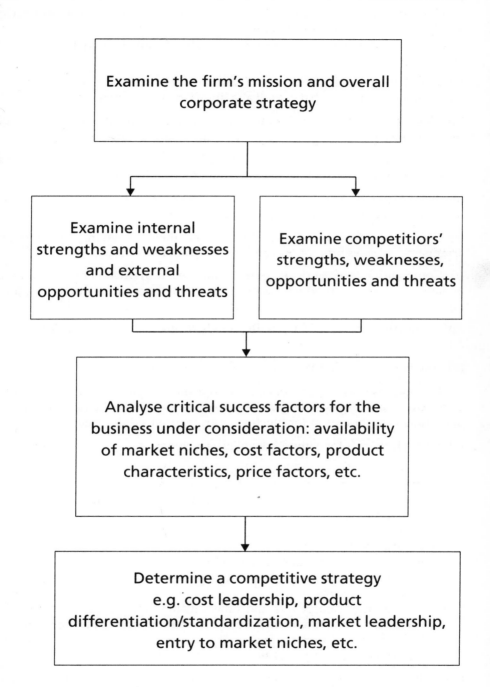

Figure 3.6 Competitive strategy

methods and asset structure. Some of these (strategies and objectives for example) can be inferred from competitors' observed behaviour. Otherwise a considerable amount of desk research is required. Competitor analysis needs to encompass the following:

(a) Prices and pricing history of competitors' brands, particularly the environmental changes that caused alterations in pricing strategies.

(b) Timing of competitors' promotional campaigns, and the implications of these timings for how competitors perceive their target audiences.

(c) Themes and concepts used in competitors' promotional materials. This requires the collation of a folio of each competitors' advertisements.

(d) Information on the strengths and weaknesses of rival firms' products and how these compare with the outputs of the firm in question.

(e) Market sectors covered by competitors, their packaging, distribution arrangements, sales promotions, and public relations events.

(f) Competitors' product development strategies. Introduction by competitors of new products or product features, or competitors' acquisitions of other businesses in order to obtain their brands.

(g) Competitors' terms of sale, credit periods, levels of after-sales service, and so on.

(h) The financial performance of competing firms.

(i) The reasons why competitors choose to operate in particular markets. How competitors are organised: their distribution systems, whether they have departments for brands or for functions, nature of subsidiaries, etc.

Information sources for competitor analysis include:

- press clippings (possibly purchased from a press clippings agency);
- published company reports and literature;
- published or specially commissioned market research studies;
- government reports;
- competitors' advertisements;
- trade association data;
- industry exhibitions and conferences;
- detailed examination of competitors' products;
- consumer surveys;
- reports from salespeople and others in the field. These are especially useful for evaluating competitors' distribution arrangements: the numbers of outlets carrying their products, shelf space allotted, customer service levels, sales promotions, and so on.

It is easier to obtain information on limited companies (which must publish their accounts) than for other types of businesses. Trade magazines frequently publish market surveys with analyses of the major businesses in particular markets. Such articles present estimates of the total extents of markets, the market shares of various firms, competitors' histories, profitabilities, selling and distribution methods and advertising style. Lists of competing firms' distributors are usually given out freely in response to customer enquiries. Also competitors' advertisements often specify where and how their products may be purchased. Much useful information is available from competitors' brochures, leaflets and other promotional literature and/or through purchasing their products. To evaluate competing brands a firm could ask a sample of its own customers to comment on the quality of competitors' outputs.

It is important not to underestimate competitors' strengths and overstate their weaknesses in consequence of wishful thinking on the part of the management concerned.

Progress test 3

1. Define incrementalism.

2. Who are the major stakeholders in a business?

3. What are the problems facing worker directors on company boards?

4. What is 'organic growth'?

5. List six reasons why a firm may wish to diversify its operations.

6. What factors should be taken into account when selecting takeover targets?

7. What is a 'reluctant bid'?

8. Explain the difference between a management buy-out and a management buy-in.

9. What is a 'sale and leaseback arrangement'?

10. Give four examples of critical success factors (CSFs).

11. What are the main criticisms of Porter's theory of competitive strategy?

12. How did the Boston Grid originate?

4
FORECASTING

1. Nature of forecasting

Forecasts are predictions of future situations or events, in contrast to 'plans', which frequently (but not always) contain statements of predetermined responses to anticipated future eventualities. Forecasts may be based on past events, or involve pure speculation (e.g. when there are no data on relevant previous occurrences or when something completely novel and unprecedented is foreseen). Short-term predictions are normally more accurate than long-term projections. The latter are subject to greater uncertainty, so larger margins of error must be allowed. Hence, many firms prepare both short and long term forecasts; the former in detail, the latter only in outline. It is not worth spending enormous amounts of money on long-term predictions of highly uncertain events.

Both internal and external forecasts might be necessary. Internal forecasts could relate to expenditures, equipment breakdown, maintenance requirements, labour productivity, plant utilisation, materials costs and usage, overheads, working capital requirements, returns on capital employed, cash flows, etc. External forecasts might involve national economic growth rates, price levels, foreign exchange rates, consumers' expenditure and other macroeconomic variables, plus market share and assessments of competitors' likely future behaviour. Often the forecaster's task is to identify connections between variables (i.e. 'what causes what') and hence to generate predictions of future outcomes. Hopefully this will enable management to determine the consequences of its intended policies and thus select the best course of action. In a formal forecasting procedure the pre-assumptions of the exercise are clearly laid out, so that inaccurate forecasts can be examined in order to establish which of the assumptions were incorrect. Then it becomes possible to learn from past mistakes and so improve future forecasts.

Note how professional forecasters have been in business throughout the ages, and it seems to be a natural desire of humans to want to predict the future. A belief that one knows what is about to happen seemingly helps the individual feel secure and confident, even though the prediction may have little scientific foundation.

2. Justifications for forecasting

Senior managers inevitably have to take certain decisions the consequences of which depend on the states of environments and factors that are not known at the time the decisions are made. In these circumstances, managers typically apply their experience of similar past situations to the decision-making process. The need for forecasts arises wherever decisions have to be made in conditions of uncertainty, so that managers cannot really avoid forecasting because uncertainty is an essential ingredient of business life: numerous decisions have to be taken on the basis of incomplete information and on inadequate knowledge of the factors that cause a situation.

A major reason why forecasting is inevitable in many business situations is that strategic decisions often take several years to exert their full effects, especially capital investment decisions and matters pertaining to the introduction of new products. This type of decision needs to be taken not in relation to current conditions but rather in the context of the situation that the decision taker believes will apply at the time the results of the decision begin to be felt. Therefore, future conditions have to be considered when making such major long-term commitments. Further justifications for forecasting are as follows:

(a) Forecasting facilitates the co-ordination of policies.

(b) Arguably, effective planning is impossible without sound forecasting procedures.

(c) Forecasting encourages strategic vision (see 3.5). Proactive managers are naturally curious about the future. Logically-constructed projections will assist them to think clearly and sensibly and to weigh up all alternative possibilities.

(d) Forecasting need not be prohibitively expensive. Straightforward and low cost forecasting methods are frequently as good as (indeed often outperform) complex and sophisticated statistical techniques.

(e) Clear patterns and relationships among variables can be observed in many business situations, so it makes sense to utilise them to the best advantage. The problem, of course, is predicting breaks in trends and/or the precise timing of turning points in trend cycles.

(f) The alternative to forecasting is to take decisions on the basis of current conditions, which is inappropriate in a fast changing world: there will always be some aspect of the future situation that differs from anything experienced in the past.

In the early 1980s the UK's Acorn Computers forecast big increases in the demand for personal computers in the US and thus decided to enter the market. What it failed to predict, however, were (i) aggressive competitive responses by the American computer manufacturer, Apple, and (ii) refusal by the American Federal Communications Commission to approve Acorn's product, necessitating costly modifications and delaying entry by eight months! Eventually Acorn had to withdraw from the US, at an estimated cost of £6 million.

Source: *Financial Times*, 6 December 1984.

3. Long-range forecasts

Long-range forecasts are needed to facilitate decision making *vis-à-vis* such matters as major long-term investments in capital equipment (especially the introduction of new technologies), plans for acquiring or merging with other businesses, research and development projects, new product development and introduction, and the withdrawal of existing products. A long-range forecast is as much an act of faith as a statistical prediction – it is a statement of intent, not a prognostication. Plans extending over several years will never be realised unless positive measures (human resource policies, management by objectives procedures, new product development, management training, etc.) are initiated to secure their achievement. Yet because of the numerous and severe difficulties necessarily attached to long-term planning and forecasting, and the uncertainty of the benefits likely to result from the exercise, these matters are frequently overlooked. Management becomes preoccupied with shorter-term problems and ignores the need to consider longer-term issues.

Policy committees

To overcome this problem, some organisations deliberately constitute 'policy committees' to prepare long-range forecasts and plans and to inaugurate the policies needed to achieve long-run objectives. Such committees meet periodically to speculate about the future. Their membership usually consists of senior managers who are not concerned with routine company administration but rather with diagnostic and organisational duties. Hopefully, such individuals will possess broad outlooks and be able to assess objectively the future prospects of the company. Policy committees might then be able to make valuable inputs to future corporate strategy statements since they will already have carefully considered the key variables affecting the business's survival and profitability in the long term.

Long-range forecasts are quantified in general terms, e.g. expected rate of return on capital employed resulting from successful implementation of strategic policies such as increasing market share, diversification, or the introduction of new technology.

4. Technological forecasting

This is the assessment of the likelihood of new developments in relation to products, processes, and the technological infrastructures of industries. It is an essential ingredient of the strategy formulation processes of high-tech firms (indeed any business operating within an environment of rapid technical change). The procedure involves management adopting long-term perspectives and (importantly) having to consider wide-ranging technological trends and issues. Aims of technological forecasting are to identify existing products and methods that are liable to be overtaken by new developments, to establish a research agenda for the organisation, to avoid the trauma of having to switch to a new technology without notice. Methods of technological forecasting include brainstorming, use of the Delphi technique (see 8), and the examination of the development of a particular technology over a long period (which might be several decades) and extrapolating this into the future. The points at which one technology was overtaken by another need to be analysed in order to identify the causal factors involved. Also, technological 'life cycles' might be discerned. A technological life cycle will have a development phase as a new technology is introduced, followed by a technological 'peak' and subsequent decline as the technology becomes redundant and is replaced by alternatives. Forecasts might consider three possible future situations: that which is most optimistic in terms of the consequences for the firm; that which is most pessimistic; and that which is most likely.

There are two general approaches to technological forecasting: 'exploratory' and 'normative'. The former assumes that the present level of technical and scientific knowledge in a particular field will progress steadily, and predictions of new developments are based on that assumption. Normative forecasts, conversely, create radical scenarios of what might happen to a technology in the future (e.g. that it will be entirely replaced) hence generating fresh research and development objectives for the organisation. This latter type of forecasting is valuable because a firm's commitment to an existing technology may cause its management to adopt biased perspectives when evaluating potential new methods: so much has been invested in the current technology that without the obligation to prepare a normative forecast the managers involved cannot bear to think of the consequences of radical technical changes.

5. Sales forecasts

Probably the most important of all business forecasts is that of future sales. This will indicate anticipated revenues, and will determine current purchases of raw materials, employment of labour and other resources needed to produce the goods. Expenditure on input is incurred now; sales revenue is realised later. Therefore, finance is needed to bridge the gap and the firm must borrow to meet its short-term expenditure obligations. Contracts are signed and must be honoured even if expected sales do not materialise. Forecasts themselves are normally based on past sales, with appropriate allowances for expected consumer reactions to advertising campaigns, predicted behaviour of competitors, likely changes in consumer incomes, and so on. Obviously, sales forecasting is difficult because there are so many uncontrollable variables involved. It is sensible, therefore, to register several forecasts, each contingent on the occurrence of particular events. Then the firm can decide today how it will react to future environmental changes such as price cuts by competitors, tax alterations or changes in fashion. Sales forecasts are used to set targets for the marketing department and for individual salespeople.

In preparing a sales forecast, management will seek information from:

(a) external sources such as trade reports, journals, trends in prices, competitors' behaviour, government statistics and statements of intent;

(b) internal data from market research, opinion surveys, views of hired consultants and from extrapolation of past trends.

The many difficulties associated with sales forecasting include the following.

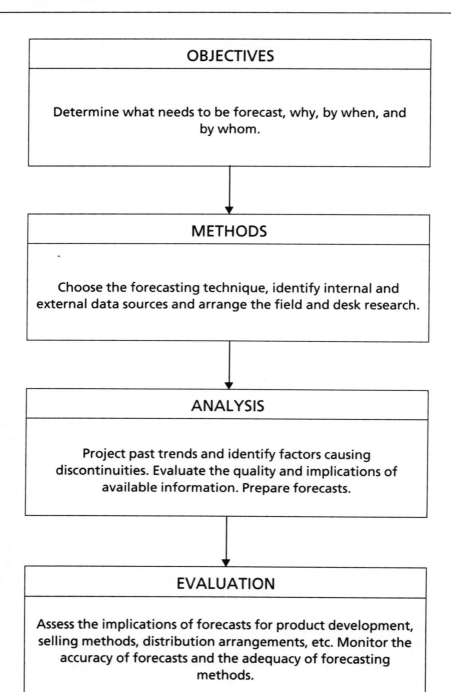

OBJECTIVES

Determine what needs to be forecast, why, by when, and by whom.

METHODS

Choose the forecasting technique, identify internal and external data sources and arrange the field and desk research.

ANALYSIS

Project past trends and identify factors causing discontinuities. Evaluate the quality and implications of available information. Prepare forecasts.

EVALUATION

Assess the implications of forecasts for product development, selling methods, distribution arrangements, etc. Monitor the accuracy of forecasts and the adequacy of forecasting methods.

Figure 4.1 Sales forecasting

(a) Sales, normally, are influenced by consumer incomes, which are mainly determined by government policies and other macroeconomic variables outside a firm's control.

(b) Consumer tastes can alter quickly and in seemingly unpredictable ways.

(c) Political and legal superstructures can change overnight. New taxes might be introduced.

(d) Competing firms may alter their prices or increase advertising expenditures. Foreign firms could enter the market.

(e) New production techniques might become available which require complete re-estimation of future output constraints.

(f) Forecasts of the future are usually based on what happened in the past: there is no guarantee that previous trends will continue.

A UK personal computer manufacturer experienced massive sales growth over a period of six years. Recruitment of additional sales staff had proceeded in line with the expansion in demand, and each extra salesperson had generated a proportional rise in sales. Demand was forecast to increase by 25 per cent annually over the following four years, so plans were made to hire the appropriate number of extra salespeople. Sales forecasts were not met, and the subsequent investigation revealed that this was due to poor performance by recently recruited sales staff. The reasons for this were as follows:

(a) Other computer companies had achieved similar rates of growth, and were also recruiting salespeople. Hence there were not enough experienced salespeople to go round so that the sales staff included a higher proportion of untrained and inexperienced employees than previously.

(b) Rapid expansion of the business had strained its resources and led to a proliferation of red-tape, inefficiency and low-quality back-up services.

(c) Sales training for newly recurited staff had proven inadequate.

(d) The firm's most recent models were far more technically sophisticated than before, requiring extensive product knowledge in order to achieve sales.

None of the above had been considered while drafting the sales forecast. In a desperate attempt to meet sales targets (which formed the basis for the production plan) the firm introduced huge bonus incentives to induce experienced salespeople to work extensive overtime, at great financial cost to the company.

Techniques for forecasting sales include regression analysis (see 7), moving averages, and subjective predictions by salespeople 'in the field'. The latter method is especially useful in fast changing markets and/or where data on causal variables are difficult or expensive to obtain. Typically, each salesperson will be asked to give an estimate of how they believe sales will move (and the probability of this happening), independent of other people. Then, individual predictions are analysed by a third party and a compromise forecast determined. Often a subjective evaluation is used in conjunction with the results from quantitative forecasting models. Other common devices for forecasting sales include:

(a) The use of key indicators. Here the forecaster identifies economic, social or other indicators known to relate to the variable being forecast. Indicators might be 'lead indicators' which move in advance of the forecast variable, or 'tied indicators' that move in conjunction with the variable in question.

(b) Marketing models which focus on trends in consumer behaviour, research into the effectiveness of the firm's advertising, and customer awareness of the company's products. Model building is discussed below.

6. Model building

Most forecasts rely on the use of some sort of model constructed to facilitate predictions.

Nature of models

A model is a representation of reality. It reduces an issue to just a few key variables which the analyst may then study in great depth. Model building requires that a number of assumptions about the nature of the problem be made, for example that people are motivated by certain rewards, or that observations follow a normal probability distribution or some other prespecified statistical form. The model constructed will predict events and describe the circumstances in which they might happen.

Schematic models use graphs, charts, decision rules, algorithms, etc., to help management predict the future and run an organisation in the most efficient way. Mathematical models are analogues of relationships between variables, seeking to identify cause and effect and hence to predict values for the forecast ('dependent') variable. An example of a 'causal' mathematical model is a sales forecast determined by such variables as product price and the prices charged by competitors, rate of growth of consumer expenditure, inflation and unemployment levels, etc. The forecast will change as values of these 'independent' variables alter. Problems with this type of model include:

(a) the difficulty of specifying the model, i.e. deciding what causes what and which variables to include in the forecasting equation. Note how a very large number of variables will affect most business outcomes, so that selecting just a few of them runs the risk of ignoring important influences;

(b) biases in forecasts resulting from technical deficiencies in the statistical model or methods adopted, e.g. if the independent variables are themselves interrelated and/or partially determined by the dependent variable.

Schematic models are frequently (but not necessarily) non-causal, i.e. they assume that forecasters do not need to specify or even understand the factors which determine the values of a variable in order to predict its future levels. Thus the paths of variables are carefully recorded, trends identified and extrapolations intuitively charted. This type of model is often cheap and convenient to construct, and can be reasonably effective. And they are essential in situations where the underlying causal structure of a system cannot be established, or where there are no data on the independent variables.

Model building has a number of advantages:

(a) Analysts are compelled to list and evaluate all the assumptions underlying their suggestions. Rational approaches to decision taking are thus encouraged.

(b) Problems are presented concisely, precisely, and in a clearly understandable form.

(c) Complex situations are reduced to a handful of manageable variables, peripheral issues are excluded from the analysis.

(d) Decisions based on the model may be taken quickly.

The disadvantages are as follows:

(a) Many human emotions that affect people's behaviour (fear, greed, discomfort, etc.) are extremely difficult to incorporate into a model.

(b) Usually, a model represents a situation only at a specific moment in time. In reality, however, business situations are constantly changing, so that the results from a model will be continually out of date.

(c) Important aspects of a problem might be ignored in order to make it fit neatly into the confines of a narrowly defined model.

7. Quantitative and qualitative forecasting techniques

Quantitative techniques include regression analysis whereby a dependent variable is said to be determined by a number of independent (causal) variables: the analysis of moving averages over time; exponential smoothing, and other extrapolative devices. Projections based on moving averages assume that history will repeat itself and past trends continue. This obviously is inappropriate in most situations, so that predictions of any future events likely to disturb current trends must be incorporated into the analysis. Models involving the extrapolation of a variable on the basis of its own past values are said to be 'naive', although this word is not to be interpreted pejoratively. For further information on such methods see the M&E volume, *Statistics*, by W.M. Harper.

The normal procedure is to gather data on the variables in question; then to select an appropriate forecasting model, identify causal relationships among variables, and finally to extrapolate into the future – including an assessment of the reliability of the forecast in the reported projection. In the natural sciences it is common for forecasts to be extremely accurate (predictions of the timing of sunrise and sunset or the movements of sea tides for example). Business forecasts are notoriously unreliable, however, for a number of reasons:

(a) Relationships among variables change over time: environments alter and new influences regularly emerge.

(b) Social events depend on human behaviour which can be irrational and unpredictable.

(c) Rival firms are constantly changing their policies in order to gain competitive advantage, causing initial forecasts to be incorrect. New firms enter the market and existing ones go into liquidation.

(d) Technical change can lead to the complete restructuring of industry sectors.

It is common to 'fine-tune' statistical forecasts via the discussion of critical issues pertaining to them by teams of experts in various fields, the integration of opinion, and the participation in discussions of people who will be affected by important decisions resulting from the forecasts.

Sensitivity analysis involves the study of key assumptions upon which intended actions are based. These assumptions are systematically altered and 'what if' questions then asked. Most optimistic, most pessimistic, and most likely outcomes are estimated, and the probabilities of each possibility assessed. The main problem with sensitivity analysis is perhaps the explosion in the number of potential outcomes that occurs when all the uncertainties attached to a large number of key variables are combined. Numerous permutations are generated each with a particular end result.

Qualitative forecasts

Examples of qualitative forecasting techniques are the Delphi method (see below) and similar devices for canvassing expert opinion; estimates provided by salespeople and other employees of the organisation; questionnaire and telephone surveys; scenario building (see **9**); brainstorming (see **10**); and the analysis of historical analogies.

8. The Delphi method

This is an approach to forecasting based on consultation with experts on the subject in question, rather than on numerical extrapolation and statistical technique. The name derives from a famous oracle at Delphi in Ancient Greece. Use of the Delphi technique was developed by the US Rand Corporation. It takes advantage of the knowledge and experience of experts in the field, but because it involves committee work there is a danger that 'group think' will occur and lead to irrational conclusions. Group think means the tendency for like-minded people within a cohesive group to agree on issues without challenging each others' ideas or realising that the consensus which seemingly emerges may not represent the actual views of the group. The problem is commonest in groups with strong, charismatic leaders and when group members devote little mental effort to analysing the situation in hand. Acting individually, each panel member is likely to come up with a different forecast to the others. One of these forecasts might be correct, and the compromise prediction resulting from the pooling of ideas serve merely to dilute this correct conclusion. Also the assumptions behind the forecasts that emerge from discussions might not be clearly laid out.

To overcome some of these problems the principle of anonymity might be applied, so that expert opinion is canvassed via questionnaires distributed and collated by a non-participant – hence reducing the influence of dominant individuals and the pressure to conform. The co-ordinator summarises the opinions expressed at the first round of the exercise and informs the participants, who then revise their opinions in the light of this information. Members remain anonymous, and the process is repeated until consensus emerges. If no agreement is reached the reasons for divergent opinions are investigated.

9. Creation of scenarios

Instead of attempting to predict the future it might be better to accept that forecasts are extremely unlikely to be realised and to concentrate instead on constructing a variety of scenarios each describing a possible future state. The process is analytical, and hopefully will pinpoint the basic forces that create particular environments. Scenario building is said to stimulate creative thinking and help identify major opportunities and threats. It is a highly practical approach to forecasting, unhindered by statistical confusion or complex econometric technique. A major advantage is that scenario building enables the combination of an extensive range of political, economic, social and technological factors into predictions of the future.

Problems with scenario creation are that:

- very many scenarios may be required, each costing time and money to investigate;
- the managers whose job it is to examine the various possible scenarios may become overloaded with complex information involving numerous 'ifs and buts';
- although scenarios describe various possible situations, they might not indicate the best possible courses of action.

Royal Dutch Shell has over 100 operating companies around the world. Each subsidiary has a high degree of autonomy, so that co-ordinating the plans of the diverse elements of the enterprise is a major management task. In 1970 the firm's Group Planning Department (GPD) developed the technique of scenario planning as a means for predicting future trends. GPD realised that long-term patterns of oil production, pricing and consumption were about to change: the West was increasingly dependent on oil imports, while many oil exporting countries were openly questionning the propriety of existing oil prices and were concerned about declining reserves. Such factors were built into scenario projections, but the results of the latter were rejected by most operational managers – who had experienced nothing but smooth growth in oil demand and supply throughout their working lives. Accordingly, managers in operating units were challenged to specify all the assumptions that would need to be met for the present stable environment to continue. GPD then demonstrated that these assumptions could not possibly hold. Subsequent feedback from unit managers was incorporated into the scenarios currently under construction. This exercise helped Shell to cope with the OPEC oil price rises of 1972/73. The oil crisis could not be predicted exactly, but the types of change that were likely had been foreseen. It was obvious from the scenario analysis that exploration for oil would have to be undertaken in new countries while investment in refineries had to fall as the demand for oil decelerated. Hence Shell's well-thought-out response to the OPEC oil embargo was to reduce investment, rebuild existing refineries to enable them to process several different classes of crude oil, and step up exploration in non-OPEC countries. The results were spectacular. In 1970 Shell was the least profitable of the world's seven largest oil companies; by 1980 it was ranked number one.

10. Brainstorming

Most qualitative methods involve group brainstorming at some stage. Brain-storming is the process of generating a large number of new ideas, without considering their feasibility at the time they are put forward. All the ideas brought up by participants during a brainstorming session are listed, but not discussed. A separate meeting is then convened to evaluate the costs, benefits and implications of each idea. Only the most promising ideas are eventually followed up. Participants in a brainstorming session are encouraged to be as inventive and imaginative as possible, looking at problems from different angles rather than head on. Hopefully, one idea will generate others so that ideas build on themselves. Group brainstorming sessions are useful only if participants take them seriously and are competent to contribute fresh ideas about the problem. However, members should never be criticised for suggesting (superficially) absurd or trivial ideas.

11. Morphological analysis (MA)

This is an extension of brainstorming which seeks to discover fresh ideas by cross-referencing concepts. Consider for example a manufacturing firm that is considering an extension to its range of products. Suppose three new products, A, B and C are technically feasible and that three markets – teenage consumers, the middle-aged, and retired people – exist. To conduct a morphological analysis, management lists the products and states how each might be used in each market, thus creating $3 \times 3 = 9$ new ideas for desirable features for the intended new products. Then a third dimension could be added, consisting of (say) three ways of designing the packaging of the products, hence enabling the generation of still further ideas (e.g. how best to package product C for the teenage market). This will generate $3 \times 3 \times 3 = 27$ ideas, and so on. Each idea is then critically evaluated, leaving only the best for critical investigation.

Morphological analysis adds form and structure to a brainstorming exercise. As many dimensions may be added as are deemed necessary, with a consequent proliferation of ideas. The problems with MA are that:

(a) too many ideas might be generated – more than can be properly evaluated in the time available;

(b) possibly, only one or two options can realistically be implemented so that the remainder of the ideas are superfluous.

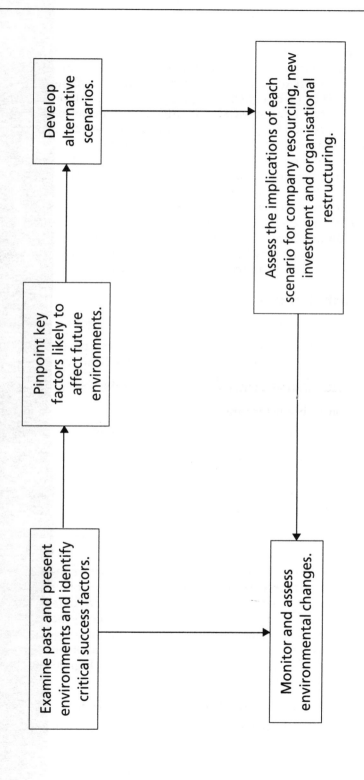

Figure 4.2 Scenario analysis

12. Heuristics

A heuristic system is one that uses current experience to guide future plans, applying *ad hoc* rules of thumb in order to solve problems. Heuristic methods are common in situations where formal and systematic decision-taking procedures cannot be applied. They do not attempt to present definite solutions, but rather solutions that are tentative and subject to alteration as circumstances change. The need for heuristic methods frequently arises in business because management problems often lack structure and are subject to great uncertainty.

To illustrate the concept consider the game of chess. All chess problems can be solved with certainty using algorithms (i.e. exhaustive computational procedures that examine every aspect of the state of play) – provided powerful computing facilities and plenty of time are available. Yet a competitive chess player cannot use a computer. He or she is constrained by time and must rely on intuitive rules of thumb, based on experience, and which offer no guarantee of success. Thus, chess is like many business situations in that it is a deterministic game, which in practical terms must be played heuristically.

13. Problems with forecasting

Accurate business forecasts are extremely difficult to achieve, for several reasons:

(a) Many variables (tax levels, business laws, interest rates, consumer incomes, etc.) are determined by government and thus beyond the firm's control.

(b) Consumer tastes can change quickly and unpredictably.

(c) New technical inventions may occur.

(d) Competitors might alter their behaviour; fresh competition could emerge.

(e) Past occurrences upon which forecasts are based might not continue in the future.

(f) Existing suppliers, distribution options, harmonious industrial relations, and so on, could suddenly disappear.

(g) Technical difficulties (unreliable data, incorrect choice of statistical forecasting technique, etc.) might arise.

(h) Often the data on which forecasts are based are themselves highly aggregated and do not reveal the precise factors relevant to specific problems confronting the firm. For example, data might be available on demand for (say) pet food within a certain region, but not on pet food with respect to moist and dry varieties, premium and basic, tinned versus soft carton, brand categories, and so on. The same difficulty applies to variations in local conditions within an area. Thus, for instance, economic growth rates may be extremely high for a region as a whole, but negative for certain localities.

(i) Data might be available, but extremely expensive to obtain.

Forecasting technological change is especially difficult, as typically very little information is available on likely future developments. Note in particular how competitors' research and development activities will be secret, and when they come to fruition the results will immediately be patented. Another difficulty is that often there are several alternative forecasting techniques that can be applied to any given forecasting situation, without any hard criteria for determining which of them is most appropriate. This problem is confounded by the fact that few managers have received formal training in forecasting techniques. (Note that a background in mathematics and/or statistics is not of itself sufficient to ensure expertise in business forecasting.) Further problems with forecasting are as follows:

(a) People preparing forecasts may be tempted to simplify forecasting problems in order to make them fit into a conventional forecasting model. This cuts costs, but also reduces the reliability of decisions taken on the basis of forecasts.

(b) Attempts to increase the accuracy of forecasts can be extremely expensive: more data has to be collected, additional time and research are required.

(c) Arguably there is little point in trying to predict the unpredictable. The OPEC oil price increases of the 1970s and 80s (which severely disrupted world trade) are good examples of the impossibility of forecasting events with major international consequences.

14. Evaluation of forecasts

The accuracy of predictions should be monitored by comparing them with events as they occur, and sources of error (inadequate or incorrect data, faulty forecasting techniques, poor judgements by forecasters, etc.) should be identified. It is useful to know whether forecasts are on average persistently overestimating or underestimating actual performance. There are two aspects to the use of forecasts in corporate planning. One is analogous to a traveller obtaining a weather forecast prior to a long and difficult journey: the forecast may not be realised but the traveller needs to know the sorts of weather he or she is likely to confront. The other is where it is possible to influence future outcomes, so that forecasts lead to the implementation of policies intended to alter future events in line with the decision taker's best interests. An example is a forecast of low sales which causes the firm to increase its advertising, reduce prices, offer special discounts, introduce sales promotions, and so on. Note how the success of these measures will necessarily mean that the initial forecast of poor sales will not be observed. This is not to say that the initial forecast was 'inaccurate', only that the entire configuration of circumstances leading to the forecast has changed. Evaluation of the accuracy of forecasts is difficult under such circumstances. Indeed, forecasts that do not correspond with actual future events are inevitable if the initial forecast causes the firm to implement policies intended to reverse forecast outcomes. Also, to the extent that a firm's forecasts are accurate its strategies should be well-founded and hence the business should succeed in the market place, which fact will itself cause competitors to react aggressively and hence confound the original forecasts! Note moreover that in a competitive situation it is simply impossible for all firms' forecasts to be accurate, as there are bound to be winners and losers in any truly competitive market. Other factors that can invalidate business forecasts are economic recessions, unexpected changes in government policy, random occurrences, entry of new firms to a market, and technological innovation.

Clearly, the closeness of real and predicted future happenings as a criterion for evaluating forecasting activities is only valid in certain circumstances, and the fact that forecasting is fraught with difficulties does not mean that there is no cause for engaging in the activity. Arguably, inaccurate forecasts do not mean that forecasting should be abandoned, only that there are deficiencies in the firm's forecasting technique that need to be remedied or that the results of forecasting are being misinterpreted. Forecasts will never be perfect, but can be greatly improved in very many situations. Forecasts can be evaluated in terms of their usefulness for decision making, understandability and, in appropriate circumstances, their accuracy. If forecasts are inaccurate, their underlying assumptions need to be examined, since if the selection of a different set of assumptions would have generated accurate forecasts this indicates that it is not so much the forecasting technique that is at fault; rather that the wrong assumptions were chosen. More general evaluative criteria are:

- the financial costs of forecasting relative to proven benefits;
- how much useful ancillary information the forecasting system generates;
- estimates of what would happen if no forecasts were prepared;
- whether the business is achieving its objectives and, if not, the role of forecasts in the explanation of shortcomings.

Progress test 4

1. Explain the difference between forecasting and planning.

2. Why do some firms establish policy committees?

3. There are two approaches to technological forecasting. What are they?

4. Why is the sales forecast the most important forecast that a firm has to make?

5. What is a schematic model?

6. Define 'groupthink'.

7. What is a morphological analysis?

5

MANAGEMENT AUDITS AND ENVIRONMENTAL ANALYSIS

MANAGEMENT AUDITS

1. Nature of management auditing

A management audit is a systematic appraisal of the effectiveness of an organisation's strategies, policies and administrative procedures. Management auditing encompasses a range of function-specific audits (manufacturing, marketing, etc.), the strategic audit (see below), and more general aspects of administration. The purposes of management auditing are:

- to assess the effectiveness of current strategies and the relevance and feasibilities of present objectives;
- to identify strengths and weaknesses with a view to removing impediments to improved performance;
- to ensure that the enterprise's management system is appropriate for current and likely future environments;
- to revise corporate plans in the light of recent developments;
- to reorganise resources – material, financial and human – and redirect effort towards the more efficient attainment of the enterprise's goals.

Major strategic audits might be undertaken every three or four years; departmental and/or functional audits more frequently – possibly on a 'rolling basis'. Typically an audit will require answers to a series of questions concerning various aspects of the company and designed to pinpoint problems and highlight strengths and weaknesses.

2. The strategy audit

This takes an overall look at the effectiveness of the company's strategies with particular reference to the following issues:

- Attainment or otherwise of key strategic objectives (market share, profitability, etc.).
- Roles and performances of senior executives.
- Accuracy of the mission statement *vis-à-vis* the firm's current activities.
- Operations of the board of directors.

- Extent and speed of feedback on the consequences of strategic decisions.
- Reasons for deviations of actual from planned overall company performance.
- Identification of external strategic threats and opportunities.
- Whether the company's mission and core goals are properly understood by employees.
- Consistency of strategic objectives with the firm's mission, the external environment, and with each other.
- Relations between policies, strategies and objectives.

Strategy audits need to be conducted at set intervals, and whenever there is a major environmental change and/or failure to attain prespecified targets or performance levels. Routine and periodic strategy audits enable managements to fine-tune the progress of existing strategies and to learn from experience. The strategic auditing process is outlined in Figure 5.1. This begins from the analysis of key quantitative and qualitative performance indicators (sales, rate of return on investment, earnings per share, etc.) and the comparison of actual and expected performance. Trends in performance need to be examined and the firm's current position *vis-à-vis* its competitors assessed. Thereafter the more mundane aspects of corporate strategy must be re-appraised. The latter include an assessment of the usefulness of the management style of the enterprise, organisation structure, business systems, etc.

The sorts of questions to be asked when conducting a strategic audit include the following:

(a) What are the strategic options currently available to the firm and what are their implications for organisational structure; resource requirements; control procedures, etc?

(b) Are the lines of business the company is actually pursuing compatible with its stated mission?

(c) Are the firm's strategies still valid considering recent changes in external circumstances?

(d) Does the company's present organisation structure facilitate or hinder the implementation of strategies?

(e) Are the firm's core strategies understood and endorsed by all management levels, and if not why not?

(f) How clear are the relationships between strategies and policies?

(g) Has the process of determining strategies revealed company strengths and weaknesses?

(h) Have priorities for action been highlighted?

(i) Have key performance indicators (sales, profits, return on investment, earnings per share, etc.) improved or worsened since current strategies were implemented?

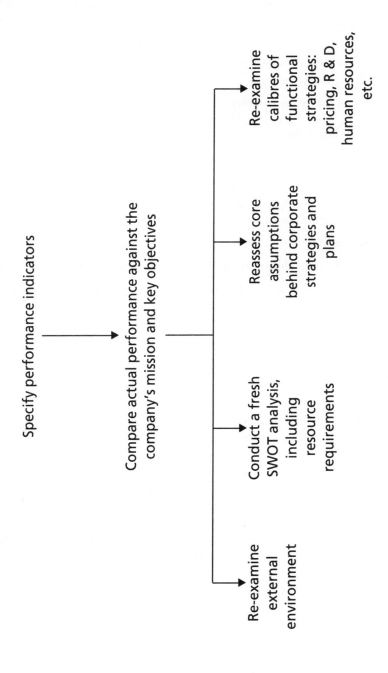

Figure 5.1 The strategy audit

(j) How does the company's track record compare with those of competitors?

(k) Have the strategies adopted unified and co-ordinated the firm's operations?

(l) Is the company's management style compatible with the implementation of its strategies?

(m) Is the process of overseeing strategy implementation absorbing too much top management time and effort?

(n) Are new ideas for future operations being generated?

3. Audits of operations

Two types of operational audit are needed: internal and external. External audits examine the general environments – legal (the effects of changes in employment law for example), economic, market opportunities, behaviour of competitors, etc. – surrounding the organisation. Internal audits investigate operational systems within the firm. A typical audit will examine such things as:

(a) communication systems;

(b) whether organisation charts and job specifications are clear and up to date;

(c) whether organisational and departmental objectives are understood by all department members;

(d) possible duplication of activities;

(e) operational efficiency within sections;

(f) plant and/or office layout;

(g) output quality.

Typically, SWOT analysis is used to complete operational audits.

4. SWOT analysis

SWOT is the acronym for 'Strengths, Weaknesses, Opportunities and Threats'. Typically, strengths and weaknesses exist within the organisation; opportunities and threats normally originate outside. Table 5.1 lists examples of areas in which a firm might have weaknesses and strengths.

Opportunities and threats are normally to be found in the external environment. Examples of opportunities are possibilities for:

- developing fresh markets;
- introducing new products;
- cutting costs;
- exporting;
- taking over competing firms;
- mergers;
- improving relations with suppliers;
- controlling distribution networks.

TABLE 5.1 Sources of strengths and weaknesses

Customer care	Distribution arrangements
Production efficiency	Availability of useful management
Staff resources and skills	information
Delivery periods	Advertising and sales promotion
Ability to introduce new products and	Dealership and discount systems
working methods	Research and technical development
Ability to raise funds	Market research facilities
Supply of components and materials	Cash flow situation
inputs	Managerial efficiency
Plant, equipment and vehicles	Age structure of senior management
Flow of work between departments	Delegation systems
Suitability of premises	Control methods
Stock control	Relevance of the organisation structure
Product attractiveness	Financial structure
Quality control	Asset utilisation
Internal communications	Administrative system
Warehousing	Human resources
Packaging and transport	Procurement systems

Threats might arise from competitors, from impending legislation that could damage the firm, from dangers of technical obsolescence or from sudden changes in public taste. Further examples are:

- possible overdependence on certain suppliers or large customers;
- risks of economic depression;
- dangers in the physical environment;
- stock market collapses (increasing the costs and difficulties of raising equity finance).

A common first step in conducting a SWOT analysis is the preparation of a breakdown of the contributions to company profits of each of the firm's sections, products and major functional activities, followed by an examination of the resources devoted to each one of these. Then the firm might investigate the market share held by each of its brands, and the reasons explaining each product's relative position. Note however that meaningful SWOT analysis involves far more than the mere listing of company strengths and weaknesses, opportunities and threats. The fundamental natures of the SWOTS identified need to be examined in depth. What exactly must be done in practical terms to deal with each factor revealed by the investigation?

5. Advantages and problems of SWOT analysis

Advantages to conducting a SWOT analysis are:

(a) Even though nothing can be done about certain weaknesses, knowledge of them enables the firm to avoid bad decisions based on ignorance of their existence.

(b) Resources may be allocated more efficiently.

(c) The company can build on its strengths.

(d) The feasibilities of expansion and/or acquisition strategies become evident.

(e) Key factors determining the business's profitability are pinpointed.

(f) Important decisions can be taken on the basis of facts rather than opinions.

Problems with SWOT analysis include the time and cost of conducting the investigation; the difficulty of obtaining accurate information (note the reluctance of heads of department to pinpoint weaknesses in the work of their sections, fearing subsequent accusations of personal failure); and the fact that certain weaknesses may be such that it is not possible to correct them. And the typical company has so many strengths, weaknesses, threats and potential opportunities that the enumeration and detailed analysis of each and every one is unlikely to be feasible. Selection of particular SWOTs for exhaustive study is necessarily subjective. Note moreover that the completion of a SWOT analysis does not always lead to actions intended to improve the company's situation. The individuals who allocate resources might not be the same as the people who conducted the investigation. Indeed, there could be antipathy between the two other groups. Another problem is that it may be unclear whether a situation represents a threat or an opportunity. Difficulties can sometimes be exploited to serve the firm's best interests.

Some companies engage external consultants to conduct SWOT investigations. Outsiders possess less detailed knowledge of the firm's operations, but bring to their work an objective and independent perspective (especially where comparison with competitors is concerned).

6. Value chain analysis

Value chain analysis is one means for identifying SWOTs. The term 'value chain analysis' was first used by Michael Porter in his book *Competitive Advantage* (Free Press 1985) to describe how particular resource categories contribute to a firm's strategic performance. According to Porter there are five primary activities that occur in most business organisations:

(*i*) inbound logistics of raw materials and input components (storage, inventory control, materials handling, etc.);
(*ii*) operations that transform inputs into products, e.g. manufacturing, packaging, assembly, and so on;
(*iii*) outbound logistics of the finished goods; transport and distribution for example;
(*iv*) marketing and sales;
(*v*) customer service, including after-sales activities, warranties, installation, repair facilities, customer training, etc.

These primary functions are supported, Porter asserts, by four types of activity: procurement; technology development; human resource management; and the management system that embraces, inter-alia, planning, accounting and quality control. Linkages among primary and support activity need to be examined in depth in order to pinpoint areas of competitive strength and to identify possibilities for synergy from the sharing of value chain activities. Economies of scale and economies of scope might be available. The former result in reductions in unit production costs resulting from large-scale operations. Common examples are discounts obtained on bulk purchases, benefits from the application of the division of labour, integration of processes, the ability to attract high calibre labour and the capacity to establish research and development facilities. Economies of scope are unit cost reductions resulting from a firm undertaking a wide range of activities, and hence being able to provide common services and inputs useful for each activity.

7. The Seven-S system

This is an overall framework for analysing the core determinants of the performance of an enterprise. It was developed by the McKinsey management consultancy and has been extensively used for auditing the strategic and operational configurations of organisations. The title of each element was selected so as to begin with the letter S (as a memory aid), providing a convenient checklist of the major areas where decisions may be required. Components of the taxonomy are listed below, alongside examples of the matters that need to be examined under that heading.

(a) Strategy – how the company allocates its resources in order to achieve its strategic aims. Its mission and strategic policy statements. The corporate plan. Strategy development processes and the interface between strategy formulation and implementation.

(b) Structure – organisation structure, line and staff relations, degree of decentralisation, authority and responsibility arrangements, etc. Ability to reorganise quickly in response to environmental change. Relations between strategy and structure.

(c) Systems – the firm's management information systems, budgetary and other control mechanisms, methods for managing projects. Internal communications. Accounting, procurement, marketing and other functional systems. Whether the company's operational systems help or hinder the implementation of strategies. Efficiency and cost-effectiveness of operations.

(d) Style – leadership style, degree and type of supervision, interpersonal relationships within the firm. The overall ambience towards employees displayed by the management team.

(e) Staff – human resource programmes: recruitment, induction and training policies and the effectiveness of these. Promotion systems and the general culture of the organisation. Calibres of management development and succession programmes.

(f) Skills – the capabilities of the enterprise taken as a whole and the particular areas in which it excels. The term is used to describe the totality of a business's particular skills, acting in unison, which determines its general competence and capacity to outperform the competition. Innovativeness and the ability to acquire fresh skills in a short period.

(g) Shared values – group cohesiveness within the firm: morale and the extent to which employees adopt common perspectives towards issues. Whether all employees are working towards the same corporate objectives. The 'sense of purpose' of the organisation: its basic concepts, goals and aspirations.

The 7-S approach emphasises the inter-connectedness of the factors leading to successful business. It is not sufficient to be excellent in just one or two areas, as a deficiency elsewhere can disrupt the entire system. The first three of the above, strategy, structure and systems, are known as the 'hard' elements of the configuration. Excellence in relation to the hard components is not sufficient for high calibre performance overall. Rather, the hard elements need to inter-relate with the 'software' to produce an integrated and mutually re-inforcing management system as a whole: neglect of any one of the factors can cause the business to fail.

Advantages to the 7-S approach are its practicality and comprehensive coverage – while focusing on the key determinants of business success. It has been used extensively in real life situations, and formed the basis for a best selling book written by two McKinsey consultants (*In Search of Excellence*, by T.J.Peters and R.H.Waterman, Harper and Row, 1982). Limitations of the system are its lack of precision and guidelines on how any particular element should be examined in depth.

EXTERNAL ENVIRONMENTS

A change in any one of an organisation's external environments can create difficulties. Indeed, entire industries have been devastated by external change.

8. The political environment

A country's political system will define the manner in which its industry is organised. In a socialist country there is much state intervention, planning and government control. Under capitalism, market forces prevail. The political superstructure defines the legal environment in which business operates, particularly with respect to:

(a) the law of contract;

(b) rules on advertising;

(c) consumer protection;

(d) forms of business ownership;

(e) laws on employment protection;

(f) laws on health and safety at work and working conditions.

Figure 5.2 Environmental influences on strategy formulation

Governments, moreover, might pressurise firms into providing job opportunities for the disabled or other minority groups, and government rules define, ultimately, the limits of business activity. There are government regulatory bodies, codes of practice, review boards, agencies, etc. Political change can affect, *inter alia*:

(a) the regulatory framework within which the business operates;

(b) government industrial policies: investment allowances, cash subsidies, regional development incentives, etc.;

(c) methods and procedures for setting technical standards;

(d) the legal environment of business.

9. The economic environment

The interfaces between a business and its economic environment are numerous. Firms are taxpayers, suppliers of goods and services, buyers of raw materials and other factor services, employers of labour, and providers and consumers of technology. Economic conditions have enormous implications for business strategy. They influence the sizes and profitabilities of markets and the firm's abilities to serve its markets. Economic factors affect costs, consumer demand, financing options, availability of raw materials, pricing possibilities, and many other matters. Note how the economy is to a large extent the consequence of other environments. Technology, for instance, can alter firms' levels of outputs; changes in government might lead to higher inflation; the degree of competition within an industry may affect efficiency.

10. Demographic factors

Large populations may be essential for sales of low-value mass-produced items. Age structures can be crucially important for products that appeal to particular age groups. Demographic change is particularly important to suppliers of consumer goods because alterations in average age levels, rates of population growth, numbers of people in education, etc., frequently generate new consumer requirements.

The average age of the populations of most industrialised countries is rising. This will have the following consequences:

(a) Additional demand for products consumed by middle-aged and elderly people and reduced consumption of goods normally purchased by the young.

(b) Recruitment difficulties in relation to young workers, plus possible skills shortages in certain fields.

(c) Fewer young families and hence less demand for housing (i.e. fewer 'first-time buyers') resulting in spillover effects on house prices, the demand for mortgages and hence the financial services market overall.

(d) The need to retrain older workers and extend training to high unemployment ethnic minority groups.

(e) Greater female participation in the workforce.

(f) Possibly an oversupply of people in middle management.

11. The technological environment

New technologies affect materials, processes, work locations and organisational forms. Change might result from new inventions, or from discoveries or increased accessibility of resources not previously available. 'Technology' means the utilisation of the materials and processes necessary to transform inputs into outputs. Understanding technology requires knowledge; operating a technology requires skills. Technology is created by people and it affects people; especially through the goods it produces and the working conditions (extent of division of labour, employee involvement in operational decision making, use of discretion a work, etc.) it creates.

Typically, new technologies benefit some people through giving them jobs, higher incomes and/or a wider variety of goods, and harm others by creating technological redundancy or making worse the boredom and alienation they experience at work. Technology affects the products emerging from an industry and the processes used to produce these items. It can also influence consumer attitudes and lifestyles, and the structure and functions of organisations, as follows:

(a) Advanced technologies need more professionally qualified and well-educated employees and fewer manual workers.

(b) Different technologies might demand differing forms of group leadership and management style.

(c) As the technology used within an organisation increases, so too will the demand for specialisation of functions in order to cope with the growing complexity of the problems it confronts. This creates the need for better co-ordination in order to integrate activities and unify effort towards the attainment of the organisation's goals.

(d) New technologies require new work patterns, incentive systems, occupational mobility and fresh attitudes towards acceptance of change.

Technical change and environmental turbulence mean that decisions taken according to existing rules are often meaningless. Rather, a strategic approach is necessary, transcending business functions and operational areas and fitting long-term intentions to the realities of fast-changing environments.

12. The social and cultural environment

Society regulates relationships within and between organisations, both formally through its legal system and informally through customs and norms. The social environment affects personal behaviour, including behaviour at work. Thus, social conventions define how management/labour relations and relations between firms and their customers and suppliers are conducted. Attitudes formed by social intercourse influence many economic variables: productivity, consumer demand, competitive conditions, and so on.

A country's culture will affect its residents' perceptions of correct behaviour. Culture is easier to recognise than to define, involving as it does a complex set of interrelating beliefs and ways of living. A nation's culture represents a collective frame of reference through which a wide range of issues and problems are interpreted. Culture affects what people buy (taboos, local tastes, historical traditions, etc.), when they buy (e.g. the spending boom around Christmas in Christian countries), who does the purchasing (men or women), and the overall pattern of consumer buying behaviour. Culture can also affect which consumer needs are felt more intensely; which family members take which purchasing decisions; and attitudes towards foreign supplied products. On a wider level, cultural influences are evident in some aspects of a country's demographic makeup (e.g. household size, kinship patterns, social mobility and social stratification), and in authority and status systems that emerge from the management styles of firms.

13. Environmental scanning

All the above inter-relate to form the company's overall commercial environment, which is constantly changing. Environmental change can create problems or opportunities for the firm. Technological change, for example, can lead to product obsolescence, demographic change can create or destroy markets, while changes in input costs may significantly increase or decrease profits.

Environmental scanning is the process of searching for and gathering information on significant changes in the company's environments. Its purposes are to:

- facilitate planning;
- monitor the relevance of current strategies;
- identify the implications of environmental change for the firm's operations.

Effective environmental scanning requires:

(a) A definition of which environments are most important to the company. Not all environmental factors can be investigated (there are too many of them) so a handful of relevant external variables must be selected for research.

(b) A sound management information system (see 12.**16**).

(c) Precise identification of critical environmental issues, including assessments of which issues might develop into major opportunities or threats.

There are two approaches to searching for relevant environmental change. The first is to predict the external changes that might occur and then detail: (i) how the organisation would be affected by them; and (ii) how the organisation should respond. Alternatively, the planner may begin with a list of the firm's functions, followed by a listing of all the environmental factors that might affect these functions. The latter course is usually the easier of the two since it is concrete, and named individuals can be made responsible for listing relevant factors in each functional department. However, some important variables may be overlooked.

Progress test 5

1. What is a management audit?

2. There are two types of operational audit. What are they?

3. Explain the meaning of the term 'value chain analysis'.

4. What do the S's stand for in the 7-S system?

5. List some of the consequences for businesses of an increase in the average age of a country's population.

6. Define 'technology'.

7. What is 'environmental scanning'?

6

CHANGE, CHAOS AND THE LEARNING ORGANISATION

1. Nature of change

More than ever before, organisations function in an environment of change. New products are introduced, new materials discovered, new markets and competitors constantly emerge. The cultural, political, economic and legal frameworks within which firms operate are today liable to rapid and far-reaching alteration. Enormous technological advances have occurred during this century, and particularly during the last thirty years. New economic alliances have developed; there has been an explosion in world trade. Economically and politically the world is now a much smaller place.

Change is inevitable. The problem from a managerial point of view is how best to harness change and use its force for the benefit of the organisation. Some change can be initiated by management itself. Otherwise the organisation must learn how to respond to externally induced change; and adapt quickly and effectively to the requirements of completely new circumstances. Change can be smooth, uneven or discontinuous. 'Smooth' change is that which is predictable and the result of slow and systematic developments in the business's environments. Examples are the effects on consumer markets of rising living standards or changes in the calibres of fresh recruits to firms due to improvements (or deteriorations) in a nation's education system. Uneven change is predictable, but its timing erratic. Management knows that a new development is likely, yet cannot say when it will happen or how extensive its consequences will be. Discontinuous change results from trend breaks and/or major shocks in technical, legal, social or other environments.

The most widely documented example of a large business forced to respond aggressively to external change is perhaps that of the US AT & T company following its compulsory breaking-up in 1983 under US anti-monopoly legislation. Prior to that date, AT & T was consistently profitable and had a reputation for being well-managed and a good employer that generously rewarded hard work and staff loyalty. The firm was an efficient bureaucracy, with precise written procedures covering every eventuality and organisation charts and manuals for all aspects of the business's operations. Following the dismemberment of this giant telephone company around 75,000 jobs were lost. The core business remained as AT & T, other sections became multi-billion dollar companies in their own right. Morale within AT & T plummeted. Employees had previously prided themselves on providing a public service; now they were expected to adopt a market-driven approach.

AT & T's chief executive convened an emergency meeting of the firm's 27-strong senior management team, following which each individual was required publicly to state his or her support for the new strategies necessary to revitalise the organisation. Existing divisions of the company were merged, administrative policies and procedures harmonised and a fresh corporate image determined. The firm's product range was rationalised and, for a time, it became a market follower rather than market leader in a number of product areas. Mass meetings between the chief executive and employees were convened in seven cities at which the company's problems and their proposed solutions were explained. Organisational systems were restructured and a new company-wide employee training programme implemented. An entrepreneural culture was encouraged within the firm, in conjunction with a stringent cost-cutting exercise and a big investment in computerised management control systems and IT.

2. Technological change

The overall technological environments of business are discussed in 5.11. This section briefly examines the implications of technical change. New technologies affect materials, processes, work locations, and organisational forms. Change might result from new inventions, discoveries or the accessibility of resources not previously available. Technical change is necessary for progress, though acceptance of change among those who will be affected by it may be extremely difficult to achieve. If possible therefore, the organisation should itself seek to initiate technical change, since then its economic and human relations consequences can be partly controlled. Technological change can alter the shape of an entire industry, and have far-reaching effects on everyday life. Otherwise, change might involve modifications to existing products or methods, or the need to replace entirely those items that have been rendered obsolete. Increasingly, technical change implies organisational change. Recognition of the inevitability of change should therefore be incorporated into an enterprise's long-term organisational development and overall corporate plans. If a firm fails to update its products, production methods and choice of markets its competitors will quickly take advantage of the fact. A major implication of the rapid product obsolescence characteristic of so many contemporary markets is the need either for individual firms to spend more on research and development (of markets as well as products) than previously has been the norm, or to imitate quickly the activities of successful competitors.

3. Other environmental change

Environmental change can involve alterations in laws, consumer attitudes, tastes and fashions, taxes, and a whole range of demographic variables. Consider for example the effects of a change in government. Income and other taxes might alter thus changing consumers' incomes and spending patterns. New laws to protect consumer interests might be passed, as might laws that alter relationships between management and trade unions (redundancy schemes and payments or Employment Protection Acts, for example), or between a company and its shareholders. Competitors might cut prices, introduce new products, or embark on large-scale advertising campaigns. Other environmental changes that might affect a firm include the following:

(a) A change in the age structure of the population. Spending patterns of younger people typically differ from those of the older section of the community.

(b) Changes in lifestyles. Basic attitudes towards fundamental aspects of life – diet, family size, style of clothing, form of occupation of dwellings (leasehold or freehold, houses or flats, independent or joint occupation), attitudes towards work and leisure – all alter over time.

(c) Changes in the labour force. Developments in the educational system can improve the competence of new workers entering the labour market. The structure of the labour force can alter. A government could raise or lower the compulsory retirement age, or encourage the employment of ethnic minorities or women workers.

4. Planning for change

Recognition of the inevitability of change naturally leads to desires to plan the business reorganisations and alterations in activities that change might necessitate. There are five steps in the process of planning and implementing change:

1. Precise definition of the operational changes that are needed.

2. Specification of how new working methods will affect particular people and groups.

3. Identification of attitudes and perspectives currently held by employees and how these support current working practices.

4. Statement of the attitudes and perspectives necessary to enable people to adapt successfully to new environments and working methods.

5. Implementation of measures designed to change existing attitudes.

Four strategic alternatives are available:

1. Altering technologies by introducing new equipment, methods, materials and systems. Existing staff may need to be retrained to handle a new technology, or different staff might be required.

2. Altering structures. This can involve organisation design; centralisation or decentralisation of functions, respecification of authority and accountability systems, etc.

3. Altering tasks, i.e. changing the content of employees' jobs, increasing or decreasing the extent of the division of labour within the organisation, and so on.

4. Altering the people who do the work. Here management focuses on solving the human problems created by change.

5. Force field analysis

Effective management of change requires an understanding of the dynamics of change and its root causes both within the organisation and in the wider business environment. Hence it is necessary to explore the forces that facilitate or inhibit the implementation of change. This exercise is sometimes referred to as force field analysis, the idea for which was first developed by K. Lewin in 1935. Lewin's model focused on the identification and systematic analysis of those elements within an organisation which seek to promote change ('driving forces') and those which resist new methods ('inhibitors'). Organisational behaviour, Lewin suggested, depends on the relative strengths of driving forces and inhibitors, and the equilibrium that emerges from their opposition. Examples of driving forces are improved inputs and working methods, pressures exerted by senior management, competition between groups, and the introduction of new technology. Inhibitors to change include the existence within an organisation of an inappropriate organisational culture, fear of the unknown, inadequate training of workers, and the narrow-minded pursuit of self-interest by individuals at the expense of attaining organisational goals.

A force field analysis can be illustrated in a diagram that shows the strengths of the enabling and constraining factors as arrows proportional in length to the perceived relative force of each element. Figure 6.1 is an example. Advantages of force field analysis are that:

- it recognises the dynamic nature of the change process;
- key factors facilitating or impeding change are (hopefully) highlighted;
- the method is straightforward, understandable, and applicable in very many situations;
- a wide range of people can be consulted in order to identify relevant constraints and enablers.

Problems with the method include the following:

(a) A force field diagram represents a 'snap-shot' of a particular situation at a specific moment in time. By the time decisions are taken on the basis of this snap-shot the entire situation might have changed.

(b) The analysis says nothing about the costs of implementing change or of the techniques necessary.

(c) Attention focuses on enablers and inhibitors and not on whether the intended change is itself worth undertaking, i.e. it is 'process-driven' rather than results-orientated.

(d) Quantification of the values of change factors is crude and subjective.

(e) Sometimes a factor can be interpreted either as an enabler or a constraint. Also factors might inter-relate and affect each other.

(f) The lists of possible enablers and inhibitors are so extensive that important variables might be missed.

Force field analysis might be effected via special brainstorming sessions or

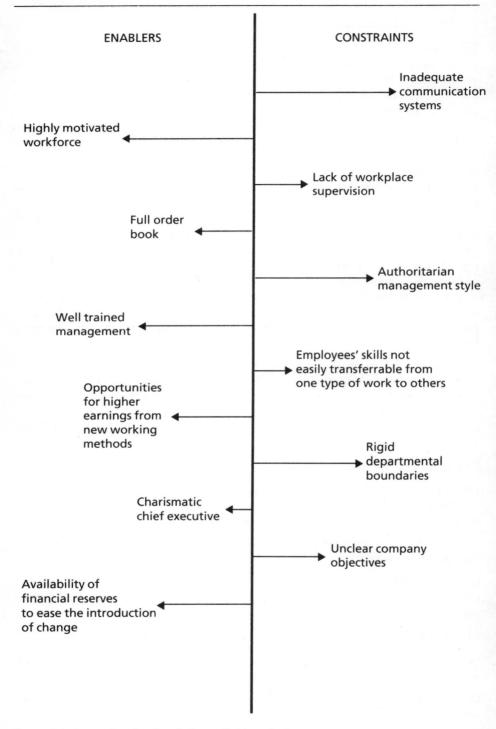

Figure 6.1 Example of a simple force field analysis

as part of a firm's overall strategy formulation and corporate planning processes.

6. Resistance to change

As an organisation matures it becomes, typically, more formal and bureaucratic, set in its ways and generally resistant to outside pressures. Employees resist change for many reasons, including the following:

(a) feelings of insecurity generated by an intended change;

(b) disruption of existing relations and patterns of behaviour;

(c) threats to individual status and financial reward;

(d) the influence of group norms and values that oppose change;

(e) doubts regarding the technical feasibility of proposed changes;

(f) the threat of having to retrain and acquire new skills in order to cope with altered working methods;

(g) feeling of personal inadequacy *vis-à-vis* new technologies, e.g. fear of not being able to understand a recently installed computer system;

(h) resentment over not having been consulted about a change;

(i) the realisation that skills and experience acquired at great effort over many years are no longer of value to the organisation.

7. Management systems and resistance to change

R.M. Kanter completed a celebrated study of 115 examples of successful innovation occurring within American companies, concluding that certain management attitudes and practices invariably inhibited the introduction of change. Examples of these attitudes and practices were:

(a) suspicion of new ideas or of suggestions emanating from the base of the organisation;

(b) management through committees;

(c) allowing one department to criticise and interfere with another's proposals;

(d) assuming that high-ranking employees know more about the organisation than low-ranking employees;

(e) assigning unpleasant tasks (dismissal of employees for example) to subordinates;

(f) not involving subordinates in decisions to restructure the organisation;

(g) exercising tight supervision and control;

(h) perceiving subordinates' problems as indications of their failure, and treating a subordinate's discussion of a problem as an admission of his or her incompetence;

(i) telling subordinates that they are not indispensable;

(j) regularly criticising subordinates but only rarely praising them.

8. Overcoming resistance to change

Lewin (see 5) suggested three steps for overcoming resistance to change:

1. Unfreezing – getting rid of existing practices and ideas that stand in the way of change. Unfreezing can occur through dramatic events (a number of a company's employees being declared redundant for example), or by gradually making people aware of the need for and benefits of change. The latter might be achieved via training, team briefing sessions, videos or other communication devices. Workshops are a common device for unfreezing existing perceptions of issues. A workshop will highlight the nature and extent of the problems confronting the organisation, devise action plans, identify barriers to the implementation of change and suggest means for overcoming them. Often the participants in the workshop will divide into groups to discuss specific issues.

2. Changing – teaching employees to think and perform differently.

3. Refreezing – establishing new norms and standard practices. Refreezing involves the consolidation and stabilisation of the new situation.

Implementing change can involve the reshaping of strategies, organisational restructuring, measures to alter the culture of a business, or the introduction of new working methods. Specific techniques for introducing and overcoming resistance to change include the following:

(a) Maintaining existing work groups intact wherever possible.

(b) Employee participation in decisions concerning the practical implementation of change.

(c) Improved communication with workers, regularly informing them of intended alterations.

(d) Human resource planning, i.e. predicting the consequences of changes to working practices and redeploying workers to alternative functions. HRP is discussed in Chapter 16.

(e) Creation of financial reserves specifically earmarked to pay for the retraining of employees adversely affected by new methods. The reserve could also be used to encourage natural wastage, e.g. through the early retirement of older workers.

(f) Careful explanation to employees of the benefits of change and of the technical superiority of new systems.

(g) Preparation of detailed records on each employee's qualifications, attributes and experiences, thus enabling management to assess a worker's suitability for alternative duties.

(h) Encouraging flexible attitudes in employees though training programmes and through arranging work in such a manner that the skills and experience acquired in one job can be quickly and easily transferred to others.

(i) Application of wage payment systems that encourage the adoption of new and better working methods.

(j) Ensuring (as far as possible) employees' security of tenure and informing workers of the measures that have been implemented to achieve this.

(k) Instructing employees in how to cope with change, emphasising the need for transferable rather than purely job-specific skills.

9. Change agents

A change agent is a person who fosters change within an organisation. Usually (but not necessarily) the change agent is an external management consultant who specialises in this type of work. Outsiders might be more objective and dispassionate than internal employees of the company, but will lack the detailed knowledge of day-to-day operations that the latter usually possess. Also, internal staff know exactly where to look for information, and they are fully accountable for their actions in the long term. (Outsiders move on as soon as an assignment is completed.) On the other hand, in-house staff may lack the necessary insights, creativity and management skills, and will not be exposed to penetrating independent criticism.

External consultants should have extensive experience of implementing change in other organisations, so that the firm in question will benefit from other companies' work. Outside consultants have no vested interests in the welfare of particular departments and are not concerned with internal organisational politics. They have up-to-the-minute knowledge of the latest techniques, and need not be afraid of asking questions of anyone in the organisation. Note how internal staff can benefit simply by observing a top-class external consultant at work.

The change agent may advise on job and organisation design, on improving the firm's communication systems, or on the need for retraining and management development.

RESTRUCTURING ORGANISATIONS AND PROCESSES

10. Re-engineering

This means the radical redesign of business processes, normally via the use of the latest information technology, in order to enhance their performance. Conventional approaches to efficiency improvement sometimes fail because they focus on automating and speeding up existing systems and processes, merely perpetuating old ways of performing operations rather than addressing fundamental deficiencies and replacing out-of-date systems as a whole. Often, moreover, firms seeking efficiency gains do little more than tinker with the prevailing organisation structure in the naive belief that this alone will lead to the desired result. Problems with simple organisation restructuring are:

(a) The revised structure is likely to become out-of-date very soon after it is implemented.

(b) Frequent alterations in company structure destabilises the organisation and demoralises workers.

(c) Existing employees are likely to be thrust into new and unfamiliar roles for which they lack experience and/or training.

(d) Significant time periods are needed for people to adjust to each restructuring.

Re-engineering, conversely, involves challenging underlying assumptions and changing the basic rules and philosophies concerning the ways a business is managed. Examples of re-engineering include:

- abolition of job descriptions and departmental boundaries;
- widespread use of empowerment (see **11**);
- integration of a large number of operations;
- finding new ways of achieving specific outcomes;
- creating organisation structures based on desired results rather than on the functional duties needed to attain them, e.g. by having one person overseeing several types of task and assuming full responsibility for reaching a specific objective;
- involving users of the outputs to processes in the design and execution of those processes. For example, departments that work on raw materials could be made partially responsible for selecting and controlling suppliers of the raw materials;
- centralisation of control procedures using computers;
- having decisions taken on the spot, where work is performed. Note how this implies the removal of some layers in the management hierarchy and hence a 'flattening' of the organisation.

11. Empowerment

An employee's feeling of being in control and of significantly contributing to an organisation's development can be greatly enhanced by 'empowering' that person to complete tasks and attain targets independently, without constantly having to refer back to management for permission to take certain actions. The employee is trusted to take sensible decisions. Hence, for example, salespeople might be empowered to offer special discounts to prospective customers, production operatives can be empowered to decide the speed of an assembly line, and work teams may be empowered to determine the extent and intensity of the use of robots within a section of a firm. The aim is to enable employees who actually have to deal with problems to implement solutions quickly and without recourse to supervisors and/or higher levels of management. This is increasingly necessary as large and bureaucratic organisations 'delayer' management hierarchies in the search for administrative efficiency and lower costs. Removal of one or more entire layers of the management pyramid is a fast and sometimes highly effective means for streamlining management communication and control.

Empowerment differs from 'delegation' in that whereas the latter is the devolution of duties from boss to subordinate (albeit with the authority to implement decisions), empowerment is a general approach to operational management, requiring not just the passing down of power and responsibility through a hierarchy but also that the individual workers actively contribute to improving the performance of tasks. Benefits to empowerment include:

- the encouragement of individual creativity and initiative, commitment to the enterprise and team spirit;
- decision taking at the most suitable levels;
- facilitation of performance management.

A UK specialist bicycle manufacturer was confronted with the most ferocious competition experienced during its 40 year history following the completion of the European Single Market. In order to survive, the firm's production costs would have to be cut by a quarter, implying a big reduction in staff. However, the firm was a family business with many long-serving employees, and management was unwilling to dismiss anyone simply to reduce costs. Hence a radical productivity and quality improvement programme was implemented, based on empowerment. Authority to take decisions on quality control was delegated to workers and jobs redesigned so that individuals routinely inspected their own work and implemented whatever measures for remedying defective production might be necessary. An agreement was struck with employee representatives whereby 20 per cent of all financial savings achieved through workers' higher productivity would be paid to employees. Productivity rocketed. Workers responded to their new decision-making powers by implementing scores of labour-saving innovations, and the firm quickly became one of the most efficient bicycle manufacturers in the world.

CHAOS AND THE LEARNING ORGANISATION

12. Chaos

Arguably, disorder and confusion are endemic to business situations; so that management theory and practice should focus on the best means for responding to uncertainty and change. Scientists have been interested in the theory of chaos for generations, seeking to understand the effects on macro-systems of micro events (e.g. a butterfly flapping its wings in northern Siberia can generate a chain of events leading to a hurricane in the USA). The number of possible combinations of micro events and potential outcomes was so immense that new thinking on the nature of 'prediction' and 'uncertainty' was required, taking into account the fundamental instability of nature. These ideas have begun to influence management theory as the pace of organisational and environmental change has accelerated to unprecedented levels.

The 'chaos approach' challenges the conventional scientific emphasis on seeking to discover relationships between cause and effect, since the conventional approach assumes regular mechanistic 'laws of the universe'. Rather it is necessary to recognise that every event affects every other event in some way or other, so that there are no clear and direct chains of causality: the consequence of a change in one variable causes something else, which affects other things which themselves have implications for numerous further variables, including that which altered in the first instance. Thus, nature is a continuous feedback system with inputs and outputs mutually interacting. 'Laws of nature' exist, but are far too complex to be explained in terms of straightforward cause-and-effect relationships. Consider for example the determination of the shape of a snowflake as it drifts towards the ground. The surrounding air quality, temperature and other environmental conditions affect the snowflake, which itself is simultaneously influencing the environment (by lowering its temperature, changing the humidity, etc.), which affects the form of the snowflake, and so on.

A state of equilibrium (balance) in a business situation can be upset by seemingly trivial events (staff transfers, personal disagreements, changes in procedures, etc.) that have knock-on effects which interact and multiply in an extremely complicated manner. Chaos theory has been offered as an explanation for unexpected turmoils on stock exchanges and foreign exchange markets, the instability of world oil and other commodity prices, and the sudden collapse of organisational structures. The chaos approach has many implications for management, including the following:

(a) Managements cannot control long-term future activities because future environments are totally unpredictable (in consequence of the complexity of cause/effect linkages).

(b) Stable environments can suddenly explode into unstable environments for no seemingly apparent reason, and vice-versa. Hence it is necessary to recognise that 'anything can happen' and plan accordingly.

(c) Organisations can appear to be stable and then suddenly become highly unstable.

(d) Unstable organisations need not be unsuccessful.

(e) Dynamic forces are constantly pulling a business in different directions. Examples of such forces are market conditions, regulatory frameworks, decentralisation of decision making, and human desires for excitement or for a quiet life. An organisation that moves towards stability is likely to ossify and lose its innovative edge. Equally, however, movements towards extreme instability can lead the organisation to collapse.

(f) Firms must be flexible and responsive to environmental change. They need to have effective information-gathering systems and to focus on short-term rather than long-term activities.

(g) Long-term planning is basically useless, as it is not possible to predict future environments.

(h) Mission statements should be regularly updated.

(i) Statistical forecasts will typically be wrong. Simulation and scenario building is preferable as a means for taking decisions.

To cope with chaotic situations firms need to be able to learn from past and current activities, systematically review the lessons learned from recent experience, and hence develop rapid and flexible responses to fast-changing environments.

13. The learning organisation

The term 'learning organisation' is sometimes applied to companies operating in turbulent environments that require transformations in working methods and which – in order to facilitate the introduction of new systems – train and develop their employees on a continuous basis. Hence the very essence of the business – its products, markets, processes and orientations – is likely to alter totally from period to period. Learning organisations discover the key characteristics of their environments and are thus better able to plan ahead. The learning organisation will attempt to identify interactions between the firm's sub-systems that facilitate or inhibit the management of change and is better able to cope with environmental and other change because it can accommodate unpredictability. It is not encumbered with rigid and out-of-date plans and procedures.

Nature of organisational learning

To learn means to absorb knowledge, acquire skills and/or assume fresh attitudes. Learning results in permanent changes in ability or behaviour, as opposed to short-term changes which are soon reversed. Organisational learning means all the processes whereby freshly discovered solutions to administrative problems pass into the firm's 'managerial memory', hence becoming integral parts of the organisation's mechanism for reacting to future events. A consequence is that decision-making procedures are continuously modified and adapted in the light of experience.

One of the most notable businesses to take up the idea of the learning organisation has been the US Hanover Insurance Company; a giant firm that nearly went into liquidation in 1969, then acquiring a new managing director greatly influenced by Argyris' thinking. Hanover was seemingly beset by organisational politics, bureaucratic inertia and unwillingness of managers either to discuss significant issues seriously or to take decisions. From 1969 onwards all Hanover's middle and senior managers had to attend a three day seminar on the principles and practice of action learning intended to compel individuals to question their underlying assumptions about, perspectives on, and approaches towards fundamental management concerns. These seminars were supplemented by an extensive management training programme focusing on 'systems thinking' (i.e. analysing processes rather than snapshots of situations), reflection, and honest face-to-face discussion by managers of sensitive events. Conversion of theory into practice occurred via a network of 'internal boards of directors' comprising three or four managers who would advise regional general managers, plus internal boards advising senior executives direct. The system was intended to increase the flow of information throughout the organisation, stimulate creativity, and encourage individuals to articulate their views and consider alternative opinions. Hanover claims that adherence to the learning organisation philosophy helped it re-establish itself as one of the world's leading insurance firms. It bettered the average insurance industry profit performance in eight out of ten years between 1970 and 1979, and throughout the 1980s. By 1991 it ranked fifteenth among 68 US insurance companies.

Source: Adapted from Senge, P.M., *The Fifth Discipline*, Century Business, 1992.

14. Single loop and double loop learning

According to Chris Argyris, organisations can be extremely bad at learning, unless the learning is simple and routine. Hence an organisation quickly loses the benefits of experience and reverts to its old bad habits. 'Single loop' learning, according to Argyris, is the learning necessary for an employee to be able to apply existing methods to the completion of a job. This is contrasted with 'double loop' learning that challenges and redefines the basic requirements of the job and how it should be undertaken. Single loop learning typically involves the setting of standards and the investigation of deviations from targets. Double loop learning means questioning whether the standards and objectives are appropriate in the first instance.

Implementing DLL

DLL inevitably occurs within organisations as they experience crises, fail to attain targets, and experience environmental change. Learning about mistakes in these situations however is costly and inefficient: decisions are taken too late to be effective, and all the benefits of forward planning are lost. Rather the organisation needs to:

(a) educate its managers in the methods of learning by doing;

(b) formulate its objectives and standards in such a way that they can be evaluated on a continuous basis and the basic assumptions that underlie them can be empirically tested;

(c) seek to learn in advance of environmental turbulence or, if this is not possible, adapt its behaviour systematically through trial and error as situations develop. The first loop in the double loop system is the discovery of facts, acting upon them and evaluating the consequences. Knowledge gained is formal, systematic and explicit. The second loop involves the development of skills and 'know-how' resulting from the first loop and hence a change in fundamental perspectives on the matter under consideration. This feeds back into the interpretation of the facts embodied in the first loop and the actions taken thereafter. Hence, both behaviour and understanding of events and environments will change.

Training, employee relations and staff development

Companies operating in fast-changing environments require regular transforma-tions in working methods and (in order to facilitate the introduction of new systems) must train and develop their employees on a continuous basis. Note however that a learning organisation is far more than a firm which spends large amounts on training. Rather, it requires the unqualified acceptance of change at all levels within the business, including basic grade operatives. Implications of the learning organisation for training, employee relations and staff development are as follows:

(a) Current policies should be open to question and challenged by all grades of employee. Indeed, management should welcome and actively support such questioning.

(b) Individuals should not necessarily be penalised for experimenting on their own initiative and making mistakes.

(c) There is a need for heavy emphasis on employee communication, with management diffusing information on current environmental trends throughout the organisation.

(d) Employee appraisal and reward systems need not be linked to the attainment of existing goals but rather to finding new and profitable fields of activity.

(e) Workers must possess an understanding of customer requirements.

(f) Employees need to 'learn how to learn'; taking their example from top management.

Note how an organisation is, at base, a group of individuals, so that the manner whereby groups within it learn is affected by social, interpersonal and other intangible factors as well as information systems and other formal learning facilities.

Problems of implementation

Creating a learning organisation is difficult, for a number of reasons:

(a) Employees at all levels within the organisation must want to learn. Thus, the establishment of a learning organisation is a bottom-up process that may not fit in with the culture of a pre-existing bureaucratic and hierarchical system.

(b) Inadequate information gathering and internal communication systems.

(c) Organisational politics (see below) that might impede widespread acceptance of the idea.

Fatal disasters are frequently cited as examples of organisations' failures to learn. The 1986 explosion of the Challenger space shuttle, for example, was due to a faulty ring seal between segments of its booster sockets allowing flame to escape and trigger the explosion. It subsequently emerged that managers of the project had been aware of the problems for a long period. The supplier had criticised the design of the ring seal, had complained, written memoranda and raised the matter in meetings. All this was ignored, management regarding the proper role of the supplier as *implementing* design decisions, certainly not questioning them. Management was so concerned with meeting schedules that it overlooked quality control considerations. There was no forum for constructive disagreement with decisions.

The Zeebrugge ferry disaster of 1987 similarly illustrates the dangers resulting from management apathy in relation to safety matters. Like other ferries, the mv Herald of Free Enterprise received its load through its bow doors, which had not been shut prior to setting sail. This resulted in the capsize of the vessel and 188 deaths. The Herald of Free Enterprise was commanded by five Masters, who took it in turn to manage the vessel. Several different sets of Chief Officers, Deck Officers and crews manned the vessel at various times. One of the Masters complained formally in writing that there was little co-ordination between on-coming and off-going Deck Officers, that no fewer than 30 different Deck Officers had worked on the vessel over a three month period, and that a permanent complement of Deck Officers was urgently needed. It became clear that Officers were under pressure to turn the vessel around in the shortest possible time, and the roles of various Officers were not clearly defined. Masters met only intermittently; management and senior Masters had meetings just once every couple of years. The Masters had complained formally to the company's management about four serious matters: overloading of passengers, inadequate door status warning lights, overloading of cargo, and inadequate ballast. Numerous memoranda had been sent to the company's operations manager and requests for face-to-face meetings advanced, but nothing happened. All of the four subjects of the complaints contributed to the Herald of Free Enterprise's capsize.

15. Organisational politics

The term 'organisational politics' is used to describe negotiations and settlements within organisations made necessary by the existence of contrasting interests and the differing perceptions of various organisation members. Political activities lead to compromises, toleration, and a stability of relationships which enables the organisation to survive.

Organisational politics typically involved the building of coalitions around issues, persuasion and advocacy, and the skilful deployment of resources and power. Control over information is a key tool in the process. Coalitions rise in consequence of bargaining among various interest groups, and a dominant coalition will emerge. Organisational politics affect which issues assume prominence within the organisation and how they are discussed and interpreted. The manner in which a problem is diagnosed may be determined primarily by the self-interests of influential individuals and coalitions. Hence organisational politics influences how decisions are taken as well as the decisions themselves. Note how certain rules, procedures and interpersonal relationships might develop outside the official management system.

A company's political power system can affect its organisation structure, even to the extent that the latter becomes unsuitable as a means for realising the enterprise's goals. Internal politics helps shape the ideas about organisation structure that are deemed acceptable and, once implemented, the organisation design most favoured by the dominant political group might perpetuate itself indefinitely. Organisational politics can affect planning (see Chapter 16) in the following respects:

(a) disputes over who should undertake corporate planning activities;

(b) the status of the planning function in the overall company hierarchy;

(c) possible misuse of planning mechanisms by individuals wishing to pursue their own personal objectives;

(d) resistance to planning on the grounds that it could pose a threat to vested interests within the firm and/or may expose personal weaknesses;

(e) conflicts between various functions (marketing and finance for example) regarding which department's plans are to be paramount;

(f) use of a corporate plan as a means for making redundant people who otherwise would be dismissed for underperformance.

Organisational politics are perhaps most likely to develop where:

(a) the organisation faces severe resource constraints, so that individuals and departments are compelled to fight hard for their budget allocations;

(b) environments are fast changing and uncertain;

(c) there is a lack of leadership at the top of the organisation;

(d) the firm does not have clear objectives;

(e) key managers have fundamentally different opinions about the basic purpose of the organisation;

(f) there is little accountability and inadequate management control.

Organisational politics can damage a company in a number of respects:

(a) Certain individuals may come to act as 'gatekeepers'. An organisational gatekeeper is someone who (i) communicates with the outside world on behalf of an organisation (formally or informally), (ii) gathers information from external sources and (iii) through being able to withhold this information from certain of the organisation's members is able to influence the decisions it makes.

(b) Departments are encouraged to seek to make other sections dependent on them, regardless of whether these inter-relationships benefit the firm as a whole.

(c) Sectional goals might be inconsistent across the organisation and not shared by all individuals and departments.

(d) Managers may become obsessed with ideological struggle, conflict and gaining the upper hand, at the expense of getting on with their work.

(e) Bad decisions might result from the internal political bargaining process.

(f) Interpersonal relationships may deteriorate.

(g) Inaccurate information might be deliberately circulated.

(h) Decision processes can become disorganised and disorderly.

CULTURE

16. Corporate culture

The culture of an organisation (sometimes referred to as 'organisational climate') consists of its customary ways of doing things and its members' shared perceptions of issues that affect the organisation A firm's culture evolves gradually, and employees may not even be aware that it exists. Organisational culture is important, however, because it helps define how workers feel about their jobs. In particular it affects:

- leadership styles applied within the organisation;
- individual perceptions of colleagues and situations;
- assumptions about how work should be performed;
- attitudes towards what is and what is not correct.

Culture affects business strategy formulation and planning mechanisms in a number of important respects, including:

(a) how well the company's goals are understood and supported by employees;

(b) decision making processes (participative, autocratic, etc.) and the management style applied within the enterprise;

(c) whether individuals can be relied upon to be self-motivated and to implement strategic plans and decisions;

(d) attitudes towards risk;

(e) how senior management perceives the very character of the organisation: as a market leader or follower, as traditional and conservative, innovative and trend setting, etc.;

(f) organisational drive, vigour and vitality.

Organisational culture may be innovative, conservative, or somewhere between the two. A conservative culture is likely to generate low risk strategies heavily reliant on what has gone before, tried and tested solutions to problems, and possibly a tall management hierarchy and authoritarian management style. Organisational culture creates norms of behaviour, attitude and perception, myths and rituals, and (importantly) feelings within employees of the value of being associated with the firm. Myths arise from exaggerated stories about past incidents, rumour and innuendo, the consequences of past mistakes (dismissal of certain employees for example), and from lack of communication and accurate information within the organisation.

Influence of culture

Positive aspects of organisational culture are that it furnishes employees with a sense of corporate identity, helps generate commitment to the attainment of organisational goals, provides employees with a frame of reference through which to evaluate issues and, by influencing individual perspectives and perceptions, stabilises interpersonal relationships within the firm. Equally, however, a culture might be highly resistant to change, encourage bureaucracy and inflexibility, and lead to short-sighted thinking within the firm. The organisation's needs and activities will regularly alter, but its underlying culture might remain constant. The continuing existence of out-of-date attitudes and perspectives among employees following changes in organisational structure and working methods is known as 'cultural lag'.

17. Types of organisational culture

Charles Handy distinguished four types of culture: power; role; task; and person. One of these might dominate the entire organisation, or different cultures may exist in various parts of the firm. The power culture stems from a single central source, as in a small business that has begun to expand. Here, there are few rules and procedures and few committees. All important decisions are taken by a handful of people and precedents are followed. A role culture, in contrast, is highly bureaucratic. It operates through formal roles and procedures and there are clearly defined rules for settling disputes. Organisations dominated by a role culture offer security and predictability, but since they are rigidly structured, cannot adapt quickly to accommodate change (as can a power culture organisation).

The task culture is job- or project-orientated and manifest in matrix organisation structures (see 7.24). There is no single dominant leader; all group members concentrate on completing the collective task. A task culture will encourage flexibility in approach and is ideal for an environment of change. Job satisfaction is high and there is much group cohesion. A person culture might arise in an organisation which exists only to serve the people within it. Examples are partnerships, consultancy firms, and professional organisations.

According to Handy, none of these cultures is better than the others. A culture arises, he argues, from historical circumstances, the existing environment, technology, and the human needs of people within the organisation.

18. Formation of culture

A culture will have risen within a particular environmental context and be related to specific organisational needs. Factors contributing to the formation of a culture include the following:

(a) Management's stated objectives and core values. Employees who wish to progress within the organisation will tend to adopt these values in order to win the approval of their superiors.

(b) Induction systems and organisational socialisation techniques (e.g. selection methods and methods for training employees).

(c) Procedures for status symbols and fringe benefits, superannuation schemes, company housing loans, possibly the wearing of company uniform, and so on.

Ideally the values, beliefs and expectations shared by employees should be consistent with the firm's mission, strategies and objectives. Indications that this is not the case might emerge from communications breakdowns, excessive bureaucracy, resistance to change, underperformance and poor quality output. This will require that the prevailing culture be changed.

19. Changing the corporate culture

To alter an existing culture the following measures may be required:

(a) injection of new staff into the organisation;

(b) introduction of incentive schemes to encourage the acceptance of new approaches and working methods;

(c) emphatic managerial endorsement of new ideas, plus an increase in the flow of information between management and workers;

(d) deliberate promotion of individuals who possess flexible and appropriate cultural attitudes.

Although it is clearly important for management to understand and, if possible, determine the culture that exists within an organisation, a preoccupation with cultural matters can itself create difficulties. Employees may feel they are being manipulated, and hence react in a negative manner. Also the process of culture change is never-ending, so that enormous amounts of time and resources may be devoted to relatively minor cultural problems and issues.

Progress test 6

1. List some of the environmental changes that might affect a business.

2. In force field analysis, what is the difference between a driving force and an inhibitor?

3. Specify six examples of management attitudes and practices that could inhibit the introduction of change.

4. According to K. Lewin, what three steps are necessary to overcome resistance to change?

5. What is a change agent?

6. How does re-engineering differ from conventional organisational restructuring?

7. Explain the difference between empowerment and delegation.

8. How does chaos theory differ from conventional approaches to change mangement?

9. Distinguish between single-loop and double-loop organisational learning.

10. How might organisational politics affect business planning?

11. What factors are likely to influence an organisation's culture?

7

STRATEGY AND STRUCTURE

1. Organisation structure

The system for breaking down the totality of a firm's work into units and for allocating these units to people and departments constitutes the 'organisational structure' of the enterprise. This structure defines the framework within which activities occur. Organisational theory is the study of organisation structures, of how organisations function, the performance of organisations and how groups and individuals within them behave. Organisation structure is a means whereby a company can attain its objectives. The latter change over time, and the firm's organisation should also change in order to keep in step. When structuring an organisation, management needs to consider the following issues:

(a) whether the firm should have departments (i) for particular functions (marketing and personnel departments for example), (ii) for products (each of the company's products representing a cost centre in its own right), (iii) for geographical regions, or (iv) for teams of individuals concerned with specific projects;

(b) the best organisation structure for the firm in terms of the number of levels of authority in its hierarchy and how many immediate subordinates each line manager should personally control;

(c) whether each member of the organisation should specialise in and be responsible for a single function or whether duties and responsibilities should overlap;

(d) how individuals, sections and departments are to be appraised and controlled;

(e) whether employees should be closely supervised, or left alone to complete broadly defined tasks;

(f) how activities are to be co-ordinated (communication systems, the extent of delegation of work to lower levels) and by whom;

(g) whether decision taking is to be centralised or devolved to decentralised units;

(h) sizes of departments;

(i) the shape of the management hierarchy;

(j) groupings of activities;

(k) the extent and nature of delegation.

An outline of the major steps involved in determining the structure of an organisation is shown in Figure 7.1.

2. Structure and strategy

'Structure follows strategy' in the sense that once a strategy has been selected the organisational framework of the business will usually have to be amended in order to implement that strategy. Thus, expansion may lead to divisionalisation; diversification can result in the establishment of subsidiaries and SBUs (see **23**); new product development might necessitate a change in departmentation, and so on. Examples of how strategy can affect structure include the following:

(a) Divisionalisation of a firm may create a large number of levels in its overall management hierarchy, and widen the spans of control (see **12**) of individual senior managers. The former is due to the imposition of an extra layer between the chief executive and operational units in conjunction with the inevitable emergence of employee grading systems within divisions themselves; while the latter results from the proliferation of specialist staff advisers at head office, all reporting to a handful of senior executives.

(b) Diversification strategies can greatly increase the numbers of departments and divisions within a firm.

(c) The size of a company's core business might depend on the extent to which it is diversified.

(d) Acquisition strategies determine how many quasi-independent subsidiary units a firm has to operate.

(e) Doing business in geographically separated and culturally disparate markets can cause a business to organise itself in a distinct and complex way.

It is especially important for structure to follow strategy, perhaps, in high-tech firms operating in conditions of rapid change. Here, structure needs to keep up with the requirements of the latest technological innovations, so that the business's organisational infrastructure must be flexible and capable of speedy alteration as circumstances change.

3. Purposes of organisation structure

The essential purposes of an organisation structure are:

- to have the right people taking the right decisions at the right time;
- to establish who is accountable for what and who reports to whom;
- to facilitate the easy flow of information through the organisation;
- to provide a working environment that encourages efficiency and the acceptance of change;
- to integrate and co-ordinate activities.

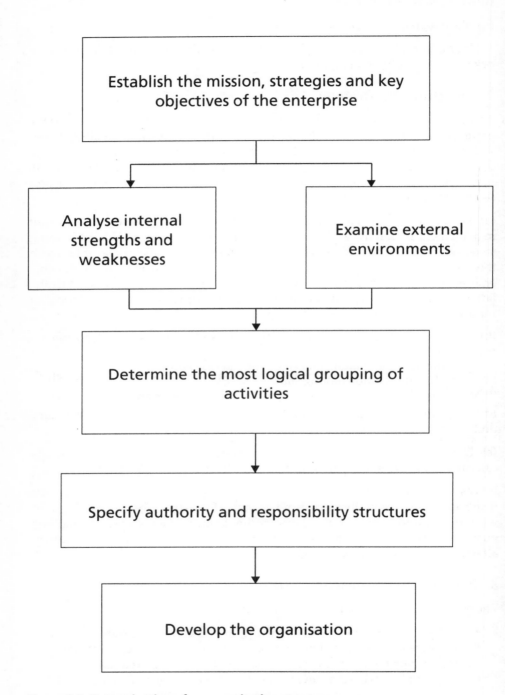

Figure 7.1 Determination of an organisation structure

The chosen structure must balance order and innovation. On the one hand, it must avoid the duplication of effort, standardise procedures, monitor the quality of work, etc. On the other hand, it should encourage initiative among the staff and generate job satisfaction in employees through presenting them with an interesting variety of disparate tasks. There is no single ideal structure that is universally applicable to all businesses. What works in one firm may not be suitable elsewhere because of differences in mission, strategies, and the calibre of personnel. In the ideal situation:

- each unit will act as a self-contained cost/profit centre;
- the performance of units can be easily appraised;
- information about units is readily available (meaning they can be controlled without difficulty);
- units are 'organic' in that each contains homogeneous elements and/or elements with a common purpose (e.g. putting all marketing activities together into a single department);
- work passes from one unit to the next in a logical sequence;
- the resource needs of each unit are clearly visible so that resources may be deployed where they are most urgently required.

4. Identifying organisational problems

Manifestations of an inappropriate organisation structure include:

- poor internal communication;
- slow decision making and frequent bad decisions;
- lack of motivation among staff;
- poor co-ordination of the work of various divisions and departments;
- high administrative costs due to inefficiency and/or duplication of effort;
- bad relations between line and staff managers;
- management not being able to appraise the efficiencies of certain functions (accounting, marketing, etc.) or activities (e.g. launching a product, changing a production technique) because of the complexity of organisational interrelationships within the firm;
- staff not knowing the organisation's true objectives;
- absence of procedures for interdepartmental consultation and/or joint departmental decision-taking;
- a single favoured department dominating others, even to the extent that other departments feel they require its permission prior to initiating certain actions;
- conflicts between individual and organisational goals, and the pursuit by individuals of personal rather than company objectives;
- slow and ineffective decision-taking within the business;
- excessive numbers of meetings necessitated by people not being sure what they are expected to do;
- poor co-ordination of projects;
- non-implementation of strategic plans.

5. The pioneering empirical studies

The thesis that a change in corporate strategy will (or should) lead to an alteration in organisation structure (i.e. that 'structure follows strategy') was first advanced by A.D. Chandler, an American business historian who studied the growth and development of a number of large US companies in the early and middle years of the twentieth century, concluding that common patterns of organisational adjustment to changes in strategic requirements could be discerned. New strategies led, it seemed, to new administrative problems that the existing organisation structure could not solve. Hence inefficiencies emerged and financial performance declined. This would trigger the introduction of fresh and more appropriate organisation systems until profits returned to their previous levels.

Chandler argued that there exist natural tendencies towards particular degrees of centralised control within large organisations. According to Chandler the decentralisation of operations via the creation of divisions to deal with particular functions, products or markets resulted from the needs of the mass markets and automated production methods characteristic of the twentieth century. The day-to-day operations of a big firm's constituent parts, Chandler suggested, are more efficiently handled by managers who are close to the firm's operational base, whereas long-term strategy is best undertaken by those who can take an overall, birds-eye, view of the organisation. As firms develop new products, acquire their own sources of supply, create their own distribution networks, etc., they become too complex to be managed through a highly centralised system. Hence, multi-unit businesses emerge. At the same time, responsibility for purely strategic matters will be centralised. Senior executives thus have the time and facilities to consider properly the firm's long-term future. Chandler examined the growth and development of four large American corporations. Initially, these firms centralised their administrative structures but then, confronted with the enormity of the control problems associated with very large organisations, they decentralised their operations into separate divisions. Top-level management thus involved centralised co-ordination rather than detailed administrative control. According to Chandler, market and technological pressures have, in general, led very large businesses to adopt fundamentally similar structural forms, although each organisation will develop its own particular variations within market and technological constraints. An 'adaptive' response, Chandler noted, involves the retention, as far as possible of existing working methods, customs and practices. 'Creative innovation' on the other hand is an interventionist response, whereby top management deliberately imposes greater decentralisation.

John Child, in a study of 82 British companies, also concluded that large firms seem to gravitate towards divisionalised organisational forms. The greater the degree of environmental variability, he suggested, the more control devices a firm needs in order to integrate its activities. Large firms with diverse activities, he asserted, need relatively formal structures, and if they organise themselves into divisions they will generally improve their performance. A highly influential study supporting the 'structure follows strategy' thesis was that of A.P. Sloan who chronicled the structural changes occurring at the US firm General Motors in the 1920s and 30s. Operations were decentralised to individual divisions (Buick, Chevrolet, etc.) which were free to determine the policies whereby strategies would be implemented, while strategies for the corporation as a whole were developed centrally by top management. This, Sloan argued, was administratively efficient and especially effective for the development and introduction of new models

P.R. Lawrence and J.W. Lorsch presented an 'environmental' approach to the explanation of how organisations are structured. According to Lawrence and Lorsch, organisations are created to solve 'environmental problems'. Thus, organisations develop separate units (departments, divisions, functions or whatever) for dealing with various aspects of the outside world. Lawrence and Lorsch studied ten American firms drawn from three very different industries: plastics, wood, and containers; concluding that more departments and functions will be created, and the more precisely defined will the duties and responsibilities of each sub-unit be, the greater the degree of change and uncertainty in a firm's environment. This process of 'differentiation', as the authors put it, results in the various sub-units having different attitudes, patterns of inter-personal communication, formal hierarchies, and time horizons – some units react more to short-term problems than to long-run opportunities. Of the three industries, plastics was found to be the most diverse and unstable and hence the plastics firms had greater differentiation within their organisation structures. The existence of differentiation created the need for 'integration' of an organisation into a unified whole capable of achieving its objectives. Thus, firms in the plastics industry had many more 'integrative devices' – rules, codes of conduct, standard procedures, appointed co-ordinators, etc. – than others.

T. Burns and G.M. Stalker investigated the attempts made by a number of Scottish firms to introduce electronics work into their existing manufacturing systems during the late 1950s finding, like Lawrence and Lorsch, that the rate of change of the outside environment affected organisational effectiveness. In stable environments, the authors asserted, structured 'mechanistic' organisational forms will emerge. Here, individual tasks are clearly defined, there is specialisation and the division of managerial labour, formal hierarchies, and rigid administrative routines. The emphasis is on vertical communications, with only the very senior management having overall knowledge of how the organisation works. Firms operating within volatile environments, however, find that new and unfamiliar problems which do not fit conveniently into existing structures, constantly arise. These firms need to respond quickly to external change. Bureaucratic organisations, according to Burns and Stalker, cannot accommodate the demands of new technology. Working methods frequently change, individual roles need continual redefinition. Looser, horizontal communications systems are appropriate for these circumstances, which demand 'organistic' rather than mechanistic organisational forms. Organistic structures are flexible, relatively informal, have overlapping individual responsibilities and hence a great capacity to cope with change.

6. Subsequent research

These primary empirical studies provoked much discussion and subsequent research. Results have been mixed; some supporting and others refuting the proposition that structure follows strategy. Studies have tended to focus on whether a change in structure immediately following the introduction of a new strategy significantly increases a firm's financial rate of return. A number of factors have, unfortunately, obscured the results, including the following:

(a) Firms facing very little competition might be able to have inefficient organisation structures while continuing to earn high profits! The same applies to companies in receipt of large government subsidies.

(b) Big businesses frequently take a large part of their total profits from foreign operations, so that currency fluctuations, transfer pricing (see 14.6) and other international trading considerations can affect the levels of profits observed.

(c) It is undoubtedly the case that firms in the same industry tend to organise themselves in a similar fashion, following the latest management theories and trends, regardless of their particular situations.

Note moreover that structure can affect strategy in the following respects:

(a) Firms with organisation systems based on advanced IT (see Chapter 12) can use the latest information technology to support (and hence influence) the strategy formulation process.

(b) Small and/or uncomplicated businesses are often dominated by a single manager who takes all major strategic decisions. This might not be possible in more complex situations. The structural form of a company (line and staff, matrix, market or product departmentation, etc.) can affect internal communications, interpersonal relations and (importantly) the perspectives adopted during the strategy formulation process.

(c) A stable bureaucracy might be essential for the long-term survival of the firm.

7. The organisational life cycle

Chandler's basic proposition that successful companies tend to follow a distinct pattern of organisational development as they age and expand subsequently became known as the 'organisational life cycle'. The stages of the life cycle (suggested by a number of writers) are as follows:

1. *Birth.* The business is created by an entrepreneur who takes all important decisions personally. He or she controls and supervises all significant activities, and there is little formal structure. Plans are short term, although the owner/manager might have a clear vision of what he or she wishes to come. The firm is flexible, dynamic and able to grasp whatever opportunities arise. Administrative systems are simple and routine. Usually the firm will be serving a niche market and/or supplying a limited range of products.

2. *Growth.* As the firm expands it becomes necessary for the founding entrepreneur to hire a team of managers to take charge of various key functions, and a bureaucracy emerges. The business is specialised and continues to supply a small number of products. Strategy focuses on developing these products and increasing the company's market shares. A functional organisation structure (see **16**) is established. There might be conflict between the original owner/manager and recently hired managerial employees as the latter demand more and more discretion to take decisions. General policies are agreed and decision making follows rational procedures. A budgetary control system might be installed, as might appraisal, audit and management by objectives systems. The firm may acquire other businesses to protect its sources of supply and outlets for distribution.

3. *Diversification.* The business now begins to expand its product lines and to operate in other industries and geographical regions. Decision making is increasingly devolved to divisions and decentralised units, which are themselves controlled and co-ordinated from a central headquarters. Units are given precise objectives, and reporting systems are implemented. Operations become increasingly complex; administrative systems inflexible and somewhat bureaucratic. Management is undertaken impersonally by professional managers operating formal systems according to well-established rules and procedures.

Transitions between stages **1** to **3** in the life cycle are likely to be traumatic and might even cause the business to collapse, especially if the original founder/owner refuses to delegate and resists bringing in expert professional managers.

4. *Decline.* A variety of problems can beset a company during its growth and diversification phases. It might become complacent, resistant to change, unwilling to take risks and organisationally inflexible. The founder and/or existing senior management could be aging, and refuse to delegate to younger and less experienced people. Departments and divisions within the company might formulate their own objectives, and pursue these at the expense of the overall welfare of the firm. The senior management team might lack ability and strategic vision, may not grasp opportunities, and be unable to cope with turbulent environments. Existing control systems might prove inadequate. Hence the organisation begins to decline.

At this point the firm stands at a crossroads between failure and revival. The latter may occur through re-engineering the corporation (see 6.**10**), the recruitment of able and vigorous managers, divestment (see 3.**22**), new product innovation, and/or by entering fresh markets. Otherwise sales will fall; well-qualified staff leave the organisation; morale collapses, and the company eventually goes into liquidation.

Problems with the organisational life cycle hypothesis are as follows:

(a) It is based on the evidence of just a handful of successful (mainly US) corporations. The experiences of millions of other businesses worldwide may be entirely different to the patterns suggested.

(b) There are notable examples of owner/managers retaining tight personal control over all their businesses' substantive operations at all stages in company development.

(c) The initial culture of a business is likely to continue unaltered as operations expand. People hired by the founder to help in running the company might themselves be very similar in outlook and background to the founder, so that the process of 'professionalisation' of company management may not proceed as the theory predicts. Note how the prevailing culture can remain even after the founder has left the scene.

(d) The impact of IT and computerised production processes can revolutionise a firm's operational and administrative structures in a very short period. Management systems and procedures in a high tech environment may be entirely different to those suggested by the life cycle hypothesis.

FACTORS INFLUENCING THE DESIGN OF ORGANISATIONS

8. Problems of organisation design

Detailed and protracted attention to organisational design might result in the drafting of a theoretically perfect organisational model which in reality is so impractical that it can never work. Further problems with organisation design are:

(a) The people who design an organisation might not themselves subsequently have to work within the structure.

(b) Staff implementing the structure might not possess any knowledge of the theories on which it is based, leading perhaps to contradictory and inconsistent organisational policies.

(c) Informal or 'shadow' organisational structures might grow up alongside and subvert the official system. The formal organisation is that established by management and embodied in organisation charts, official hierarchies, company rule books, operating manuals, etc. Formal organisation is intended to be permanent, to contribute directly to the attainment of organisational goals, and to facilitate the smooth flow of work. Informal organisation, conversely, arises naturally and spontaneously as individuals begin to interact. Thus, informal groups emerge to represent people with common interests, each group possessing its own norms, perceptions and internal communications. Informal organisation is important because the informal structures that emerge may develop goals and work routines that run contrary to the interests of the formal system.

9. Advantages and problems of informal organisation

The disadvantages of an informal organisation are that it might:

- establish standards and objectives beyond management control;

- encourage conformity and lack of initiative;
- be highly resistant to change;
- generate rumour and malicious gossip;
- create conflicts of loyalty between a person's role in the formal system and his or her role in the informal organisation.

Nevertheless, informal organisation offers a number of benefits:

(a) It can supplement and improve the operation of the formal system.

(b) Informal groups can help individuals relate to their colleagues more easily and thus might assist people in fulfilling personal ambitions and needs.

(c) Communications within the organisation may be greatly improved through the existence of an informal system.

(d) The workloads of formal leaders might be lightened, since some important managerial responsibilities (co-ordination of work, for example) may be undertaken by the informal organisation.

10. Choice of organisation system

Four major factors need to influence the design of an organisation:

1. How much information flows through the firm. If information flows smoothly through the business and if interpersonal and interdepartmental relations are good, a relatively complicated organisation structure may be appropriate.

2. Employees' attitudes, morale, abilities and educational attainments. Organisations which use highly qualified staff for specialist tasks may need to adjust their organisation structure to meet the emotional requirements of this type of worker.

3. The firm's goals. A change in objectives might create the need for a new organisation structure. Consider, for example, a business which operates in a fast-moving, technically sophisticated industry and finds that a competitor introduces a new product which renders all existing models obsolete. The firm must react instantly by altering its own product line. This can involve complete reorganisation of methods of production, marketing and administration. A flexible structure that can be quickly altered is most appropriate in this case.

4. The nature of the external environment. Examples of variables affecting wider commercial environments are the laws and/or customs of society, market structures, the degree of market uncertainty, local practices, perhaps even the local political system.

11. Designing a structure

Typically the design of a new organisation structure involves the following steps:

(a) Examinations of:

- internal decision-making procedures;

- interpersonal relations within the company and senior executives' management styles;
- external threats;
- the culture of the business. Organisational cultures evolve gradually, and members of organisations may not even be aware that cultures exist. Yet culture is important because it helps define how workers feel about their jobs. A culture will have arisen within a specific environmental context and be related to particular organisational needs. The problem is that an organisation's needs and activities necessarily alter, while its underlying culture might remain unchanged. Culture involves common assumptions about how work should be performed and about appropriate objectives for the organisation, for the departments within it and for individual employees. Changing an organisation's culture may be the most pressing of the organisational designer's tasks.

(b) Determination of which of the firm's activities belong together, and how the efforts of the new groupings can be co-ordinated in order to achieve the organisation's goals.

(c) Specification of the duties and responsibilities of various sections and individuals.

(d) Consultations with staff to discuss proposals (followed by amendments to the draft scheme).

(e) Production of documentation: organisation charts and manuals, job descriptions, etc.

(f) Implementation. This could mean employees having to change job or take on new and/or additional duties. Spans of control may be widened or narrowed; decentralised units might be created or wound up. Responsibility for taking key decisions may be shifted, upwards or downwards, to different personnel.

ISSUES IN ORGANISATIONAL DESIGN

In the past it was sometimes argued that there exist a handful of fundamental principles of organisation that should always be applied regardless of the nature of the firm or the industry within which it operates. Nowadays, however, few analysts would adopt so dogmatic an approach, although a common set of issues need to be addressed in all organisations, as outlined in the following sections.

12. How wide should be managers' spans of control

A manager's span of control is the number of immediate subordinates who report directly to that person. Narrow spans involve just two or three subordinates; wide spans have perhaps twelve or fifteen subordinates reporting to a single manager. Most analysts suggest that any more than six or seven subordinates represents too wide a span of control because of the complex relationships and competing demands on the controlling manager's time that result. Four factors are relevant to the choice of a span of control: organisational diversity, complexity of work and the calibres of the manager and his or her subordinates.

Organisational diversity affects the efficiency of internal communication. If face-to-face contacts between manager and subordinates are impossible, communication depends on telephone calls, letters, memoranda and similar indirect means. Interruptions in information flows and other communication breakdowns cause loss of effective control, especially if people and departments are geographically separated. Complex work means that managers need time to assess the reports and suggestions of subordinates and they ought not to be overburdened with minor problems arising from lower levels. A narrow span of control is appropriate in this case. Note however that the imposition of narrow spans of control throughout the organisation necessarily creates many more levels of authority than in 'flatter' structures, resulting perhaps in long channels of communication and in important information not being passed up and down the chain of command. Hence top management may lose touch with what happens at lower levels within the organisation.

Some managers are better able to handle large numbers of subordinates than others, depending on their training, experience and personal qualities. The degree of authority given the manager is also relevant to this point. Similarly, well-trained, enthusiastic and competent subordinates need less control and supervision than others, so that wide spans of control may then be applied.

Narrow spans of control recognise that an individual's capacity to supervise others is limited and that it is better to deal with a small number of subordinates properly than to have contact with many subordinates but only in casual ways. However, wide spans also offer advantages – they force managers to delegate (so that subordinates acquire experience of higher levels of work), subordinates may experience a higher degree of job satisfaction, and the cost of supervision is low. On the other hand, co-ordination of subordinates' activities may be poor. Communication between subordinates of equal rank could be inadequate and lead to much duplication of effort.

13. Should the principle of 'unity of command' be applied ?

Unity of command means 'one person one boss', i.e. that nobody should report to more than one superior. Its justification is that if a subordinate is accountable to several superiors then conflicting orders might be issued from different sources and the subordinate may not know which order to obey. Practical application of this principle is difficult because of the strong influences that informal authority systems can sometimes exert. A person might in theory be responsible to a single superior, but in reality behave according to standards determined by someone else. Moreover, the principle cannot normally be applied to individuals who belong to several project teams.

14. To what extent should managers specialise in a specific field?

The advantages of a conventional line and staff system (see **17**), with narrow spans of control and carefully delineated authority and responsibility structures, are (i) that specialist skills develop among managers (who acquire extensive knowledge of specific functions), (ii) that they are logical, coherent and easy to understand, and (iii) that a clear line of authority runs from the top of the organisation to its base. Unfortunately, however, communication in line and staff systems can be slow, and they might not be able to accommodate change.

15. Tall versus flat structures

Narrow spans of control create numerous levels of authority within the organisation and hence long chains of command. The advantages of a 'tall' organisation with many levels between top and bottom are as follows:

(a) Managers may devote their full attention to the demands of their subordinates.

(b) There is proper supervision and (hopefully) effective control.

(c) There is less need to co-ordinate the activities of subordinates than in a flat structure.

(d) Duplication of effort among subordinates is unlikely.

(e) Communications are facilitated.

(f) Employees are presented with a career ladder and thus can expect regular promotion through the system.

(g) It facilitates specialisation of functions and the creation of logically determined work units.

Flat organisations have the following advantages:

(a) Managers are forced to delegate work, so that subordinates acquire experience of higher level duties.

(b) Morale may improve on account of the majority of employees being on the same level.

(c) Low supervision costs.

(d) Subordinates are given more discretion over how they achieve their objectives.

(e) Few personal assistants and staff advisors are necessary because there are fewer levels.

(f) Managers and subordinates meet directly without having to communicate via intermediaries. Thus, information will not be lost or misinterpreted as it passes up and down the organisation.

(g) Managers remain in touch with activities at the base of the organisation.

16. Departmentation

A 'department' is a set of activities under a manager's jurisdiction. Division of the firm's work into units creates the need for departments, which can be defined in terms of: function performed, a product, market, or person.

(a) Functional departments are established to deal with particular varieties of work. Examples are production, accounts, advertising, transport, and administrative departments. Major functional departments contain sections. Thus an advertising department can be subdivided into sections for media selection, sales promotions, package design and other promotional activities.

Definitions of the responsibilities of functional departments follow logically and naturally from the work of the organisation. Normally, divisions will parallel occupational distinctions so that, for instance, everyone concerned with selling will be in the marketing department, everyone involved in manufacture will be in production, and so on.

Although it is easy to understand, functional departmentation may encourage narrow and introspective attitudes. Departments with wider responsibilities could provide staff with challenging environments that stimulate effort and initiative.

(b) Product departmentation means creating departments each of which deals with a single product. Staff within the department control all activities associated with the good, including the purchase of raw materials, administration, processing, and the sale and distribution of the final output.

Senior departmental managers acquire a wider range of general managerial skills than they would in functional departments and they accumulate expert knowledge of the problems involved in the design and manufacture of their own product. Such specialised experience might be essential for efficient administration in firms producing technically complicated goods. A further advantage of product departmentation is that it makes co-ordination between relevant management functions and stages of production easier to achieve.

(c) Market departmentation can occur by geographical region or customer type. Regional sales departments are an example. Local factors can then figure in decision making, and it might be cheaper to locate offices near to customers. Otherwise the departmentation could relate to customer size (e.g. having special facilities for large buyers), or to retail or wholesale distribution channels, export or home markets, etc. Problems of co-ordination might ensue, and control could be difficult.

APPROACHES TO ORGANISATION STRUCTURE

17. Line and staff organisation

Line managers are directly responsible for achieving the organisation's objectives and exert direct authority over their subordinates. Line authority flows through the chain of command from the apex of the organisation to its base. Often, the chain of command is illustrated via an 'organisation chart'.

Typical line management positions are: managing director, production director, general manager, works manager, sales manager, first line supervisor. Each position in the line system identifies points of contact between a manager and his or her subordinates, showing the authority of its occupant and to whom that person is responsible. Vertical communications proceed only through the line system; if a manager cannot handle a problem it is referred upwards to superiors. Equally, work may only be delegated to the subordinates of a specific position.

Staff managers

Staff managers advise line managers but do not possess authority to implement important decisions. Line executives might ask staff managers for advice, but are not obliged to accept their recommendations. Examples of managers likely to occupy staff rather than line positions are lawyers, researchers, industrial relations specialists, or technical experts.

18. Advantages and disadvantages of line and staff organisation

The advantages of having a line organisation are:

(a) There is an unambiguous chain of command.

(b) Each person's area of responsibility is clearly defined.

(c) Everyone knows to whom they are accountable.

(d) It is coherent and easy to understand.

(e) It embodies a logical division of labour.

(f) Decision taking can be fast and effective (orders have to be obeyed immediately).

Disadvantages of line systems include the following.

(a) Staff advisors are relegated to subsidiary roles which, as highly qualified specialists, they may resent having to occupy.

(b) Line systems rely heavily on a small number of key personnel whose resignation or illness may cause great disruption.

(c) Power is concentrated into the hands of a few line managers who might not be sufficiently mature, experienced or competent to exercise it responsibly or effectively.

(d) Line managers might be overworked, have to take too many decisions, and thus be subject to excessive amounts of stress.

For staff organisation the advantages are:

(a) Line managers do not become immersed in detailed analysis of what to them are secondary issues.

(b) Staff specialists are left free to develop their personal expertise.

(c) Executive decisions are taken by people who have been trained and are sufficiently experienced to take them.

Disadvantages are as follows:

(a) Possible confusion over who is responsible for what and who has authority over whom.

(b) Line managers might rely too heavily on staff specialists' advice.

(c) Line managers may receive so much advice from staff specialists that vital points are missed.

(d) Experts are not able directly to implement their expert recommendations.

19. Bureaucratic versus flexible structures

An organisation operating within a rapidly changing environment may have to alter its organisation at short notice and for all aspects of its work. Consider for instance a computer manufacturing company which finds that a competitor has introduced a cheaper and superior model. This business must completely reorganise its design, production, marketing and administration systems almost at once. Thus, it should adopt flexible organisation structures possessing total labour mobility, overlapping responsibilities, and fragile and transitory departmental structures that can be altered at will. The employees of such a company must be capable of taking on different types of work at short notice, and be culturally attuned to accepting change.

Conversely, organisations in relatively stable environments, or which employ poorly educated and/or apathetic staff, or which are concerned with routine assembly line or equally mundane activities that cannot be made more interesting, may opt for rigid, formal and bureaucratic organisational forms. Rules will exist covering every aspect of the firm's work. There will be clear divisions of work and close supervision. All procedures will be standardised and stated in writing: workers will not be allowed discretion over how they undertake their tasks. Relationships are extremely formal in such a system; everyone knows their place and exactly what they are expected to do.

Such measures relieve employees of the burden of having to think for themselves, and there is certainty that work will actually be completed. But individual initiative is stifled and this type of organisation is not capable of accommodating change: people 'pass the buck' whenever they are confronted with new ideas.

20. Centralisation

In a centralised organisation, all major decisions are taken by a central administrative body which issues binding directives to lower levels of authority. Sections of the firm are bound by fixed rules and procedures, and exercise little discretion in the course of their work. Note however that as organisations grow, it becomes physically impossible for top management to take all decisions, so that some decentralisation – via delegation of decision-making responsibilities to subordinates – becomes inevitable. Nevertheless, some organisations prefer to centralise decision taking as tightly as possible, for the following reasons:

(a) All employees are subject to direct and immediate control.

(b) Departments and sections can be provided with detailed operating instructions.

(c) There is no question of decentralised units competing with each other to undertake similar tasks.

(d) Employee's performances can be rapidly appraised.

(e) There is unified decision making, since the activities of all sections can be related to the objectives of the organisation as a whole.

(f) Correct working methods can be imposed on all units within the organisation.

(g) The efforts of diverse units can be synchronised.

(h) Administration is simplified.

(i) New strategies can be implemented quickly.

The disadvantages of centralisation include the following:

(a) Local expertise is not fully utilised.

(b) The organisation becomes less flexible and possibly more bureaucratic and incapable of accommodating change.

(c) Centralised managers will receive so much information that important points might be misinterpreted or overlooked.

(d) Subordinates might deliberately disobey the detailed instructions they receive, preferring to operate through unofficial and informal decentralised organisation systems.

21. Decentralisation

There is perhaps a natural tendency for large organisations to decentralise, since this allows 'local' control over operations – thus enabling the central authority to concentrate on long-term strategic plans. Decentralisation may occur through the creation of subsidiary companies, through increasing the decision-making authority of individual managers, or through the divisionalisation of a firm. Factors encouraging decentralisation include the following:

(a) Rapid growth of the organisation. The larger the organisation the harder it becomes for top management to take all important decisions.

(b) Variability in the external environment, hence causing the need for rapid response to external change.

(c) The need to allocate separate budgets to functions, sections and departments.

Advantages of decentralisation are:

(a) Senior executives can devote their time to strategic planning while leaving operational matters to expert local managers. Those at the top can take an overall bird's-eye view of the situation. The word 'local' in this context need not refer to geographical location. Rather it means nearness to operations and to the units where the decisions taken have to be applied.

(b) Local initiative is encouraged.

(c) The organisation becomes responsive to local conditions.

(d) There is less red tape and hence faster decision taking.

(e) Local circumstances are taken into account when policies are determined.

(f) Managerial jobs in decentralised units become more interesting so that the organisation can attract better quality managerial staff.

(g) Decentralised managers acquire the experience needed for more senior positions.

22. Divisionalisation

This is a popular form of decentralisation. It avoids the cost and inconvenience of setting up subsidiary companies, and divisional managers can be made subject to close central control.

Divisions may be established for different products, for geographical markets, customer type (retail or wholesale for example), organisational function (purchasing, finance, etc.) or method of production. Heads of division are given targets, but are left to achieve them in their own ways. Organisation within a division may itself be centralised or decentralised.

There is a difference between divisionalisation and decentralisation in that the latter simply means passing authority to others – perhaps to the bottom levels of a conventional line and staff system – whereas the former is the consequence of growth and diversification and involves the creation of new and quasi-autonomous organisational units.

The advantages of divisionalisation, apart from the general benefits of decentralisation already mentioned, relate to:

(a) its value as a training medium for the development of divisional managers for top level posts in the parent organisation;

(b) the relative ease with which divisional activities can be integrated at higher levels of control;

(c) the motivation afforded to local managers who are encouraged to use individual initiative involving local problems. Note however that total decentralisation of an organisation via divisionalisation is impossible, since any decision arising at the divisional level that has policy implications for the organisation as a whole must be endorsed by central control.

Disadvantages of divisionalisation include the following:

(a) Senior managers may lack the training and expertise necessary to co-ordinate decentralised units effectively.

(b) Divisions might not be large enough to justify each one providing a full range of their own internal services, and thus may not be cost effective.

(c) Divisions might fight each other for control over resources and to undertake certain functions.

(d) Bad external publicity attracted by one division will rub off on the rest.

(e) Activities might be duplicated.

(f) Potential economies of scale (e.g. cost savings through the integration of processes, discounts for bulk purchasing of supplies, etc.) could be lost.

(g) The benefits of specialisation of functions become difficult to obtain. Each division might have its own accountant, administrative staff, etc., rather than these people being centralised into single units serving the entire organisation.

23. Strategic business units

These are groupings of a business's activities which are then treated as self-contained entities for the purposes of strategic planning and control. An SBU could be a division of a company, a department, a collection of departments, a subsidiary, or a function undertaken within the firm (e.g. all the firm's marketing activities might be regarded as an independent SBU). Often, SBUs cut across existing divisional, functional and departmental boundaries. Having defined SBUs, management then gives each unit a budget and the authority to administer its own resources. Criteria for establishing SBUs might involve:

- common markets or product types;
- shared resources;
- shared know-how;
- common concerns (with customer care or impending government legislation for example).

The idea was invented by the US General Electric company which, dissatisfied with its existing divisional structure, rearranged all the enterprise's activities into SBUs, some of which bore little relation to traditional departments, divisions or profit centres. Thus, for example, a number of food preparation appliances previously manufactured and sold through several independent divisions were merged into a single 'housewares' SBU.

Similarly, a firm might produce television sets in one division, radios in the next, and car stereo systems in another. Yet for strategy and planning purposes all three activities could be conveniently lumped together into a self-contained administrative unit. To make sense, an SBU should:

- comprise compatible elements each possessing a direct and identifiable link with the unit as a whole;
- be easy to appraise (which requires that its performance can be compared with something similar within or outside the organisation);

- contribute significantly towards the attainment of the organisation's goals.

By 1968 the giant US General Electrical Company (GEC) was operating in 23 of the 26 standard industrial classification (SIC) categories, had ten groups, 46 divisions and 200 departments. It possessed highly sophisticated planning mechanisms, and had become the tenth largest US based corporation. Yet financial performance was disappointing. Sales had almost doubled since 1960, but net profit had risen by only 63 per cent. Return on total assets was actually falling. Company policy through the 1950s and 60s was (i) to decentralise, and (ii) to make rather than to buy. This led to a proliferation of marketing, finance, R&D and manufacturing units around the world. Growth and diversity inevitably created problems of control, and *overall* company planning became increasingly problematic. Accordingly, GEC in 1969 commissioned a study by the management consultants McKinsey and Co. intended to analyse the efficiency of planning undertaken at the operating level. The outcome was a complete reorganisation of the company into 43 Strategic Business Units (SBUs) each of which was, in effect, a self-contained business constructed from an appropriate sub-set of GEC's operating units. Each SBU then reported direct to the chief executive, who was assisted by a head office staff support unit divided into four components: finance, strategic planning, technology, and legal and administrative services. The SBU structure itself was superimposed on the existing line management reporting system. Thus section managers reported to department managers; the latter to divisional managers; and heads of division to the manager of an SBU. However, very large departments or individual divisions could also be designated as SBUs. Only SBUs (rather than units within them) prepared strategic plans. Problems experienced during the implementation of the new organisation system included disputes concerning which particuar sections should join which SBU, determination of the powers of SBUs, and deciding who exactly should prepare SBU strategic plans.

SBUs are most appropriate for highly diversified businesses the activities of which can be grouped under distinct headings.

Advantages to the creation and use of SBUs are:

(a) They reduce the total number of administrative units that senior management has to monitor and control.

(b) Use of SBUs enables management to operate two levels of strategy: overall corporate decisions that affect the nature and direction of the enterprise; and unit level strategies relevant to specific operating environments. This facilitates the linking up of strategy development with strategy implementation.

(c) Important decisions can be taken in discrete business units.

(d) SBU organisation provides a planning framework that cuts across organisational boundaries.

(e) Units are encouraged to behave entrepreneurally.

(f) Decision making can be related to specific consumer groups and resource categories.

The main problems with SBUs are how to co-ordinate many disparate activities simultaneously and how to assess the financial and other contributions of various activities to a particular unit. SBUs are not suitable for vertically integrated companies supplying a limited range of products.

24. Matrix organisation

This seeks to create project teams with members drawn from several different departments. Teams are then made responsible for particular functions. A firm's advertising team, for example, might comprise members from marketing, finance, design and sales departments: the 'health and safety at work' team could consist of representatives from the production department, personnel, quality control and (possibly) finance. In consequence, committees are assembled to oversee each of the organisation's key projects and/or operational activities.

Matrix organisation violates the classical principle of unity of command (i.e. that employees should only report to one manager) since team members have a number of different bosses, namely the heads of their 'home' department plus the team leaders of the various committees on which they serve. Teams are multidisciplinary, cutting across traditional occupational divisions, departments and distinctions between line and staff. Matrix structure, moreover, creates numerous opportunities for employee participation in decision taking and the rapid development of general managerial skills. The system is extremely flexible (teams can be set up and disbanded at will). Matrix structures are especially useful for:

(a) managing complex projects where immediate access to several highly specialised professional skills is required;

(b) managing strategic business units (see **24**). Often, SBUs do not correspond to existing divisions or departments so that it becomes necessary to establish a team representing each aspect of the work of the unit to oversee its activities.

Royal Dutch Shell is a global business with 135,000 employees, around 5500 of which are likely to be working outside their own country at any one time. The group operates in over 100 countries across six disparate industry sectors, and participates in about 1000 joint ventures worldwide. Control and co-ordination of such a vast business empire is of course a gargantuan task. The company has a decentralised management structure, with each business unit fully responsible for its own operations. Head office provides advice and support services to operating units. Decentralisation has been adopted in recognition of the near impossibility of effectively controlling such a diverse organisation from a single central point, and because experience has shown that local decisions based on local information from the local environment work well for Shell's lines of business. The firm claims to be highly responsive to external change and to be able to implement decisions quickly.

Shell was a pioneer of the matrix approach to organisation. Its matrix system has three dimensions: for regions, industry sectors and business functions. Regions combine to determine company-wide strategies, to agree acquisitions and divestments, approve major capital projects, and appoint and decide the remunerations of senior group executives. Business sector specialists select policies, research programmes and technologies appropriate for particular industry sectors. They advise regions on the feasibilities of planned investments in various sectors, and support local subsidiaries. Functional managers are professional experts possessing expert technical knowledge of their respective fields, and are expected to disseminate their knowledge throughout the organisation. Also they formulate operational standards and working procedures. Executives from the three dimensions combine to form multidisciplinary teams capable of supporting local operating units and/or addressing specific issues. Head office periodically reviews how the various teams inter-relate and the roles of particular individuals within the matrix system. The matrix principle is applied within operating units as well as at higher levels.

25. Advantages of matrix approaches

Matrix organisation offers a practical and coherent device for analysing the make-up of an enterprise. Personal and departmental contributions to the organisation are systematically classified and crucial activities that absorb large amounts of effort and resources are highlighted. The method is commonly used where several departments performing related duties are grouped together into divisions. In this way, interdepartmental communications are enhanced and duplication of effort can be avoided. Further advantages are that:

(i) there is much face-to-face communication between managers with interests in the same projects;
(ii) project teams can be immediately disbanded following a project's completion;
(iii) departmental boundaries do not interfere with the completion of projects;
(iv) team leaders become focal points for all matters pertaining to particular projects or functions;
(v) it encourages flexible attitudes;
(vi) specialised professional knowledge relevant to a project or function is instantly available;
(vii) interdisciplinary co-operation is encouraged;
(viii) junior managers develop broad perspectives on problems and issues;
(ix) top management is left free to concentrate on strategic planning.

26. Disadvantages of matrix structures

Matrix organisation deliberately violates the principle of unity of command (see 13). Team leaders are responsible for projects, though heads of department retain executive authority over their staff. In consequence, team members might receive conflicting instructions from heads of department on the one hand and project team leaders on the other! Thus it is important to establish at the outset (i) who, ultimately, each individual should obey, and (ii) whether subordinates are to

143

regard themselves first and foremost as members of a department or as members of a particular project team. (Usually, departments take precedence since projects last only for limited periods, and individuals will normally be assigned to a number of projects at the same time.) Other problems are that:

(a) matrix systems are more complicated and costly to administer than other forms of organisation;

(b) they might offer fewer discrete promotion opportunities than do hierarchical systems;

(c) teams rather than individuals are appraised (unsatisfactory employees may thus be difficult to identify);

(d) unofficial links between members of various project teams may emerge which subvert teams' abilities to achieve their objectives;

(e) staff need to be trained in the methods of matrix management and the cost of such training could be substantial;

(f) there could be much duplication of effort within the organisation;

(g) managers need to spend much time in committees;

(h) disputes may arise regarding who should do what and who is in charge of whom;

(i) conflicts may occur between the decisions of individual line managers and the collective decisions of project teams (which normally are given their own budgets and authority to implement decisions);

(j) matrix structures might encourage managers to develop their political and negotiating skills at the expense of their managerial abilities;

(k) the system may severely overwork certain key managers;

(l) team members may be unclear about the precise nature of their roles in the team and in the organisation.

Progress test 7

1. List some of the issues dealt with by the subject of organisational design.

2. In what sense does 'structure follow strategy'?

3. What problems might emerge from inadequacies in a firm's organisation structure?

4. What is the 'organisational life cycle'?

5. State the disadvantages of informal organisation.

6. What factors should determine a manager's span of control.

7. Explain the meaning of the term 'line and staff' in the context of organisation.

8. What is a strategic business unit (SBU)?

9. List some of the problems associated with matrix organisation.

8

ETHICAL CONSIDERATIONS

1. Business and society

No organisation can divorce itself from the society within which it operates. Businesses provide goods and services to the general public, which has therefore a vested interest in how businesses behave. Customers want the products and services they purchase to be of reasonable quality. They demand fair prices, prompt delivery, good after-sales service, and so on. Other interest groups, moreover, make similar demands: suppliers expect fast settlement of bills, shareholders want high dividends, employees ask for better wages and conditions of work. The problem of course is that some of these requirements conflict; they cannot all be achieved simultaneously. Thus priorities must be specified and compromises negotiated. In some cases the state will decide how businesses should behave. There may be laws prohibiting specific acts of consumer exploitation or pollution of the environment. Collusion between firms to fix prices or output levels might be illegal. Often, however, individual managers have to take ethically problematic decisions, and in doing so will be influenced by the social norms and attitudes of the society in which they live.

2. Ethics

Ethics concerns the study of moral principles and how individuals should conduct themselves in social affairs. Thus, it requires a definition of what constitutes human well-being, and the identification of the factors that cause it to exist. Having formulated a definition, rules of conduct conducive to the attainment of human well-being can then be devised. Ethical considerations in decision taking involve the decision taker's personal feelings about how human affairs ought to be organised, about what – in his or her subjective opinion – is 'good'. An ethical approach to an issue requires an evaluation of its morally good and bad features.

The question of what represents ethically proper business behaviour is enormously complex because ethical standards vary over time and among cultures and nations. And there is, of course, no way of proving what is ultimately good, since such values are assumed in advance by individuals. People interact; they depend on others and will be influenced by other people's attitudes and norms. Managers of organisations are members of a society – as consumers, voters, owners of property, members of families and so on. When they purchase goods for their own personal use they expect certain standards to apply, and it would be inconsistent of them not to feel obliged to adopt similar standards in their own business affairs. A manager will want to feel that he or she is behaving properly and in socially acceptable ways.

Criticisms of the debate

Critics of the contemporary debate on ethics in business allege that it is superficial and fails to challenge the *real* issue, i.e. the propriety of private enterprise and its effects on the distribution of wealth in society, on the dignity of labour, the overall allocation of economic resources, and the human condition as a whole. The mercenary aspects of human nature are regarded as normal. Businesses are merely expected to minimise the damaging consequences of the anti-social behaviour that sometimes results from competitive situations. If there were no private enterprise and everyone co-operated with each other – so the argument goes – then social harmony would prevail and concerns regarding 'business ethics' would be irrelevant.

3. Ethics and strategy

Ethical issues play an important role in strategic management for a number of reasons:

(*i*) Big corporations sometimes have incomes larger than those of many nation states. How these companies use their wealth has numerous implications for the well-being of the countries in which they operate.

(*ii*) Power and responsibility are necessarily intertwined. Typically, senior managers in big firms occupy positions where they can hurt or promote the interests of large numbers of employees, and might take decisions affecting entire communities.

(*iii*) Consumers increasingly judge the worth of a company in terms of how it deals with ethical and environmental problems.

(*iv*) To the extent that cultural factors affect managers' moral philosophies, strategic management decisions will in part be determined by the cultural influences of the societies in which they reside.

Certain business practices are considered unethical throughout the world. Examples are the 'dumping' of products, i.e. selling them at less than cost price in order to drive competing firms out of business; covert involvement in the political affairs of a country; or knowingly breaking the law *vis-à-vis* consumer protection, health and safety of employees, equal opportunities, pollution of the physical environment, etc. Other forms of ethically questionable behaviour are more problematic: when the welfare of employees or the general public are endangered, *even though* this is technically lawful, and when a practice is considered acceptable in some countries but reprehensible elsewhere.

4. Personal professional ethics

Ethical conundrums regularly arise in managerial situations. Some examples are listed below:

(a) Should a manager report to the authorities (police, government agency or whatever) an illegal act deliberately performed by the manager's employing firm?

(b) If an individual is a member of a committee that takes a decision with which the individual fundamentally disagrees, should that person feel bound by the normal conventions of confidentiality of committee proceedings and collective responsibility for decisions? If, for instance, some of the manager's colleagues are to lose their jobs through a committee decision, is the manager morally entitled to warn them of what is to happen and thus possibly enable them to prevent implementation of the committee's plans?

(c) Should senior managers always back the decisions taken by subordinates even if those decisions turn out to be wrong? Bosses who overturn subordinates' decisions may impose fairer and more just solutions on specific problems, but in so doing will lose the trust and confidence of their subordinates, who will become increasingly reluctant to take decisions on their own without first seeking approval from higher levels.

(d) To what extent (if any) is it reasonable to bribe representatives of client firms in order to win orders? If payment of such inducements is regarded as a normal part of a business's marketing effort, should similar bribes be offered to government officials who are capable of helping or hindering the work of the firm? If it is not considered permissIble to bribe government officials in one's own country, is it reasonable to bribe government officials in other countries to secure export sales?

(e) How truthful should the manager be when describing the firm's activities or products to outsiders? Note that deliberately withholding relevant information can be as misleading as actually telling lies.

5. Resolution of ethical problems

A person's behaviour depends substantially on the culture, institutions, norms and collective perspectives of the society to which he or she belongs. Managers have been born to a particular social group, have been educated in a certain tradition, might subscribe to a specific religion, and will have absorbed some of the values expounded by peers. All managers possess, therefore, a philosophy of some sort, even if they are not aware of the fact. This philosophy will help the manager determine hierarchies of personal objectives, identify good and bad occurrences, and evaluate the desirabilities of various courses of action. Also the philosophy should help the individual establish ethical criteria against which particular events can be assessed. There are two approaches to the problem. Either, the manager must predetermine strict moral principles and adhere to them always – regardless of extenuating circumstances; or must consciously decide to vary his or her behaviour according to the demands of particular situations. The former option has the advantage of consistency, and it avoids managers having to wrestle with their consciences each and every time an ethical problem arises. Having once decided on a set of moral values the manager simply applies these without exception, and does not worry about the results. Managers who behave in this way might be accused (perhaps justifiably) of obstinacy, and intolerance of the human weaknesses of others. And they will not attract much sympathy if they themselves break their self-imposed moral codes. The alternative, more flexible, approach requires changes in managers' moral outlooks according to the needs of the situation. Inconsistent decisions could result, and managers will never be really sure in their own minds whether they did the right thing. Those affected by a manager's ethical inconsistency might resent and retaliate against the decision.

6. Individual preferences

Some people are intellectually independent and innovative; they do not accept that the *status quo* is necessarily just, and they experience feelings of guilt when they perceive something as wrong. Others accept without question existing social norms and adapt – perhaps unconsciously – their views to fit in with the prevailing culture. The social order as it stands is seen as equitable and its moral standards, therefore, as sacrosanct. Managers who feel this way will tend to cling to traditional values and always interpret events (and the ethical problems they generate) in manners that support the norms of contemporary society. Thus for example they will *always* obey the law, regardless of what the law is or its effects on other people. They will always implement the orders of their superiors, and will not generally accept the proposition that what might be ethically correct in one set of circumstances could be totally inappropriate in others.

7. Codes of Practice

A Code of Practice is a document published by a government agency, professional body, trade association or other relevant authority outlining model procedures for good practice in a particular field. Some large organisations issue their own in-house Codes of Practice on particular matters (the receipt by employees of gifts from outside companies for example). Codes give examples of excellent and bad behaviour, and recommendations regarding how things should be done. Government Codes of Practice (e.g. those issued by the Equal Opportunities Commission) are not legally binding, but will be looked at by Courts when adjudicating cases.

The obvious advantage of Codes of Practice is that they provide guidance to people who genuinely want to behave properly but who do not know what they should do in order to achieve this aim. Advice contained within a Code can be quite detailed. For example, the UK Equal Opportunities Commission Code on the avoidance of sex discrimination in employment has sections covering:

(a) the legal background, coverage of the legislation, exemptions from the Sex Discrimination Act;

(b) definitions of direct and indirect discrimination, with examples;

(c) good employment practice in relation to recruitment (wording of advertisements and so on), selection, training and promotion;

149

(d) terms of employment, benefits, facilities and services;

(e) grievance procedures and victimisation;

(f) dismissals, redundancies and other unfavourable treatment of employees.

The Code also contains practical guidance on formulating, implementing and monitoring equal opportunities policies. Note how a firm that visibly adheres to a recognised Code of Practice can use this fact in its corporate image advertising (companies that claim to be 'equal opportunity employers' for example).

Problems with Codes of Practice are (i) that their implementation is voluntary and not a statutory requirement, and (ii) that however well-intentioned and clearly drafted a Code might be, it can never be composed in sufficient detail to cover all possible situations.

Swiss food processing giant Nestlé was accused in the 1970s of contributing to the deaths of large numbers of infants in Third World countries via its sale of powdered milk without explaining the circumstances in which its use is justified. Hence, it was alleged, mothers were discouraged from breast feeding and the powder was frequently mixed with contaminated water and overdiluted. Nestlé replied that it was being unfairly blamed for the effects of all sorts of hygiene and infant health problems common in Third World nations and that *all* its products carry a statement that breast feeding is best and that powdered milk shoud be used as a *supplement* rather than alternative to the mother's milk. Also women in very poor countries on average produce only half the daily amount of breast milk than women in affluent countries, on account of dietary deficiences, so that it is not surprising that Third World infants are frequently malnourished. Nevertheless, criticisms persisted and Nestlé phased out its advertising of powdered milk. Then the World Health Organisation drafted a code of practice on the marketing of powdered milk in Third World countries. This code forbade, *inter alia*, all direct advertising of powdered milk to the general public, point-of-sale advertising, distribution of free samples, commissions on sales or other inducements to promote the product, and the use of pictures of babies on labels. Also the hazards of incorrect usage had to be clearly stated. Nestlé agreed to adhere to the WHO code in 1981. Criticism of the company ceased and groups refusing to buy any Nestlé product lifted their boycott. Thereafter Nestlé's share of the international powdered milk market grew steadily, despite the company not engaging in advertising.

Source: Adapted from Greer, T.V., 'International Infant Formula Marketing', in *Advances in International Marketing*, Vol. 4., 1990.

8. Role of professional bodies in regulating members' activities

Professionally qualified people (lawyers and accountants for example) often belong to professional bodies which attempt to regulate their members' behaviour. Professional bodies are organisations which seek:

(a) to maintain or improve members' occupational status; and

(b) to enhance members' standards of performance through training and a system of certification, usually (but not always) involving a series of examinations.

Traditionally, professional workers have performed service roles (accountants, lawyers, etc.) and have worked for many 'clients' rather than a single employer. Today, however, it is common for professionals to spend their careers in large firms.

Three fundamental criteria normally applied when defining 'professional' functions are:

(a) Activities should be based on an established, systematic body of knowledge the acquisition of which requires several years of substantial intellectual training.

(b) Certain ethical ('professional') standards must be maintained and Codes of Practice applied to members' work.

(c) Entry should be restricted to persons possessing predefined qualifications, experience and/or characteristics and with common training and perspectives.

The latter criteria enables the traditional professional body to control access to particular types of work. In the UK, for example, accountants cannot audit company accounts unless they have passed the examinations of a chartered body; doctors may not treat patients until they belong to the British Medical Association (BMA); unqualified lawyers cannot represent clients in Court. A 'profession' is as much concerned with controlling an occupation as with the occupation itself.

An essential ingredient of this process is the specification and maintenance of 'professional standards', backed up by disciplinary procedures and the threat of sanctions (up to and including expulsion from the body) against those who break the professional body's rules. Hence, professional bodies publish Codes of Practice and advise their members on what is and is not considered ethically correct.

Note the important differences between professional work, in the sense previously discussed, and general management. The latter is not 'professional' in that no formal qualifications are needed to become a manager; indeed, many successful managers (especially entrepreneurs) have received only a rudimentary formal education. There are no generally accepted norms of conduct for managers (other than those imposed by government), and there are no uniform management principles that all managers need apply to their work.

SOCIAL RESPONSIBILITY

9. Nature of corporate social responsibility

The doctrine of corporate social responsibility demands that firms behave as 'good citizens' as well as pursuing purely commercial goals. Unfortunately there is no clear-cut definition of what *exactly* is meant by the 'public good', and there is no consensus on the question of whether the common good is maximised or harmed via the selfish pursuit of personal gain. Nevertheless, most people would probably agree that certain fundamental principles should govern the conduct of business affairs, principles such as:

(a) concern for the quality of life, including life at work and the satisfaction derived from the work experience;

(b) concern for the physical environment;

(c) fair reward for effort and enterprise;

(d) involvement with and interest in the activities of the wider community;

(e) no misrepresentation in advertising or other fraudulent activities;

(f) absence of unfair discrimination in hiring, promoting or dismissing employees;

(g) adherence to the laws and established customs of the community.

Further examples of how a business can behave in socially responsible ways are listed in Table 8.1.

There are however many grey areas in the field of corporate social responsibility. Consider for example the following issues.

(a) Privately owned firms compete with each other for market share. Successful businesses acquire bigger market shares, others go into liquidation or are taken over by remaining firms. Governments and the public at large dislike monopoly because of the opportunities it provides for consumer exploitation. Monopoly is said to increase prices to artificially high levels, to concentrate wealth in the monopolist's hands, reduce output, diminish the quality of goods, reduce consumer choice, inhibit innovation, and retard overall national economic growth. At what point in its development should a firm cease to expand and instead stabilise its market share in order to avoid giving the impression that it is seeking to become a monopoly? Why indeed should not an efficient, successful business simply continue to grow and eat up its failing competitors?

(b) Large profitable firms contribute much revenue to the state, and they provide the community with goods and income from employment. Why, then, should their economic and social importance not be paralleled by political influence? Perhaps the state should recognise the community's dependence on big business by explicitly favouring the business community when drafting legislation. A related question is the extent to which firms should be allowed to buy political influence through sponsorship of political parties. Businesses have the resources (human as well as financial) to present their views effectively. Thus they might be able to influence individual politicians – independent of direct financial contributions – more convincingly than other social groups (unions or consumer groups for example) that do not have the same wealth or persuasive skills.

(c) Business decisions affect local communities. Shut-down decisions cause unemployment, loss of incomes and social distress. Wage policies help determine local spending power which in turn determines local demand for the outputs of other firms. Should, therefore, the local community be directly involved – via

TABLE 8.1 Examples of how businesses can act in a socially responsible manner

Towards customers
Concern for improving
product safety over
and above minimum legal
requirements.
Relating prices to costs
of production and not
exploiting shortages of
products.
Maintaining a high quality
of output or service.
Not engaging in misleading
advertising.
Providing value for money.

Towards society
Not polluting the environment.
Contributing to community
activities.
Not engaging in restrictive
trade practices.
Obeying the spirit as well
as the letter of the law.
Not undertaking unfair
industrial espionage.
Using natural resources
frugally.

Towards shareholders
Making available the
maximum amount of accurate
information on company
performance.
Not concealing earnings.
Resisting takeover attempts
potentially detrimental to
shareholders' interests.
Creating a sound capital base.

Towards suppliers
Prompt payment of invoices.
Giving long periods of notice
of termination of contracts.
Offering advice on how to
satisfy input specifications.
Maintaining confidentiality.
Not exploiting monopoly power.

Towards employees
Paying fair wages.
Providing continuous
employment.
Concern for employees'
health and safety.
Designing jobs to make
them interesting.
Provision of training and
opportunities for internal
promotion.

Implementing equal opportunity
policies.
Respecting individual privacy.
Treating employees with dignity
and respect.

elected representatives – in the decision-making processes of local businesses? Local government does have some power through its ability to pass by-laws relating to prevention of pollution, control of traffic, planning permission for buildings, and similar matters, but it is not normally directly involved in forming the strategic policies of local firms. These policies might affect local people just as much as the construction of a new road or rearrangement of traffic flow, yet their voice is not heard when policies are formulated.

(d) Some private firms provide public services, under government protection. They do not operate in a free market environment, yet they are not subject to direct government control. To what extent should the objective of profit maximisation be modified in these organisations to take account of wider social concerns, say by:

- offering cut price output to those in need;
- employing the disabled;
- providing a good or service at the same price regardless of the customer's location or the marginal cost of supply;
- offering extended credit to customers currently unable to pay their bills, and so on?

(e) Should a foreign company utilise child labour in host countries where this is permitted? Are social responsibility standards transferrable between nations: should a company adapt its methods to conform to local norms (e.g. by paying very low wages in underdeveloped countries) or act as a 'shining example' to rival local firms? Typically firms operating internationally adopt the norms of the host country, even if these involve standards of behaviour lower than in the head office nation. Examples are countries where there is direct discrimination against certain ethnic groups, or minimal employee health and safety requirements.

(f) If consumers are ignorant of the risks attached to the use of certain products, should this lack of knowledge be exploited?

Thousands of people were killed by an accidental release of poisonous gas from the Union Carbide plant at Bhopal in India. Union Carbide's safety standards satisfied local law, but were hopelessly inadequate given the size and nature of the company's operations. The valves of a tank containing pesticide had burst open, enabling a cloud of lethal gas to envelop a large shanty town alongside the plant. Prior to the accident the management of the plant had been under intense pressure to reduce costs. Short cuts were taken in relation to employee training, shift rotas and the maintenance of equipment. Instead of superintendents receiving the recommended two years of training, they were trained in one month. When the valve problem was noticed it was not addressed, and the staff in charge had little appreciation of the danger of the situation. It seems however that no laws were broken. Indeed, Union Carbide was subsequently granted immunity from all civil and criminal prosecution by India's Supreme Court. Union Carbide had set up the plant and trained its first staff, but then withdrew from day-to-day operations – as required by Indian government regulations. No parent company officials were on-site at the time of the accident.

Should Union Carbide have exercised tigher supervision over its Indian subsidiary? Why were large numbers of people allowed to squat in such a potentially dangerous location? Should the company have imposed safety standards over and above those required by local law? To what extent did the parent organisation owe a duty of care to shanty-dwellers who — without the company's approval – chose to live alongside the plant?

Sources: Chakravarty, S.N., 'The Ghost Returns', in *Forbes Magazine*, Dec. 19, 1990.
Kurzman, D., *A Killing Wind Inside Union Carbide*, McGraw-Hill, 1987.

For managements committed to the adoption of a socially responsible approach the basic issue is whether to regard it as a *supplement* to existing policies or to build it into the heart and mission of the enterprise, *even if* this results in lower profits for the firm. Normally the former approach is applied, with social objectives assuming a secondary role and modifying rather than driving managerial behaviour.

The Body Shop is a supplier of personal hygiene and cosmetic items produced by methods that avoid cruelty to animals, that are environmentally friendly, and which minimise waste. It is mainly a franchise operation that trades in 39 countries. The parent organisation is committed to community involvement in areas of high social need. Examples of its involvement have included the setting up of a soap factory in Easterhouse, a district of Glasgow then experiencing 70 per cent unemployment and intense urban deprivation; and a hand paper making project in Nepal. Body Shop provided the management expertise, production, finance and marketing skills necessary to run these factories, both of which were highly successful in terms of profitability, job creation and growth. Yet each of the projects attracted bad as well as favourable publicity. The Easterhouse operation was criticised for (i) having created a 'third world' type of business in what was once a proud industrial area, (ii) its naivety in supposing that such a project could *seriously* address the social problems associated with 70 per cent unemployment, (iii) seeking publicity for the parent organisation, and (iv) generally adopting a patronising approach. Similar comments were made about the Nepalese paper making factory, which was accused of developing out-of-date craft skills (rather than high technology employment) and fostering dependence on western markets. Such a project, it was alleged, could make no significant impact on the difficulties confronting the local area, and merely served to divert attention from the *real* problems involved.

Source: Adapted from Cannon, T., *Corporate Responsibility*, Pitman, 1992.

10. Managerial responsibility

The exercise of 'managerial responsibility' means the deliberate restraint of corporate power in order to benefit particular groups. People and organisations often consciously limit their activities in order to please others. Such self-regulation can stabilise inter-personal and inter-group relationships and be mutually beneficial in the long run. For example, a monopoly firm could, if it wanted, raise its prices to unreasonably high levels; a company operating in an area of very high unemployment might be able to impose wage cuts and worsening terms and conditions of employment on its employees; businesses that sell on credit sometimes have the ability to force into liquidation slow paying customers. Frequently however businesses which are in a position to exercise such power abstain from so doing because they recognise the destructive long-run consequences of such actions for the system as a whole. They accept that some loss of immediate benefit is necessary to avoid provoking other interest groups (unions, consumers, the government) into retaliatory action. Indeed, such considerations might even cause an individual or organisation not to respond to external attack.

155

Whitbread Ltd pioneered the use of compact schemes in schools in deprived inner city areas. A compact scheme is an agreement between a company and pupils in a local school whereby pupils are guaranteed a job with the company provided they attain prespecified goals in relation to attendance, standard of school work, punctuality, etc. Students spend short work experience periods with the company. Hence the firm is seen to be endorsing the role of education in personal development while simultaneously creating job opportunities for young people and ensuring a steady supply of good quality recruits to the organisation.

11. Resolution of social responsibility issues

There are various approaches to how best these and other social responsibility dilemmas might be resolved. Free marketeers for example argue that *laissez-faire* government policies will in normal circumstances guarantee the attainment of a just and equitable society. Business people, they argue, are in business to maximise their profits, not to make moral judgements about others. Thus, through constantly seeking to improve their own profitability, firms will increase not only their own returns but also the overall wealth of society. Goods that are most wanted by consumers command the highest prices. Accordingly, firms will consciously seek to satisfy consumer demands. Social considerations should not concern individual firms. Managers are not trained or competent in social work, and business is not part of the social security system.

12. The interventionist position

The opposing view asserts that state intervention is essential for ensuring that firms do not behave in irresponsible and socially damaging ways. Large businesses possess enormous economic and – by implication – social power. They can manipulate communities and appropriate for themselves revenues far in excess of those justified by their contributions to the wider society. Firms are able to initiate social change, and it is reasonable therefore that society, through its elected representatives, determine the directions that changes should take. Businesses, moreover, are components of a wider economic, social and legal system. As social organisations they must necessarily be concerned with social issues – education and training, occupational health and safety, incomes and employment, labour relations, equal opportunities and so on. Thus, some managerial prerogatives must be surrendered for the common good. Examples are:

(a) state insistence that employers do not discriminate unfairly in respect of sex, race, disability, religion or other criteria not relevant for particular types of work;

(b) state provision of arbitration, conciliation and advisory services to help settlement of industrial relations disputes;

(c) government restrictions on firms' freedom to trade with certain countries. These restrictions may be voluntary or have the full weight of law;

(d) state encouragement of certain modes of behaviour for firms domiciled in one country that operate in other, less developed, countries. For instance, the government could require firms to pay specified minimum wages to their foreign employees.

13. The profit motive

Private businesses must at least break-even if they are to survive. The overwhelming majority of private firms also want to earn substantial profits, and they make the maximisation of profits their primary objective. Earning high profits makes the firm attractive to outside investors, generates rewards for employees, provides resources for expansion, and is an unambiguous testament to the overall competence of the organisation. Comparisons of the profits of businesses in the same industry may generate meaningful insights into the competitive strengths and weaknesses of individual firms. It is clear, nevertheless, that profit maximisation is not the only factor that explains business decisions. Peter Drucker for example sees profit as a retrospective test of a business's success. The pursuit of profit, he argues, is not the *cause* of behaviour and does not explain all management decisions. Management, Drucker suggests, has two dimensions: short-term economic performance and long-term survival. Managerial competence is judged on economic criteria, but in achieving economic success managers have to take risks; and the assumption of excessive risk can lead to long-term failure.

Japanese companies, it is sometimes alleged, value market share in preference to short-run profits. Their desire to offer long-term employment to their workforces arguably causes them to seek continuously to expand their overseas market shares in order to provide work for their employees. Hence Japanese companies have an ongoing incentive to invest in sound long-term projects, to modify and adapt products to serve new market segments, to introduce new products on a regular basis, to market aggressively and to develop efficient international distribution systems.

Rapid growth is another strategy that reduces profits in the short run. Apart from the costs of the investments necessary to achieve a larger operating base a growth strategy might take the firm into markets that will not generate revenues for many years.

14. Profit and entrepreneurship

Profits induce people to accept and organise economic activity. Without profit, no production (using the word production to cover any form of business activity, including the supply of services) will occur. Goods which customers most want will command the highest prices and hence generate large profits. Thus, high business profits actually *benefit* consumers through indicating to firms which goods they should produce in order to satisfy current consumer demand. These profits provide the resources necessary for expansion and enable the business to pay higher wages and improve the quality of its output.

Ostensibly, the pursuit of profit should cause entrepreneurs to compete. But individual firms do not necessarily seek to maximise their profits all the time.

Rather, a business might want to guarantee its continuing existence (and hence refrain from belligerent competition), or to increase sales (which is not necessarily the same as increasing profit), or to expand the scale of its activities. Salaried managers are perhaps more likely to opt for such strategies than are owner/ entrepreneurs, since paid managers will typically be looking for job security and higher salaries (linked probably to performance indicators such as higher sales or the rate of expansion of the firm's assets) rather than maximum profit per unit of capital employed. Conflicts of interest may thus arise between entrepreneurs and the managers they employ to help them run their businesses, and such conflicts might dampen the entrepreneurial enthusiasm of firms.

Entrepreneurs themselves might be inspired by factors not directly related to profit. The continued ownership of a relatively unprofitable business (a newspaper for example) could spur a person to intense effort simply because of the prestige and social status that continuing ownership provides. Sometimes, individuals seek to emulate their peers, perhaps by acquiring various types of business or through adopting specific forms of entrepreneurial behaviour. Most entrepreneurs seek a comfortable living for themselves and their families, but not necessarily one that is exceedingly luxurious. Inventors who personally produce and market their inventions may be driven on by the urge to have their ideas accepted by the public, or by the desire to achieve further technical breakthroughs and may be uninterested in social status or high material reward. In yet other cases, the creation and expansion of a business might become the dominant passion in a person's life – feeding a restless spirit while simultaneously enlarging that person's appetite for commercial success.

15. Advantages to firms of acting in a socially responsible manner

It can be argued that it benefits a firm financially in the long term to behave in socially responsible ways, since only through being a good neighbour can a business acquire from the wider community the co-operation it needs for long-term survival and commercial success. Visible concern for social responsibility is useful, moreover, for a business that wishes to lobby government on matters that affect its vital interests; that seeks political influence; or which aspires to a position of leadership in the local community. Also a large organisation with a virtual monopoly of a certain market might identify itself with the moral high ground and thus avoid adverse criticism by government representatives. Examples of benefits that arise from the adoption of a socially responsible approach include the following:

(a) Projection of a 'green' image of a company is itself good for business, leading to higher sales.

(b) Energy conservation and avoidance of environmental pollution through industrial waste and spillage cuts production costs and increases corporate efficiency.

(c) Being a good employer helps the firm attract and retain high-calibre workers.

(d) Sponsorship of charitable and community events attracts valuable publicity.

Another powerful argument for business involvement in community affairs is that the more that companies contribute to the wider society the less has to be done by government, resulting perhaps in greater freedom and less state bureaucracy. If businesses do not adopt a proactive role in the wider society then social problems may emerge that government (and ultimately the taxpayer) will have to deal with. Many businesses are wealthy organisations, and managers within them are skilled and experienced administrators. Why not utilise this wealth and talent for the social benefit?

16. Arguments against firms adopting social responsibility approaches

Arguments against corporate involvement in local communities are that:

(a) it can create overdependence of the community on company handouts, which might be withdrawn at short notice;

(b) it leads to businesses assuming a disproportionately influential role in local affairs;

(c) it could undermine normal democratic processes in local government;

(d) local services should be supplied by democratically accountable bodies and not by private firms;

(e) social responsibility objectives may be so vague as to be meaningless;

(f) if businesses initiate social ventures that affect the general public then they should be accountable to the general public;

(g) there is no such thing as a 'free lunch' where these matters are concerned. At the end of the day any business expenditures on social improvement have to be recovered through higher prices, which detrimentally affects consumers of the goods;

(h) individual firms which do not behave in a socially responsible manner (which pay very low wages, cut corners in relation to product safety, engage in misleading advertising, etc.) obtain an unfair competitive advantage over others;

(i) internationalisation of business has resulted in a large number of firms having to compete in world markets where rival companies are not expected to engage in any social activities at all;

(j) when dealing with social issues business executives might apply unsuitable working methods and procedures and see things from perspectives entirely inappropriate for social (rather than economic or technical) problems;

(k) any social intervention by a business is likely to be regarded as 'good' by some people, and 'bad' by others. Compact schemes for example (see p.156) benefit the school students who participate in them, but in so doing necessarily deny employment opportunities to other school-leavers. Equally there is no universal consensus regarding *whose* social values should be respected. And the social values of any given group or individual typically have several aspects and dimensions.

Note moreover that it is easy to *claim* that an organisation is behaving in a socially responsible manner (how many businesses would admit to being socially irresponsible?), but social responsibility is such a nebulous and unmeasurable concept that it is extremely difficult to establish whether a particular firm is exercising social responsibility or not. Often, management accepts that it should be concerned over a particular social issue; but how extensive should be the magnitude of that concern?

17. Social audits

The term 'social audit' is sometimes used to describe the systematic appraisal of all of a company's activities that have an impact on the wider community. Certain elements of a firm's social policies will be prescribed by law, e.g. pollution control, equal opportunities in recruitment; others are implemented on a voluntary basis. An audit needs to cover all the main operations and functions of the firm, plus its relationships with national and local government and with consumer and local community welfare organisations. Problems arise from the fact that virtually *all* the activities of a typical business have an impact on the wider society in some way or other, and that the mere identification of cause-effect relationships has little consequence: *money* is needed to facilitate social involvement. Nevertheless, social auditing places ethical issues at the top of the management agenda and (importantly) it *institutionalises* concerns for social responsibility.

Outputs to a social audit might include changes in policy on particular issues, formulation of Codes of Practice (see 7), training and staff development for certain employees, and possibly the establishment of task forces to investigate specific problems.

CURRENT ISSUES IN BUSINESS ETHICS AND SOCIAL RESPONSIBILITY

The following sections discuss a number of contemporary issues that illustrate the many problems that arise for business and for social institutions where questions of ethics and social responsibility have to be addressed.

18. Determination of executive pay

Senior managers are sometimes criticised for paying themselves very high salaries, while severely restricting the remunerations of lower ranking employees. Directors may be able to set their own pay levels with little regard for market forces in the short term, and minimal accountability to shareholders (perks and fringe benefits are frequently not revealed to outsiders). Criticism is markedly severe in situations where there are few clear relationships between organisational performance and executive pay. The case for providing extremely high salaries to senior managers rests on the following propositions.

(a) They are necessary in order to motivate individual executives (e.g. through performance-related pay).

(b) High remuneration implies high status and recognition of individual worth.

(c) Competent top-level managers are in great demand and likely to be head-hunted, so that high wages are needed to secure their loyalty and long-term commitment to the organisation.

(d) Senior management involves taking risky decisions which, if wrong, have serious adverse consequences both for the organisation and for the individual executive. A high salary is needed to compensate for the assumption of such a high level of risk.

(e) Only a small number of executives possess the management skills, knowledge and contacts necessary to succeed in competitive situations, and market forces of supply and demand naturally raise the remuneration levels of these people.

(f) Failure to attract the best managerial talent available will damage the firm in the longer period.

(g) Senior management is at the top of the managerial pyramid, so that high salaries are needed to maintain differentials while enabling lower levels to earn a reasonable reward.

(h) High salaries generate a culture of effort and achievement within the firm.

19. Bribery

Bribery is said to distort market mechanisms, create unfair competitive advantage for certain firms, and hence lead to an inefficient allocation of national resources. Inducements paid to public servants are subject to particular criticism, as in this case it is the innocent taxpayer (rather than private shareholders) who ultimately foots the bill. Although bribery is officially frowned on throughout the world (including those countries in which it is extensively practised), it is not illegal in many nations. Indeed it might even be tax deductible as a business expense! Hence a case can be made for adopting a liberal approach to bribery, based on the following arguments:

(a) Distinguishing between a 'bribe' and a 'gift' is problematic. The giving of small gifts is common in Western countries. But what constitutes a 'small' gift; and where should the line be drawn between low and high value items? An expensive gift to a managing director with a million pound annual salary might be considered reasonable; yet the same gift to a lower ranking employee could be deemed corrupt!

(b) There is in reality no reliable means for ensuring that all gifts are reported, so why bother attempting to control the practice?

(c) Bribery is a way of life in many countries and business situations. Firms *not* engaging in bribery stand to lose money, resulting in job losses and other detrimental economic effects in certain geographical areas.

(d) Consultancy and agency fees remitted to third parties might in fact be bribes, yet be virtually undetectable as improper payments.

(e) Arguably, bribes should be seen as an integral part of the market system. If firms find it worthwhile to offer bribes they will do so, and a 'market price' for bribes will emerge in any given situation depending on the supply and demand for favours. Note that because bribes are 'unofficial' in nature, there is no guarantee that the recipient will in fact fulfil his or her part of the bargain.

20. Disclosure and confidentiality

The need to transmit and receive information is common to all organisations. Management has to pass instructions to the workforce, to explain its policies and objectives to shareholders, and to tell workers if their jobs are threatened. An action that a business is ashamed to admit is necessarily suspect on ethical grounds. It might be illegal or unprincipled: if it is not then presumably the firm should be willing openly to discuss the matter with anyone concerned. At the same time management has to maintain confidentiality in certain respects and prevent competitors obtaining trade secrets. Arguments in favour of management disclosing large amounts of information are that:

(a) If information is not revealed then outsiders may suspect that management is deliberately withholding relevant facts and will *assume* that the firm's position is much better or worse than might actually be the case. Disclosure can help dispel workers' misconceptions about the company's affairs, especially its profitability and the extent of competition.

(b) Lack of sound management information encourages the circulation of rumours amongst the workforce.

(c) Employees, consumers, government and the general public are likely to react more favourably to a company that is frank and open about its affairs.

The arguments against the free disclosure of management information are that:

(a) it might give competitors an unfair advantage;

(b) the costs and inconvenience of preparing detailed information for employee representatives could be substantial;

(c) the people receiving the information might not be capable of understanding it;

(d) the fact that information is disclosed does not mean it will be believed.

21. Insider dealing

This is the situation that arises when buyers or sellers of stock (equities, debentures, convertibles or whatever) execute transactions on the basis of knowledge not available to the public and which, were it generally known, would cause the price of the stock to change significantly. The prevention of insider dealing in practice is extremely difficult. Incontrovertible proof that it has occurred is almost impossible to obtain; financial policing is expensive; and the practice itself is seen as a 'victimless crime' by many people. In fact, the victim in the case of a price increase is the person who sold the stock to the insider not knowing the price was almost certain to rise; while in the opposite case the victim is landed with stock the price of which is about to fall sharply.

The European Commission has long recognised that efficient pan-European capital markets are impossible without the removal of insider trading, which has constituted a major problem on the European Stock Exchanges. Neither the investing public nor capital seeking firms can have full confidence. Accordingly, the 1989 EC Directive on Insider Dealing (effective from 1 June 1992) compelled member states to make insider trading illegal and to co-operate by exchanging information in order to enforce the Directive. The Directive covers both 'primary' insiders (who acquire knowledge through their employment) and 'secondary' insiders who knowingly receive inside information. Specifically, the Directive prohibits insiders from:

- improperly making use of inside information when buying or selling securities;
- passing on insider information;
- recommending others to buy or sell on the basis of insider information.

Enforcement

Despite the draconian penalties for insider dealing that exist in many countries the fact is that very few cases involving alleged ID ever come to trial, and when they do the accused persons invariably declare themselves bankrupt and thus unable to compensate victims. Cases can last for months, and juries are often unable to understand the complexities of insider trading legislation. Acquittals are common. Note moreover that the suspension of a company's quotation while allegations of insider dealing are being investigated disrupts capital markets and punishes the ordinary shareholders, not the individuals responsible for the insider dealing.

22. Consumerism

The modern consumer movement emerged in the 1950s and 1960s consequent to allegations that certain motor and other manufacturers were deliberately building into their products structural defects which guarantee failure within predetermined periods (use of corrosive metals instead of long-lasting plastics for example). Note however that the ethicality of 'built-in' obsolescence can be viewed in differing ways. One interpretation is that short product life cycles ensure continuing employment and income for workers, who not only make the goods, but also consume them; unemployment reduces aggregate consumer income and hence aggregate demand. The opposing argument is that planned obsolescence wastes valuable resources that could be better applied elsewhere.

As the consumer movement grew it extended its activities (lobbying of governments, press campaigns, consumer boycotts, etc.) to cover a wide range of issues concerning marketing, advertising, the environment, and general customer care. Examples of malpractice that have attracted the interest of the consumer movement include:

(a) failing to test goods properly for fire, toxic and other potential hazards;

(b) not revealing the possible harmful side effects resulting from long-term use of certain products (tobacco or alcohol for example);

(c) not recalling defective products after dangerous faults have been discovered;

(d) not marking safety instructions clearly on packages (manufacturers are reluctant to do this because of the implication that goods might not be safe);

(e) advertising which exploits the vulnerabilities of the young;

(f) misleading and deceitful advertising;

(g) high pressure selling, especially to customers who are ignorant of the nature of the products;

(h) packaging goods in indestructible containers, or in explosive aerosols, or in materials that become highly flammable as they deteriorate.

Consumerists demand four basic rights: information, choice, safety and redress. Lack of competition, they argue, denies consumers the ability to choose between products, while advertisements that focus on images at the expense of information create ignorance (including ignorance of the potentially harmful effects of using certain products) among consumers. Thus, laws are needed to prevent wealthy companies gaining the upper hand and to guarantee basic consumer rights.

23. Benefits and problems of consumerism

Consumerists have been able to draw public attention to the needs for quality, safety and reliability in products; so much so that many firms today consciously anticipate the reactions of consumer groups when drafting marketing plans. Indeed, in a sense the consumerist movement provides businesses with free market research – informing firms of customers' desires for better labelling, more effective after-sales service, reusable containers and so on. Consumerist activities, moreover, have induced several major industries to devise Codes of Practice covering such matters as product safety, quality control, avoidance of environmental pollution, and the establishment of independent procedures to investigate complaints.

Opponents of consumerism allege that it encourages groundless petty complaints, creates unfounded fears about product safety, and that consumerist interference with commercial decisions causes inefficiency and increased production costs. If customers do not want the goods on offer – albeit with built-in obsolescence and extensive advertising – then they will not be bought! Market forces, they assert, will ensure that customer requirements are met.

THE PHYSICAL ENVIRONMENT

24. Environmental issues in management

There are two reasons for managerial involvement in environmental issues:

(a) Environmental regulations (e.g. emission standards, constraints on packaging materials, antipollution laws) impose large financial costs on firms, which have therefore a vested interest in the outcomes to environmental debates. Thus, businesses frequently lobby the government in attempts to influence environmental legislation in their favour.

Some companies have adopted affirmative action programmes in relation to the protection of the physical environment, i.e. they conduct audits of their activities intended to identify any practice detrimental to the natural world. Examples of the consequences of these measures include Unilever's decision not to use non-biodegradable chemicals in detergents, MacDonald's refusal to purchase packaging materials that incorporate CFCs, and Heinz declining to buy tuna fish caught in a non-approved manner.

(b) Many consumers regard a company's publicly stated concern for environmental protection as an important selling point for its goods.

Companies can demonstrate their support for environmental conservation through incorporating 'green' messages into their advertisements, and by including environmental factors in their strategies and plans. Other measures might include:

(a) reductions in the amounts of goods packaging, perhaps even the loose display of certain items;

(b) conspicuous promotion of the energy-saving aspects of goods;

(c) provision of bottle and paper banks in retail outlets;

(d) adoption of technologies and working methods that reduce pollution;

(e) incorporating environmental considerations into new product design.

The above might be implemented in consequence of a sense of social responsibility, or for purely commercial reasons. Note how free marketeers treat concerns for the environment in much the same way as demands for particular goods. If people want the environment to possess certain characteristics they will pay for those characteristics, and organisations will naturally spring up that (in return for payment) will seek to manipulate the environment to satisfy the public's desires.

The knock-on effects of the bad publicity surrounding Union Carbide after the Bhopal disaster (see above) hurt nearly every aspect of the company's worldwide operations. It became difficult to recruit top calibre staff; share price plummeted, senior managers were eschewed by government leaders, and local communities around every other Union Carbide plant in the world demanded information and reassurances concerning safety. The international media highlighted the differences in safety standards in Union Carbide plants in the USA and in poorer countries and the company's seeming lack of concern for local people likely to be affected by the company's foreign operations.

Following the tragedy, Union Carbide appointed the former head of the US Environmental Protection Agency as its vice-president responsible for safety and the environment. It also launched a massive damage limitation public relations exercise and developed an in-house Code of Practice relating to environmental concerns.

25. The Valdez principles

The sinking of the oil tanker *Exxon Valdez* with the consequent spillage of 300,000 barrels of oil that devastated the wildlife and coastline of Prince William Sound in Alaska catapulted corporate environmental matters to the forefront of public debate. A major outcome was the publication by the leading US investment institutions of a list of general principles which multinational companies have been asked to follow when dealing with the physical environment. Firms that accept the principles undertake to:

(a) conserve energy;

(b) minimise and safely dispose of waste;

(c) recycle materials wherever possible;

(d) protect the biosphere and eliminate air and water pollutants;

(e) produce environmentally friendly goods and services;

(f) reduce health and safety risks to employees and the local community;

(g) pay full compensation to victims of environmental malpractice;

(h) undertake an annual audit of how the firm's products and policies affect the environment;

(i) disclose full information to employees and the general public about incidents that may harm the environment and/or damage public or employees' health;

(j) make at least one member of the company's board responsible for environmental matters and for implementing these principles.

Progress test 8

1. Define ethics.

2. Why do ethical issues play an important role in strategic management?

3. What is a Code of Practice?

4. Explain the concept of corporate social responsiblity.

5. What is meant by the term 'managerial responsibility'?

6. List the main arguments against corporate involvement in community affairs.

7. What are the arguments in favour of adopting a liberal approach to bribery?

8. The consumerist movement has four basic demands. What are they?

9. List the Valdez principles.

Part Two

FUNCTIONAL STRATEGIES

9

MARKETING STRATEGY

1. Nature of marketing

Marketing is far more than just selling, although higher sales are obviously the ultimate aim. Rather, marketing is a whole collection of activities including advertising, selling and sales promotion, marketing research, introduction of new products, pricing, packaging, distribution and after-sales service.

Approaches to marketing

One approach to marketing is to regard it as the process of finding customers for goods which the firm has already decided to supply. In this case there is much emphasis on face-to-face customer contact, price cutting, heavy advertising and sales promotions. It might be assumed that customers will always want to purchase well-constructed items that are made available to them at low cost: that all a firm needs to do is offer for sale high-quality, sound-value products with many attractive features, provide effective after-sales service, and then the goods will 'sell themselves'.

The marketing concept

Alternatively, the firm might seek to evaluate market opportunities before pro-duction, assess potential demand for the good, determine the product character-istics desired by consumers, predict the prices consumers are willing to pay, and then supply goods corresponding to the needs and wants of target markets more effectively than competitors. Businesses adopting the latter approach are said to apply the 'marketing concept'.

Adherence to the marketing concept means the firm conceives and develops products that satisfy consumer wants. Note however that:

(a) consumer demand can be and frequently is created and manipulated through advertising campaigns;

(b) unquestioning adoption of the concept could lead to the production of items that are highly attractive to consumers but which nevertheless are expensive to supply and thus generate negligible profit.

Practical application of the marketing concept implies the full integration of marketing with other business activities (design, production, costing, transport and distribution, corporate strategy and planning) so that the marketing department assumes extraordinary importance within the firm. Numerous conflicts with other functions could arise from this situation.

2. The marketing mix

In 1965 Professor N.H. Borden coined the phrase 'marketing mix' to describe the combination of marketing elements used in a given set of circumstances. Appropriate mixes vary depending on the firm and industry, and over time. Professor E.J. McCarthy subsequently summarised the notion under four headings (known as the 'four Ps' of marketing), as follows:

(a) *Promotion* – including advertising, merchandising, public relations, and the utilisation of salespeople.

(b) *Product* – design and quality of output, assessment of consumer needs, choice of which products to offer for sale, after-sales service.

(c) *Price* – choice of pricing strategy, prediction of competitors' responses to changes in the supplying firm's prices.

(d) *Place* – selection of distribution channels, transport arrangements.

Marketing is the primary interface between the firm and its customers, guiding resources towards appropriate product offers and facilitating the satisfaction of customer requirements. Selection of the particular mix to be used forms the basis of the firm's marketing strategy. Examples of marketing strategy are:

- developing new products for existing markets;
- deeper penetration of existing markets;
- entering new markets for existing products;
- developing new products for new markets;
- attacking competitors head-on (rather than following competitors' norms and behaviour);
- serving particular market niches.

Marketing myopia

In 1960 Theodore Levitt published in the *Harvard Business Review* an article entitled 'Marketing Myopia' in which he argued that firms should adopt broad industry orientations rather than focusing their attentions on narrowly defined products or technologies. Thus a railway company should regard itself as being in the transportation business, oil companies as in the energy business, and so on. This has many implications for corporate strategy, as outlined in Chapter 3, particularly in relation to the question of diversification. Problems with Levitt's approach are that:

(a) whereas it extends the vocabulary used to describe a business's activities, it does not necessarily alter the things the firm actually does;

(b) often it is easy to define a market opportunity in a widely defined industry sector, but extremely difficult (perhaps impossible) to exploit it in practice.

3. Market segmentation

The term 'market segmentation' describes the breaking down of a market into self-contained and relatively homogeneous sub-groups of consumers, each with its own special requirements and characteristics. Products and advertising messages can then be altered to make them appeal to particular segments.

Markets may be segmented with respect to consumers' locations, ages, incomes, social class, or other demographic variables; or according to consumer lifestyles, attitudes, interests and opinions as they affect purchasing behaviour. It does seem that many consumers buy goods that fit in with a chosen lifestyle (healthy, sophisticated, rugged, etc.) and with their perceptions of what they ought to purchase in order to pursue that lifestyle. Once the lifestyle to which potential consumers aspire is identified, advertising messages can be modified in appropriate ways.

Differentiated versus undifferentiated marketing strategies

A *differentiated* marketing strategy requires the firm to modify its products for various market segments and to operate in all sectors. Production and promotion costs are normally higher when this approach is followed. Concentration strategies involve focusing all attention on one or just a few market segments. *Undifferentiated* marketing means that the firm offers exactly the same product using identical promotional images and methods in a wide range of markets. Differences in market segments are ignored. Products are designed and advertised in order to appeal to the widest possible range of consumers.

4. Positioning

The term 'market position' describes how a product is perceived and evaluated by consumers in comparison with the products of competing firms. As a management process, positioning means finding out how customers think about the firm's products, with a view either to modifying the product (plus associated advertising and other publicity) to make it fit in with these perceptions, or to changing the product's position in consumers' minds. Positions depend on the nature of the product, competing products, and on how consumers see themselves (the lifestyles to which they aspire, role models, etc.). A great deal depends on the decision where to try to position a brand relative to competitors' outputs. The positioning statement determines the target market groups to be contacted, the creative strategy that will underlie the campaign and the cost of the firm's advertising effort. Firms operating in several different foreign markets need to decide whether to locate their products in similar or disparate positions in each country. Factors influencing the choice should include the following:

(a) The scope of the product's appeal: whether it sells to a broad cross-section of consumers (in relation to their ages, sex, income level, lifestyle, etc.) or only within small market niches.

(b) Special advantages the advertised brand has to offer.

(c) The extent to which a product's selling points are perceived similarly in different nations.

(d) Whether the item fulfils the same consumer needs in each market.

(e) The degree of direct and immediate substitutability between the advertised output and locally supplied brands (if this is high the appropriate position for the product should be self-evident).

(f) Whether the brand name and/or product features need to be altered for use in different markets.

5. Market leaders and market followers

A market leader is a firm that dominates a particular market, decides the level of price to be charged for the product, the intensity of advertising, how the item will be promoted (discounts, special offers, etc.), essential product characteristics, and so on. Market followers charge similar prices to the market leader and do not attempt to take market share from it. They exercise great care in not provoking the leader into taking aggressive action against them. This might even involve followers delaying the introduction of new models until the leader has developed a similar item. Market leadership requires the abilities to introduce new products before competitors, alter prices without provoking price wars with rival firms, and to vary advertising expenditures at will. The company may wish to expand its share of the existing market (through sales promotions for instance) or to increase the total size of the market (e.g. through finding new users or uses for the general type of product that the industry in question supplies). Increasing the firm's market share typically necessitates price reductions, additional advertising, sales promotions, and a building up of the firm's sales force. The numbers of wholesalers and retailers carrying the company's products need to increase and (where appropriate) extra retail shelf space must be devoted to the product. Serving a particular market niche may require attacking and displacing specific rival firms currently dominating the niche. This could involve aggressive price cutting, discounting, special offers and various forms of sales promotion.

PRODUCT STRATEGIES

A product is anything a business has to sell, whether this be a physical good or a service. 'New' products could be completely fresh innovations, or modifications of existing products, or copies of other firms' products. Branding a product means giving it a trade name and/or logo and then seeking via advertising and other sales promotions to associate certain attractive characteristics with the branded item. Customers then recognise the product and, having once been satisfied by it, need not subsequently re-evaluate its worth. Thus, little fresh information about the product has to be provided to the customer after it has been branded.

6. Product choice

Complacency about current models is a common cause of failure in otherwise competent and efficient firms. To assess the relevance of existing products to market needs a firm should ask itself two questions.

What images of the firm do current products create?

Images of old fashioned, conventional, uninspired products should be avoided. Products should create impressions of innovation, imagination and market leadership.

Are production costs of individual products high relative to their contributions to profits?

Sometimes, firms expand their product ranges faster than increases in their aggregate sales. New versions of existing products are introduced, but old models are not phased out. This results in complicated production and organisation systems, which are expensive to administer and add little to the corporate images of the firm. Possibly, the features of one model can be incorporated into another, thus removing the need for the first. In general, products should be retained only if at least one of the following conditions applies:

- they contribute significantly to total profits;
- substantial future sales are expected;
- they are necessary for, or by-products of, other profitable products.

Otherwise, scale economies made possible by product standardisation will probably be worth more than the benefits derived from the provision of a wide selection of models. Note, however, that firms seeking to penetrate new markets must offer products that possess special features compared to versions already available. Rationalisation and standardisation are more appropriate for firms presently holding large market shares.

The introduction of new products is risky and expensive. Not surprisingly, therefore, many firms copy the successful products of more adventurous rivals. Innovation demands research, acquisition of extra equipment, learning new skills, initiation of training programmes and the recruitment of extra labour.

7. Product development

This has two aspects: (a) extension of the market for existing products through improving their attractiveness, and (b) altering the product range to reach completely new markets. Ideas for new products or markets might emanate from research workers, salespeople, customers, suggestion schemes or quality improvement teams. A common stimulus is the sight of another firm successfully launching a new good. Other firms then market thinly disguised copies of the original. To prevent this happening, the initiating firm could simultaneously launch several versions of the product under completely different brand names. Consumers will then believe they have a choice of competing products whereas, in fact, all are produced by subsidiaries of the same firm. Competitors cannot easily enter a new market in these circumstances.

Product development policies derive from a company's strategic objectives, resources and market opportunities. The firm's strategic objectives are relevant to product development policy because they determine the organisation's attitudes towards risk, expected returns on new products, and the particular markets in which the firm does business. Resources affect product development policy as they determine the business's capacity to engage in technical and market research, to advertise and otherwise promote new items. Market opportunities arise from changes in consumer demand and/or economic circumstances, and from lack of competition in specific markets.

8. The product life cycle (PLC)

Products have been likened to living organisms; they are conceived and born, they mature, decline and eventually die. Marketing strategies and policies should, it is sometimes argued, be systematically varied with respect to the phase in its lifecycle that the product currently occupies. The *introductory phase* is characterised by high expenditures (for market research, test marketing, launch costs, etc.) and possibly by financial losses in the early stage. The first customers will be attracted by the novelty of the good. Typically, these customers are younger, better educated and more affluent than the rest of the population. Technical problems are likely and, realising this, many potential consumers will delay purchasing the good. No competition is experienced at this stage. Advertising is normally the most important element of the marketing mix during the introduction. The aim is to create product awareness and loyalty to the brand.

There should now follow a period of *growth*, during which conventional consumers begin to purchase the product. Competition appears, so advertisments should attempt both to reinforce customer loyalty and to broaden the product's appeal. Next, the product enters its *maturity* phase. Here the aim is to stabilise market share and make the product attractive (through improvements in design and presentation) to new market segments. Extra features might be added, quality improved, and distribution systems widened. Most consumers have by now either tried the product or decided not to buy. Competition intensifies; appropriate strategies now include extra promotional activity, price cutting to improve market share, and finding new uses for the product.

Eventually, the market is saturated and the product enters its phase of *decline*. Consumer tastes might have altered, or the product may be technically obsolete. Sales and profits fall. The product's life should now be terminated, otherwise increasing amounts of time, effort and resources will be devoted to the maintenance of a failing product.

9. Objections to the PLC hypothesis

The following difficulties apply to the concept of the PLC:

(a) Many products cannot be characterised in life cycle terms (basic foodstuffs or industrial materials for instance).

(b) The length of life of a new product cannot be reliably predicted in advance.

(c) Variations in marketing effort will affect the durations of life cycle phases and determine the timing of transitions from one stage to the next.

(d) Competitors' behaviour may be the primary determinant of the firm's sales, regardless of the age of the product.

(e) Products do not face inevitable death within predetermined periods. Termination of a product's life is a management decision. A product's lifespan may be extended by skilful marketing.

(f) Management can never be sure of the phase in its life cycle in which a product happens to be at a particular time. How for instance, could management know that a product is near the start and not the end of its growth phase, or that a fall in sales is a temporary event rather than the start of the product's decline?

(g) Many random factors can influence the duration of phases, turning points and levels of sales.

Note, moreover, that the expected demise of a product can become a self-fulfilling reality; management may assume wrongly that sales are about to decline, and consequently withdraw resources from the marketing of that product. Hence, in the absence of advertising, merchandising, promotional activity, etc., sales do fall and the product is withdrawn!

10. Branding strategies

Firms operating in several foreign markets must choose whether to allocate separate brand names to individual products or establish a generic 'family' brand covering all versions of their outputs. The latter approach can be highly cost effective, especially if the various products are closely related through associated usage (toiletries for example) or a common channel of distribution, a common customer group or similarity of prices. This is because their entire product range may then be advertised under a single brand name, thus cutting the cost of advertising individual brands separately. Moreover, additions to product lines are introduced easily and inexpensively since no extra advertising or promotions need be incurred. The new product is simply incorporated into existing literature. It is not necessary to establish a completely new individual brand image. Separate brands are essential, nevertheless, if the company wishes to appeal to different market segments (e.g. in consequence of culture differences) or where products are markedly dissimilar.

Proctor and Gamble sells its outputs in nearly 150 countries worldwide. Branding and brand management is a major feature of the firm's business, necessarily leading to complex control and communication systems. Each of the company's divisions had up to 15 brand managers, who were frequently required to go through four levels of divisional management when important decisions were required. Market opportunities were lost through faulty communication, decision making had become slow and bureaucratic, and there was much duplication of effort. In order to address these problems the company streamlined its brand management system by introducing a new grade of executive, the 'category manager' each of whom was deemed to head a quasi-autonomous SBU (see 7.**23**). Twenty-six category managers were appointed to look after 39 product groups (detergents for example). Individual brand managers now report to a category manager, who is a cost/profit centre in his or her own right. Thus the entire brand management function was delayered, with category managers taking all significant brand decisions. For the development of global brands, teams are formed to analyse opportunities for the standardisation of the product and the manner in which it is to be promoted, and a lead country is selected. A team will include individual brand mangers from the countries in which the new global brand will be marketed, technical experts, a divisional manager and a branch category manager.

PRICING STRATEGIES

Price is an important factor in the purchasing decision, but it is not necessarily paramount. Much depends on customers' perceptions of the unique attributes of a product: its quality, reliability, image, and 'need fulfilling' characteristics.

11. The options available

A number of pricing strategies are available, as follows:

(a) *Penetration pricing*, whereby a low price is combined with aggressive advertising aimed at capturing a large percentage of the market. The firm hopes that unit production costs will fall as output is expanded. The strategy will fail, however, if competitors simultaneously reduce their prices.

(b) *Target pricing*, where the firm predetermines a target level of profits, estimates its potential sales at varying prices, and then charges a price to generate target profits.

(c) *Skimming*, which is a high-price policy suitable for top-quality versions of established products. The firm must convince high income consumers that the expensive model offers distinct improvements over the standard version.

(d) *Product life cycle pricing*. Here the price is varied according to the product's stage in its life cycle (see **8**). Initially, a high price may be set to cover development and advertising costs. The price might then be systematically lowered to broaden the product's appeal.

(e) *Loss leading*. This means selling an item at less than its production or purchase cost in an attempt to attract custom and hence induce consumers to buy other items.

(f) *Price discrimination* involves charging different prices in different markets for the same good. It can only work if there exist barriers (consumer ignorance or high transport costs for instance) that prevent intermediaries buying in low price markets and reselling elsewhere.

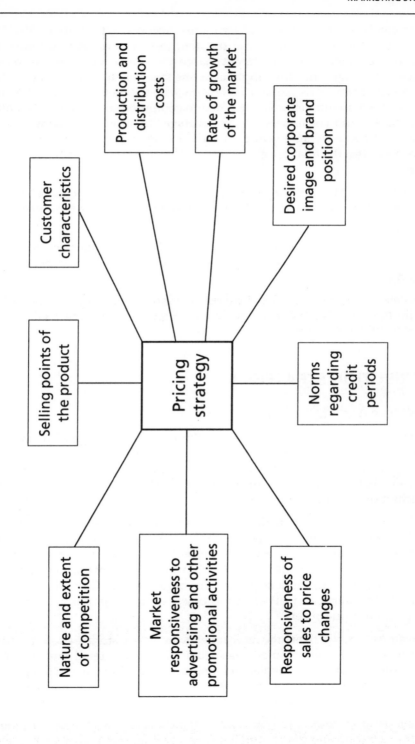

Figure 9.1 Influences on pricing strategy

(g) *Marginal cost pricing* means charging the customer a price that reflects the extra cost to the firm of supplying the item to that particular customer. For example, a telephone company might charge a low price for installing an inner city line, but a high price for supplying a line to a remote rural location where much additional work is required. Problems with the method include the difficulties and extra administration attached to computing marginal costs, and its unpopularity with consumers. Hence, average cost pricing is more common whereby all costs are aggregated and divided by expected sales to derive a common base for the final price. This is simple to apply and readily accepted by customers.

(h) *Limit pricing.* Here, existing firms in an industry collectively choose to charge lower prices than the market would bear in order to discourage the entry of new firms to the industry.

(i) *Variable (stayout) pricing* is used by firms wishing to discourage custom when they have too much business. Hence, prices are increased when order books are full, and vice-versa.

(j) *Customary pricing* is occasionally used in inflationary situations. Price is held constant but the volume of contents of a package is reduced, in the hope that customers will not notice.

DISTRIBUTION STRATEGIES

12. Nature of distribution

A distribution channel is a route from the producer of a good to the final consumer. The functions of a distribution channel include the physical movement of goods, storage of goods awaiting transit and/or sale, transfer of title to goods, and their presentation to final purchasers. There are three main categories of distribution system, as follows:

(a) *Direct to consumers,* e.g. mail order or if the producer owns and controls its own retail shops. No intermediaries are involved, so prices can be lower and suppliers can ensure their goods are properly presented to consumers. The method is commonest among firms (i) with large volumes of business (and thus able to justify establishing a separate sales organisation), (ii) with technically complicated products, and (iii) where customers are geographically concentrated and place high value orders.

(b) *Producer to retailer.* Here the retailer bears the cost of storing goods awaiting sale. The supplier must employ salespeople to canvass retail outlets and to merchandise the product. Retailers sell the goods, possibly offer credit, provide product information to customers, and ensure that goods are available in small quantities throughout the year. Franchising is a special case of this method.

(c) *Producer to wholesaler.* The advantages of selling to a wholesaler include (i) less administration (there is no need for a salesforce, no warehousing costs, fewer

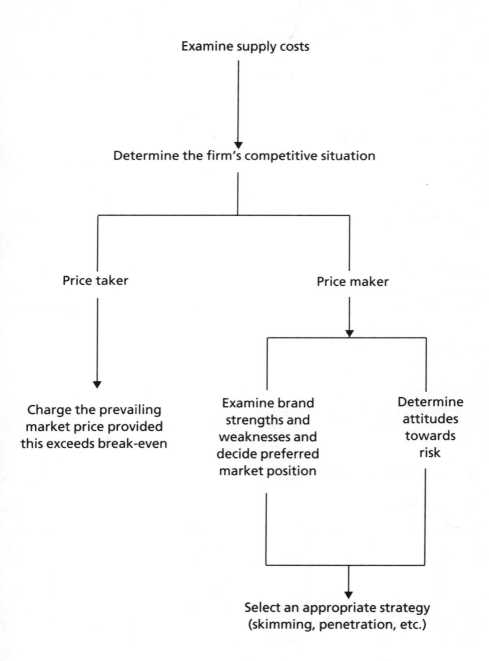

Figure 9.2 Pricing decisions

deliveries, and negligible invoicing and debt collecting) and (ii) the transfer of the risk of product failure from the supplier to the wholesaling firm. However, final prices will be higher and wholesalers typically hold competing lines.

The *intensity* of a distribution system is the number of sales outlets it involves. Intense (many outlet) systems are appropriate where there is regular demand, where customers are widely dispersed and where little product information is needed.

13. Choice of method

In selecting a distribution system the producer should consider the following characteristics in respect of each alternative:

(a) Cost of the channel. This is affected by the sizes of customers' orders (discounts are necessary to secure big contracts), salespeoples' salaries and travelling expenses, costs of credit given, inventory holding costs of unsold output, and administrative costs (invoicing, debt collection, bad debts, etc.).

(b) Extent of the control that can be exercised over the channel.

(c) Whether the channel improves or worsens the image of the goods (e.g. high-quality expensive output would not be congruent in a low-price cash and carry discount store).

(d) Geographical coverage of the channel.

(e) Reliability of distributors in relation to:

(*i*) product presentation and the provision of information to customers;
(*ii*) ensuring continuity of supply;
(*iii*) adequacy of customer care and after-sales services.

PROMOTIONAL STRATEGIES

14. Advertising

The European Union's definition of advertising is 'the making of a representation in any form in connection with a trade, business, craft or profession in order to promote the supply of goods or services, including immovable property, rights and obligations' (EC Directive on Misleading Advertising, 1984).

Formulation of an advertising strategy requires the clear identification of target consumers and a definition of the product attributes they desire. Then, media (newspapers, TV, magazines, posters, etc.) are chosen to carry messages. Factors relevant to the choice of a particular medium include its:

- overall coverage of target markets;
- capacity to penetrate specific market segments;
- cost in relation to the enquiries and orders it generates;
- frequency of appearance, e.g. daily versus weekly newspapers;

- atmosphere, e.g. newspapers have an atmosphere of urgency and authority;
- timing, e.g. most personal letters are written at weekends so advertisements requiring a written response are best placed in media that appear over the weekend.

15. Advertising strategy

A firm with a coherent advertising strategy is better able to co-ordinate diverse promotional activities, allocate resources effectively, and monitor the progress and cost efficiency of campaigns than is a business that organises its advertising on an *ad hoc* basis. Results from campaigns may be compared against logically formulated targets, the research that has to be undertaken when preparing an advertising strategy itself generates large amounts of information that will be useful in other fields, and the existence of a strategy provides a focal point towards which all the company's promotional efforts may be directed. Key elements of an advertising strategy include the selection of advertising media (press, television, etc.), product positioning (see **4**), choice of market segments (see **3**), whether to confront or avoid competitors during advertising campaigns, deciding whether to use an advertising agency and, if so, for which purposes and to what extent, and choice of the criteria to be adopted to determine whether a campaign has been a success.

16. Advertising objectives

Basic advertising objectives are to increase sales, obtain new customers, and possibly to alter consumer behaviour, e.g. by increasing the proportion of customers who buy directly via mail order rather than through retail outlets. Specific campaign targets might involve the capture within a predetermined period of a certain market share, the creation of brand awareness and/or inducing consumers to switch brands, or persuading distributors and other intermediaries to stock up with the advertised item. Further aims might be to:

- encourage consumers to increase the frequency of their purchases;
- induce customers to buy at different times of the year in order to even out seasonal fluctuations in demand;
- create the belief among consumers that a brand is the leader in its field;
- defend an existing market, e.g. through maintaining brand loyalty via a creative strategy that focuses on reminding consumers of the key advantages of the brand;
- stimulate impulse purchases;
- improve the firm's corporate image among a particular target customer group;
- increase consumer awareness of the firm's products;
- generate a certain number of enquiries from specific customer types.

17. Direct marketing

Direct marketing covers direct mail, telephone selling, catalogues, and 'off-the page' selling via cut-outs in newspaper and magazine advertisements. Direct mail is perhaps the major activity within direct marketing. It offers a flexible, selective and potentially highly cost-effective means for reaching consumers. Messages can be addressed exclusively to a target market; advertising budgets may be concentrated on the most promising market segments; and it will be some time before competitors realise that the firm has launched the campaign. Also the size, content, timing and geographical coverage of maildrops can be varied at will. The company can spend as much or as little as necessary to achieve its objectives. There are no media space or airtime restrictions, and no copy or insertion deadlines to be met. All aspects of the direct mail process are subject to the firm's immediate control, and the firm can experiment by varying the approach used in different markets. Direct mail is personal, selective; useful for informing customers of special discounts, credit packages, maintenance agreements, etc; and versatile since a variety of items and information can be included in the envelope – including any one of a number of possible response mechanisms.

18. Sales promotion

Sales promotion covers the issue of coupons, the design of competitions, special offers, distribution of free samples, etc. The objectives of sales promotion campaigns include:

(a) stimulation of impulse purchasing;

(b) encouraging customer loyalty;

(c) attracting customers to the firm's premises;

(d) penetration of new markets;

(e) increasing the rate at which customers repeat their purchases.

Promotional techniques need to relate to the specified aims of the exercise (free samples to enter new markets, reduced-price offers to encourage repeat purchase, money-off coupons to attract customers to the premises, etc.). The use of sales promotion has increased rapidly throughout the world over the last decade. Factors contributing to the expansion in sales promotion expenditures include:

(a) greater competition among retailers, combined with increasingly sophisticated retailing methods;

(b) higher levels of brand awareness among consumers, leading to the need for manufacturers to defend brand shares;

(c) improved retail technology, e.g. electronic scanning devices that enable coupon redemptions, etc., to be monitored instantly;

(d) greater integration of sales promotions, public relations and conventional media campaigns.

Progress test 9

1. What is the marketing concept?

2. List the main elements of the marketing mix.

3. Explain the difference between a differentiated marketing strategy and an undifferentiated marketing strategy.

4. There are two aspects to product development. What are they?

5. List the characteristics of the introductory phase of the product life cycle.

6. Define 'skimming'.

7. What are the benefits to having an advertising strategy?

8. List the advantages of direct mail as a means for selling a firm's products.

9. Why has the use of sales promotions increased so rapidly during recent years?

10

FINANCIAL STRATEGY

1. Nature of financial strategy

Effective strategies are crucial to the well-being of the firm, and need to address the following issues:

(a) How, where and when the business will obtain funds, plus (for public companies) the timing of share issues and the determination of share issue prices.

(b) The best use of financial resources.

(c) Gearing (see **3**).

(d) How to maximise the market valuation of the firm.

(e) What to do with accumulated cash.

(f) Long-term financial planning for business expansion.

(g) The capital structure of the business (see **2**).

(h) The extent to which internally generated profits are reinvested within the company.

(i) Choice of financial criteria for selecting major capital investments.

Also companies operating in several countries need to formulate strategies and policies for dealing with the risks associated with exchange rate fluctuations, the management of long-term financial investment, and the cross-border administration of working capital and liquidity. Manufacturing businesses in particular have to plan the purchase of large amounts of raw materials, components and capital equipment, frequently sourced from abroad.

Successful implementation of financial strategies will enable the firm to:

- replace capital assets when necessary;
- cover loan and debenture interest as this falls due and repay the capital on maturity;
- build up sufficient reserves to meet contingencies;
- facilitate steady long-term growth;
- ensure that funds are available at the right time and the lowest cost.

2. Capital structure

A public limited company (one that sells shares to the general public) can finance expansion in several ways: shares, debentures (i.e. loans to the company secured against its assets, normally – but not necessarily – fixed term and fixed interest) or other loans, or through retained profits. Shares have the advantage that dividends need not be paid in loss-making periods. However, outsiders gain votes as shares are issued, so that existing majority shareholders may lose control. Debenture financing involves no loss of control since debenture holders have no votes. But the risk of liquidation is higher because debenture interest must be paid in full, on time, regardless of current financial circumstances. Overdrafts and similar loans may be recalled.

Against this background, companies are sometimes tempted to finance themselves entirely by ploughing back their own profits. There are no interest payments on retained earnings and there is no possibility of takeovers from outside. The danger is that while the value of a business goes up as profits are ploughed back, market prices of the company's shares may fall, since high retentions of profits necessarily reduce dividends. Shareholders are not interested in buying shares in companies that do not pay good dividends. Demand for such shares will be weak. Thus, paradoxically, increases in a firm's physical assets: land and buildings, plant and equipment, vehicles, work in progress, etc., might be accompanied in the short term by declining share prices.

Of course, in the longer run, shareholders (who own these physical assets) are entitled to extra shares to cover increases in company asset values. These are known as bonus shares and are issued, periodically, in proportion to shareholders' existing holdings. In the short term however, dangers exist that outsiders might be able to buy a controlling interest in the firm for less than the monetary value of the company's physical assets.

Public companies must consider carefully, therefore, the relative proportions of debentures, shares, and retained earnings they should include in their capital structures. Debenture financing is appropriate for steady, low risk industries (usually offering comparatively poor returns) whereas shares are better for riskier, less stable, high return environments where profits fluctuate and money for interest payments may not be available in some years. An advantage to debenture financing is that they can be redeemed from reserves specially accumulated for this purpose, or through the issue of fresh debentures. Retained profits are a free source of business finance (no interest or dividends are payable) but must be administered judiciously bearing in mind the consequences of lower dividends on share price. Companies whose shares are highly valued in relation to capital employed and which are earning high returns are likely to retain substantial parts of their profits. Note moreover that the maintenance of a high level of financial reserves results in a company being better equipped to resist unwanted attempted takeovers.

Factors determining the choice of an appropriate capital structure might include:

- the riskiness of the markets in which the business operates;
- estimates of future profits and capital requirements;

- attitudes and perspectives of senior managers and major shareholders;
- tax considerations;
- the extent of the need for flexibility (i.e., how quickly the capital structure can be changed as circumstances alter).

During the 1970s UK-based electronics and defence giant GEC improved its turnover by 400 per cent and profits by 600 per cent, generating large amounts of cash that could be deposited at the high rates of interest prevalent during that period. Earnings per share doubled. The company then decided to limit dividend payouts over the next ten years, and more than half of each year's profits was retained within the company (much of it in the forms of cash and short-term financial investments). This had a sharp adverse effect on the company's share price, which fell from 225 pence in 1983 to 166 pence in 1988 – even though operations were highly successful. The decline was even more disturbing considering the huge overall rise in share prices that occurred in all industrial sectors during the early/mid 1980s. As a profitable and cash-rich company with a declining share price, GEC became vulnerable to unwanted attempted takeovers. GEC reacted to this situation by buying back large numbers of its own shares in order (i) to bolster the market share price by creating additional demand for the shares, and (ii) reducing the number of shares over which existing levels of profit payouts would be distributed, thus increasing dividend per share and so making GEC shares more attractive to investors.

---

3. Gearing of the firm

A critical strategic financial management decision is the ratio of a company's borrowing to its total share capital. This is known as the 'gearing' of the business, although the term is also used, loosely, to describe the ratio of borrowing to assets in sole traderships and partnerships.

Companies that borrow heavily relative to their share capital are said to be highly geared, and vice versa. Lenders typically impose on borrowing companies a contractual restriction on the latter's ability to borrow from other sources, i.e. borrowers' gearing ratios are limited to agreed maximum values. This ensures that the lender has first claim on a borrowing company's assets if it goes into liquidation, and there will be no other lenders with secured claims on the failed business's funds.

FINANCING THE BUSINESS

A firm's requirements for financial capital may be divided into two categories: fixed capital, i.e. the money used to purchase assets such as land, buildings and other items that are for use within the business (rather than for resale at a profit), and working capital that is necessary to buy stock, pay wages, meet day-to-day operating expenses, and so on. Fixed and working capital interrelate. The former represents an investment in items that enable the business to earn profits which themselves generate further working capital

– part of which can be used to acquire further fixed capital thus creating a continuous cycle between the two.

Time elapses between the purchase of raw materials, hire of labour, leasing of equipment, etc., and the sale of final goods. Finance is necessary to bridge the gap. In general, the source of business finance should be related to the purpose for which it is intended. Short-term finance should be used to bridge short-term deficits; long-term finance should be used for purchasing long-lived capital assets. Thus for example a machine expected to last six years should be bought using a six-year loan (during which period the machine is generating the profits needed to finance repayments); a ten-year asset should be purchased with a ten-year loan, and so on. This will balance the company's cash outflows in relation to interest and capital repayments against the earnings created over similar periods by the equipment purchased.

4. Short and long term capital

Short-term finance can be obtained via overdrafts, fixed-term bank loans, sale of debts to credit factoring companies, and through trade credit. Each option has its own particular advantages and drawbacks (for details see the M&E volume, *Management*, 2nd Edition, Chapter 9).

Long-term finance mainly comprises funds raised through the sale of shares and debentures. The commonest type of share is the 'ordinary' share. Ordinary shareholders carry the risks of the business and receive dividends only if profits are made. And if the company collapses they are repaid their investment only after all the firm's other debts and obligations have been settled Normally each ordinary share carries one vote, although non-voting ordinary shares (called 'A' shares) may be issued.

Multi-option facilities

Here a consortium of bank and/or other lending institutions guarantees the company immediate access to low cost funds during a predetermined period. This is possible because, at any moment in time, certain members of the consortium will possess idle balances that may be used for short-term lending. Thus, funds can be made available on a continuous basis. A consecutive series of such short-term loans from various lenders represents long-term finance as far as the borrowing company is concerned.

Note moreover that firms can purchase 'financial futures', i.e. options purchased today to borrow money at predetermined future dates for specified periods at rates of interest fixed in advance in the option contract (which is known as a 'forward rate agreement'). Large businesses can buy a variety of futures, using the ones they eventually need and reselling the others.

Factors influencing the selection of sources of funds include:

- cost and flexibility;
- how quickly the funds are required;
- extent of the business's assets that can be offered as security for loans;
- repayment periods;
- levels of risk associated with the company's operations;

- stability of the firm's income;
- the extent to which outside providers of funds will be able to control the company's policies;
- tax considerations.

5. Share dilution

As more shares are issued, profits have to be distributed to increasing numbers of shareholders so that if earnings remain stable, the dividend payable to each shareholder must decrease. This process is known as share dilution, and leads to the company not being able to provide an adequate rate of return on the capital invested in the firm. Share dilution (also known as over-capitalisation) can result from additional shares being issued to finance acquisitions, or from management overestimating the amount of capital required by the company in relation to its actual trading prospects. Adverse consequences of over-capitalisation include:

- a decline in the market price of the company's shares (perhaps making it more vulnerable to takeover);
- general lack of confidence in the business and a poor public image;
- a lower credit rating.

Dixons plc used convertibles to finance the acquisition of the US electrical retailer, Silo, for which it paid $311 million. The purchase price represented 25 times Silo's historical annual earnings and included a staggering $220 million for goodwill. Issue of additional equities by Dixons to pay for this acquisition would obviously lead to severe share dilution (as Silo's earnings could not finance the extra dividends that would have to be paid on the new shares), so convertibles seemingly offered an ideal solution. Dixon's existing market share price would not be affected and earnings per share would remain unaltered. Hence, zero interest convertible loan stocks in Dixons with a £1 face value were issued which, when fully paid up in two years time, could be converted into five per cent redeemable preference shares, which themselves could be converted into ordinary shares in Dixons at a predetermined price at set dates in the future. This gave Dixons two years in which to boost Silo's revenues (which it confidently expected to be able to do through integrating the firm into Dixon's wider international operations) during which no interest payments were necessary. Silo's shareholders were attracted to the offer because the £1 convertibles significantly exceeded the value of their shares in the company, and the acquisition was quickly completed. Unfortunately for Silo's shareholders, however, Dixon's share price tumbled (in consequence of a number of external factors) so that they were not able eventually to convert into ordinary shares at a profit.

Under-capitalisation

This is the opposite of share dilution. Profit per share will be high, but the business's capacity to expand will be restricted. Under-capitalisation might result from an underestimation of the firm's potential, or from superefficient operations that lead to the need to increase the scale of activity. Problems with undercapitalisation are as follows:

(a) It could cause cash shortages within the firm and hold back lucrative new investments.

(b) Employees will observe the high profitability of the business, and interpret this as the consequence of unfair exploitation of labour and thus demand large wage increases.

(c) Customers might expect selling prices to be reduced.

(d) Credit customers might assume the supplying firm has plenty of money and thus not settle their bills on time.

6. Obtaining a quotation

Public companies may or may not decide to seek a listing on the Stock Exchange. The Stock Exchange is a market place for shares. It is privately owned and has nothing to do with the government. The owners (members) of the Exchange will not allow the shares of any company to be traded using its (now fully computerised) facilities: only approved shares can be transacted via the Exchange. The process of obtaining approval is known as 'obtaining a quotation'. Once a company has a quotation, the current prices of its shares are 'listed' each day by the Exchange and hence published in national newspapers.

In order to become a listed company the firm must have traded profitably for a certain period and have a specified minimum share capital. Once it is listed, at least 25 per cent of all its share issues must thereafter be made available to the public.

The shares of quoted companies are readily sold through the Exchange, and this marketability enhances the attraction to investors of quoted securities. Thus, listed companies should find it easier than others to sell their shares to the investing public. Other benefits associated with a quotation include:

- an improved public image through having the company's name mentioned in the *Financial Times* and other national newspapers;
- the fact that quoted securities are generally acceptable as payment for takeovers;
- a quick and convenient mechanism for assessing the worth of the company through the interplay of market forces;
- reduced dependence on banks and other lenders for business finance.

The disadvantages of becoming a quoted company include the subsequent administrative costs of new issues, and possible loss of control (outsiders may freely purchase shares in the business).

7. Share issue

Public limited companies wishing to raise money by share issue will normally do so through the 'new issues market', which consists of institutions that specialise in the sale of new shares, although other methods are available (see below). First the company will (normally) consult a merchant bank for advice on (i) the timing of the issue, (ii) an appropriate issue price, and (iii) how best to underwrite the flotation. Underwriters are institutions that guarantee to buy (at a predetermined price below that of the official issue) any shares not purchased by the public.

Share issues may proceed in any one of several ways:

1. *Issue by prospectus*
A 'prospectus' is published in several newspapers detailing the company's past record, recent accounts, its senior management, and the purposes for which the money is intended. Members of the public are invited to subscribe for shares at a single stated price.

2. *Rights issue*
This means selling extra shares to existing shareholders. New shares are offered (usually at an attractive price made possible by the low administrative cost to the company of raising capital in this manner) in proportion to shareholders' present holdings, e.g. one new share for every five held.

3. *Issue by tender*
The procedure here is the same as issue by prospectus, except that investors are invited to bid for the shares above some specified minimum price. Shares are then allocated to the highest bidders. Any shares not allocated (because there are not enough bidders above the minimum stated price) go to underwriters.

4. *Offer for sale*
This method is identical to issue by prospectus, but initially all the shares are taken up by an 'issuing house', i.e. a financial institution – which may or may not be a merchant bank – that specialises in floating new issues. The issuing house subsequently offers the shares to the general public.

5. *Placing*
An issuing house places the shares with investment trusts, insurance companies, pension funds and other large institutional investors rather than advertising them to the general public.

Scrip issues

A scrip issue (sometimes called a 'bonus' issue) is a 'free' issue of shares to existing shareholders to account for the increase in the value of the company that has occurred in consequence of it ploughing back large parts of its profits into land and buildings, new machinery and equipment, etc. Dividends in a company pursuing this sort of policy will necessarily have been lower than was possible, although the worth of the business will have been going up.

By definition, the extra assets purchased with retained earnings belong to shareholders, who are thus allocated bonus shares to acknowledge their property rights over the additional value of the company. Note however that the firm's profits must henceforth be distributed over a greater number of shares so that future dividends per share will have to be lower.

The Virgin Group is a good example of an enterprise that obtained a Stock Exchange listing only to decide shortly thereafter to reverse its strategy. Entrepreneur Richard Branson had established a highly successful music publishing and retailing business that he wished to expand and diversify. Hence a share flotation occurred in 1986, the general public acquiring one third of all the shares in the company. The company's market share price was hit badly by the 1987 Stock Market crash, and a number of other factors seemingly contributed to a general lack-lustre share price performance, including:

(a) the decision not to include Branson's airline company, Virgin Atlantic, in the original flotation (the airline remained Branson's private property);

(b) public perceptions that Virgin was a fashion-related high-risk enterprise;

(c) low earnings per share due in part to Branson's desire to reinvest profts in the company rather than pay high dividends.

Branson felt constrained, moreover, by the Stock Exchange rules and bureaucracy relating to quoted companies, and the listing had a considerable administrative cost. Also Branson resented the need to adopt short-term perspectives on business operations simply to please the share market. Accordingly, in 1988 Branson offered to buy back shares in the company at the initial flotation price, which was considerably higher than their current market value. This drained Virgin (and the associated airline) of resources that were needed for long-term investment. Hence Branson sold ten per cent of Virgin Atlantic to Seibu Saison, a Japanese conglomerate; 25 per cent of the music division to another Japanese firm, Fujisankei; 50 per cent of Virgin's UK retail stores to W.H.Smith; and minority stakes in other parts of the Virgin group of companies.

8. Use of venture capital

With venture capital financing, an outside body (a merchant bank for example) takes shares in a business in order to inject capital, then takes an agreed proportion of the profits for a prespecified period, and sells the shares back to the company at a predetermined future date at a price agreed in the initial contract. Venture capitalists are looking to invest in sound businesses that wish to expand rapidly.

Problems with venture capital are as follows:

(a) The high cost (possibly in excess of 30 per cent) of capital raised in this manner.

(b) Borrowers must regularly submit detailed reports, containing much confidential information, on the progress of their businesses.

(c) Lenders typically impose contractual restrictions on borrowing firms' gearing and minimum values for net assets and the maintenance of financial reserves. (This is to enable venture capitalists to recoup their initial investments if borrowing companies go into liquidation.)

(d) If the firm fails to achieve certain specified targets the contract may provide for the venture capitalist taking control of the company. The venture capitalist is a shareholder in the business, and as such may be keen to liquidate it (in order to sell off the firm's assets to raise money to redeem share capital) at the first sign of financial difficulty.

9. Forward exchange

Firms which import goods from foreign suppliers have to pay their bills in the currencies of the foreign suppliers' countries (e.g. a French firm will want payment in French Francs, a German supplier in Deutschemarks, etc.) which means that the importer must run the risk of a depreciation in its country's currency between the moment an order is placed and when the resulting debt has to be settled. A depreciation in the exchange rate means that more units of domestic currency have to be spent in order to purchase a given amount of foreign currency. Similar risks apply to an exporting firm that invoices its foreign customers in the currencies of the latters' own countries. For example, a UK exporter to Germany who invoices in Deutschemarks will receive less Sterling than anticipated if Sterling depreciates against the Deutschemark between now and when the Deutschemarks are converted into Sterling following settlement of the invoice. To be sure of how much Sterling its invoices will yield the exporter can sell in advance to its own UK bank the foreign currency its customers have been invoiced to pay. The bank will quote a fixed 'forward exchange rate' for these transactions. This predetermined forward rate will apply to the conversions regardless of the actual 'spot' exchange rate in force 90 days (say) from today. The bank requires a reward for its services and hence will quote an exchange rate for forward currency transactions which differs from the current spot exchange rate by an amount sufficient to cover the bank's exposure to risk and to make a profit.

If the exporter expects the spot exchange rate to move in favour of Sterling, so that it stands to raise more Sterling when it eventually comes to convert the foreign currency than it would get if the money was converted today, it may decide not to bother with forward cover.

A firm expecting to receive payments from a foreign customer over a long period can enter an 'option contract' with a UK bank whereby the exporter is given the right to sell to the bank foreign currency up to an agreed limit at a predetermined rate at any time within the next 12 months. If the spot exchange rate moves in one direction the exporter will exercise the option; if it moves the other way the option will not be taken up – forfeiting thereby the fee paid to the bank to purchase the option.

SHORT- AND LONG-TERMISM

10. Short-termism

In Britain and the USA companies are regarded as commodities to be traded in exactly the same way as any other marketable item, leading – so advocates of the Anglo-American system allege – to optimum efficiency as the forces of supply and demand direct scarce resources towards the most efficient businesses. On the Continent of Europe, conversely, shares become locked into family and institutional investors, making it difficult to acquire companies on the open market. Continental European share markets are 'thin': Stock Exchanges have low capitalisations compared with the UK; share trading is irregular and share price movements infrequent. The total value of shares quoted on the London Stock Exchange (i.e. its aggregate 'market capitalisation') is more than double that of the German, Italian and French Stock Exchanges combined. Banks in many EU states invest directly and heavily in companies (especially in Germany). Representatives of banks occupy seats on company boards and help control businesses. There is much debenture and loan financing in continental countries, and many medium/large-sized enterprises are family owned.

Arguably, all this enables Continental businesses to adopt long-term perspectives, to plough back profits and to expand and diversify without having to worry about hostile takeover attempts by other firms. Conversely, the ease with which outsiders can acquire significant shareholdings in UK companies results in the latter being obliged to incorporate plans for avoiding being taken over into their overall corporate strategies: causing them perhaps to rely too heavily on debenture financing; to distort their market share prices; or to assume obligations intended to make them unattractive to predators (selling-off valuable assets for example) when they should instead be concentrating on developing the firm. This 'short-termism', as it is known, is also blamed for the continuation of old production methods and the failure to exploit new technologies, since to the extent that managements seek quick financial returns they will be unwilling to invest long term in advanced manufacturing techniques.

Examples of measures that might lead to short-run increases in profit at the expense of long-run growth include:

(a) not advertising at all for several months (possibly longer). This saves substantial amounts of money, boosting short-term profits at little cost because sales will continue at previous levels for some time in consequence of consumer loyalty to a brand and the firm's pre-existing reputation. Eventually, however, sales will decline as competitors attack the market and as the brand in question loses public exposure. The cost of subsequently recapturing market share could be enormous;

(b) cancelling or running down research and development projects;

(c) not maintaining buildings, plant and equipment.

Germany's Deutsche Bank has a 'blocking minority' shareholding in Daimler-Benz (the country's leading industrial group), and ten per cent shareholdings in Germany's largest insurance company (Allianz) and in Münchner Ruckversicherung, the world's biggest reinsurance firm. It also holds 25 per cent of the share capital of the retail chain Karstadt, a third of the shares of the German construction giant Philipp Holzmann, and significant shareholdings in many other notable German businesses. Senior managers in Deutsche Bank, conversely, occupy about 400 seats on the Supervisory Boards of German companies. The figure would be higher were it not for a government regulation restricting to a maximum of ten the number of external directorships held per person. Numerous German shareholders give Deutsche Bank (DB) their proxy voting rights in relation to their shareholdings in companies, and opinions expressed by DB proxy holders carry great influence at shareholders meetings. DB justifies its power by claiming that it stabilises industry and enables company management to concentrate on running the business (rather than on financial management) and to avoid the constant threat of restructuring forced on the firm from outside. Also the system has created two-way communication between finance and industry, and a degree of collaboration between bank and company representatives unparalleled in most other parts of the world.

Source: Adapted from Lessem, R., and Neubauer, F., *European Management Systems*, McGraw-Hill 1994.

11. Problems with the Continental approach

A number of problems are created by the Continental (especially the German) company financing system, including the following:

(a) The absence of an active share market means there is no market mechanism for valuing companies objectively. Share prices represent an acid test of how the astute and commercially knowledgeable outside investor sees the worth of a company and its future prospects.

(b) The high proportion of Continental firms owned by private families and/or that have large blocks of their shares in the hands of large banks and other institutional investors creates a shortage of companies available for sale in certain countries.

(c) As there are so few companies listed on Continental Stock Exchanges there has been little to encourage the development of the company research and information-gathering facilities that exist in Britain, Ireland and certain non-EU nations (especially the USA).

(d) An 'uneven playing field' *vis-à-vis* merger and takeover activity in different EU nations has emerged. British firms sometimes find that the need to concentrate on short-term issues causes them to lack cash and immediately realisable assets, placing them at a disadvantage compared to Continental rivals that possess extensive reserves accumulated over many years. Also the corporate cultures of many European countries are not attuned to the cut and thrust of hostile acquisitions, and shareholders often have to be cajoled and seduced into parting with their shares. Interest rates differ among countries, so that funds for financing acquisitions can be borrowed less expensively in some countries than elsewhere. Moreover, profit retentions by firms that do not have to worry about the adverse effects of internal financing on dividends (and hence the market price of the company's shares) have resulted in a large number of cash-rich predator companies in certain nations.

12. Prospects for Continental equity financing

To some extent, the paucity of share markets in Continental countries over the post-Second World War period is due to historical circumstance rather than to conscious choice. In the past there have been relatively few private pension schemes (which are big investors in equities) in certain European nations; while the non-availability of extensive share trading systems has encouraged insurance companies to invest in regional savings banks or government bonds rather than in shares. German insurance companies, for example, only hold about five per cent of their funds in the form of equities.

There are however a number of reasons for believing that Continental attitudes towards equity issue and share trading might change:

(*i*) Affluence has resulted in many Continental Europeans having high disposable incomes, some of which is now being invested in shares. For instance, the number of German shareholders increased by 50 per cent between 1987 and 1994 (albeit starting from a low base).

(*ii*) Younger Europeans are perhaps less risk-adverse than the older generation and hence more willing to purchase equities.

(*iii*) Political stability and steady economic growth during the last 40 years means that Europeans born in the richer EU countries in the next century will inherit wealth, much of which will be invested.

(*iv*) Long-term economic growth could lead to demands for finance so extensive that they outstrip the capacities of banks, families and institutional investors to satisfy them.

(*v*) The emergence (hopefully) of vibrant European high technology industry sectors which require risk capital that (risk averse) banks are not willing to supply might boost the call for equity finance.

(*vi*) More and better information is becoming available on EU companies (facilitated by EU Directives compelling greater company disclosure) possibly creating a greater willingness among Continental Europeans to purchase shares.

(*vii*) Because of their economic power and increasing importance in the global financing system, France and (particularly) Germany are naturally becoming leading financial centres in their own right. This should create an environment generally conducive to the development of financial services industries in these countries and, concomitantly, to more extensive international as well as domestic share trading.

Note also that the extents of UK companies' reliance on equity financing could diminish as the detrimental effects of having to concentrate on short-term objectives causes them (possibly) to lose out to Continental rivals.

Progress test 10

1. List some of the benefits to having a financial strategy.

2. Define 'gearing'.

3. What are the major sources of short-term finance?

4. What are financial futures?

5. Explain the negative consequences of share dilution.

6. What are the problems associated with venture capital?

7. What is meant by the term 'short-termism' and what are its effects?

8. List some of the factors that have stimulated the demand for equity financing in Continental European countries?

11

HUMAN RESOURCES STRATEGY

1. Nature of human resources management

Human resources management (HRM) concerns the human side of the management of enterprises and employees' relations with their firms. Its purpose is to ensure that the employees of a company, i.e. its human resources, are used in such a way that the employer obtains the greatest possible benefit from their abilities and the employees obtain both material and psychological rewards from their work. Human resources management has strategic dimensions and involves the total deployment of human resources within the firm. Thus, for example, HRM will consider such matters as:

(a) the aggregate size of the organisation's labour force in the context of an overall corporate plan (how many divisions and subsidiaries the company is to have, design of the organisation, etc.);

(b) how much to spend on training the workforce, given strategic decisions on target quality levels, product prices, volume of production, and so on;

(c) the desirability of establishing relations with trade unions from the viewpoint of the effective management control of the entire organisation;

(d) the wider implications for employees of the management of change (not just the consequences of alterations in working practices).

The strategic approach to HRM involves the integration of personnel and other HRM considerations into the firm's overall corporate planning and strategy formulation procedures. It is proactive, seeking constantly to discover new ways of utilising the labour force in a more productive manner thus giving the business a competitive edge. Practical manifestations of the adoption of a strategic approach to HRM might include:

(a) incorporation of a brief summary of the firm's basic HRM policy into its mission statement;

(b) explicit consideration of the consequences for employees of each of the firm's strategies and major new projects;

(c) designing organisation structures to suit the needs of employees rather than conditioning the latter to fit in with the existing form of organisation.

Possession of a human resources strategy implies recognition of the crucial importance of the HR function and the need therefore to have an HR specialist in the senior management team, e.g. as a member of the firm's board of directors. More than ever before, human resource managers are expected to contribute to productivity and quality improvement, the stimulation of creative thinking, leadership and the development of corporate skills.

Zeneca Pharmaceuticals employs 14,000 people worldwide. Its human resources strategy is to integrate all HRM activities into a coherent and fully integrated whole, aiming to create shared values, a common work culture, targets that are understood throughout the organisation, and a simple and straightforward system for allocating work. The firm employs many researchers, scientists and other professionally qualified staff in numerous nations and from widely disparate cultural backgrounds. Thus, a global HRM strategy generating standard policies and procedures (subject to local variation in appropriate circumstances) is required. Minimum standards have been established in each of five areas: performance management, training for an individual's current role, personal development, communication, and performance-related pay. Standards are broadly defined, leaving local business units to work out the detail in appropriate ways. Overall HR targets are included alongside other key objectives in the company's strategic plan. Also a 'people development strategy' is appended to the firm's mission statement. This HR strategy statement includes, *inter alia*:

(*i*) a commitment to provide the resources necessary to develop human resources, particularly in the training field;
(*ii*) the requirement that individual managers be responsible for developing their subordinates;
(*iii*) procedures for drafting a personal development plan for each employee;
(*iv*) an assurance that individual efforts to extend skills and experience will be encouraged;
(*v*) provision for the regular auditing of human resources development activities.

Singapore International Airlines (SIA) employs 23,000 people and is Singapore's largest private sector company, contributing nearly four per cent of that country's GDP. Its human resources strategy focuses on the provision of continuous training and staff development and the encouragement of innovation, especially in relation to customer care. This fits in with SIA's overall corporate strategy which is to position the airline at the quality end of the market – emphasising excellent service, the provision of first-class in-flight facilities, and use of the very latest information technology. Concern for customers is promoted via teamwork and an appraisal system based on group rather than individual achievement. There is much job rotation intended to help employees develop a wide range of skills. The company is organised into units no larger than the minimum necessary to complete the tasks assigned to them. This reduces bureaucracy and facilitates fast local decision making. Recruitment procedures for cabin crew are stringent, although Singapore's tight labour market sometimes creates difficulties in this respect. Stewardesses are regarded as key employees (the firm's corporate image is heavily reliant on the sarong-clad 'Singapore Girl' figure from a highly successful advertising campaign broadcast throughout the world) and senior managers participate in the final selection of this category of staff. Long service with the company is highly valued, and recognised via gifts and medallions. Staff turnover is low by Singapore standards, at around six per cent per annum.

Source: Adapted from Torrington, D., *International Human Resource Management*, Prentice-Hall 1994.

2. Devising a human resources strategy

The first step in devising an HR strategy is to assess the size, nature, scope and human resources requirements of the *future* organisation (rather than the business as it stands) and to define the measures necessary to supply the human resources needed to attain company goals. Human resources strategies should be formulated *after* other major functional strategies have been determined. Thus the firm must decide its strategic objectives; specify its production and marketing strategies, organisation structure and operational plans; and *then* address the issue of how best to manage the human resources required to implement the chosen options. The selected organisation system is particularly important as it defines accountability and responsibility structures, job descriptions and performance requirements, possibly the firm's culture and management style, and recruitment and training requirements.

Next, the firm must compare its present human resources with the demands implied by the above. The comparison needs to examine:

(a) existing and desired organisational climates (cultures) including leadership style and employee participation mechanisms;

(b) the types of people required in terms of skills, attitudes and performance capabilities;

(c) motivation and reward systems;

(d) current and anticipated skills requirements;

(e) management succession programmes;

(f) the firm's training and employee development capabilities.

Further matters requiring examination include potential obstacles to the efficient use of the firm's human resources, the quality of internal communications, techniques for measuring performance, and general personnel policies. Gaps between actual and desired situations will become apparent. Measures for bridging these gaps should now be defined.

3. Influences on HRM strategy

HR strategies are necessarily affected by a variety of environmental factors. *External* influences include the following:

(a) *The legal framework.* Laws on collective bargaining, the right to strike, employment protection, employee participation in management decisions, minimum wage levels, etc.

(b) *Political factors.* Government attitudes, guidelines and Codes of Practice on employment matters. The general ambience of the political party in power towards industrial relations and employment matters.

(c) *The economy.* Unemployment and inflation rates (both of which affect employee demands for wage increases), competition within industries (intense competition implies the poaching of rival firms' staff), growth prospects, and so on.

(d) *Social trends.* Extents of female participation in the labour force, part time working, attitudes towards work and working hours, demands for improvements in the quality of working life, changes in living standards, educational opportunities, etc.

(e) *The technological environment.* Changes in working methods, effects of computerisation and IT (see Chapter 12), needs for reskilling and greater flexibility of labour, and the implications of various technologies for management style.

Internal factors affecting HR strategy are the degree of centralisation of the organisation; the present state of morale; whether jobs can be completed by unskilled people; the nature of the workforce in terms of background, education, perspectives, etc.; the degree of trade union density within the firm; ownership (company shareholders, individual proprietor, partners) and the attitudes of owners towards employee relations; and the perspectives of individual employees.

4. Need for human resources strategies

A company's success or failure depends to a large extent on its ability to select, train, motivate, develop and manage its human resources, and it is axiomatic that no business can attain its mission without employees who are competent to complete the necessary work. Specific reasons for having a human resource strategy include the following:

(a) Firms with the most productive workforces possess a competitive advantage over rivals.

(b) Expenditures on personnel typically represent a very large proportion of total company spending.

(c) A business's capacity to adopt new technologies, enter fresh markets and/or undertake different lines of work frequently depend more on the availability of appropriate people than on capital investment.

(d) Increasing organisational complexity requires a suitable mix of specialist skills, which cannot be obtained overnight.

(e) Employment protection legislation imposes many constraints on how managements may treat their workforces.

(f) Only through having coherent HR strategies will a company be able to provide its employees with career prospects, job security and a reasonable quality of working life.

(g) Computerisation of manufacturing and administrative processes has greatly influenced the nature of work and the structure of employment within enterprises. Communication and control systems have altered; there is less demand for unskilled employees completing routine duties. Strategic HR planning is necessary to cope with the resistance to change that new technologies might engender and the possible displacement of labour that might result.

(h) It is highly desirable to maintain a balanced age distribution within an enterprise, avoiding thereby the problem of too many competent and experienced people all retiring at the same time and/or having too many young or elderly workers.

5. Advantages and problems of HRM strategies

Advantages to having a human resources strategy are:

(a) It places human relations at the top of the management agenda.

(b) Personnel policies and procedures should be standardised throughout the firm.

(c) There ought to be better co-ordination of HR activities.

(d) A professional approach to human resource issues is encouraged.

(e) Employee morale might improve in consequence of workers perceiving that management is taking a genuine interest in developing the firm's human resources.

(f) The company will be better prepared to deal with collective bargaining and other industrial relations concerns.

Problems with devising and implementing HR strategies are:

(a) Human behaviour is frequently unpredictable and sometimes (seemingly) irrational, hence disrupting the best laid human resources strategies and plans.

(b) Strategies are sometimes formulated ritualistically, without genuine commitment to their implementation. Management might be as much concerned with *being seen* to possess an HR strategy as actually having one *per se*. Statements to the effect that organisations are 'equal opportunities employers', for example, may be made cynically and with no intention of applying the principle in practice (the real purpose being to create a good image with government equal opportunity agencies and other outside bodies).

(c) Major differences of opinion over what constitutes an effective HR strategy may emerge between personnel specialists on the one hand and line managers on the other.

(d) There is little point in having an HR strategy if it is not properly communicated to *everyone* working for the firm. Lack of management/worker communication and employee involvement in HR management issues can make the implementation of HR strategies extremely problematic.

(e) Managers might pursue their own self-interests *vis-à-vis* personal pay, status, prospects, etc., when devising the firm's HR strategies and plans.

(f) Although a company may have an HR strategy 'on paper' and under the overall supervision of a personnel department, line managers might simply ignore the strategy at the departmental or production unit level. Note how line managers can be extremely hostile towards personnel department staff, whom they may perceive as challenging their authority over subordinates.

(g) Difficulties caused by failures in a business's human resources strategy might not be as obvious as, say, the consequences of a collapse in financial strategy – at least not in the short term.

Note how immediate crises in human resources management can often be overcome by short-term measures such as compulsory early retirement for everyone above a certain age, extensive overtime working to meet staff shortages, emergency recruitment, etc., but only at a heavy long-term cost to the firm.

EMPLOYEE RELATIONS STRATEGIES

The modern approach to the management of employee relations is to emphasise co-operation rather than conflict and to integrate employee relations (ER) policies into the overall corporate strategy of the firm. This requires that management (a) recognise the critical importance of harmonious relations with the workforce, and (b) relate its ER activities to the achievement of increased competitiveness, improved quality and better customer care.

6. Human resources strategy and employee relations

Human resources strategies affect employee relations in a number of important respects:

(a) HRM strategies determine the aggregate size of a company's labour force, how the firm is organised and structured, and so on.

(b) The firm's HRM strategies establish the basis of its relations with trade unions, including whether to recognise trade unions and if so for what purposes.

(c) Employee relations policies are needed to cope with the human implications of the introduction of new technology, especially with regard to the encouragement of flexible attitudes and the acceptance of new working practices. It is desirable to create within an organisation a *culture* that is conducive to employee commitment and co-operation. Note how conventional approaches to industrial relations have been criticised for being overly concerned with *imposing* rules and procedures on employees rather than encouraging their loyalty and commitment to the firm.

7. Elements of employee relations strategy

Major decisions that have to be taken when formulating an employee relations strategy include:

(*i*) whether to recognise trade unions;

(*ii*) managerial approaches to personnel policies and procedures that affect employee relations (recruitment and promotion; appraisal; selection of workers for training, redundancy, etc.);

(*iii*) whether management is prepared to use external bodies to arbitrate and help resolve disputes;

(*iv*) the levels of expenditures to be devoted to employee training and development;

(*v*) the basic formulae to be applied to the division of the firm's profit between the owners of the business and workers;

(*vi*) the methods to be used for communicating with employees;

(*vii*) the organisation, structure and scope of collective bargaining;

(*viii*) whether to have a personnel department (as opposed to leaving human relations matters predominantly in the hands of line managers) and, if so, the extent of its power to initiate activity in the employee relations field;

(*ix*) the degree to which employee representatives are to be involved in management decision-making;

(*x*) the roles and functions of workplace representatives;

(*xi*) the contents of procedural agreements and how these are to be determined.

Effective employee relations management requires top-level involvement of the firm's most senior executives, since only they have the ultimate power to take important decisions and implement strategic change. Also, top management needs to be kept fully informed of attitudes among employees and current developments in the workplace situation. Policies should be clear and explicit, and management must be committed to their implementation. They must be communicated to middle and junior executives and their effectiveness periodically assessed.

8. Advantages to having an ER strategy

The advantages to management of having a systematic employee relations strategy include the following:

(a) Consistent policies will be applied within all the firm's sections, divisions and establishments.

(b) Individual line managers will know precisely where they stand in respect of employee relations matters.

(c) Procedures for controlling grievances and conflict are rationalised.

(d) The emergence of informal *ad hoc* systems that operate in parallel with, yet tend to undermine, official lines of authority can be avoided.

(e) Employees will receive much more information about the company's structure, operations and level of performance than otherwise might be the case. This can greatly contribute to the establishment of common perspectives throughout the organisation.

(f) Management becomes proactive rather than reactive, may plan ahead and will not have to take critically important decisions during crisis situations when accurate information cannot be obtained.

(g) Policies affecting employees can be dovetailed into an overall corporate plan.

9. Union recognition strategies

The management of a non-unionised firm must decide whether it is willing to recognise trade unions and, if so, needs to have a well-planned strategy for introducing union recognition in an orderly manner. The objectives of this strategy should include:

(a) the efficient dovetailing of management/union negotiating procedures into the administrative structure of the firm;

(b) establishment of mechanisms for defusing potentially dangerous conflict situations and for ensuring that appropriate unions represent the workers;

(c) the systematic extension of collective bargaining to encompass issues of greater substance as both management and newly elected union representatives gain experience of formal negotiation. Initial management/union meetings consider grievance and disciplinary matters only. Thereafter, working conditions, pension schemes, sick pay and holiday arrangements, overtime and shift work systems and (eventually) wages and conditions of service will be gradually incorporated into the negotiating agenda.

A critical aspect of the strategy is to determine appropriate bargaining units, i.e. to establish whether negotiations should occur at departmental, divisional or company-wide levels. Clearly, disputes regarding working practices specific to a particular section of the firm should be dealt with initially by the workplace representative and supervisor of the section concerned, whereas workplace representatives and supervisors are not normally allowed to negotiate fundamental changes in wages or contractual conditions of work. Also, management and employees must jointly agree which unions should represent various categories of workers.

10. Collective bargaining

Collective bargaining means that representatives of groups of workers seek to negotiate with and influence employers on matters relating to pay, working hours and conditions, indeed on any issue that affects working life. It recognises the weakness and ineffectuality of the individual worker as a negotiating unit and, implicitly, accepts the existence of conflicts of interest between management and employees.

National and local agreements

Bargaining can occur at national, industry or plant level. At national or industry levels a combination of employers will negotiate with a panel of unions to establish national wage rates and conditions of work. Quite often, however, these national agreements are looked on as representing minimum rather than actual terms. Thus, local union branch secretaries and employee representatives try to negotiate extra bonuses and better conditions with managements in individual workplaces.

Frequently, national agreements are formal and in writing, whereas local agreements are informal and unwritten. A major problem with national agreements is the difficulty of drafting them in sufficient detail to make them applicable to all firms and circumstances. Hence, they are usually formulated in very general terms. Note also that national agreements can quickly become out of date as business conditions change. Another difficulty with national-level collective bargaining is that since it typically involves a large number of employers and trade unions there is a significant probability that some members on either side will subsequently renege on agreements, or at least not enforce them enthusiastically. Negotiating panels often lack cohesion and are badly organised.

Local agreements have the advantage that they are immediately and directly relevant to existing circumstances and may be altered at short notice. Agreements negotiated by local union officials should enjoy the backing of local employees who, after all, elected local officials to office. However, the informality of local agreements might encourage negotiating parties to break agreements soon after they have been reached. Further problems with local bargaining are:

(a) It is usually disjointed and disorderly, lacking the formal rules of procedure applied at national or industry level.

(b) It encourages unofficial industrial action within particular enterprises.

(c) Productivity and pay are not linked at the national level, possibly leading to inflation.

(d) There is leapfrogging of settlements among enterprises in the same industry sector or geographical area.

The UK chemical industry is a good example of the application of national collective bargaining. About 200 companies belong to the Chemical Industries Association (CIA), collectively accounting for half of total employment in the chemicals sector. The CIA oversees three national agreements, signatories to which *automatically* apply to the letter nationally determined terms and conditions of employment relating to working hours, holiday entitlement and holiday pay, and overtime premiums. Nationally agreed terms concerning basic and shift pay and call-out payments tend to be regarded as minimum rather than actual levels. The CIA claims that this two-tier system effectively sets a wages floor for the industry and a solid framework for subsequent company agreements. Actual pay in member firms is typically well above the nationally determined basic level. However, the CIA contends that there is no evidence of national negotiations contributing to inflationary pay settlements and, it asserts, it has prevented pay leapfrogging and 'companies being picked off by the unions'. Changes in working practices are applied nationally, and the system provides employers with immediate access to senior trade union officers. A spirit of co-operation between managements and unions is encouraged, especially in relation to health and safety, training, and the analysis of measures intended to improve productivity. The nationally agreed procedure for settling industrial disputes is widely used and, the CIA claims, a major cause of the low incidence of strikes in the sector.

Source: 'Developments in Multi-Employer Bargaining', in *Industrial Relations Review and Report*, 443, March 1993.

Managements of large firms that engage in collective bargaining with trade union representatives need to determine the degree of centralisation of bargaining procedures that is to occur. The term 'decentralised collective bargaining' is sometimes used to describe the practice adopted by many big companies (with numerous divisions and subsidiaries) of empowering the management of each subsidiary, division, etc., to conclude separate deals with the union(s) in that unit, independent of agreements struck by 'local' managers and unions in the firm's other subsidiaries and divisions elsewhere. Reasons for decentralisation of collective bargaining within the same firm include the following:

(a) Management's desire to relate employee remuneration to productivity levels achieved in *local* operations.

(b) The trend towards overall decentralisation and diversification of activities in large companies, with quasi-autonomous profit centres, budgetary control by local managers, decisions on industrial relations management being taken at the establishment level, etc.

(c) Increasing competence in the human resources management field of the line managers employed by large blue chip companies, consequent to more extensive training and better staff development than in the past.

(d) Effective teamwork within a local unit can be accompanied by team-based bonus systems.

(e) Local circumstances can be taken into account during collective bargaining.

(f) From management's point of view, decentralised bargaining has the advantage that unions find it more difficult to organise industrial action at the enterprise level because of the need to arrange ballots at each place of work, and the fact that workers in at least some decentralised units are likely to vote against and hence not become involved in strikes, etc. With centralised bargaining, conversely, a union need gain only an overall majority of votes in favour of industrial action at the company rather than individual workplace level.

(g) Increasing competition among businesses, recession and declining profit margins have led many enterprises to overhaul entirely their negotiating procedures in order to try and cut costs.

11. Advantages to single-company decentralised bargaining

These are as follows:

(a) Local factors can be taken into account during negotiations.

(b) Operational managers in divisions, subsidiaries, etc., become closely involved in employee relations decision-making.

(c) It is suitable for large companies with divisions that conduct differing types of work and hence employ disparate categories of employee, each with its own set of terms and conditions of employment.

(d) Unit-level performance-related pay can be introduced more easily.

(e) The firm's most highly valued groups of employees can be properly rewarded.

(f) Plant-level management/employee representative communications are facilitated.

(g) It might strengthen managerial authority at the local level.

12. Disadvantages of single-company decentralised bargaining

Decentralised plant-level bargaining tends to be informal, fragmented, heavily dependent on unwritten rules, and often undertaken by individuals without any training in negotiation or employee relations. The specialist expertise that a head office industrial relations unit may provide is sacrificed. Other problems are:

(a) Whereas managements are often keen on decentralised bargaining when there is high unemployment and little union activity, their enthusiasm can wane when the situation is reversed and unions in local units successfully leapfrog each other's pay settlements.

(b) Changes in working methods and terms and conditions of employment might by introduced to local units in an uncoordinated and haphazard manner.

(c) The stability of a firm's relationships with national trade union officers could be endangered.

(d) To the extent that a company uses job evaluation, this will have to be applied at the local rather than company level leading perhaps to many inequalities in the pay of employees doing similar work but in different establishments.

(e) There is duplication of effort within the bargaining process.

(f) Regional labour shortages can enable unions to exploit the situation and obtain large wage increases, which then become benchmark figures for unions negotiating in other areas.

(g) The issues discussed during decentralised negotiations are likely to become parochial, ignoring matters relating to corporate strategy, planning and investment.

13. Use of decentralised bargaining

Decentralised bargaining is more likely where:

(a) there is little integration between the production systems of decentralised units (as sometimes happens when a business has expanded via mergers and acquisitions of other firms);

(b) the company has many products and operates in multiple markets;

(c) the impact of technical change is felt predominantly at the local workplace than at the company level;

(d) there is no overall corporate identity to which workers in decentralised units can relate;

(e) the skills and competencies needed to undertake a decentralised unit's work are found in local rather than national labour markets;

(f) there are big regional disparities in wage levels;

(g) a company's activities are spread over a wide geographical area;

(h) there are poor communications between workers in various decentralised units;

(i) different unions operate in different units;

(j) disputes and grievance procedures operate at the local and not the company level;

(k) major changes in working practices need to be introduced in some sections of the company but not in others.

14. Single table bargaining (STB)

This is the situation where the pay and conditions of all groups of workers employed by an establishment are determined around a single table in a single set of negotiations. It might involve a single union representing both manual and non-manual employees, although it is more common for single table bargaining to mean several unions negotiating at a single table in order to bargain as a single unit. Bargaining arrangements are unified and usually relate to a common pay and grading system, which encompasses all employees from unskilled labourers to junior managerial staff.

STB makes sense in single-status situations where all workers have the same hours, holidays, sick leave and pension entitlements, etc., so that alterations in these can be settled for (nearly) everyone in the organisation at a single sitting. It is interesting to note that British trade unions have been generally supportive of multi-union STB because it represents a credible alternative to the single union deals increasingly imposed by managements on their workers. Often, STB is offered by an employer as part of an overall package intended to streamline the firm's employee relations. Hence STB might only be available if accompanied by the introduction of flexible working practices, teamworking, new quality assurance procedures, etc.

For more information on single-table bargaining, single-status, and single union deals see the M & E volume, *Employee Relations.*

CMB Speciality Packaging has operated single table bargaining since 1982. The division has about 3250 employees belonging to nine different trade unions. Prior to 1982 a wide range of bargaining arrangements applied; at industry, company, divisional and plant levels. Decentralised bargaining and single status were introduced alongside STB—which was generally supported by the unions, one representative of which described it as 'an antidote to single unionism and non-unionism'. There is equal representation for the various unions; usually one seat each. Management grades are not covered by STB. Matters determined at STB meetings include pay, group bonuses, working conditions and practices, consultation procedures, and collective (though not individual) grievances. There is a joint consultation procedure quite separate from STB. The firm reports that since 1982 the pace of negotiations has been slower but outcomes quicker to implement and more sensible. Also STB was said to prevent leapfrogging in relation to pay at the plant level.

Source: *IRS Employment Trends*, 436, May 1990.

DOWNSIZING

Changes in technology and economic recession have led to large numbers of workers in western countries losing their jobs. Even in Japan – where security of employment is an integral feature of the economic system – redundancy is increasingly common. The dismissal of employees is an extremely serious matter for which careful planning is required. Procedures must be fair and seen to be fair, otherwise great disruption can ensue, followed perhaps by legal action. Effective strategies for dealing with employee redundancies are thus essential.

15. Redundancy

A redundancy can result from the firm's human resources plan, or unexpectedly through alterations in market forces or government policies. Note how it is a worker's job that becomes redundant, not a particular worker. Redundancy can sometimes be avoided through work-sharing or early retirement schemes. If not, criteria for selecting redundant personnel must be determined. These criteria should be fair and objective. Among the criteria commonly applied are length of service, age, capabilities, qualifications, experience, past conduct, and suitability for alternative employment within the organisation. Naturally, trade unions and governments are concerned that redundancy procedures be impartial, and many laws and codes of practice have been introduced including (usually) the following requirements:

(a) Workers' representatives must be informed immediately redundancies are proposed. Selection criteria should be disclosed and timetables for layoffs clearly stated.

(b) Management should provide reasons for the redundancies, and be prepared to negotiate on union proposals for their avoidance. In particular, management should seek alternative work for workers threatened with the sack.

(c) Before contemplating redundancies, management should stop recruitment, ban overtime, introduce short-time working, and insist that all employees over normal retirement age retire. Volunteers for redundancy should be sought. As far as possible, the workforce should be cut via natural wastage rather than compulsion.

Some firms negotiate redundancy procedure agreements with trade unions, stating:

- management's commitment to avoiding redundancies wherever possible;
- specific measures to be taken to prevent redundancies (banning overtime for example);
- periods of notice and settlement terms to be applied when redundancies are inevitable;
- the extent of the management information to be disclosed to unions;
- criteria to be used when selecting workers for redundancy;
- procedures for appeal against selection for redundancy.

RECENT DEVELOPMENTS IN HUMAN RESOURCES MANAGEMENT

16. Trends in HRM

A number of important factors have altered the scope and nature of human resources management in recent years, notably the following:

(a) Greater involvement of line managers in personnel management and a general decentralisation and devolution of the personnel function. Increasingly, line managers are required to undertake duties previously completed by personnel specialists. This results in part from firms seeking to cut costs through reducing the sizes of their personnel departments, and partially in consequence of the view that line managers *ought* to be able to complete this work (see below).

(b) Economic recession in the early 1990s, the downsizing of organisations and hence a shift in the nature of the relationship between management and labour.

(c) New working methods based on flexible labour practices.

(d) Recognition of the importance of the development of a firm's human resources as a means for securing competitive advantage, spurred on by the successes achieved by Japanese companies which pay great attention to the role of HRM.

Decentralisation and devolution

Many personnel and HRM functions can be undertaken by managers in local units rather than through a central personnel department (decentralised collective bargaining [see 10 to 13 for example]). Note that the individuals completing such duties in subsidiaries, divisions, etc., might themselves be personnel specialists rather than general line managers, although in practice this is rare because of the duplication of effort involved. The main problem with devolution of personnel and/or HRM work to non-specialist line managers is that they may be neither competent nor interested in personnel or HRM issues, and might not be motivated to complete HRM duties properly so that critically important personnel tasks are neglected. Bad HRM decisions lead to a poor corporate image, higher long-run costs and loss of output due to industrial conflict. Also line managers might focus all their attention on immediately pressing personnel problems, at the expense of long-term HRM planning, and it could result in HRM considerations not influencing strategic management decisions.

Effective devolution requires:

(a) the provision of back-up services in relation to technical problems arising from contracts of employment, legal aspects of redundancy and dismissal, union recognition, etc. An outside consultancy might assume this role;

(b) acceptance by everyone that line managers' workloads will have to increase following their assumption of personnel responsibilities;

(c) training of line managers in HRM concepts and techniques.

17. New developments in employee relations

Traditional approaches to employee relations have focused on collective bargaining between management and employees; on the establishment of procedures for handling grievances, disputes and disciplinary matters; and on the introduction of new working arrangements and techniques. Such matters have often been associated with conflict between management and workers. However, it is increasingly recognised that in the modern world, employee relations need to focus on harmony and co-operation among all the firm's interest groups, and on the common pursuit of a business's goals. Nowadays, employee relations need to be based on shared understanding of a company's objectives and on mutual trust between management and labour.

Manifestations of the new approach include the following:

(a) Improved employee communications plus extensive consultation and employee participation in workplace management decisions.

(b) Stronger links between individual pay and organisational performance.

(c) Provision of incentives and training to encourage flexible attitudes and working practices. Employees need to have inculcated within them attitudes and perspectives which make them willing to assume personal responsiblity for quality control and problem-solving at their places of work.

213

(d) Single status, single-table negotiation (see **14**) or the recognition of just a single trade union covering all occupations and grades of employee.

(e) The creation of company environments wherein all issues and problems can be discussed and analysed at every level of the organisation.

(f) Regarding trade unions as *insiders* of the firm.

MANAGEMENT DEVELOPMENT

18. Motherhood versus honeycomb approaches

A critical strategic decision in the HR field is whether to develop people within the firm, or recruit from outside. The former (known as the 'motherhood' approach) involves long time horizons and high expenditures on training, and the staff concerned might then leave the company. However it is often less risky than hiring outsiders. Firms adopting the motherhood approach will seek to hire young, inexperienced but promising people and train them in generalist management methods. Staff are then committed to their employing organisation, undertake a wide variety of assignments, and become steeped in the employer's culture and working practices. There is guaranteed continuity of operations within motherhood firms, but staff might lack the expertise of specialist outsiders – especially in narrow functional areas. Also, because of the long periods necessary to train new entrants, motherhood firms cannot expand or alter the scope of their operations at short notice.

A 'honeycomb' approach, conversely, seeks to base the firm's organisation on a conglomeration of 'cells' each corresponding to some specialist area of expertise. The advantage of a honeycomb system is that the business can expand or contract its operations quickly and conveniently through hiring or firing the individual employees engaged in this manner. On the other hand, individual employees might feel little commitment to the firm (highly qualified and experienced experts can easily move on to other businesses) and labour turnover could be high.

19. Nature of management development

Companies that decide to undertake management development need to implement systems and procedures for its orderly implementation, including:

- analyses of present and future management requirements;
- assessments of existing and potential skills of managers;
- practical means whereby individuals can acquire the knowledge, skills and competencies to undertake higher level work.

Needs may be met either by activities arranged within the company or through external courses. The latter appear to be losing favour because they are unable to take into account a company's particular systems, traditions or general management style. In-company programmes are growing in popularity, especially those which include a team of people who normally work together. Note however that formal management training has been criticised for creating unrealistic job and career expectations among junior managerial employees. Opponents of management training allege that the environments in which training occurs are necessarily artificial, and too remote from real life managerial situations to be of practical value.

Arguably, most aspects of management can only be learned by doing. In particular, the entrepreneurial attitudes that are essential for commercial success cannot be inculcated through academic management training ; many of the most innovative of all entrepreneurs and managers have received no management training whatsoever. According to this view, normal competition between managerial employees should ensure the emergence of the most able at the top.

Progress test 11

1. What are the main steps to be followed when devising a human resources strategy?

2. Why do companies need human resources strategies?

3. How do human resources strategies affect employee relations?

4. List the advantages to having an employee relations strategy.

5. Explain the difference between national and local collective bargaining.

6. Define 'decentralised collective bargaining'.

7. What are the criticisms of management development?

12

INFORMATION TECHNOLOGY STRATEGY

1. Information technology in business

Information technology (IT) is the acquisition, processing, storage and dissemination of information using computers. IT has revolutionised office work, and is about to revolutionise telecommunications (i.e. the transmission of information via radio waves or electric cables). Information technology, moreover, lies at the heart of computerised manufacturing systems using robotics (see 13.8), and of modern management information systems.

IT has transformed management practice: indeed it has changed the way managers think about their work. Effective managerial control requires the collection, summary, and evaluation of data prior to taking decisions. Not only can computers handle enormous amounts of data, but also they enable the application of sophisticated control techniques which previously were not feasible because of difficulty and cost. In today's world, therefore, the successful manager is not necessarily someone who works at a desk sifting through information propagated by reports, memoranda, and production and other statistics, but rather is increasingly likely to sit before a computer visual display unit, requisitioning and summarising instantly huge quantities of data, formulating models for analyzing likely consequences of various courses of action and selecting criteria on which final decisions will be based. Decisions can be fed into computerised systems and implemented instantly.

The dramatic impact of IT on an established industry is well-illustrated by the experience of courier and express parcel delivery services which in the 1980s moved very quickly from manual to computerised package handling and control. Effective use of IT became a critical competitive weapon within the sector, being used, *inter alia*, to:

- schedule deliveries and help plan the most efficient routes to destinations;
- track shipments from the moment they are picked up from the consignor through to their final delivery;
- provide instant two-way communication between van drivers and their depots using hand-held computers. Such systems allow drivers on the road to receive parcel pick-up details and to send proof of delivery back to a central tracking unit;

- link customers directly to whoever is in charge of their consignments at any moment in any part of the world;
- provide on-screen facilities for booking space with carriers.

2. Integration of data

A great benefit of computerised data processing is the integration at source of each piece of information into the management control system of the entire organisation. Data is recorded once but then used for many different purposes in different departments. Thus, information on production costs will be diffused simultaneously to the accounts department, the purchasing manager, stores and stock controllers, and any other interested party. The data itself will be presented to each of these recipients in a form which is precisely relevant to their particular needs. It is not necessary for several departments to collect and prepare what is essentially the same information. This has implications for the structure of departmentalisation within the firm, since many functions which previously were independent may, with the assistance of an integrated data presentation network, be combined.

3. Improved quality of information

Information systems collect, store and retrieve data. In the past, the volume of data handled within a system has been constrained by limitations on available clerical labour and the inability of many people to comprehend and assimilate large quantities of information. Hence, various summary statistics were developed to ease the burdens of data collection and interpretation. Aggregate figures only were available, however, because of the difficulties and expense of cross-tabulation. Comprehensive detailed analyses with respect to various categories and subheadings were not generally possible.

Computerisation has cut the cost of data collection, and has made the reduction of large amounts of data into summary numbers easy. Cross-tabulation has become effortless, and the precise form in which data is presented can be chosen at will.

4. Need for an IT strategy

The need for computerisation of administrative processes can become apparent in several ways: excessive amounts of management time spent on collecting and interpreting information, inaccurate or out-of-date records, non-availability of essential information needed for important decisions, high clerical costs for particular functions, and so on. Yet the consequences of computerisation may not be so clear. Installation of a new system can itself create the need for major organisational change, requiring new accountability and appraisal procedures, new departments, documentation, staffing levels, etc. The use of IT in companies implies rapid and drastic changes in equipment, attitudes and working practices and, in consequence, the need for an IT *strategy* designed to facilitate the introduction of change.

Determination of an IT strategy is one of the most important of all senior management functions, due to the ever-increasing complexity of modern business and the enormous efficiency improvements that the effective utilisation of IT can create. Further stimuli to the development of an IT strategy might include:

(a) rival firms gaining competitive advantage;

(b) information overload within the organisation;

(c) environmental turbulence accompanied by an increased need to gather and analyze information from external sources;

(d) organisational restructuring and/or being taken over by another firm;

(e) ferocious competition in markets both at home and abroad.

Products have to be supplied quickly, economically and at a high level of quality; and only by using modern technologies can most companies keep up with rival firms. Judicious use of IT can lead to a first-rate administrative system, effective decision making, efficient use of resources, and high productivity levels within the firm. IT helps businesses cope with complexity, uncertainty, and the explosion in the volume of information (internal and external) that has become available to companies in recent decades. As organisations become more sophisticated, so too must the techniques and procedures of organisational control – techniques that in today's world are invariably based on IT.

Information technology can be an important source of competitive advantage through:

(a) linking the firm to its customers and suppliers;

(b) improving operational efficiency;

(c) helping management devise and implement high calibre strategies;

(d) creating a fresh entry barrier for firms outside the industry;

(e) making it difficult for business customers to switch to alternative suppliers that have incompatible IT systems;

(f) facilitating business re-engineering (see 6.**10**);

(g) improving quality management (see 13.**24**). Note how modern TQM systems rely heavily on computerised production and IT;

(h) enabling the firm to respond quickly to environmental change;

(i) facilitating the monitoring of key performance indicators (see 16.3);

(j) enabling the firm to service niche markets via product differentiation and flexible manufacturing (see 13.**8**);

(k) monitoring suppliers and reducing procurement costs;

(l) integrating marketing with production;

(m) improving management control.

Rapid conveyance of control information facilitates fast and effective decision taking. The quality of decisions should improve because computerised systems enable operations research models and solution techniques to be applied, and advanced methods of planning and co-ordination to be implemented. Decisions are taken on the basis of more comprehensive information and the likely consequences of a wide range of alternative courses of action can be explored.

One of the classic examples of a company gaining a competitive edge through IT is American Airlines' use of its SABRE reservation system, the stimulus for the development of which was the threat of US travel agents developing their own computerised booking facility. SABRE began operation in 1963 handling 85,000 telephone enquiries, 40,000 reservations and 20,000 ticket sales. Demand for SABRE was phenomenal. American Airlines reduced significantly the number of clerks engaged in handling reservations, could increase the number of passengers on each flight without the risk of overbooking, and *guarantee* each passenger a seat. The system developed in sophistication during the 1970s and was extended to cover flight plans for aircraft, crew scheduling, the tracking of spare parts, and decision support systems for managers. It was installed in travel agencies and enlarged to incorporate new services for hotels, rental cars, rail bookings, etc. By 1988 American Airlines was making more money from SABRE than from flying aircraft. A subsidiary was set up with sole responsibility for managing and marketing the system. The subsidiary's turnover exceeds $US 6 million annually, handling reservations for nearly 750 airlines.

Source: Adapted from Peppard, J., *IT Strategy for Business*, Pitman 1993.

5. IT strategy and corporate strategy

IT strategies need to derive from the firm's corporate strategies as a whole. Systems selection and development should relate directly to such matters as choice of product distribution channels, nature and extent of automation of production lines (especially the use of robotics), total quality management, competitive situation of the firm (e.g. whether it is planning a major expansion) and its short/medium-term objectives. The IT strategies and systems adopted significantly affect the overall strategic options available to the company and play a crucial role in the implementation of corporate plans. Decisions taken when determining IT strategies have implications for a wide range of matters, including:

- the business's costs and competitiveness;
- changes in the status of various managers and departments;
- individual tasks and responsibilities;
- appraisal, accountability, control and co-ordination systems;
- working practices;
- training needs;
- reward systems;

- recruitment and other personnel issues;
- management decision making procedures.

Also they help determine organisation structures, management style and patterns of inter-personnel communication within the firm.

6. Devising an IT strategy

In order to devise an IT strategy, management needs to examine the role of IT in comparable firms, assess the extent and relevance of available information, identify the critical areas in which IT can generate a competitive advantage for the company, and analyze the potential impacts of various IT systems on operating efficiency. Thereafter the main steps in formulating an IT strategy are as follows:

1. Specification of key IT objectives in the context of the business's overall corporate plan.

2. Identification of the options available in relation to systems and procedures.

3. Examination of the implications of the various options for human resource management, organisation structure, etc.

4. Development of a systems architecture that matches the company's requirements.

5. Selection of appropriate methods and procedures, plus the format of the information reports generated by the system.

6. Choice of an organisation structure that best facilitates the effective utilisation of IT.

Typically, IT strategies are drafted and implemented by teams comprising IT specialists, general planners, and representatives of the departments that will be major users of the system. It is crucially important when selecting a system to look ahead and predict the firm's IT requirements in future years. Once installed the system will prescribe very many of the organisation's operating procedures, which cannot be changed until the system is replaced. Note how it is possible to skip a generation of new technology by not upgrading, and then devote significantly more resources to IT the next time round.

7. Purposes of IT strategy

The purposes of an IT strategy are:

(a) to utilise internal and externally generated information in a manner that gives the firm a competitive edge in its various markets. This will involve improving existing information flows *and* using the information strategically;

(b) to understand customers needs and preferences;

(c) to integrate all the information available to the firm in order to make the best decisions. Note how several of the strategy formulation techniques discussed in other chapters (e.g. environmental scanning) benefit from IT support.

Strategic use of information

As well as needing strategies for managing IT, information itself can be used to obtain a competitive advantage. In other words, information may be managed in such a way that it develops and supports the strategy formulation process. Information management plays a crucial role in:

- competitor analysis;
- the provision of databases for corporate planning;
- environmental scanning (see 5.**13**);
- construction of scenarios (see 4.**9**);
- SWOT analysis (see 5.**4**);
- understanding customer requirements;
- assessing and liaising with suppliers.

Management information systems generally are discussed in **16** below.

Elements of an IT strategy

Strategies for managing IT systems need to encompass the total resources of the organisation, having particular regard to the following matters:

(a) Staffing. Selecting recruits best equipped to handle IT-based management systems. Determining training requirements. Deciding how those competent in IT are to be rewarded and their salaries differentiated with respect to other categories of staff.

(b) Determining the extent of the modifications to existing products, administrative arrangements and working methods required to obtain maximum benefit from an IT-driven organisation.

(c) Altering organisational structures, including spans of control, delegation arrangements, number of levels of authority, etc. in order to make the best use of the latest IT.

(d) Integrating IT into all aspects of the firm's operations.

(e) Deciding whether to develop a unique system in-house or to purchase a standard commercial system.

(f) Determination of how frequently the system is to be upgraded.

The strategy adopted will determine *how* information is to be used in order to support the business, how new systems are to be implemented, and the performance standards expected from new and existing systems. IT strategies need to be realistic, understood by all affected parties, and cost effective. Strategies will only succeed if they have wholehearted support from top management, are implemented by technically competent staff, and endorsed by a significant majority of affected workers. Note the ability of quite junior staff vexatiously to disrupt a computerised system. The policies emerging from strategies should:

- ensure that the IT function comfortably dovetails into the organisation structure of the firm;

- facilitate the management of change (see chapter 6);
- wherever possible, present quantifiable targets.

8. Problems with IT strategies

A frequently experienced problem in the formulation of IT strategies is that key decisions are taken by senior managers who do not possess technical expertise in the subject. It has to be recognised, however, that IT strategy is too important to be left solely to IT technicians, in view of the extensive financial investments in IT that large firms typically have to make and the high cost of maintaining systems. IT specialists might recommend a system that incorporates the latest developments and which greatly enhances the status of IT staff, but which is not really appropriate for the organisation! Note moreover that heavy investment in a new and successful IT system can cause competitors to respond by introducing even better systems, hence generating 'IT wars' and removing the firm's initial competitive advantage.

9. Practical problems

Intelligent use of computerised systems will reduce costs, inventory holdings, manufacture and delivery times, and will improve product quality and reliability. Computerised procedures do, however, present special problems to those responsible for their control. Invariably, computerisation is accompanied by standardisation of methods and processes. Deviations from standards may be impossible even if such deviations are desired. Note that a hardware malfunction can disrupt totally the work of a firm. Destruction of files through accident or negligence can lead to major financial losses and enormous difficulties in trying to make good the damage caused. Software can also be a source of problems; errors might continue to exist even after programs have been officially debugged. Large programs often contain subroutines which are hardly ever used so that mistakes might be discovered several years after a system has been implemented.

A common problem in IT management is that of constantly escalating costs and (importantly) the absence of concrete measures of the efficiency of the IT function. For example, a large pharmaceuticals manufacturing company once discovered that its IT hardware and software costs were approaching a staggering five per cent of annual total expenditure. A detailed analysis of the firm's IT spending revealed that there were no measures of IT efficiency in any of the company's user departments; that control over IT expenditure was in the hands of individuals more interested in improving data processing services than in attaining the company's wider business objectives; and that costs leapt whenever suppliers announced the availability of new equipment, regardless of the company's actual computing requirements. Increases in the power of the firm's IT system made available by improvements in each generation of computer technology were not reflected in lower operating costs. Rather the savings released were used to expand the system, to hire additional computer staff and to develop even more applications. To deal with these problems a member of the firm's main board of directors was given exclusive responsibility for controlling all aspects of the IT function. Targets and appraisal systems were introduced and a more commercial approach applied to IT matters.

Source: Adapted from Grindley, K., *Managing IT at Board Level*, Pitman 1991.

HUMAN RESOURCES ASPECTS

10. IT and human resources management

Those who operate IT-driven administrative and production systems typically require a higher level of education and training than the traditional manufacturing worker. At the same time, however, the need for conventional craft skills has diminished. Labour flexibility within a computerised working situation requires *technologies* rather than crafts people. In particular, the range and quality of the information potentially available to everyone in the organisation is greatly increased. Hence, traditional dividing lines between occupational categories break down, and the demarcation of jobs can become irrelevant: vertically as well as horizontally. Other important possible consequences of computerisation with implications for human resources management include the following:

(a) Deskilling of tasks in certain parts of the enterprise while new types of skill are required elsewhere, leading perhaps to resentments and conflicts between various categories of worker.

(b) Total integration of all phases of production, office administration and internal communications, causing more frequent and perhaps closer interactions among employees in different sections of the firm and between various levels in the managerial hierarchy.

The competencies needed to succeed within a computerised work environment are general in nature and not necessarily related to particular occupations. Hence there is much scope for job rotation, undermining thereby employees' specific control over what were previously highly specialised jobs that could not easily be given to other categories of worker.

11. Possible HRM problems

IT staff (and computer literate employees generally) frequently occupy key positions in organisations whereby they can cause great disruption through taking industrial action. This could induce management to treat computing personnel more favourably than other categories, and to try and arrange the division and pattern of work so as to ensure that not too much disruptive potential lies in a few pairs of hands.

To the extent that computer staff are treated differently to other types of worker, a number of sources of conflict may arise, as follows:

(a) Sometimes, computer literate staff with specialist qualifications have the same status, earn similar salaries, and occupy the same grades as line managers who – although they contribute a great deal to the organisation's work – are not as well certificated academically and have not had to spend several years studying for professional examinations. Accordingly, those who operate the computerised system might treat with disdain the work of line managers and resent the fact that computing staff and line managers are graded and paid equally. Conversely, line managers may begrudge the computer worker's self-assumed intellectual status.

(b) Those who manage the computerised system might expect to be able to exercise discretion and judgement in the course of their work, but at the same time must comply with the bureaucratic rules and demands of the wider organisation. They are subject to the authority of senior administrators, yet usually are not fully involved in the formulation of the administrative processes that determine the rules.

(c) Other categories of employee (including line managers) might form a coalition against computing staff whose level of education and social status they resent and whom they do not feel should be taking significant decisions on behalf of the company.

12. End-user computing

End-user computing means the imaginative manipulation of computer packages and systems by employees who have no special qualifications or expertise in computing or IT, so that non-specialist package users have maximum discretion in determining the outputs of the system. The implications of end-user computing for business organisation and for human resources management include the following:

(a) There is a levelling out of the performances of the firm's best and worst employees, since the computer will do a lot of the employee's basic work. This makes it difficult to appraise workers' performances accurately and to determine a fair system for rewarding employees.

(b) Opportunities are created for greatly increased productivity among white-collar workers, who will be able to choose how they complete IT-related tasks. This should make their jobs more interesting.

(c) Staff require a flexible approach to their work, must undertake tasks relating to a wider variety of business functions, and need to be able to assess the reliability of outputs from systems that contain information on topics with which they are not familiar.

(d) Workers' capacities to choose *how* they complete IT-related tasks should motivate them and provide numerous possibilities for acquiring experience of higher-level work.

(e) There is less need for middle managers.

(f) Employees have open access to a wide range of the firm's databases. Note how this can create data security problems and possibilities for the deliberate disruption of systems.

(g) Decision making is much faster.

(h) Employees are presented with:

- new alternatives regarding how work can be completed;
- more interesting tasks, challenges and responsibilities;
- a wider range of duties to be completed;
- the need to take an increased number of decisions;
- fresh possibilities for restructuring the working day.

Introduction of end-user computing is often accompanied by the 'downsizing' of systems, i.e. the increased use of small but powerful personal computing systems and applications, made possible by the enormous expansion in the capacity of the typical PC that has occurred in recent years. Downsizing implies greater systems flexibility, decentralisation of costs, and improved responsiveness to local needs. On the other hand it can involve a substantial capital outlay, weaken central control, and impose additional workloads on staff in user departments.

Strategic issues related to end-user computing are as follows:

(a) Definition of the role of end-user computing in attaining corporate objectives.

(b) The extent of central management control over end-user computing activities.

(c) Who is to select hardware and software (i.e. the degree of user involvement in the process).

(d) How the system is to be developed, how quickly and by whom (users or specialist IT staff).

Advantages and problems of end-user computing

Advantages of end-user computing are:

(a) Individuals are able to develop their IT skills.

(b) Each section of the firm can use IT at a level of sophistication appropriate for its particular requirements.

(c) The approach encourages creativity and innovation among employees.

Problems with end-user computing include duplication of activities, higher costs, the possible emergence of inconsistencies in working methods, and perhaps a general lowering of the quality of the firm's overall IT activities. Users might not define problems in an appropriate manner, with consequent waste of computing time and resources. Training needs are extensive (and costly) and money has to be spent on technical support (either from a centralised unit or from outside consultants). Note moreover that some individuals might be extremely reluctant to become involved in the system, creating extra work for other people. Further difficulties are that:

225

(a) end users might not be competent to select the decision support tools that are objectively the best to apply in complex circumstances;

(b) users might concentrate on short-term issues at the expense of long-term systems development;

(c) bad IT working practices may be passed on from department to department.

SELECTION OF SYSTEMS

13. Selection procedures

Choice of an appropriate IT system has crucial significance for the firm. First it is necessary to examine all the financial and other costs and benefits involved, followed by an appraisal of the implications of candidate systems for employees and the firm's organisation structures. The study needs to investigate:

(a) all the tasks that need to be undertaken;

(b) employee retraining requirements;

(c) the form in which output information will be required, and how data flows can be arranged to meet output requirements most efficiently;

(d) all the costs involved: equipment, software, retraining and extra recruitment;

(e) implications of the new system for management control;

(f) longer-term side effects of the proposed system.

A major cost in the early stages is that of running the existing system alongside the new scheme. The firm cannot risk the failure of untested procedures unless a back-up system is available and thus has to operate the two systems simultaneously.

Custom-built software

Few companies (especially small businesses) employ people to write company-specific application programs as there now exist a wide variety of ready-made packages, and many standard commercial programs contain menu-driven procedures which enable them to be adapted to meet particular users' requirements.

If greater specialisation is needed, 'custom-built' software may be commissioned from professional software designers. However, the high cost of this relative to the straight purchase of existing programs encourages firms to alter their internal routines to make them compatible with available software programs rather than vice versa. Changing an existing administrative system is often cheaper than commissioning designer software, and has the added advantage that well-established commercial programs are usually error-free whereas custom-built software can contain many errors. Relevant factors to be considered when deciding whether to purchase a standard commercial system include:

(a) capacity of the system;

(b) speed of operation;

(c) quality of output, especially if the output consists of written documents that will be seen by outsiders;

(d) ease of use. Ideally the system should be capable of operation by inexperienced people;

(e) flexibility. Good systems allow the user to modify, via menus, the basic structures of their operations and output;

(f) availability of support services from the system supplier;

(g) whether the system is user-friendly, how much training (if any) is required prior to its use, and any problems or drawbacks associated with its operation.

When the Japanese motor giant Toyota first established significant manufacturing and distribution arrangements in Europe and the USA it decided to use in-house Japanese developed software, rather than purchasing locally produced packages off-the-shelf. This resulted in incompatibilities between imported software and local systems, creating many difficulties as the firm's European and US operations began to expand. In response, the company introduced a private satellite-based communication system to link its various factories and distribution units with each other and with head office in Japan. Nevertheless, the firm could not divorce itself from its local IT environments and increasingly found itself having to hire and train local computer programmers – greatly increasing the overall costs of IT. Also the shortage of local people with the high-level programming skills necessary to cope with the satellite system and computer interfaces between this and the IT systems of other firms made recruitment extremely difficult. And since Japanese software specialists required work-permits to enter Europe and the USA it was not generally possible to bring over in-house IT employees from Japan. Inevitably, therefore, local subsidiaries began to purchase off-the-peg software compatible with that used by local firms. It was simply not feasible to develop and maintain in-house software for every new application necessary.

Use of consultants

IT consultants may be categorised as follows:

(a) Equipment and/or software producers who provide consultancy services regarding choice of model, installation of the system, training of the customer's staff in equipment/package use, and post-installation troubleshooting, maintenance and advice.

(b) Specialists in particular areas, e.g., CADCAM, optimised production technology, management information systems, etc. Ideally the specialist will be mainly concerned with the technical aspects of his or her subject and not committed to installing any specific make of equipment. Often, however, these firms take commissions from equipment manufacturers in exchange for recommending their clients to purchase certain models and types of equipment.

(c) General management consultancies and accounting firms with IT divisions.

The role of the IT consultant is to investigate inadequacies in existing information flows and to design new systems to overcome them. He or she will take a broad view of the situation, from data input through distribution channels right up to the final recipients of the processed information. The consultant will ask why information is needed, how best it might be used, and will devise and implement new methods for its analysis and presentation. An IT consultant will:

(a) explain the new technology and (importantly) how jobs will change in consequence of its introduction to a firm;

(b) demystify computer functions and create within the client company feelings of self-confidence about computer use;

(c) develop a *common* understanding of the purpose of the new system among all its users.

ORGANISATIONAL ASPECTS

14. Implications for organisational structure

Often the introduction of a new IT system necessitates the rearrangement of the departmental structure of the firm. Computerisation tends to encourage centralisation of administrative procedures. Data is summarised and distributed automatically, circulating around a central control unit which can receive and monitor management information continuously. Requirements for local data interpretation and decision taking might diminish. Less delegation from senior to junior managers is likely in a computerised system because higher management obtains better, faster and more comprehensive information. Consequently senior managers exercise much tighter personal control. Indeed the great bulk of senior managerial work in some industries can, in principle, be conducted from a computer terminal.

15. Organisation of IT staff

The basic issue here is whether to concentrate IT resources into one or more centralised units, or to disperse IT expertise throughout the firm. Some firms have 'information centres' to support sectional IT activities (especially end-user computing). Each centre gives specialist advice to a number of departments, has access to sophisticated software, and may undertake more difficult computing tasks. The problem is that the centres could lack detailed knowledge of sectional IT requirements and become 'marginalised' within the organisation. Other alternatives are the creation of a single centralised department to oversee all IT activities, or widespread dispersion of responsibility for IT throughout the firm.

Centralisation

Advantages to the creation of a centralised department include:

(a) rapid responses to systems failures;

(b) cost savings made possible through the avoidance of duplicated activities;

(c) better security;

(d) clear responsibility for IT activities;

(e) tight control over the system;

(f) accumulation of technical expertise within the central unit, together with the application of sophisticated support facilities and software;

(g) the ability to recruit highly qualified IT staff, whose talents can be fully utilised in a centralised IT department (a career ladder will exist within the unit);

(h) improved prospects of IT procedures;

(i) the fact that staff can be quickly redeployed within the department.

However, centralisation can lead to a splitting off of IT development from the rest of the organisation, and costs may run out of control as IT specialists pursue their particular interests. 'Chinese walls' might be erected between IT and other functions, with IT not being regarded as an integral part of the management structure of the firm. Further problems with centralisation are:

(a) Inflexible attitudes and administrative bureaucracy may emerge.

(b) The centralised unit might lose touch with the goals of major IT user departments.

(c) Long delays may occur before user departments experiencing difficulties can be serviced.

(d) It can be difficult to allocate the costs of the centralised unit to user departments. Should these costs be regarded as a general overhead to be spread across the entire firm (thus penalising sections that do not use the unit's services), or should IT intensive departments pay more than the rest?

(e) If the central unit fails the company's entire IT system will collapse.

The Automobile Association is a major user of information technology, spending over £1 million on IT each week. A centralised approach to IT management is applied. Reasons advanced for centralisation include the ability to buy supplies in bulk at high discount, faster internal communication, better response to customers' requirements, and the fact that staff in the centralised unit have intimate knowledge of all aspects of the Association's IT operations. The centralised unit has a section that develops in-house software. This section has to compete with outside suppliers vis-à-vis price, quality and speed of delivery. Such competition, it is alleged, ensures that the AA receives only the very best service from its in-house facilities. Costs are automatically kept to the absolute minimum.

Decentralisation

Factors encouraging dispersion of responsibility for IT (via the creation of Information Centres for example – see above) include:

(a) massive increases in the power of desktop computers;

(b) the development of high-quality end-user computing software;

(c) growing computer literacy among middle managers;

(d) the large variations in the IT needs of certain departments.

Dispersion results in IT specialists being closer to end-users and (hopefully) more in tune with their everyday needs. Users are involved with devising and operating the system and should in consequence be better motivated towards making it succeed. Further advantages are that:

(a) systems that emerge should be immediately relevant to the business's operational requirements (rather than being selected for their purely technical excellence);

(b) systems are more likely to be flexible and responsive to changing circumstances;

(c) computer awareness is encouraged throughout the organisation;

(d) end-user computing is facilitated (see 12);

(e) creativity is stimulated;

(f) information is processed close to where it is to be used;

(g) decentralised units can tailor their activities to the specific requirements of particular functions and/or departments;

(h) IT costs are directly related to user sections;

(i) IT is more closely integrated into the organisation system of the enterprise.

Problems with dispersion include communication difficulties, computer illiteracy among certain types of staff, and duplication of effort. Costs may be higher and (importantly) not as visible as when the IT function is concentrated into a single unit. Other difficulties are that:

(a) working methods in various units may become incompatible and lead to poor co-ordination;

(b) dispersed facilities might not be able to cope with complex and technically sophisticated IT problems;

(c) the role and status of IT specialists might be unclear;

(d) arguments between dispersed IT staff and functional line managers might develop.

A large engineering company had a centralised management control system which it decided to decentralise via the creation of self-contained business units within the enterprise. Each business unit was constructed around one of the firm's major products. However, IT remained a centralised function, paid for jointly by the various product divisions. After the new structure was implemented product divsion managers began to complain about the escalating costs of the centralised IT they were required to finance; about their inability to impose targets and accountability systems on the IT department; and about the nature of the information generated by the centralised unit (information was processed according to categories not directly related to the firm's products). IT personnel were accused of adopting arrogant and patronising attitudes and of not dealing with divisional requests for computing systems as quickly as was necessary. Hence, IT was turned over to the product divisions. It emerged that:

- the belief that divisions could themselves provide a superior service was misfounded, as no single division had the technical IT expertise necessary to deal with complex difficulties;
- overall company spending on IT actually increased;
- the distribution of IT costs among divisions was very uneven. According to the nature of the product handled, some divisions found they were spending far more on IT than before; others much less. This had repercussions for divisional budgets, profitabilities and the pricing of products;
- it became difficult to make comparisons of the relative efficiencies of the IT systems of different divsions;
- divisions began bringing in outside consultants to solve problems, adding to IT costs.

Facilities management

Firms that need to rely heavily on IT and more general computer services (companies with very large databases for example) but which lack experience and expertise in computing and information management sometimes elect to use the services of an outside facilities management company which takes over the client firm's entire computing function and becomes, in effect, the data processing department of the company. The client may or may not own the system and/or employ its own computing personnel. Hardware, software and computer operatives could be provided – possibly via third parties – by the consultant's firm. A client will (usually) pay:

- an annual lump sum fee;
- rental charges on equipment (when the client does not directly own the system);
- equipment maintenance costs; and
- an hourly charge while the system is in use, covering the wages of computing staff plus general support services.

Invariably, responsibility for providing data in a form acceptable for input to the system lies with the client company – the facilities manager simply processes the information and presents the results.

The client obtains a complete electronic data processing facility at low overhead cost and is relieved of all the burdens of training, organising and controlling computing staff. And the cost need not be prohibitive because the consultant might use the system for processing other clients' work thus enabling the consultant to reduce his or her total fee. Equally, a consultant could arrange for a part of the client's own computing work to be done on another firm's system.

Advantages to using a facilities management company is that it will:

(a) possess expert knowledge of the latest technical developments;

(b) have its own commercial objectives and be driven by the need to keep its customers satisfied;

(c) have incentives to keep costs to a minimum.

Problems with using a facilities manager are that the client (i) becomes entirely dependent on the former's services, and (ii) loses control over computing costs. Also the facilities manager might use the client firm's system to complete work for other clients without the knowledge or permission of the firm in question.

STRATEGIC MANAGEMENT AND THE MANAGEMENT INFORMATION SYSTEM

Computers and information technology play a vital role in the operation of the firm's management information, although it is important to note that a management information system has many non-IT dimensions: assessment of competitors' products and marketing abilities, evaluation of customer attitudes, environmental scanning (see 5.13), etc.

16. Functions of a management information system

Efficient management information systems (MIS) enable management to plan, co-ordinate, organise and control. They provide the information needed for strategic planning and for day-to-day operations. Strategic information requirements include data on business ratios (return on capital employed, ratio of debt to equity capital, interest payable on borrowed money, etc.), on current trends in external capital markets, the firm's liquidity position, aggregate cash flow forecasts, market research data and so on. Tactical information needs might involve ratios of profits to working capital, stock to current assets, sales to output; rates of return on specific investment projects; information on production bottlenecks, capacity constraints, etc.

An important MIS function is to highlight potential difficulties with debtors and suppliers. What, for example, is the average delay between delivery of goods and the issue of invoices? How quickly do customers settle their accounts? What are the effects of offering discounts for prompt payment? What is the ratio of creditors to purchases? How long, on average, do suppliers take to deliver goods, and to what extent can payments to suppliers be delayed?

Other categories of information that an MIS should supply include the following:

(a) Market information:

(*i*) effectiveness of sales personnel;
(*ii*) responsiveness of sales to price changes;
(*iii*) market trends;
(*iv*) behaviour of competitors;
(*v*) adequacy of distribution channels.

(b) Financial information:

(*i*) whether budgets are being adhered to;
(*ii*) length of trading cycles;
(*iii*) adequacy of cash inflows;
(*iv*) need for external financing.

(c) Work-in-progress information:

(*i*) ratios of work in progress to production, stock to sales, etc;
(*ii*) identification of slow-moving stock;
(*iii*) frequency and causes of stockouts;
(*iv*) stockholding costs;
(*v*) causes of machine breakdown and other interruptions in production.

17. Installation of an MIS

To install an MIS it is necessary to consider when, how and to whom information has to be transmitted, and how best to summarise data in a form that enables its fast and accurate evaluation prior to taking decisions. In practice, however, difficulties emerge, including the following:

(a) Relevant information might not reach the right people. Managers commonly assume that colleagues and subordinates have been informed of particular facts when, actually, they have not.

(b) Breaks in the chain of command. Information should flow vertically through the enterprise from its top to its bottom via the channels illustrated in the organisation chart. Often, information 'bottlenecks' occur at supervisory and middle management levels since supervisors and middle managers not only receive information from above (and have to decide whether to act on it) but also collect feedback from lower levels.

(c) Horizontal flows of information among colleagues of equal rank may be interrupted if certain individuals deliberately conceal information or – through incompetence – do not pass it on.

(d) The *culture* of the organisation may be resistant to change. This could create special problems if the MIS cuts across existing departmental boundaries, challenges informal information transmission systems, or creates 'information gatekeepers' (i.e. individuals who handle large amounts of information and become powerful through being able to withhold vital information from colleagues they dislike).

The effectiveness of an MIS should be evaluated against its capacity to assist in taking decisions; particularly through enabling the comparison of various possibilities in new and meaningful ways. Note that there is little point in confronting, for example, a sales manager with an array of figures on market trends, promotional costs, survey results and so on if he or she cannot understand what they mean. In the IT-driven firm the skill of the manager lies in recognising what summary data are relevant and useful, and the format in which they are required.

Progress test 12

1. Define (i) information technology, and (ii) telecommunications.

2. What are the relationships between IT strategy and corporate strategy?

3. State the purposes of an IT strategy.

4. List the human resources problems that might be experienced when implementing IT strategies.

5. Define 'end-user computing'.

6. Why does the introduction of new IT systems often necessitate organisational restructuring?

7. List the main problems connected with the centralisation of the IT function.

8. What are the main purposes of a management information system?

13

MANUFACTURING STRATEGY

1. Nature of manufacturing strategy

Manufacturing strategy should derive from the firm's overall corporate strategy and has many crucial implications for the financing of the business, for its organisation, management style and human resources. A successful manufacturing strategy is one which results in the production of the correct amount of output in the right place at the right quality, cost and time. Absence of a coherent manufacturing strategy is likely to result in loss of market share, high inventories, expensive and inefficient working practices, outdated production methods and ineffective management.

Manufacturing strategy and operations management

Manufacturing is a key element of the wider function of 'operations management', i.e. the family of activities that concern the transformation of material resource inputs into outputs of goods and services. These activities add value to goods while they are being processed, moved or converted. Thus operations management encompasses manufacturing, storage, physical transport and distribution, and the deployment of physical items such as shelving, refrigerated cabinets and checkout tills in a retail outlet. Issues that need to be addressed by a manufacturing strategy include the following:

(a) The role and status of manufacturing within the organisation.

(b) Make versus buy decisions (see 18).

(c) The technology to be used in manufacturing.

(d) Criteria for selecting capital investment projects.

(e) Whether to lease rather than purchase major capital items.

(f) How the workforce is to acquire appropriate technical skills.

(g) Whether to produce for stock when order books are empty.

(h) When to introduce new technologies and how quickly.

(i) The calibres of the plant and equipment to be employed in manufacturing.

(j) The nature of quality control and quality assurance procedures.

(k) How to integrate marketing research with new product development and generally relate manufacturing activities to marketing.

(l) Delivery/reliability/price trade-offs.

(m) How best to integrate computer assisted manufacturing into the firm's overall organisation system.

PRODUCTION

Manufacturing concerns the conversion of materials, components and other resources into finished products. The markets for the products must be researched and their potentials evaluated, and manufacturing activities have to be financed (see Figure 13.1). Normally, responsibility for the manufacturing function is vested in a production department.

2. Role of the production department

Typical activities within a production department are work planning and scheduling, technical aspects of manufacture, product choice (in conjunction with the marketing department), and factory layout. Further duties might include design, research and development, standardisation procedures, maintenance, inspection and quality control. The range of tasks undertaken by the staff of a production department is extremely varied. In managerial grades, professional engineers, designers and functional specialists are employed, together (usually) with their administrative and clerical support units. At the other end of the spectrum are shop-floor supervisors, skilled, semi-skilled and unskilled workers, and maintenance and inspection personnel.

Often, senior staff in the production department possess more technical knowledge and are better qualified academically than colleagues in other departments, especially in high-technology industries. Further characteristics of production department are outlined below.

(a) They absorb large proportions of firms' expenditures. Apart from operating costs (raw materials, wages, electricity, etc.) there are the capital costs of fixed plant, equipment, vehicles, warehouses and so on. Thus, production managers must be familiar with the techniques of cost control: standard costing, ratio analysis, budgetary control, and so on.

(b) Production managers must liaise with many other departments, since production decisions normally involve marketing (what goods should be produced); finance (how production is to be paid for); personnel (recruitment, training and control of staff); and a variety of other departments – security, secretariat, legal services, etc.

Thus, effective production management involves much co-ordination and communication with other departments, as well as specific functional responsibilities.

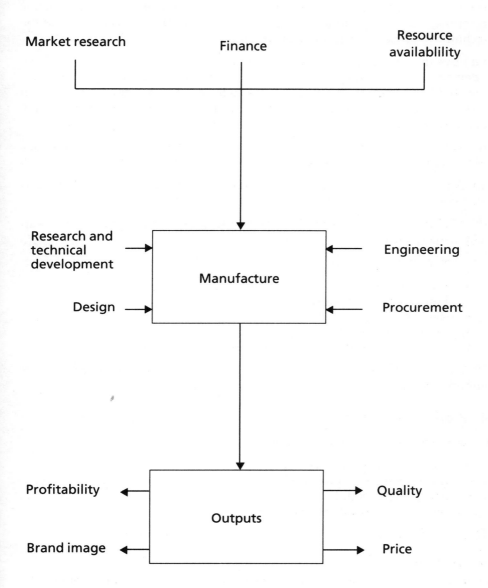

Figure 13.1 The manufacturing process

3. Technology

'Technology' is the utilisation of the materials and processes involved in the transformation of inputs into outputs. It determines the physical and economic resources that an organisation has at its disposal. The characteristics of the technical aspects of organisation are as follows:

(a) As the technology used with an organisation increases, so too will the demand for specialisation of functions in order to cope with the growing complexity of the problems it faces. This creates the need for better co-ordination in order to integrate activities and unify effort towards the attainment of the organisation's goals.

(b) New technologies require new work patterns, incentive systems, occupational mobility and fresh attitudes towards the acceptance of change.

(c) Advanced technologies need more professionally qualified and well-educated employees and fewer manual workers.

(d) Different technologies might demand different forms of group leadership and management style.

Technology usually affects:

- the extent of the division of labour;
- employee training needs;
- the nature of employees' tasks;
- organisation structures;
- employee job satisfaction and attitudes toward work.

Management has to choose which particular devices and techniques are best for improving efficiency and for achieving organisational goals.

4. Production methods

Choice of particular methods to be adopted will depend on:

- the use of the product;
- the quantity to be produced;
- technical possibilities;
- relative costs of alternative techniques.

Three options are available: job, batch and continuous production.

Job production

Here, articles are made to clients' precise specifications. Examples are bookbinding, shipbuilding, or the construction of buildings. Job production is not usually amenable to the application of the division of labour, so few opportunities of scale occur. Also, since many varied tasks are normally necessary to complete a job the labour used in production needs to be competent in several skill areas. Firms engaged in job production cannot plan their outputs until customers have placed orders. Thus, demand forecasting is not generally possible and production for stock cannot take place. Consequently, firms often experience long idle periods between jobs. Fixed costs, however, are still incurred during slack periods. The only way to ensure continuity of work with job production is through efficient marketing.

Batch production

Production which is not continuous, but nevertheless repetitive, is called batch production. The length of the production run is finite and determined in advance. Goods are produced to meet customers' orders, or for stock. Sales might be continuous, but of insufficient volume to justify uninterrupted production. Batch production occurs where a product's design or specification is altered regularly. Some specialisation and division of labour is possible; economics of scale might be obtained.

Continuous (flow) production

This is mass production using assembly lines, conveyor belts or other continuous supply systems. Mass production is appropriate for standardised, relatively homogeneous products. The division of labour can be applied and significant economies of scale should result. Often, mass produced goods are made in anticipation of future orders. It is essential therefore that reasonably accurate sales forecasts are prepared. The economics of mass production demand that plant, equipment, and labour be continuously and fully used to reduce overheads per unit of output. Hence, the firm must be prepared to accumulate large amounts of stock whenever sales fall.

5. Production planning

Production planning involves first 'preproduction programming' which concerns (i) production specification, deciding the quantity and rate of production, and (ii) process engineering: choosing production methods, work study, design of tools and equipment. It further involves work planning, including the determination of project completion dates, the drafting of networks, arrangement of tools, materials and equipment, and the scheduling of activities. Production plans result from sales forecasts. Obviously, businesses should produce only those goods they can sell; sophisticated production techniques, efficient working methods, good labour relations and so on are wasted if the goods produced cannot be sold.

6. Standardisation

Standardisation of production seeks to remove unnecessary differences between produced items. Larger production runs, lower unit manufacturing costs, easier movement of goods and more efficient stockholding are possible with standardised units. Component parts become interchangeable and can be used for several purposes.

Producers gain many advantages from standardisation:

(a) Fuller use of existing machines and labour, easier work planning and scheduling.

239

(b) Quicker inspection, better quality control.

(c) Reduced average stockholdings.

(d) More specialisation and division of labour.

(e) Simplification of clerical records.

Diversification is the opposite approach. Here, firms seek actively to alter existing products or add new lines to satisfy changing consumer wants. Product variation may require new manufacturing techniques, skills and materials; so obviously the economic benefits of homogeneous outputs cannot be obtained. Nevertheless, new market segments become available while existing products gain additional unique selling points.

FLEXIBLE MANUFACTURING

7. Relevance of the focused factory

Computerisation and the use of robots have revolutionised manufacturing and enabled a wider range of items to be produced within the same factory. This has many implications for the general approach to manufacturing that was adopted by many firms prior to the era of computerised robotics. Wickham Skinner, for example, argued that production units gained competitive advantage through focusing on a narrow range of activities rather than tackling several diverse lines of work all at the same time (Skinner 1974). Firms would benefit, Skinner argued, from the application of the division of labour, experience curve effects (see 3.28), and the specialist use of resources. Through focusing on just a few types of output, businesses are presented with a handful of key targets and do not have to trade-off one objective against others. Further benefits might include:

(a) use of familiar and proven technologies;

(b) the ability to identify and satisfy a small number of specific customer requirements;

(c) a constant flow of orders from a known market;

(d) development of human resources in particular specialist fields;

(e) capacity to serve niche markets.

If a company has an extensive product range then, according to Skinner, its factories should be segregated into small, self-contained and specialist production units.

Problems with Skinner's approach

In the modern world however, computerisation, robotics and the extensive use of information technology have altered the basic framework in which manufacturing is conducted. Specialisation of tasks, standardisation of output and long production runs to secure economies of scale are in many cases no longer necessary in order to reduce manufacturing costs. And today's circumstances demand fast responses to rapidly changing environments, close attention to quality, customer-driven product design and characteristics, a wide range of models to place before customers, and speed of delivery as well as an attractive price. Increasing competition has resulted in consumers being presented with numerous product options, so that suppliers must be more customer-oriented than in the past and willing to adapt their outputs to meet consumer requirements.

8. Flexible manufacturing

A flexible manufacturing system (FMS) comprises a collection of computer-controlled machine tools and transport and handling systems, all integrated via the use of a master computer. This enables the manufacture of small batches of output each modified to suit the requirements of particular market segments, while continuing to obtain manufacturing economies of scale. The essential advantage of flexible manufacturing is that it enables new production specifications to be implemented immediately, thus allowing frequent and rapid modifications to output for different orders (necessary to satisfy the needs of various markets and consumer categories). Further benefits include:

(a) lower stockholding made possible through more precise work scheduling;

(b) reductions in machining times;

(c) less need for control by (highly paid) managers and increased possibilities for tight central administration;

(d) enhanced potential for the integration of marketing and production functions.

Use of flexible manufacturing gives a manufacturing firm a wider range of strategic options.

Robotics

Most flexible manufacturing arrangements rely heavily on robots for routine production. Recent generations of robots incorporate reprogrammable computers that can quickly change the nature of the robot's activities. Hence, the same robot may be used for several different purposes: assembly line work (grasping, machining and moving goods from a fixed position), materials handling (shunting goods from one location to another), clearing up the workplace, spray painting, stamping or otherwise identifying stock items, etc. Use of multi- function robots enables the firm to avoid having to focus on particular styles of manufacturing: varying degrees of precision and quality can be required of the same production line.

9. Implications of flexible manufacturing

Flexible manufacturing has the following implications for firms:

(a) As it is possible to re-program schedules and outputs quickly and inexpensively, so the assembly line of a business using these methods comes to resemble that of a process operation (as in chemicals or food processing for example) rather than mechanical automation of the conventional sort.

(b) A different set of skills, attitudes and competencies is typically required from employees who work in such a system.

(c) Use of robots means (importantly) that workplaces do not have to be designed to suit human needs: they can be as dirty, dangerous and noisy as is necessary, and there is no need for rest areas, toilets, or facilities for workers to interact socially and communicate. Hence, humans do not have to work in these conditions, or to lift heavy weights or undertake dangerous duties. Increasingly jobs will be moved from the factory floor and into the office.

(d) Because the employment of robots is obviously labour saving, the rewards of the enterprise can be shared out among few people. However, deciding who exactly is to receive additional rewards might generate significant conflicts within the organisation.

Computerisation and robotics make it possible to implement dozens (even hundreds) of alterations in product specification simply through reprogramming factory robots – as opposed to having to retrain manual workers. Robots, moreover, can work at levels of intensity and accuracy not physically possible when the work is done by humans.

The question of whether robotics leads to loss of skills within the workforce or whether it actually increases skill levels (through multi-tasking, giving employees a wider range of duties, opportunities for greater workplace autonomy, etc.) is much disputed, and there exists empirical evidence to support either proposition. In general however the operative's role becomes one of monitoring assembly, watching to see that nothing goes wrong. This removes the human drudgery associated with assembly line work and the division of labour, but itself can create boredom and a stressful environment.

10. Computerisation

More general implications of the computerisation of production and wider business processes include the following:

(a) The ratio of managers to human operatives rises dramatically, so that each manager has fewer operatives to control.

(b) Those who operate computerised production systems typically require higher levels of education and training than the traditional manufacturing worker. At the same time, however, the need for conventional craft skills has diminished. Labour flexibility within a computerised working situation requires technologies rather than craftspeople. This has many implications for human resource strategy (see Chapter 11).

(c) Computerisation vastly increases the range and quality of the information potentially available to everyone in the organisation. Hence, traditional dividing lines between occupational categories break down, and the demarcation of jobs can become irrelevant: vertically as well as horizontally.

(d) Old skills are no longer required in certain parts of the enterprise, while new types of skill are required elsewhere, leading perhaps to resentments and conflicts between various categories of worker.

(e) There is total integration of all phases of production, office administration and internal communications, causing more frequent and perhaps closer interactions among employees in different sections of the firm and between various levels in the management hierarchy.

11. Manufacturing and other business functions

Managers in charge of manufacturing sometimes experience conflict with executives from other departments over such matters as:

- whether products should incorporate selling points that are expensive to produce;
- the time periods to be spent in developing, testing and introducing new products;
- the breadth of the firm's product line;
- the frequency of model changes;
- standardisation versus customisation of outputs;
- inventory levels of finished products;
- accuracy of the sales forecasts that determine the volume of production.

It is especially important for manufacturing and marketing to be properly integrated. Strategies for manufacturing and marketing need to be determined co-jointly if only because an overemphasis on the one may easily lead to inflexibility and the setting of infeasible objectives in the other. Integration between manufacturing and marketing might be achieved via:

- joint objective setting;
- collaboration in new product development;
- departmental staff exchanges as a management development exercise;
- creation of project teams containing representatives from both functions;
- precise specification of the markets the firm is to serve (hence facilitating the selection of products to be manufactured and their characteristics);
- incentive systems that reward interfunctional performance, e.g. production staff being penalised for failing to deliver output on time to the firm's customers, or marketing managers losing bonuses if they fail to provide accurate sales forecasts to the manufacturing department;
- having production staff attend sales conferences.

Note how the technical nature of manufacturing can result in inappropriate 'bottom-up' strategies being applied, rather than top-down approaches which take as their starting point the determination of the overall competitive strategy of the enterprise. Engineers, IT specialists, production planners, etc., may possess enormous technical expertise, but equally might focus on mundane production problems at the expense of broader strategic thinking and an innovative management style. A notable problem is that whereas technically excellent (and highly expensive) 'add-ons' to existing technologies may greatly improve current levels of productivity, they can easily lock the firm into working methods that quickly become outdated. Fundamental rethinks of the firm's entire manufacturing philosophy should be undertaken periodically.

12. Time-based competition

'Time-based' manufacturing strategies are those which focus on the rapid development of new models. In other words, firms might prefer to produce new products faster rather than make them better or more cheaply. The rationale for this is that in order to succeed in today's highly competitive world a new product not only needs to possess novel and attractive features; it must also be introduced quickly. Note how product life cycles are shortening significantly for the majority of product categories, with many product offerings now being judged as much on fashion as on any other purchasing criterion. And very many consumers are willing to pay premium prices for recently developed items.

Firms' capacities to engage in time-based competition are greatly facilitated by the use of flexible manufacturing (see 8), which means that they can produce small batches of items customised to meet the requirements of specific groups of customers. Companies employing flexible manufacturing do not need to rely on economies of scale from mass production in order to obtain competitive advantage. Hence frequent introduction to a market of small outputs of alternatives of a core product may be feasible and what the market requires. Advantages claimed for time-based competition include the following:

(a) Accelerating the pace of innovation can generate fresh ideas and thinking that lead to important new inventions.

(b) Firms can behave opportunistically, exploiting lucrative market segments as they appear.

(c) Speeding up the production process generally leads to savings in inventory and working capital.

(d) Parallel sequencing of product development and production activities is often possible.

(e) As research and technical development is so costly, the shorter the period the firm is spending money on this the better. Sometimes an item is 'good enough' even though further technical research on it would be beneficial. Also there is a tendency in certain companies to overload their product research and development departments with too many disparate projects.

Possible disadvantages to time-based competition are that it could lead to inadequate market research and product testing and poor quality output. Also the cost of rapid new product development could be extremely high, and the administrative procedures necessary for time-based competition might be very complex and/or overstretch the organisation's resources.

RESEARCH AND TECHNICAL DEVELOPMENT

13. Nature of research and development (R & D)

R & D concerns the acquisition of new technical knowledge, particularly regarding new products, processes, materials and working methods. Activities might be initiated by the marketing department (having identified new consumer demands) or by the production department as it seeks new methods of manufacture. 'Pure' research is normally funded by the state or an entire industry. Its aims are exploratory and very general; immediately applicable results are not expected. Applied research, in contrast, investigates specific practical questions. Applied work is typically initiated and paid for by the individual firm. The aim of applied research is quick improvement of a particular situation.

'Development' means the practical application of the results of research. Often, development activities require adaptation of the discoveries of other firms. In fact, much work described as research is really development, and few organisations distinguish between the two functions. Scientific and technical staff in the research and development department will be given assignments by senior managers, who must establish priorities for research and development work. This can be difficult since achievements of specific goals can never be guaranteed. Highly paid scientists might be engaged on a project for several years without tangible results.

Large-scale expenditures on research and development are obligatory in the pharmaceuticals industry because patent protection on new pharmaceutical products only lasts a few years. Thereafter anyone may produce the item. Yet the development of a new drug is extremely expensive: years of research are required, and ninety per cent of all prototypes fail prior to human testing. Accordingly, pharmaceuticals companies are constantly competing to attract, retain and motivate the best scientific personnel. One of the world's major pharmaceuticals manufacturers experienced a levelling-off of sales and, realising that it had few marketable new products in the pipeline, faced the imminent need to improve the productivity of its R & D workers and quickly to get a fresh set of drugs into the pipeline. The company adopted the following measures:

(*i*) Improvement of the atmosphere in which research scientists worked. This was achieved by finding out the sorts of working environments they wanted and implementing appropriate measures (pay and benefits were already very good).

(*ii*) Redesign of the communication system linking the firm's R & D workers in its 20 research centres spread around the world.

(*iii*) Contacting senior researchers who had left the company and enquiring why they had resigned.

(*iv*) Decentralising the R & D function in order to reduce bureaucracy, increase local autonomy over decisions concerning the direction of research, and speed up decision-making processes.

(*v*) Splitting research activities into two groups (one for basic research, the other for development) each having its own chief executive empowered to take high-level decisions.

(*vi*) Concentrating related R & D activities into specific research centres in order to avoid duplication of effort.

(*vii*) Including R & D staff in teams assembled to market the final products, and generously rewarding these teams when products eventually reached the market.

14. R & D strategy

The need for research and technical development arises from the dynamic nature of contemporary business and the inescapable fact in many commercial situations that materials and competitors' outputs are constantly improving, leading to a sharp reduction in the average life of the typical product. Strategic decisions concerning R & D include:

(a) the minimum returns that must result from R & D projects in a prespecified time period if the projects are not be be terminated;

(b) whether R & D personnel are to be involved in the determination of overall corporate strategy;

(c) whether to undertake basic or applied research, or a mixture of the two (and if so then in what proportions).

Basic strategic options are as follows:

- Purchase patents and know-how from external sources.
- Seek to invent entirely new products in-house.
- Commission another organisation to invent new products.
- Improve existing products.
- Engage an outside body to develop existing products.

Sometimes, great savings may be achieved through the firm deliberately following the innovative efforts of competitors and (instead of seeking to develop entirely new products to compete with those offered by other firms) simply modifying and – to the extent they are not protected by patent – improving competitor's designs.

Determination of R & D strategy

In determining R & D strategies, management should seek the advice of research scientists, but will need ultimately to take final decisions itself – in the context of the overall strategic objectives of the firm. This could lead to resignations among R & D workers who might bitterly resent being instructed to pursue particular lines of research. But the alternative policy – of allowing R & D scientists to determine research policy and how much to spend – can easily cause the company's liquidation in the medium term. Note moreover that without firm executive control the activities of various researchers might overlap, with consequent duplication of effort and resources.

A good example of a high-tech company that has succeeded without incurring extensive R & D expenditures is Amstrad plc, which chooses to focus instead on design and engineering and the production of mass market consumer items that consumers actually want to buy and not (as Amstrad's *Annual Report* once put it) a 'Boffin's ego trip'! According to major shareholder and chief executive Alan Sugar the company has thrived not on technical innovation but rather on supplying low-priced high-quality products assembled from (predominantly) bought-in components or items made under contract manufacture in the Far East. The firm is not afraid to incorporate 'yesterday's technology' into its outputs, provided the technology is adequate for a particular model. Amstrad is a follower where technical development is concerned, seeking to extract the essential conceptual elements from pioneering products and to repackage them in a manner that enables low-cost production. Manufacturing and assembly occur in locations nearest the main sources of supply of input components for the relevant product.

15. Costs and benefits of R & D

Possible benefits arising from R & D include improvements in the technical aspects of existing products, introduction of new products, and lower costs of production. Whether the greatest benefits accrue to pure or applied research is a perplexing question. Applied developmental research seemingly offers more scope for the immediate application of fresh knowledge, and may itself provide the impetus for major theoretical breakthroughs. Yet truly original thinking – leading to the complete overthrow of an existing technology – might not be possible using a developmental approach.

Unfortunately, the new theories that emerge from pure research may have value only to other theoreticians and be justified solely in academic terms. The sponsoring organisation may have contributed to the advancement of science; but have created no immediately tangible benefits.

Costs of R & D

Each day an R & D project continues it costs money. There is a danger that once a large amount of resources has been invested in a project that has so far been unproductive the firm will continue to fund the project in (possibly hopeless) attempts to recoup its initial investment. The situation is analogous to that of a gambler on a losing streak who gambles increasing heavily on the assumption that his or her luck must eventually change. Specific research and development timetables are thus essential. If targets are not met within a predetermined period or budget limitation then the project should be abandoned, unless there are outstandingly high probabilities of immediate success.

Research costs include salaries, equipment and facilities (laboratories for example) and the consequences of resources possibly being tied up for long periods with no financial return. Note moreover that labour turnover within a research department may be high. Scientists are frequently more interested in the subjects of their research than in building a career with a particular company, and thus might leave the firm when an interesting project has been completed. Retention of high calibre research staff may require the availability of a series of challenging new projects. Hence it might be better to arrange for projects to be completed sequentially rather than concurrently, thus employing fewer staff but accepting that overall research objectives may take longer to achieve.

Evaluation of R & D

Evaluation of R & D is perhaps best achieved through asking a series of questions, such as the following:

(a) Which of the firm's new products are the result of R & D activities?

(b) How does the firm's R & D effort compare with that of competitors?

(c) What would happen if all the organisation's R & D were to cease?

(d) What financial benefits (cost savings, increased sales, etc.) are directly attributable to R & D?

It is essential that the benefits of an R & D project be predicted at its inception, and budgetary constraints imposed in line with this prediction. Otherwise, one line of unproductive research might lead to other equally fruitless investigations which seek to correct deficiencies in the initial project. Nevertheless, the decision to terminate a project should not be taken lightly, and the long-term implications of the termination must be carefully evaluated. Will it result, for example, in the company losing market share? (This may actually be acceptable in comparison with enormous and escalating research expenditures.) Does termination mean that existing plant and processes are doomed to obsolescence? What are the implications for other research and investment projects?

16. Design

For many firms, product design is so important as a success factor that it is necessarily a strategic issue. Strategic decisions regarding design might be taken by a committee comprising representatives from the marketing, production, finance and design departments, hence ensuring that designs are saleable, cost effective and technically feasible. The composition of products should be analysed, since new methods or materials for their manufacture may have become available since the products were first conceived, thus creating fresh design possibilities.

Design can affect a product's life cycle in that planned obsolescence can be built into a design to ensure that corrosion, wear and tear, fatigue and vibration, etc., eventually cause the product to fail within a predetermined period (so that it needs replacement). Aesthetically innovative designs may appeal (initially) to large numbers of consumers but could lead to short product life cycles – especially as competitors copy the design and incorporate different and cheaper inputs to the product's construction. Further considerations are as follows:

(a) Whether the design finally selected will create special inspection or quality control difficulties.

(b) The extent of after-sales service and routine maintenance.

(c) Relations between design, material inputs and product reliability – appealing designs might create structural deficiencies that cause problems for users. There are several examples of this having occurred with aircraft, motor car and building designs.

(d) Whether the environment in which the product is to operate is likely to change over time.

Two basic considerations determine a product's design: the need for efficiency in manufacture, and its appeal to customers. Design is often undertaken in a separate section or department which is responsible for translating marketing or engineering ideas into practical specifications. Designers are able to control many variables: quality of the finished product, machining tolerances, processing time, and aesthetic characteristics. Equally, designers face numerous constraints in relation to costs, market acceptability, and available resources. Note moreover that customers may want high quality output, including a complex and visually appealing design, but not be prepared to pay the price necessitated by the cost of manufacturing such a product.

PROCUREMENT

17. The purchasing department

The role of a purchasing department is to procure the right goods, at the right time, in the correct quantities, at the right price. A department can be organised according to types of material purchased, or by particular areas of operation. In the former case, each purchasing officer buys just one variety of product, and thus develops intimate knowledge of the good and its suppliers. Otherwise, purchasing officers supply all the requirements of a specific department or production line, covering many different product categories. Staff collect current price lists, catalogues, details of delivery times, and data on materials availability. The department should be capable of obtaining emergency supplies at short notice (even at significantly higher procurement cost). Purchasing officers will constantly be on the lookout for new sources of supply and cheaper, better, or quicker deliveries.

Purchasing can be centralised or decentralised. In a decentralised system, each department is responsible for obtaining its own supplies. Here 'local' staff – with detailed knowledge of immediate requirements – place orders without reference to a central control. The method is quick and convenient, but does not allow bulk purchases; and higher prices may be paid through ignorance of alternative sources. Centralised procedures enable the employment of specialised buying staff who can pinpoint the best available products, prices and delivery dates. Note also that apart from advantages relating to purchase price, bulk buying allows customers to specify minimum quality standards and perhaps even design requirements. Centralised systems moreover can apply common administrative procedures and documentation to all buying activities. Close liaison between a central purchasing unit and user department is essential – buyers not attached to specific functional departments may be tempted to substitute cheaper but inferior goods for those really required. Purchasing officers should never ignore user departments' requests for supplies of a particular type simply because of procurement expediency.

18. Make or buy decisions

A major decision is what goods to purchase and which to make. A firm that produces its own components enjoys complete control over their specification, design, quality and time of delivery. Also, there is no profit margin as with supplies purchased from outside. External suppliers however will normally have produced far more units of output than those delivered to the individual purchasing firm, and thus will experience scale economies (and hence lower costs) not possible in firms producing their own components. Moreover, internal production of supplies often requires additional investments in manufacturing plant, and extra labour might have to be employed. A firm could invest heavily in plant and equipment needed for component manufacture only to find that outside firms offer these components for sale at prices lower than internal production costs.

Factors relevant to the decision include:

(a) costs of labour, raw materials, overheads, capacity usage and overheads;

(b) quality of purchased inputs and security of supplies;

(c) set-up costs for each production run;

(d) the need to protect intellectual property. For example, the staff of an outside firm commissioned to supply highly specialised components might be able to infer the characteristics of the main product to which the component is an input, and the purchasing company might want to keep these details secret;

(e) whether management wishes to maintain continuity of employment for the firm's workers.

A UK telephone and cable manufacturing company produced in-house around 100,000 units of a certain input component annually. One of the firm's regular suppliers developed a new method of making the component, which it offered to supply at a price nearly 20 per cent lower than the cable company's internal unit manufacturing cost (including overheads and raw materials). However, the company decided not to abandon in-house manufacture of the component, for the following reasons:

(a) The component was an essential element of a product vital to the continuing success of the business. Outside purchase would cause the firm to become dependent on a single supplier that it did not control.

(b) Additional testing equipment would have to be purchased to monitor the quality of the outside supplier's components.

(c) The machinery currently producing the item had a remaining life of five years, and no alternative uses. It could only be sold for a negligible scrap value. Tax allowances were being claimed on existing machinery and these would be lost if in-house production ceased.

(d) At present the company was able to make the component to order, in whatever batch sizes were required. The outside supplier would only produce and deliver batches of at least 25,000 items, implying significant stockholding costs. Also the warehouse space that would be occupied by the inventory was badly needed for other purposes.

(e) Employees engaged on in-house manufacture of the component would have to be made redundant or retrained and redeployed, again at considerable expense to the company.

FACTORY LOCATION

19. Selection of a location

Selection of a location for a manufacturing unit is a major strategic decision. Factors relevant to the choice normally include the following:

(a) Finance. Availability of long-term funds (greenfield sites normally require more start-up capital than the development of existing manufacturing facilities); government grants, subsidiaries and tax reliefs in various regions.

(b) Labour. Amount of skilled labour in the area. Local wage levels. Training facilities in nearby colleges.

(c) Ancillary services. Extent of local service industries, consultants, distributors, etc.

(d) Operational factors. Access to raw materials. Adequacy of energy supplies, water, road and rail networks, etc.

Once a location decision has been taken the firm commits itself to major capital expenditures. The establishment cannot be relocated in the short term.

It might be possible to extend an existing plant and/or locate a new factory alongside the present one. This may secure economies of scale, but might not be appropriate if the firm's markets are spread around the country (or throughout other nations).

20. Leasing and buying

A critically important decision is whether to lease or buy premises. Indeed, it may dominate all other criteria. Outright purchase of premises means the owner benefits from increases in the capital value of the property. Also, owned premises can be offered as security against loans. Conversely, leasehold premises require no capital outlay, and (of course) they cannot be seized by creditors if the business fails.

Tenants face restrictions on how they may use premises. They cannot make structural alterations, and they are not normally allowed to sublet. Rents will be increased periodically and the lease will occasionally have to be renewed. However, it is often easier to rent than to buy, and tenants are not usually responsible for maintenance. Also, if a rented building turns out to be unsuitable – either physically or because of restrictions on traffic, noise, local authority limits on working hours, etc. – then the business can cancel its lease and move to another location.

Acquisitions versus new business start-ups

The advantages of buying a local business outright – rather than incorporating an entirely new company – include the avoidance of start-up delays and expenses; immediate possession of a functioning administrative structure; and possibly the acquisition of an existing distribution system with staff, transport vehicles, etc. On the other hand, the acquired business will have to be integrated into the purchaser's current organisation system, and implementing changes in the purchased firm's management methods may prove difficult. Acquisition strategies are discussed in Chapter 3.

Sale and leaseback arrangements

Businesses that own their premises can inject much needed capital through 'sale and leaseback' arrangements. The firm sells its land and buildings for a capital sum equal to or just below their market value, but makes the transaction contingent on the purchaser formally agreeing to lease the land and buildings back to the selling firm for a certain period at a predetermined rent. Such a deal is not without costs – there are legal expenses and valuation fees, capital gains tax (possibly) on the disposal, the rent charged may be relatively high, and the firm loses its security of tenure.

CONTRACT MANUFACTURING, LICENSING AND THE PROTECTION OF INTELLECTUAL PROPERTY

21. Contract manufacturing

Instead of manufacturing items in its own factories, a firm might place orders with other businesses for the production of output which it then sells. This is known as 'contract manufacture', and has a number of advantages, such as:

(a) easy withdrawal from markets that do not live up to expectations;

(b) not having to invest large sums of money in capital equipment;

(c) the ability to dovetail local manufacture with local distribution systems;

(d) the potential to undertake large-scale operations from a small capital base;

(e) avoidance of involvement in industrial relations with manufacturing workforces.

Contract manufacturing is particularly suitable for companies with high-level marketing skills and facilities but little experience of physical production. Other reasons for resort to contract manufacture include the firm's existing production facilities being overloaded; the non-availability of suitable licensees in foreign markets; or in consequence of foreign government imposed barriers and prohibitions on other forms of entry. Problems with contract manufacture include the difficulties of monitoring and maintaining quality levels, of protecting any intellectual property embodied within the manufactured item, and preventing the other firm setting up in competition (perhaps covertly) once it has acquired expertise in making the product. Note moreover that the company to which the contract is awarded may require substantial technical back-up, possibly extending to the training of its employees.

22. Protection of intellectual property

The term 'intellectual property' covers rights over patents on inventions, trademarks, industrial designs and models, literary works, computer software, and any other copyright material. Protection of intellectual property is obviously important for firms concerned with research and development and new product innovation, and measures to safeguard intellectual property legally are often required. A common method for protecting the intellectual property of firms that wish to have others produce their outputs is through a licensing agreement.

Types of licence

Licensing agreements come in a number of forms. An 'assignment' requires the firm to hand over all its intellectual property rights in relation to a particular patent, trademark, design, or whatever to a licensee. The latter may then use these rights as it wishes. If the firm issues a 'sole licence', it retains rights but agrees not to extend licences to anyone other than a single licensee during the period of the agreement. 'Exclusive' licences require licensors not to use their patents, trademarks, etc., for their own businesses while licensing contracts are in force, leaving these rights entirely to licensees for pre-specified periods. Non-exclusive licences allow licensors to distribute licences to several licensees simultaneously. 'Know-how licensing' means the licensing of confidential but non-patented technical knowledge. 'Franchising' is a form of licensing whereby the franchisee adopts the parent company's entire business format: its name, trademarks, business methods, layout of premises, etc. The franchisor provides (in return for a royalty and lump sum fee) a variety of supplementary management services: training, technical advice, stock control systems, perhaps even financial loans. Hence it retains complete control over how the product is marketed, but the franchisee carries all the risks of failure, and the franchisor's capital commitment is typically low.

23. Advantages and disadvantages of licensing

The advantages of licensing are:

(a) No capital investment is necessary.

(b) Licensees avoid research and development costs, while acquiring experience of manufacturing the item.

(c) The licensor has complete legal control over its intellectual property.

(d) A manufacturing capability can be quickly established in an unfamiliar market.

(e) Licensees carry some of the risk of failure.

(f) The nucleus of the parent organisation can remain small, have low overheads yet control extensive operations.

Disadvantages to licensing are:

(a) Profits are sacrificed through allowing other firms to make the parent company's goods.

(b) The risk of a licensee company setting up in competition once it has learned all the licensor's production methods and trade secrets and the licence period has expired;

(c) Possible ambiguities and interpretation difficulties *vis-à-vis* minimum and/or maximum output levels, territory covered, basis of royalty payments (including the frequency of payment and the currency to be used), and the circumstances under which the agreement may be terminated.

(d) Deciding how to control the licensee in relation to quality standards, declaration of production levels, and methods of marketing the product.

(e) Problems arising if the licensee turns out to be less competent than first expected.

TOTAL QUALITY MANAGEMENT

24. Quality management

Quality management is often thought of in terms of statistical quality control – of tolerance and other specifications, acceptability ratios, random sampling, probability calculations, and so on. And many industries adopt 'scientific' approaches to quality matters – with close supervision of employees, specialisation and the division of labour, narrow job and output specifications, and the frequent checking of work. Yet quality 'management', as opposed to simple quality control, covers far wider issues. Note particularly that the quality of output in companies which apply 'scientific' quality control methods is often no better than in others. Workers who manage the quality of their own output save the cost of inspectors, and become inescapably involved with the quality effort of the organisation as a whole. Inevitably, some defective work will occur; yet its quantity need not exceed that normally experienced when independent inspectors are employed. Note, moreover, how quality levels invariably settle just above the minimum acceptable standards whenever minimal criteria are specified.

25. Approaches to quality management

The modern approach to quality management is to attempt to integrate practical techniques for controlling quality (inspection, statistical quality control, etc.) with the overall strategies and tactics of the firm. In particular, TQM aims to create within the organisation a culture that is conducive to the continuous improvement of quality. It focuses on the totality of the system rather than its individual parts, seeking to identify the causes of failure rather than the simple fact that failures have occurred. Great emphasis is placed on teamwork, leadership, motivation of employees, the bonding of workers to the employing firm, and the direct involvement of operatives in solving technical and/or equipment problems.

Similar concepts can be applied to the purchase of outside supplies. Indeed, it is arguable that the very act of laying down precise acceptance criteria itself implies that some defective input is acceptable provided certain predetermined minimum standards are met. In this case inspection becomes a source of low quality!

26. Quality assurance (QA)

Quality assurance concerns the total system needed to assure customers that certain minimum quality standards will be satisfied within the supplying firm. Formal QA standards have been drafted by various bodies (including the British Standards Institute's BS 5750) which specify that supplying firms must implement definite procedures for ensuring that appropriate 'quality environments' are maintained, e.g. that the tools used on certain jobs be of a particular type, and that only qualified and certified staff be employed on certain projects. Often, QA is implemented through checklists issued to various departments asking them to scrutinise their procedures and confirm that certain measures have been undertaken. Typically, a checklist question will ask, 'What have you done to ensure that ....?' and then ask the respondent to detail the measures applied.

A QA system might invite supplying firms to improve as well as provide contracted items, and to initiate themselves alterations in the appearance, design or durability of requisitioned products. The quality of a good involves its fitness for the purpose for which it is intended as well as its physical conditions on despatch. Suppliers need therefore to know the purposes of the articles they are invited to produce, and the operational circumstances of their use. Hence, a clear statement of purpose – leaving technical details (including perhaps the choice of input materials) to the discretion of the supplying firm – might have greater long term value than precise and detailed specifications of weights, sizes, machine tolerances, etc.

27. ISO 9000

BS 5750 is the UK version of the international quality assurance standard ISO 9000, which itself is based in large part on BS 5750. The latter is a detailed and extensive document with several parts and appendices. It requires the supplier to demonstrate its ability to design and supply products in predetermined ways.

Apart from design procedures, the specification covers the supplier's own procurement systems: its inspection and testing methods, the means by which customers may verify its claimed quality systems, how customers can check the supplier's records and other documents relating to quality procedures and how customers may confirm the nature and extent of quality related training given to the supplier's staff. The aim of BS 5750 is to provide suppliers with a means for obtaining BSI certificated approval that their quality management systems are up to scratch. Customers may then have confidence in a company's ability (i) to deliver goods of a prespecified quality and (ii) to maintain the quality of its output at a consistent level. This should increase the saleability of the firm's outputs. Further advantages to BS 5750 certification are that it:

- demonstrates the company's commitment to quality;
- requires the standardisation of quality procedures throughout the organisation;
- facilitates the identification of problem areas;
- improves the image of the firm;
- may increase operational efficiency;
- leads to greater awareness of customer needs;
- can cause staff to be better motivated.

Problems with BS 5750 include the following:

(a) The financial cost to a business of altering its (perhaps perfectly reasonable) quality control methods to meet BS 5750 may be colossal in relation to the overall improvement in quality that results.

(b) So called 'consultants' may attest that, in their opinion, certain firms within which they have installed QA systems now satisfy BS 5750 standards, and issue documents to that effect. Unsuspecting members of the public might confuse such attestation with that formally recognised by BSI.

(c) Firms seeking BS 5750 accreditation themselves determine the level of quality of output. BS 5750 applies to the procedures for maintaining a certain quality level, even if the quality of the final output is intentionally low.

(d) Maintenance of a new system based on BS 5750 can be expensive and time consuming.

(e) Procedures might become bureaucratic and inflexible.

(f) Staff affected by implementation may react negatively to change.

Progress test 13

1. What are the purposes of a manufacturing strategy?

2. List some of the duties typically undertaken in a production department.

3. Define technology.

4. What are the purposes of product standardisation?

5. Explain the concept of the focused factory.

6. How does the use of industrial robots facilitate the application of flexible manufacturing?

7. What is meant by the term 'time-based competition'?

8. Explain the difference between pure research and applied research.

9. What factors are relevant to the question of whether a business should make or buy its own input components?

10. List some of the advantages of buying an existing business outright rather than incorporating an entirely new company.

11. What is intellectual property?

12. State the problems associated with implementing BS 5750.

14

STRATEGIES FOR THE INTERNATIONALISATION OF OPERATIONS

1. Reasons for internationalisation

A number of factors can induce a company to begin operating internationally, including:

(a) a saturated domestic market and/or lucrative opportunities abroad;

(b) intense competition in the home market but none in certain foreign countries;

(c) the sight of foreign competitors entering the home market. As the world becomes 'smaller' in business terms, domestic customers are more likely to look abroad for suppliers;

(d) opportunities for new product development which, in today's world, typically requires so much expenditure that in many cases firms intending to introduce new products must adopt an international perspective. Also the higher turnover derived from international sales might enable a firm to initiate new product research and development that in the long term will give it a competitive edge. Corporate plans can be anchored against a wider range of (international) opportunities.

Many firms entering foreign markets for the first time do so in the hope that economies of scale will result from more extensive operations. Note however that scale economies might not be available if national consumer tastes and other characteristics in various countries necessitate numerous product modifications – depending on the product involved and its method of manufacture. Also the costs of market entry (advertising and promotion, establishment of distribution networks and so on) could themselves outweigh production savings. Further reasons for firms becoming involved in international operations are as follows:

(a) Sudden collapse in market demand in one country may be offset by expansions in others.

(b) Opportunities afforded by the completion of the European Single Market, the opening up of fresh markets in Eastern Europe, and the establishment of free trade areas in many of the world's major trading regions.

(c) Consumers in some foreign markets might be much wealthier and free-spending than consumers in the firm's own country.

(d) Internationalisation of business is today much easier to organise than previously. International telephone and fax facilities to 'remote' regions are much better than in the past; facilities for international business travel are more extensive; and business service firms (advertising agencies, market research companies, road hauliers, etc.) are to be found in all countries.

Doing business in foreign markets exposes a firm's management to fresh ideas and different approaches to solving problems. Individual executives develop their general management skills and personal effectiveness; become innovative and adopt broader horizons. The contacts and experience acquired through selling abroad can give a firm a competitive edge in its home country.

2. Production standardisation versus product differentiation

A fundamental decision that has to be taken by firms operating internationally is whether to supply to foreign markets the firm's existing product, or modify the product to suit the needs of each foreign country. Product modification is appropriate where there exist:

(a) significant differences in local consumer taste;

(b) intense competition in foreign markets (creating the need to differentiate a firm's output from that of foreign rivals);

(c) special local requirements in relation to package size, technical standards, consumer protection laws and customer care facilities;

(d) differences in local climate, living conditions, literacy and technical skill level of users, customer buying habits, incomes (buyers in poor countries might need low quality products), and in the uses to which the product might be put in various markets.

Hopefully product modification will increase worldwide sales of the firm's core products through (i) the satisfaction of different customer needs in various regions, (ii) retention of existing customers by keeping the product up-to-date, and (iii) matching the product attributes offered by competing firms. Complementary products might be introduced to stimulate sales of existing lines, e.g. by improving the usefulness of currently produced items (gardening tools or DIY power accessories for example). The need for extensive product modification is a common impetus for firms to establish local manufacturing or assembly facilities in foreign countries, as it could well be cheaper to set up a new establishment to produce what is essentially a new product near to end consumers rather than make major changes to existing production lines and procedures at home.

The case for standardisation

A number of problems apply to product modification, notably:

(a) Extra promotional costs have to be incurred.

(b) There is duplication of effort within the business.

(c) The company may possess insufficient experience and technical know-how of different products and how to market them.

(d) Technical research and development efforts might become fragmented as increasing amounts of resources are devoted to issues pertaining to the special requirements of particular national markets.

Supplying a single unmodified product can provide several advantages: economies of scale in production, concentration of technical research into a limited area, standardisation of marketing and distribution methods, fewer staff training requirements, and so on. It leads to reduced stockholding costs (because demand in any market can be met from a single inventory of the same item), facilitates the development of technical expertise in a narrow area, and allows the interchangeability of spare parts and input components between supply points in various locations. Accordingly, firms sometimes attempt to create universal products (hopefully) suitable for all markets in all regions. This might be suitable where:

(a) the essential need that the product aims to satisfy is basically the same in all national and market segments;

(b) after-sales service is easily standardised;

(c) there exists a large market across several countries and cultural differences do not necessitate adaptation;

(d) the product has a strong international brand image. Note how a particular national image can help sell an unmodified product in several markets. Japanese goods, for instance, are generally regarded as reliable, high quality and technically excellent: positive images that will help an overtly Japanese item to sell in any country.

3. International business

International business is more than exporting, because it could involve a company in the selling in foreign countries of goods locally part-manufactured or assembled on the firm's behalf; or in the import to one foreign country of goods from a second foreign country for subsequent local sale or for re-export; or the establishment of permanent establishments in foreign nations in order to warehouse and distribute products; licensing and franchising of the firm's products to local businesses; or other more general business activities in foreign states. An 'international' firm may be defined as one that engages in business across particular national frontiers. Some international businesses progress to become 'multinational corporations' (MNCs), which consciously integrate their entire worldwide activities rather than tackling particular foreign markets one by one. The MNC will pursue global strategies in relation to production, investment and marketing, and derive a significant proportion of its total revenue from foreign operations. Indeed some authorities define an MNC as any business which derives a minimum of 20 per cent of its net profits from operating abroad. Thus, an MNC will seek to maximise its revenues on the world rather than national level, locating operations wherever conditions are most favourable and regardless of the country in which the company's head office is based.

MNCs need not be large corporations; rather they are firms of any size that recognise the benefits of operating on the global level. MNCs can reduce their sourcing and distribution costs compared to national businesses, can avoid tariffs, quotas and other trade barriers faced by exporters, and are able periodically to shift operations from high cost to low cost countries. Their managements plan, organise and control company operations on a worldwide scale, with national markets being regarded as little more than segments of a broader regional customer base.

Technologies are developed in whichever countries have the necessary skills, research infrastructures and facilities; while finished goods, raw materials, component parts, know-how and managerial personnel are freely exchanged among operating units.

4. Organisation of MNCs

The organisational problem confronting an MNC is how best to integrate its worldwide operations within a single administrative system that optimises the use of company resources and enables it to take full advantage of opportunities wherever they arise. A range of organisational models may be applied as follows.

(a) *International divisional structure.* Here the firm sets up divisions to furnish support services for marketing, manufacture, finance, distribution, etc., to the company's operating units throughout the world. Divisions themselves may be organised along centralised or decentralised lines. International divisions provide the firm with a convenient device for developing a multinational strategy, and decisions on international matters are taken at the heart of the enterprise. Divisions acquire experience and expertise in international business.

Disadvantages to this form of organisation are its possible inability to handle extremely diverse international operations; the potential for conflict between domestic international divisions; and the risk that senior management at head office will not take the international divisions seriously.

(b) *International subsidiary structure.* The company establishes a number of subsidiary units each responsible for developing a particular market and for co-ordinating the firm's activities within it. However the parent organisation undertakes all major functional activities (usually including production) for the company's global operations. This is a simple and inexpensive approach to international organisation, which provides for local responses to changes in local conditions while maintaining effective central control. It is useful, moreover, for the training and development of managers within subsidiary boards.

Problems with the approach include the need for extensive liaison and co-ordination, and the tendency for subsidiary boards to mirror (perhaps inappropriately) the structure of the main company. Incorrect strategies might be imposed on subsidiaries, and local managers could lose sight of the global objectives of the organisation.

(c) *Product structure.* This involves the firm setting up a separate division for each of its products. The system is appropriate for organisations that supply several unrelated types of product or where significant product modifications for various markets are required. Product structure is useful for management development. Each product division will be a cost centre in its own right.

Problems with product structure are that the importance of marketing might not be properly recognised, and that important regions could be overlooked. Moreover, co-ordination across product divisions may be difficult.

(d) *Geographic structure.* Here the company establishes regional divisions, each responsible for a certain part of the globe (Europe, South America, the Pacific Rim, etc.). Strategies are determined at headquarters, leaving regional managements in day-to-day control. Operations can be specifically designed to suit regional conditions. Geographic structure is commonest when the countries covered by a division are in close proximity and the same product is being marketed in the area concerned. The system is clear, logical and easy to apply. There is close co-ordination between production and marketing, and local conditions are taken into account. However, it becomes difficult for managers to adopt a totally international perspective on the enterprise's worldwide activities and there could be insufficient emphasis on new-product development.

(e) *Matrix structure.* This offers a means for balancing geographic and product requirements. It is suitable for fast-changing environments and/or when complex decisions have to be made. The matrix can define groups responsible for various aspects of international operations, cutting across conventional departmental bounds. Advantages and disadvantages of matrix structure are discussed in 7:**24**.

Choice of structure

Final selection of the form of organisational structure for an MNC should depend on the following factors:

(a) The number, size, types and complexity of operating units in various countries.

(b) Ability levels and experience of the MNC's staff in each country, especially their capacities to think strategically and plan for the long term.

(c) Ease of communication with and control of operating units.

(d) Availability of local finance and other resources.

(e) Stability of local markets (the more uncertain the local market, the greater the need for local control).

Note how a straightforward functional structure (see 7.16) is not normally appropriate for an MNC, because each functional department would need to deal with several disparate territories, all possessing unique problems and characteristics.

5. MNC staffing policies

Firms with extensive multinational operations must decide whether to recruit staff in host countries, or rely entirely on expatriate personnel. Locally-recruited managers possess intimate knowledge of local conditions, but might not be of the same calibre as managers brought in from outside. Equally, managers who are recruited within and are nationals of the MNC's home country might not be competent to run all the corporation's foreign operations. There may be language problems, cultural differences between regions that home country managers cannot understand, and general lack of knowledge of foreign business conditions.

Special problems apply to recruitment in underdeveloped economies, since these might not possess the education and training facilities that generate within advanced economies technically qualified and experienced managerial staff.

6. Transfer pricing

Transfer pricing means the determination of the 'prices' at which an MNC moves goods between its subsidiaries in various countries. A crucial feature of large centralised MNCs is their ability to engage in transfer pricing at artificially high or low prices. To illustrate, consider an MNC which extracts raw materials in one country, uses them as production inputs in another, assembles the partly finished goods in a third, and finishes and sells them in a fourth. The governments of the extraction, production and assembly countries will have sales or value added taxes; while the production, assembly and finished goods countries will impose tariffs on imports of goods. Suppose the MNC values its goods at zero prior to their final sale at high prices. The government of the extraction country receives no revenue from sales taxes because the MNC's subsidiary in that country is selling its output to the same MNC's subsidiary in the production country at a price of zero. Equally the production country raises no income from import tariffs on this transaction because the raw materials are imported at zero price! The only tax the MNC pays is a sales tax in the last country in the chain. Transfer pricing at unacceptably low values has been a major problem for many developing nations. Sometimes, therefore, the government of the country in which an MNC operates will insist that a government official shall decide the price at which the MNC exports its output, and not employees of the MNC itself. Thus, the government of the host country will ensure that it receives an appropriate amount of sales tax. Similarly, importing countries might impose quantity-based instead of price-based import duties to ensure a reasonable revenue from taxes on imports of an MNC's goods.

Tax considerations aside, transfer prices need to be realistic in order that the profitabilities of various international operations may be assessed. Possible criteria for setting the transfer price include:

(a) the price at which the item could be sold on the open market (this is known as 'arms length' transfer pricing);

(b) cost of production or acquisition;

(c) acquisition/production cost plus a profit markup (note the problem here of deciding what constitutes an appropriate profit markup);

(d) senior management's perceptions of the value of the item to the firm's overall international operations;

(e) political negotiations between the units involved (a high or low transfer price can drastically affect the observed profitability of a subsidiary). Note the problems that arise if the 'buyer' happens to be the head office of the firm.

Normally the solution adopted is that which (seemingly) maximises profits for the company taken as a whole and which best facilitates the parent firm's control over subsidiary operations. Arm's length pricing (see above) is the method generally preferred by national governments and is recommended in a 1983 Code of Practice on the subject drafted by the Organisation for Economic Co-operation and Development (OECD). Note how a subsidiary that charges a high transfer price will accumulate cash, which might be invested more profitably in the selling country than elsewhere.

Problems with setting a realistic transfer price are as follows:

(a) Differences in the accounting systems used by subsidiaries in different countries.

(b) Executives in operating units deliberately manipulating the transfer price to enhance the book value of a subsidiary's profits.

(c) Disparate tax rates and investment subsidy levels in various countries.

(d) Possible absence of competition in local markets at various stages in the supply chain. Thus a 'market price' in such an area may be artificially high in consequence of the lack of local competition.

(e) There might not be any other product directly comparable to the item in question, again making it difficult to establish a market price.

(f) If a price is set at too high a level the 'selling' unit will be able to attain its profit targets too easily (at the expense of the 'buyer') and lead perhaps to idleness and inefficiency in the selling subsidiary.

Special problems arise when goods are being transferred among the partners of a joint venture. Should the various members of the venture be regarded as 'subsidiaries' or as independent businesses required to pay a market price?

MARKET ENTRY

Firms can enter foreign markets through a variety of methods, including exporting, joint ventures, licensing and franchising, establishment of foreign branches and subsidiaries, and direct foreign investment. The degree of risk that has to be assumed and the level of finance necessary varies from option to option (see Figure 14.1).

7. Exporting

Exporting means the sale abroad of an item produced, stored or processed in the supplying firm's home country. Some firms regard exporting as merely a convenient way of increasing total sales; others see it as a crucial element of overall corporate strategy. 'Passive' exporting occurs when a firm receives orders from abroad without having canvassed them. 'Active' exporting, conversely, results from a strategic decision to establish proper systems for organising the export function and for procuring foreign sales. Exporting may be direct or indirect. With direct exporting the exporter assumes full responsibility for transfer to foreign destinations, for customs clearance, local advertising and final sale of the goods. Indirect exporting uses intermediaries. *Export merchants*, for example, reside in the exporter's country, acting as principals in export transactions (that is, buying and selling on their own accounts). They are wholesalers who operate in foreign markets through their own salespeople, stockists and, perhaps, retail outlets. Exporters are relieved of administrative problems, documentation, shipping, internal transport and so on, and do not carry the risks of market failure. However, they lose control over the presentation of their products, and foreign sales may fall because of poor foreign retailing.

8. Advantages and disadvantages of exporting

Exporting is cheap and convenient to administer and carries no risk of failure of direct foreign investments. The revenues from foreign sales accrue entirely to the exporting company (rather than it having to repatriate profits from foreign subsidiaries), and the firm builds up a network of contacts with foreign agents, distributors, retail outlets, etc. Direct exporting provides total control over the selling process; avoids the need to share know-how with foreign partners; and cuts out expensive intermediaries. Exporting can be highly profitable, although the development of an export facility can place a severe strain on the business's resources.

Sound reasons for not actively exporting include:

(a) cost of financing long periods between obtaining export orders, delivering the goods to distant destinations, and getting paid;

(b) problem of acquiring and retaining staff competent to undertake the extensive paperwork associated with international marketing (except for EU firms selling within the Union) and possessing the linguistic and specialist foreign trade skills necessary for selling abroad;

HIGH RISK / HIGH OUTLAY

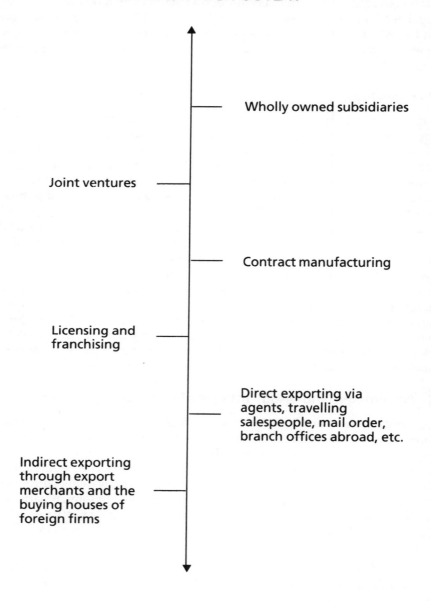

Wholly owned subsidiaries

Joint ventures

Contract manufacturing

Licensing and franchising

Direct exporting via agents, travelling salespeople, mail order, branch offices abroad, etc.

Indirect exporting through export merchants and the buying houses of foreign firms

LOW RISK / LOW OUTLAY

Figure 14.1 Market entry options

(c) managerial resources necessary to have people visit foreign markets regularly, monitor and control agents and distributors, meet important customers, attend foreign exhibitions, etc.;

(d) costs and inconvenience of finding foreign agents and distributors and of investigating the market characteristics and trading rules of various foreign countries;

(e) difficulty of forecasting sales in foreign countries rather than in the firm's home nation. Sales forecasting can be far more difficult for foreign countries than in the firm's home base. Changes in the political, legal, social and economic superstructure of other nations are hard to predict, as are the behaviours of actual and potential competing companies;

(f) higher degree of risk typically involved in selling abroad than in the home country.

Note moreover that the resources needed to sell abroad might be more profitably employed in building up the home market, and that foreign sales may encourage a company to delay introducing new products and/or to ignore the threat of domestic competition. Direct exporting in particular takes time (to establish the necessary procedures), money and commitment The firm needs to be willing to adapt its products to meet foreign requirements and to research the needs and characteristics of foreign customers. Failure to devote sufficient resources to active exporting can result in disaster. Common problems experienced with exporting are:

(a) A firm's export department might not be taken seriously by senior management. Note how export managers are necessarily involved in a wide range of functions: foreign market research, negotiation of agency and distribution contracts, product modification for foreign markets, liaison with foreign advertising media, transport, arranging the clearance of letters of credit, packaging, organising after-sales service in foreign countries, and so on. Export management, therefore, should be seen as a responsible and demanding function worthy of high status within the organisation.

(b) In consequence of its self-contained nature the export department might pursue its own objectives rather than those of the wider enterprise.

(c) Staff possessing the requisite (specialist and wide-ranging) export skills are difficult to recruit. A frequently experienced difficulty is that foreign sales increase substantially, but without any attempt to enlarge and reconstitute the export department, resulting in its staff assuming every widening responsibilities for which they are not properly prepared.

9. Use of intermediaries

The engagement of intermediaries to handle the export of a company's products has a number of advantages, including:

(a) their expert knowledge of export markets and procedures. Intermediaries

267

may be more objective when assessing the probabilities of the exporter's products succeeding in various foreign markets. Their wide-ranging experience of the export problems of other firms and industries enables them to identify solutions quickly, and to appreciate all the options available and the difficulties involved;

(b) not having to train in-house staff in the details of the export function;

(c) savings on the overheads associated with a large export department;

(d) the fact that intermediaries are driven by the need to make a profit (rather than simply drawing an employee's salary);

(e) their extensive contacts with other specialists in the export field.

The exporting firm need not possess any knowledge of export methods and procedures, or assume any financial risk of non-payment. It does not require a foreign sales organisation or visits to foreign markets. The disadvantages are the cost, and loss of control over final selling prices and marketing methods.

10. An in-house export department

Advantages to having the firm's in-house staff assume total control over exports include the accumulation of skill within the export department and (hopefully) employees' genuine commitment to expanding export sales. Staff should possess detailed knowledge of all aspects of the company's products and operations; control is straightforward, and there is continuity in the personnel employed on export work. Use of in-house facilities is perhaps most appropriate where (i) the firm has a limited number of clearly identified customers, (ii) the costs of export marketing are easily controlled, and (iii) little after-sales service is required. In-house staff know exactly where to look for information within the company and (importantly) are fully accountable for their actions in the long term: their careers within the organisation substantially depend on the success of their work. Disadvantages to using in-house staff include the following:

(a) Internal employees are not subject to penetrating expert criticism from outside. Mistakes made by in-house employees in consequence of lack of specialist skills and knowledge might never be revealed.

(b) Staff usually have limited experience of other industries and firms.

(c) Internal staff might be apathetic and lack the management skills and innovative attitudes needed to complete an unusual or exceptionally difficult project on time.

(d) The export department might become obsessed with export methods and procedures, regardless of the profitability of export sales.

11. Agents and distributors

Agents differ from distributors in that whereas the latter actually *purchase* a supplying firm's products (assuming thereby full responsibility for their condition, sale, and any bad debts), agents put their clients in touch with third parties but then 'drop out' of resulting contracts – so that the agreements are between the agent's client and third parties, without the agent being further involved. An agent will (for a commission) find foreign customers for a company's products, but if the goods are defective, damaged or delivered late it is the client and not the agent who is responsible. In practice, however, the distinction between an agency and a distribution agreement can become blurred, especially if the agent takes physical control over the goods. Distributors typically demand exclusivity. Note how exclusivity clauses in a distribution agreement can create legal difficulties, because exclusive trading arrangements are not generally permitted under the competition laws of most industrialised nations. Advantages to using agents rather than distributors are that agents (i) are subject to direct control, (ii) can conduct or commission local market research on behalf of the client firm, and (iii) can arrange for long-term customer care services. The advantages to using distributors, conversely, include:

- less (costly) supervision by the supplying firm;
- assumption by the distributor of full responsibility for selling the item;
- possibly a 'local' image for the goods;
- fewer credit risks;
- the supplier not having to pay for the long-term storage of the goods.

Note however that the contract between supplier and distributor can specify precise selling prices and marketing procedures that the distributor is obliged to follow.

12. Licensing and franchising

Licensing might be appropriate for a firm that possesses patented inventions, know-how (i.e. confidential but non-patentable technical knowledge) or valuable registered trademarks. No expertise in exporting is required; there are no delivery costs, no capital investments on the part of the licensor, and the risk of failure is shared with the licensee. Licensing offers rapid entry to a market, and can be undertaken by small firms. The income generated from licence royalties helps offset research and technical development costs, while the licensee firm does not itself have to invest in research and development.

Problems associated with licensing might relate to:

(a) maintenance of quality levels;

(b) verification of the licensee's sales figures;

(c) lower revenues compared to direct sale to the market;

(d) possible failure of the licensee to exploit fully the local market;

(e) acquisition by the licensee of the licensor's technical knowledge. Note how the licensee might subsequently set up in competition with the licensor;

(f) the need for complex contractual arrangements in certain circumstances;

(g) the numerous opportunities that arise for disagreements and misunderstandings.

269

Licensing is most likely to succeed, perhaps, where

(a) the licensee will have to purchase input components or materials from the licensor

(b) the licensor is already exporting directly to more markets than it can conveniently handle

(c) it is not feasible to establish a permanent presence in a particular country

(d) the cost of transporting goods to the local market would be excessively high

(e) images of locally produced items will improve sales.

Franchising

Here a foreign firm adopts the parent company's (franchisor's) entire business format in the local market – its name, trademarks, business methods, layout of premises, etc. Additionally the franchisor provides (in return for a royalty and lump sum fee) a variety of supplementary management services: training, technical advice, stock control systems, perhaps even financial loans. Hence the franchisor retains complete control over how the product is marketed, but the franchisee carries most of the risks of failure. International franchising allows companies to expand rapidly from a limited capital base. It combines the technical experience of the franchisor with the intimate local knowledge of the franchisee. Franchisees are self-employed, not employees of the parent company, and rarely possess rights against a parent organisation in the event of either the entire system or just an individual outlet collapsing. Also they are usually tied to supplies from the parent organisation at supply prices determined by the latter (which buys raw materials in bulk at big discounts).

Nine out of ten of all hotels owned by the international chain Holiday Inns are franchised. The company states that international franchising facilitates the establishment of an internationally consistent image and the standardisation of services and quality management systems, while allowing a centralised reservation system. Note how franchising enabled the creation of an international hotel network at a speed impossible were the parent company to have set up its own establishments in each country in which it decided to operate. Marketing and advertising are centrally administered. The reservation system links by satellite many thousands of terminals in airline reservation offices, travel agents and other travel outlets.

---

13. Branches and subsidiaries

As export sales expand, the inadequacy of exporting as a means for doing foreign business might become progressively evident. The firm will (or should) have acquired detailed knowledge of foreign markets and export procedures and thus might be capable of dispensing with export intermediaries. Accordingly, the company may set up its own branches, and/or subsidiaries, possibly to oversee production operations in other countries. The difference between a branch and a subsidiary is that whereas a branch is regarded in law as a direct extension of the parent firm into a foreign country (so that the parent is legally responsible for all the branch's debts and activities), a subsidiary is seen as a separate business from the parent company. A subsidiary is responsible for its own debts and (unlike a branch) is subject to exactly the same taxes, auditing, registration and accounting regulations as any other local business.

Branches are easy to set up and to dismantle, but complicated tax situations can arise because some nations relate the amounts of tax payable by branches to the worldwide profits of their parent companies. Normally branches are concerned with the transport and storage of goods, marketing, the provision of after-sales service; and liaison with local banks, advertising agencies, suppliers and distributors, and so on. Local assembly and/or manufacture is normally undertaken by other means. In most (but not all) countries the existence of a foreign branch has to be registered with local governmental authorities. Usually the registration is straightforward, comprising the deposit of a simple form plus translated documents attesting the whereabouts and solvency of the parent company.

Advantages to operating a branch rather than a subsidiary are that:

- a branch need not have its own capital or directors;
- assets can be transferred from the parent to the branch without incurring tax liability;
- no company formation or winding-up procedures are required;
- losses can be offset against the parent's profit.

Factors that might encourage the establishment of a subsidiary rather than a branch include:

- limited liability;
- the ability to apply for government regional development assistance and R&D grants on the same terms as any other local business;
- a local identity;
- the capacity to raise capital in the subsidiary's own name and (importantly) to sell shares to outsiders;
- not having to disclose the annual accounts of the parent organisation;
- the ability to undertake internal reorganisations without having to report this to the foreign authorities.

Major factors to be considered when selecting the precise location of a branch or subsidiary within a country include nearness to consumers and/or centres of commercial activity, availability of government investment grants and subsidiaries, and access to local sources of raw materials and input components. Other criteria might include labour and other operating costs, the availability of high-calibre labour, and the whereabouts of the competitors.

14. Joint ventures

Joint ventures (JVs) are collaborative arrangements between unrelated parties which exchange or combine various resources while remaining separate and independent legal entities. There are two types of JV: equity and contractual. The former involves each partner taking an equity stake in the venture (e.g. through setting up a joint subsidiary with its own share capital); the latter rely on contractual agreements between the partners. Joint ventures are an example of the wider concept of the 'strategic alliance', which embraces knowledge-sharing arrangements, mutual licensing, measures to control and utilise excess capacity, etc. Usually JVs are formed to undertake a specific project that has to be completed within a set period. JVs are a flexible form of business arrangement; can be quickly entered into and shut down; enable the sharing of costs; yet are frequently just as effective a means for entering markets as more direct forms of foreign investment. Often they are used to establish bridgeheads in a foreign market prior to more substantial operations within the market by individual participants. Advantages to joint ventures include the following:

(a) Firms can expand into several foreign markets simultaneously for low capital cost.

(b) Shared cost of administration.

(c) Partners can avoid the need to purchase local premises and hire new employees.

(d) Shared risk of failure.

(e) JVs may be available in countries where outright takeovers of local firms by foreigners is not allowed.

(f) Less costly than acquisitions.

(g) Higher returns than with licensing/franchising.

(h) Firms can gain instant access to local expertise and to partners' distribution systems.

(i) Possibly better relations with national governments in consequence of having a local partner.

Problems with JVs include the possibility of disagreements over organisation and control, and over methods of operation and the long-term goals of the venture. Other disputes might arise concerning pricing policy, the confidentiality of information exchanged between members, and about how underperformance by any one of the participants is to be dealt with (e.g. whether equal compensation is to be payable to each of the parties if the project is abandoned). Further possible difficulties are listed below:

- Partners may become locked into long-term investments from which it is difficult to withdraw.
- Possible arguments over which partner is responsible for budget overspends and how these should be financed.
- Problems of co-ordination.
- Profits have to be shared with partners.
- Possible differences in management culture among participating firms.
- Completion of a JV project might overburden a company's staff.

- Need to share intellectual property.
- Difficult to integrate into an overall corporate strategy.
- Partners are not free to act independently.
- The corporate objectives of partners may conflict.
- Transfer pricing problems may arise (see 14:6) as goods pass between partners.
- The importance of the venture to each partner might change over time.

A consequence of West European economic integration has been a substantial increase in the volume of air traffic and hence in the demand for equipment for air traffic control. International competition for this lucrative market intensified in the early 1990s, especially from the USA (notably IBM) and Japan. Concurrently the European Commission was pressing ahead with the harmonisation of standards for air traffic control equipment across all EU states, further adding to market demand. Standardisation created the need for a common radar tracking system, the supply of which was open to tender from any EU firm. Nobel Industries (Sweden's largest chemical and armaments company) wished to bid for the contract but was prohibited from doing so because it was a non-EU firm. A subsidiary of Nobel, NobelTech Systems, had expert knowledge of the sort of radar system required and one of the most technically sophisticated trackers in the world. Accordingly NobelTech Systems linked up with the British-based Marconi Command and Control Systems Ltd, which as a EU company was entitled to bid. Marconi is a high-tech firm with an impressive track record in radar research, but wished nevertheless to tap into NobelTech's specialist expertise. The work would be divided 50/50, with NobelTech acting as a subcontractor to Marconi in order to keep within EU tendering rules. Note the need for a clear and precise specification of the ownership of intellectual property arising from the collaboration.

Source: Adapted from Hill, E., et al., 'International Collaboration in the Market for Air Traffic Control Systems' in Preston, J. (ed), *International Business*, Pitman, 1993.

15. Criteria for selecting JV partners

Local partners in a foreign country should have proven knowledge, expertise and experience of local business conditions and practices. A prospective partner should be able to conduct or commission local market research and possess extensive contacts with local banks, businesses and providers of specialist services. Obviously the partner needs to have resources (staff, technical facilities, management systems, etc.) sufficient to undertake the collaboration. Further selection criteria are (i) the firm's track record, how long it has existed and its general business reputation; and (ii) how readily the quality of the potential partner's work can be appraised. Ideally, participants should be able to pool complementary skills. For example, one partner might supply the technological know-how, another raise the necessary finance, while the third provides local marketing expertise and facilities. Crucial to the selection process is the exercise of 'due diligence' in relation to an intended collaborator. This means verifying the other business's value and activities and will normally involve an assessment of its creditworthiness (probably undertaken by an international credit reference agency), inspection of its accounts, and the evaluation of its technical and managerial competence.

Prior to the early 1990s the German motor manufacturer BMW had never manufactured motor vehicles outside Germany, except in a very small assembly plant in South Africa. Confronted with ferocious competition in world markets from Japanese (and other) motor manufacturers who located their production sites *within* foreign markets (hence avoiding import duties and attracting substantial investment grants from national governments) the firm decided in 1992 to set up its first ever significant foreign manufacturing plant, on a greenfield site in South Carolina in America. This would establish BMW as a 'local' producer within the North American Free Trade Agreement (NAFTA) and provide a springboard for exports from the US to nations in the Pacific Rim. BMW feared high external tariffs against foreign motor vehicles resulting from the formation of NAFTA, and the company had recently experienced a sharp decline in its US sales (a major problem considering that the USA is the largest car market in the world). Other factors influencing the decision to begin manufacturing abroad included:

- the need to protect foreign markets against the appreciation of the Deutschemark. Note in particular how the exchange rates of several large EU countries frequently nosedive against the DM, meaning that BMW has to increase local selling prices by significant amounts in order to maintain its German currency revenue. A US supply point enables such markets to be serviced from a country not necessarily affected by internal EU exchange rate fluctuations;
- low labour costs in South Carolina compared to Germany;
- $150 million dollars' worth of tax reliefs offered by South Carolina's State government;
- the availability of low-cost inputs from Mexico;
- forecast expansions in the US luxury car market;
- undercapacity in BMW's German production units;
- the example of the Japanese companies Honda, Nissan, Mazda and Toyota, all of which have US manufacturing operations that now account for 30 per cent of the North American market.

---

16. Direct foreign investment (DFI)

Total ownership of a foreign subsidiary means there is no scope for arguments with partner firms; there is complete and immediate control over operations; and subsidiary operations can be fitted into the parent company's corporate strategies overall. Also, local restrictions on imports are circumvented, the local delivery of output might be greatly improved and better after-sales service provided. The close link between local production and local marketing might enable more rapid product modification in response to changing local demand. Having a permanent local presence in other countries in the form of direct investments enables the company to:

- obtain investment grants from foreign governments;
- acquire know-how and technical skills only available locally;
- minimise its worldwide tax burden;
- engage in local assembly or part-manufacture;
- project a local identity;
- spread the risk of downturns in particular markets;
- reduce production costs (e.g. because of cheaper raw materials or labour).

The essential problem with DFI is, of course, the substantial capital investment it requires. This cannot be sacrificed easily, whereas cancellation of a contract manufacture agreement is (subject to the details of the contract) a cheap and straightforward affair. Apart from the local availability of manufacturing resources (labour, materials, etc.) the decision whether to invest in foreign manufacturing capacity will normally depend on such factors as the political stability of the country being considered, the extent of government investment grants and subsidiaries, legal matters such as the ease of patent protection, wage and other costs, restrictions on the repatriation of profits, and taxation.

A UK coach company set up from scratch a new coaching firm in Lille in northern France. Lille was selected as it lies at the crossroads of northern Europe: there is an extensive transport infrastructure in the region; the Channel and North Sea ports are nearby; there is easy access to the European road network; and the proximity of Lille airport created numerous opportunities for the development of air/coach traffic. The new firm commenced operations *as if* it were a local start-up, with three brand new luxury coaches purpose-built to the very high standards that continental European coach travellers expect: air conditioning, a refrigerator, drinks machine, etc. Product profile brochures were printed in several languages and distributed to potential customers throughout the continent. The new company operated as a native organisation, forming the basis for further expansion in the EU. New start-up was considered appropriate because (i) a completely fresh corporate image could be projected from the outset, (ii) the company already possessed intimate knowledge of the technical side of the coaching business, and (iii) the new vehicles were the only major capital asset required other than premises for the head office in Lille.

A major decision that has to be taken here is whether to purchase an existing business outright, or to start up a new company. The advantages of buying a local business include the avoidance of start-up delays and expenses; immediate possession of a functioning administrative structure; and possibly the acquisition of an existing distribution system with staff, transport vehicles, etc. On the other hand, the acquired business will have to be integrated into the purchaser's current organisation system, and implementing changes in the purchased firm's management methods may prove difficult. Further potential pitfalls associated with foreign acquisitions are:

(a) Certain staff in the acquired business might not be worth employing, hence involving the acquiring company in dismissals and consequent employee compensation claims.

(b) Key employees in the acquired business might resign.

(c) New competitors may emerge (attracted perhaps by the publicity surrounding the initial takeover).

(d) Control difficulties created by having to manage a large and diverse organisation could arise.

(e) Market conditions might suddenly change following a costly acquisition.

Cross-cultural problems of mergers and acquisitions are well illustrated by the merger of the French packaging company Carnaud with the British Metal Box company to form CMB, one of the world's leading packaging conglomorates. The rationale behind the merger was that the two companies were engaged in complementary activities and that only a large business would have the critical mass necessary to succeed in the highly fragmented (and rapidly expanding) European packaging industry. Metal Box had an excellent track record in research and technical development, marketing, and in the application of computerised systems. Carnaud, on the other hand, was cash rich and had a larger market share. The merged business employed 33,000 people, and operated in 15 countries worldwide.

Human relations problems emerged almost immediately. Prior to the merger Metal Box had stagnated: motivation and productivity were low and there was a deep mistrust of senior management among lower grade employees. Carnaud, conversely, had adopted a progressive 'inverted pyramid' organisation structure, whereby senior management adopts a facilitating 'behind the scenes' role leaving operational decisions to whichever employees are *closest to the client* in relation to a particular matter. Difficulties have to be resolved at the customer interface; they cannot be referred upwards. The new system was implemented via the creation of numerous SBUs, with management by objectives, internal appraisal, and so on. All these methods had to be reconciled with the bureaucratic, centralised hierarchy of Metal Box. British staff felt they were being taken over by the French and that 'foreign' forms of organisation were being imposed on them. Rivalry and ill-will emerged between the two sides of the new company. One year after the merger CMB's market share was half the target figure, financial performance was poor, share price had fallen and restructuring costs were way in excess of the levels predicted.

Drastic measures were needed to resolve these problems. Company headquarters were relocated in Brussels (rather than Paris and London). The inverted management pyramid was applied throughout the new company and all functions decentralised apart from the recruitment of managers. In excess of 12 per cent of CMB's employees left the company during a 12 month period, counterbalanced in part by the hiring of 2000 new people in an attempt to invigorate the culture of the organisation. This was accompanied by a heavy investment programme intended to maximise market share and the payment of generous rewards to SBUs for the successful development of new products.

Source: Adapted from Landreth, O., *European Corporate Strategy: Heading for 2000*, Macmillan 1992.

17. Choice of market entry method

Criteria for selecting a market entry method should relate to the organisation's overall corporate strategy and the extent, depth and geographical coverage of its present and intended foreign operations. The firm's management needs to ask itself whether it wishes the company to have long-term involvement with international markets; or merely to exploit opportunistic export sales. Major criteria that should influence the choice include the following:

(a) How quickly the firm wishes to commence operations in the market (outright purchase of a fully operational local business is usually the speediest method).

(b) Volatility of competition and competitive intensity in the countries concerned.

(c) The ease with which intellectual property can be protected (this is particularly important for licensing and joint ventures).

(d) The degree of market penetration desired (deep penetration normally requires a permanent presence within the relevant country).

(e) The firm's experience and expertise in selling and operating abroad.

(f) Sizes of the margins taken by intermediaries in particular nations.

(g) Tariff levels, quotas and other non-tariff barriers to market entry.

(h) Availability of trained and competent personnel for staffing foreign subsidiaries.

(i) Political stability of the foreign countries the firm wishes to enter, and other risk factors.

(j) The business's financial resources and hence its capacity to purchase or set up foreign establishments.

(k) Physical and technical characteristics of the product (simple products are easy to manufacture abroad).

(l) Availability of marketing and general business services in target foreign markets.

(m) Ease of communication with intermediaries (agents, consortium buyers, etc.) in specific countries.

(n) Local constraints on the foreign ownership of businesses and/or licensing arrangements involving foreign firms.

In practice, many large companies with extensive foreign operations adopt a variety of market entry methods; exporting to some countries, licensing or operating joint ventures in others, or purchasing manufacturing plant elsewhere. A mixture of these might be applied within a particular foreign state so that, for example, export to a country and licensed manufacture within that country occur side by side. Whatever methods are adopted, internationalisation of operations will only succeed if everyone concerned with the management of the enterprise genuinely regards foreign operations as being of at least the same level of importance as domestic selling. This might imply the allocation of top jobs to foreign nationals; the integration of activities on a worldwide basis; and rewarding successful foreign subsidiaries more highly than units in the firm's home country in appropriate circumstances.

Progress test 14

1. In what circumstances might it be appropriate to modify products when selling in foreign markets?

2. Explain the difference between international business and exporting.

3. Define transfer pricing.

4. List some of the problems associated with exporting.

5. What are the advantages of using intermediaries when selling to foreign markets?

6. Explain the difference between agents and distributors.

7. Explain the difference between a branch and a subsidiary.

8. What is meant by the 'exercise of due diligence' when choosing joint venture partners?

9. List some of the criteria that should be adopted when selecting modes of entry to foreign markets.

Part Three

PLANNING AND CONTROL

15

CORPORATE PLANNING

1. Nature of corporate planning

Planning means the deliberate and systematic determination of what to do in the future in order to fulfill the organisation's mission and meet its objectives, given certain predicted or intended conditions. Planning is as much a *philosophy* as a technique, since it cannot possibly survive in a firm that is managed by intuition, last minute decisions, and without the participation in decision making of the individuals who will actually have to implement policies. Concern for planning implies a *future orientation*, faith in the viability of the firm and its products and a willingness to invest. Planning, therefore, represents a complete system for running a business. It embraces, *inter alia*:

- the evaluation of the implications of future decisions;
- establishment of performance standards;
- analysis of the environments in which the company operates;
- the precise specification of goals.

Planning involves the decomposition of problems and issues into their component parts, application of rational analysis to the interpretation of information, and the selection of actions to achieve predetermined ends. Plans can be as general or as specific as the situation requires: strategic, tactical or operational; long, short or medium term. The planning process can begin as soon as the firm's mission and core objectives have been formulated. Thereafter, planning necessarily *precedes* other managerial activities, so that changes in organisation, staffing and so on follow from planning decisions. Thus planning should be given the time and resources justified by this primary position in the overall management of the firm.

Purposes of planning

The essential purposes of planning are to:

(a) relate the business to its environment, i.e. to ensure that environmental changes do not destroy the firm. Through engaging in planning a management becomes aware of environmental factors and the influences they might exert;

(b) co-ordinate complex activities;

(c) utilise the talents of a range of people in taking important decisions;

(d) improve organisational efficiency and facilitate the implementation of change.

All managers need to plan in some respect or other (note how planning and control are inseparable), and the calibre of an individual manager's performance is likely to be appraised in part against his or her ability to formulate plans. Note however that planning is difficult because it requires forecasts of future environments and events; and expensive since it ties up significant numbers of highly paid senior executives. At the strategic level, therefore, some firms are tempted not to bother with planning, simply dealing with events as they arise. Enthusiasm for planning is greater perhaps in environments within which there is steady economic growth, a stable competitive situation, and a government which announces and then sticks to its long-term policies.

Difficulties of terminology

Unfortunately, many managers use the words 'strategy' and 'plan' interchangeably, even though they have quite different meanings. And the word 'planning' is itself often used to describe disparate things by different people. To some, planning means devising policies; to others the word is synonomous with financial budgeting, or with 'decision taking' (on the grounds that decisions taken now will help determine future events), with project management, organisational design; or simply 'management' as a whole (i.e. 'fitting things together'). The confusion arises perhaps because each term has connotations with the determination of a direction to follow; a guide for getting from where we are now to where we want to be. In this book, 'planning' *follows* the determination of overall corporate strategies, although the planning process has a strategic dimension and 'strategic planning' is a valuable activity in itself.

2. Strategic and operational plans

Strategic planning means the determination of how, in practical terms, the firm will attain its strategic objectives. Thus, strategic plans derive from the company's overall corporate strategy, from observed gaps between necessary and likely outcomes and resources (see 16.1), risk assessments, and from a situation analysis (see 3.1). Strategic plans might relate to such matters as divestment, organic growth (see 3.10), diversification, acquisitions of other businesses, research and technical development and so on. They set out the detail of how and when the firm will enter new markets, increase existing market share, improve productivity, delayer the management hierarchy, etc. The strategic plan is wider in scope and will have longer time horizons than tactical or operational plans. Its purpose is to assess the future implications of current decisions, to develop a framework for adjusting operations to changes in the wider business environment, and to link and control the various elements of complex organisations. Clearly, therefore, strategic planning has political, social and organisational as well as technical implications.

Operational planning focuses on scheduling, internal co-ordination, production and marketing, budgets and administration, schedules and project networks (see 16.8), recruitment and redundancy, formulating advertising campaigns, etc.

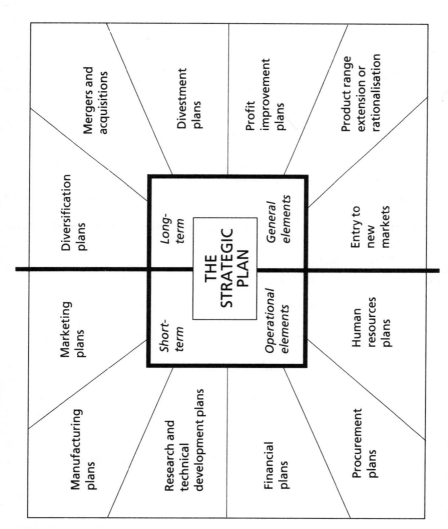

Figure 15.1 Major elements of the strategic plan

3. Reasons for planning

A number of reasons help explain why businesses engage in planning, including the following:

- to implement strategies;
- to respond to the identification of a major environmental threat;
- to facilitate the management of change;
- to cope with a new technology;
- observation of competing firms that undertake planning;
- to facilitate the administration of a growing and increasingly complex organisation;
- to convince outside organisations (banks for example) that the business is being properly run;
- to ensure that all the efforts and activities of the organisation are properly co-ordinated and directed towards particular goals;
- to ensure that a sufficient range of expertise is applied to the management process (rather than all decisions being taken by one or a few people);
- to improve internal communication;
- to ensure that everyone has a common understanding of the business's aims;
- to compel managers to think long-term and to consider the implications of possible future events;
- to facilitate control.

Planning is particularly valuable where:

- high value capital investment decisions are required;
- the firm's products may be nearing the ends of their life cycles;
- implementation of necessary changes in technologies and production methods takes a long period;
- the business has few liquid resources and is vulnerable to cash flow short-falls;
- competitors are likely to alter their policies;
- there are uneven levels of profitability among subsidiaries, divisions and other operating units;
- the firm operates in complex environments that are overloaded with information and where effective decision taking is impossible without a formal analytical approach.

Divisionalisation of organisations (see 7.22) has also encouraged managements to plan.

Note however that planning is not essential for co-ordination, which can be achieved via other means, e.g. strong central leadership by a single person, the showing of common norms and perspectives by everyone in an organisation, meetings of 'co-ordination committees', and so on.

Avoidance of planning

Managers sometimes avoid involvement in planning processes, for a number of reasons:

(a) Lack of knowledge of and training in planning methods, leading to lack of self-confidence in being able to gather accurate information, forecast the future and put together meaningful plans.

(b) Cynicism resulting from a belief that resources will not be made available in quantities necessary to implement the plan.

(c) Inadequate information about internal operations and/or external change.

(d) Fears that the outcomes to planning exercises will damage the manager's department and/or personal prospects.

(e) Assumptions that other people have already formulated the firm's plans.

(f) The desire to retain the ability to act flexibly and not to be constrained by rigid plans.

(g) Realisation that individuals are likely to be criticised for not achieving targets established in the company's plans.

(h) The fact that, to date, the firm might have been highly successful without having made any plans.

(i) Alarm at the prospect of plans leading to conclusions and decisions that are politically unacceptable to certain members of the senior management team.

Justification for planning

Henri Fayol (1841-1925) used the analogy of a sailing ship to justify the usefulness of business planning (Fayol, 1916). Winds and foul weather can force a ship to alter course; changes in route may be inevitable. Nevertheless, it is necessary to have navigational devices and firm intentions about the best course to follow, the maximum amount of information on tides, currents, seasonal variations in weather, etc., and contingency plans for alternative routes in the event of icebergs, hurricanes, and so on making impossible the realisation of original intentions. Otherwise the vessel will simply drift and never reach its predetermined destination.

Planning may be further likened, perhaps, to advertising in that while companies are extremely conscious that large parts of their advertising expenditures are wasted, they do not know which parts! Without planning, products might be advertised and aggressively marketed but not produced or imported in a quantity sufficient to satisfy consumer demand; newly acquired premises might be too small for future operations; and so on.

4. Advantages of planning

Planning compels management to prepare for future eventualities, to clarify its priorities, to develop criteria for monitoring performance and to think ahead in a systematic way. Further specific benefits to planning are:

(a) Resource deficiencies may be identified.

(b) Staff participating in planning exercises should be motivated towards achieving planned objectives.

(c) All the firm's activities will be integrated and co-ordinated.

(d) Management is forced to consider its own strengths and weaknesses.

(e) Careful consideration of possible future events may uncover new and profitable opportunities.

(f) Measures to influence future events can be initiated by the company.

(g) Criteria are established for the effective utilisation of resources.

(h) Activities are jointly directed towards the attainment of common objectives.

(i) The firm will be better equipped to respond to environmental change.

(j) Inefficiencies and duplicated effort may be identified.

(k) Team spirit is encouraged.

(l) The feasibilities of objectives are studied in depth.

(m) Departmental representatives are forced to meet and discuss common problems.

(n) The firm is compelled to look ahead, thus possibly avoiding foreseeable pitfalls.

(o) Important decisions are taken unhurriedly using all the data available and considering all possible options.

(p) It encourages strategic thinking and a rational approach to taking decisions.

(q) The specific actions needed to achieve corporate objectives are (hopefully) identified.

(r) Barriers to the implementation of strategies will be revealed.

An electronic information company specialising in the provision of networked E-Mail (electronic mail) and related facilities to businesses faced imminent collapse following the development and widespread use of fax machines. Firms simply purchased inexpensive fax units instead of subscribing to costly satellite inter-firm communication services. The company had not anticipated this development, and the experience of near-insolvency taught it a sharp lesson in the need for long-term planning. Already the enterprise's mission statement had been altered to make 'information delivery' the firm's primary concern, rather than the provision of *electronic* information services *per se*. A long-term plan was now drafted, recognising the need to broaden the company's operational base and, in particular, to enter foreign markets and acquire subsidiaries. In consequence an international cargo haulage firm with an extensive network of routes was purchased and a fleet of aircraft acquired. Warehousing facilities were purchased in key strategic locations suitable for accessing the world's most lucrative markets. Effectively the firm had become predominantly an overnight parcel delivery enterprise, with ancillary interests in a variety of transport and communication fields. Extension of the company's activities meant that a separate set of factors had to be considered when planning the future of each of its businesses. Different competitive forces applied in each area. Thus a bottom-up approach to planning (see 16.**22**) was implemented, with overall strategic planning and resource allocation occuring at the head office level.

Corporate planning should give the management of the organisation a sense of purpose. This is especially important in a firm that has no charismatic entre-preneur who leads by example and motivates employees. It should create a common understanding among different levels of management of key issues confronting the business, and facilitate sound financial management and opera-tional control. Decisions should be more consistent, and will be taken in a controlled and orderly manner; not in chaotic crisis situations.

5. Disadvantages and problems of planning

Some of the reasons for not bothering to engage in planning were outlined in **3** above. Further criticisms of planning are as follows:

(a) Strategic planning is not the same as strategic thinking, and the former does not necessarily facilitate the latter.

(b) Plans rely on data rather than market instinct to make important decisions. Data relate to the past; instincts to the future.

(c) Arguably, planning departments (see **10**) by their very nature are not able to cope with unexpected crises.

(d) Few managers have been formally trained in planning techniques.

(e) Markets are so unpredictable that it is a waste of time bothering to plan.

(f) Rigid planning systems generate bureaucracies that can inhibit creativity and lateral thinking. Plans beget plans until, eventually, a 'plan of plans' might be necessary. Each failure has to be analysed, requiring more research, more personnel, more meetings, sub-committees, etc.

(g) The mechanics of the planning process are administratively burdensome and as such might be delegated by top management to subordinates who do not possess the breadth of knowledge or experience necessary to complete these duties. Also the very act of delegating the planning function might be seen as an expression of senior management's disinterest in planning by middle and junior executives.

(h) 'Half-baked' planning is worse than no planning at all. Planning is bound to fail if proper attention and resources are not devoted to the process. Note however that this does not necessarily mean that planning should not be undertaken; rather that planning should be properly resourced.

6. The planning process

The main steps in the planning process are as follows:

(*i*) Recognition of the need to plan.

(*ii*) Situation analysis, including an identification of company strengths and weaknesses, resource constraints and limiting environmental factors (see Chapter 3).

(*iii*) Determination of possible alternative courses of action. Each option needs to be carefully evaluated to establish its feasibility in the light of the constraints revealed by (*ii*) above.

(*iv*) Specification of the assumptions behind the plan. These might relate to the continuation of present levels of inflation, growth rates, government legislation, behaviour of competitors, raw materials availabilities, etc.

(*v*) Selection of the best alternative. This may be done by an individual or a committee. Note the difficulty of defining the 'best' option in fast-changing business environments affected by numerous factors. The choice is necessarily subjective and depends substantially on the firm's willingness to take risks.

(*vi*) Implementation of the plan, involving the detailed allocation of tasks, commitment of resources, overcoming resistance to change, co-ordination of activities, etc.

(*vii*) Monitoring results and varying the plan to meet changing circumstances. Plans are rarely executed entirely as predicted. Deviations of actual from planned outcomes can be caused by inaccurate forecasts, unanticipated shortages of resources, reactions of competitors, and many other factors.

7. Planning principles

There exist certain fundamental principles of planning that should always be applied, as follows:

(a) As far as possible, plans should be based on facts and not opinions.

(b) Plans should incorporate some degree of flexibility to accommodate unforeseeable events.

(c) A plan should be as detailed as expenditure constraints allow.

(d) Plans should not extend too far into the future; accurate prediction of the distant future is simply impossible.

(e) All alternative courses of action should be considered.

(f) Side effects and implications of the actions envisaged should be examined.

(g) Instructions to individuals and departments must be incorporated into the plan.

(h) Plans should be concise and easy to understand.

(i) As the plan is executed its effectiveness in achieving stated objectives should be monitored. Differences between actual and desired positions must be quickly identified and remedial measures introduced.

(j) Targets embodied in plans should always be reasonable; overambitious targets can never be achieved and lead to low morale and cynicism among workers. Equally, targets that are too low have no operational significance.

(k) While all aspects of the firm's operations need to be considered when developing plans, the greatest emphasis should be placed on identifying and examining the key factors that are crucial to the company's success.

PLANNING SYSTEMS

8. Types of planning system

The planning system selected should relate directly to the needs of the organisation concerned. Systems may be formal or informal; quantitative or intuitive (or a mixture of both); have short period horizons or extend a long way into the future. Further differences in systems relate to:

- extent of the depth of coverage of operations, budgets, etc.;
- sophistication (and costs) of techniques;
- degree of involvement of employee representatives;
- relations with individual performance appraisal and management by objectives systems;
- number of alternatives specified;
- connections between strategic, tactical and operational elements;
- amounts of information generated.

Planning systems often evolve naturally through various phases as a company's operations expand. First the business might engage in basic financial planning, preparing annual budgets and functional plans related to specific projects. Cost accounting makes possible the orderly co-ordination of disparate activities and allows management to concentrate on exceptions to normal operations and to devise overall plans. Then, as it grows the firm may experience the need to analyse its environments, prepare forecasts, develop systematic procedures for allocating resources, and generally plan for growth. Managers begin to think strategically. Planning is extended to include detailed analyses of markets, rival companies, and the business's own competitive position. SWOTS are examined (see 5.4) and situation analyses completed. Finally the firm adopts definite procedures for evaluating strategic alternatives, combines all its *ad hoc* planning activities into an overall corporate plan and starts to be concerned about how best to inject creativity and flexibility into its planning processes. Typically the degree of formalisation of procedures increases with each stage of evolution, with more and more people becoming involved as the mechanisms become increasingly sophisticated. (Initially the chief executive is likely to take all planning decisions.) Documentation requirements become more explicit at each stage.

The planning cycle

The term 'planning cycle' is used to denote the periodicity of planning activities. Major corporate planning exercises normally occur once every three to six years (anything longer would be so uncertain as to be meaningless – except in very general terms); operational planning is typically based on annual or half-yearly time horizons. Strategic plans may have to be revised following unanticipated environmental changes (a sharp increase in the rate of inflation, sudden collapse of a market, entry of a new competitor, etc.), regardless of how long has elapsed since the last planning exercise.

9. Formal versus informal planning procedures

Formal planning procedures establish set rules for how plans are determined and hopefully will lead to consistency (all plans are developed to the same format), and ensure that issues are analysed in depth. Advantages to having formal procedures are:

(a) Everyone concerned with the planning process should have a common understanding of how plans are to be formulated.

(b) The drafting of procedures requires discussion and open communication among relevant employees.

(c) There is continuity in procedures. Note how promotions, resignations, transfers and retirements of staff mean that the managers concerned with planning will change from time to time.

Formal planning systems are sometimes based on pro-forma documents circulated to heads of department and other relevant personnel. Headings for a pro-forma based planning system might include:

- perceived departmental/divisional objectives;
- sectional strengths and weaknesses;
- opportunities and threats;
- actions needed to exploit opportunities and avert threats;
- perceived critical success factors;
- the risks involved in intended activities;
- evaluation criteria to be used;
- forecasts of relevant figures;
- who will complete which duties and by when.

The problems involved

The main disadvantage to the formalisation of procedures is perhaps that it reduces flexibility, since precedents established through following formal rules must be adhered to in future cases. A mini legal system builds up around procedures, with its own protocols, norms, case law and rules of interpretation. Further reasons sometimes advanced for not having formal written plans are that to possess them stifles creativity and innovation, discourages entrepreneurship, and generates inflexible attitudes. Another problem is that executives might feel intimidated by the need to accept the responsibilities that the precise specification of formal plans implies. Excessively formal planning procedures can become ritualistic: ends in themselves rather than aids to facilitate better management. Sub-systems may be necessary and the work can become extremely complex. Line managers might be reluctant to become involved in the process for fear of criticism should they not understand the system and/or make mistakes.

Often, formal systems rely on standard forms, which may be filled in hurriedly and without real thought. Arguably, standardisation of the layout of such forms can lead to standardisation of thought and a lack of creativity within the planning process, which may come to be seen as little more than a form-filling exercise. Also, pro-forma headings in planning documentation can, by leading a manager's thinking, introduce bias and distortion to the results.

Informal planning

Despite their not being written down, informal plans may be well-thought-out and accurately reflect the vision and aspirations of the management of the organisation. Informal planning, if sensibly applied, can have definite advantages:

(a) It recognises the need for flexibility in planning processes.

(b) The organisation becomes more adaptable, responsive and attuned to change.

(c) Fewer preassumptions are imposed.

(d) Since fewer planning decisions are taken there is less scope for mistakes.

(e) The people operating the system might be just as likely to think seriously about serious important planning issues as in a formal planning system.

(f) There is no inappropriate stereotyping of procedures.

(g) Large numbers of alternatives are considered.

(h) Informal procedures are 'user friendly' and understandable.

Problems with informal procedures include the following:

(a) The absence of pro-forma guidelines means that first-class managers are needed to operate the system.

(b) Large amounts of planning information are held in the heads of individual executives, whose resignation, illness, etc., could disrupt the informal procedures.

(c) Long-term problems are likely to be ignored.

(d) Plans might devote too much attention to particular functions (marketing or finance for example) at the expense of wider-ranging strategic planning issues.

(e) The company might start to 'drift' and lose sight of important objectives.

(f) The process may degenerate to the application of ill-conceived hunches.

(g) Plans are likely to be unco-ordinated.

(h) Critical environmental changes may be missed.

Note moreover that managements sometimes assume, wrongly, that everyone in the organisation already knows the firm's plans and objectives and that a formal statement will only complicate what is regarded as a straightforward issue. Hence there is no mechanism for communicating planning decisions, which are not implemented so that the entire system crumbles.

10. Role of the planning department

Establishment of a planning department is a convenient means for administering the planning function, but can create problems. Arguably, planning should be a line management responsibility alone, on the grounds that planning and action are two aspects of the same job. However, planning necessarily involves a substantial amount of routine administration so that even in firms that subscribe to this view it is not uncommon to establish a planning department or similar unit to co-ordinate planning activities. Planning departments typically employ well-qualified people, often with a management accountancy background. To be effective a planning department should:

(a) not be too large (otherwise, it becomes bureaucratic and out of touch with the firm's actual operations);

(b) not duplicate the functions of other departments;

(c) be closely involved in the formulation of budgets;

(d) have a head of department whose status enables him or her to discuss high-level strategic issues with members of the firm's senior management team;

(e) report directly to the chief executive;

(f) have access to expert outside help and advice (via the use of consultants for example);

(g) generate a working environment that is conducive to creative thinking.

Problems confronting a planning department are:

(a) It might be seen by top management as a convenient scapegoat upon which all corporate failures can be blamed.

(b) Departmental employees might be perceived by some of the firm's other staff as being 'trendies' brought in to implement various management fads.

(c) Benefits from planning emerge in the long term. Few immediate outcomes will be discernible, making it difficult to appraise the calibre of the department's work.

(d) The department might become infatuated with the application of the latest planning techniques, at the expense of meaningful pursuit of the company's goals.

(e) Although the department might have been set up to co-ordinate and administer the planning function, the department might in fact end up initiating and developing plans that really should be put together by line executives.

11. Planning committees

Firms without planning departments may have planning committees, since effective planning requires the application of a wide range of high-level skills and it is unlikely that a single person will have expertise in all relevant competencies. If there is a planning department a committee of senior managers from various key functions might be convened periodically to assist the planning department in its work. The role of a planning committee is to identify strategic planning issues, explore options, and draft an overall framework for the corporate plan (the detail being worked out at lower levels). The committee itself might comprise heads of divisions, subsidiaries, and major departments, plus senior executives from head office. Advantages to having a planning committee are:

(a) A wide range of views and experience are applied to the planning process.

(b) Decisions should be objective and the result of logical analysis and extensive discussion.

(c) Personal involvement in planning procedures might motivate committee members to achieve resulting objectives.

(d) The committee can take a bird's-eye view of the entire situation prior to detailed investigations.

(e) More information is utilised when taking planning decisions than might otherwise be the case.

However, planning committees are only as good as the people who sit on them, and to the extent that committee members are incompetent and/or disinterested in the work then it might be better to have all planning completed by one or more specialists in the subject – proposals being subsequently distributed to divisional and departmental heads for comment. Also the outputs of a committee might be so bland and general as to be meaningless.

12. The final company plan

This will normally be written up as a document with the following headings:

- *Introduction.* Overview of the total corporate plan. The methodology adopted.
- *Information* used in the plan; where it came from and how it was gathered.
- *Assumptions* behind the plan. Statement of how risk and uncertainty have been dealt with.
- *The strategic plan.* Details (where appropriate) of how the company will diversify, expand/contract, rationalise its operations, etc.
- *Functional plans* for:

    new product development
    marketing and distribution
    human resources
    research and technical development
    operations
    organisational restructuring.

- *Contingency plans* for various eventualities.
- *Targets, schedules and time horizons.*
- *Resourcing:* where the resources necessary to implement the plan will come from.
- *Divisional and departmental plans.*
- *Project plans*
- *Budgets*

Progress test 15

1. Give five examples of items that might appear in a firm's strategic plan.

2. Why should companies bother to plan?

3. What are the main steps in the planning process?

4. Define the term 'planning cycle'.

5. List the advantages of informal planning.

6. Why do some firms establish planning committees?

16

TECHNIQUES OF PLANNING

SWOT analysis (see 5:4) is perhaps the commonest foundation upon which firms base their planning procedures. Other planning methods include APACS (see 14), gap analysis (see 1), PERT (see 9), POISE (see 15), plus a variety of quantitative approaches (see 16). Some of the forecasting techniques discussed in Chapter 4 and the audit and appraisal methods outlined in Chapter 5 also provide major inputs to the practical planning process.

1. Gap analysis

With gap analysis, the planner sets targets based on what he or she believes to be attainable in the longer term and then compares these targets with forecasts to future achievement taken from projections of current activities – assuming that present circumstances continue. Divergences are then analysed, and measures implemented to bridge the gaps. Thus, gap analysis seeks to analyse disparities between potential and performance. Gaps might be identified, *inter alia*, in the following areas:

(a) Distribution, caused perhaps by shortages of intermediaries or outlets, or poor control over agents.

(b) Product offer, including product features, quality level and facilities for customer care.

(c) Market share, in that planned market share has not been achieved.

(d) Research and technical development, possibly involving large expenditures that have failed to generate tangible results.

(e) Rates of profitability, return on capital employed, growth of assets and profits.

Consequences of gap analysis might include:

(a) continuation of existing strategies, ignoring any minor divergences between actual and potential performance that might have been revealed;

(b) introduction of new strategies specifically designed to bridge observed gaps, while keeping the firm's core strategies intact;

(c) a complete overhaul of the strategic orientation of the enterprise.

Problems with gap analysis are:

(a) that gaps may be the result of hopelessly optimistic assessments of what is possible, leading to the introduction of inappropriate policies and the pursuit of meaningless objectives;

(b) the difficulty of accurately quantifying the magnitudes of gaps;

(c) the basic assumptions regarding future environments may be false;

(d) that actual future performance will depend on a whole range of factors apart from current strategies (entry or withdrawal of competitors for example).

Gap analysis requires the determination of performance measures for the industry average (and for specific competing businesses within the sector) in order to form a judgement on the company's potential. This is known as *benchmarking*.

2. Benchmarking

Benchmarking means the establishment of performance measures that enable a company to analyse its efficiency and compare itself against competing businesses, particularly the leading firms in the industry. There are three types of benchmark: internal, external, and functional. Internal benchmarking compares the performances of divisions, departments, etc., within the same organisation against common yardsticks. External benchmarks contrast a company's overall performance with those of competing firms, typically in terms of profitability, rates of return on capital employed, growth in market share, levels of working capital, price-earnings ratio, and so on. Functional benchmarking involves the assessment of the efficiency of the business's main functions and processes against the same functions/processes (marketing, purchasing, etc.) in other organisations – which need not be rival businesses.

For benchmarking to succeed it is essential that:

(a) reasonably comprehensive and accurate information be available on competing businesses (eg. via published accounts, commercial databases, trade magazines, newspaper reports, etc);

(b) the firm has sound internal audit procedures;

(c) benchmarks are genuinely based on industry best practice (which are not necessarily the same as targets that are easily attainable by the various sections of the firm);

(d) the benchmarks established are flexible and subject to alteration as external environments change;

(e) benchmarks directly relate to the company's overall strategies and corporate plans.

Criticisims of benchmarking are that:

(a) much effort and expense might be spent on stating obvious conclusions;

(b) establishment of benchmarks does not of itself generate the resources and/or expertise necessary to improve company performance;

(c) any benchmark is likely to be out-of-date as soon as it is determined;

(d) it is extremely difficult to benchmark creative activities (design or research and development for example).

One of the first organisations to adopt and develop benchmaking was the Xerox Corporation which, faced by a collapse in its market share in the late 1970s, systematically analysed the performances and characteristics of competing products in order to identify opportunities for improving its own product offer. Xerox pinpointed six areas that it considered critical for the company's success, relating to customer marketing and customer care, human resource management, use of information technology, quality improvement, and financial control. Sub-processes were then defined within these areas, eventually benchmarking every significant aspect of the company's operations. Comparative companies were identified and data on them collated. This enabled the discovery of gaps in competitive performance between Xerox and these other firms and hence the establishment of action plans aimed at removing them.

Xerox reported a one-third improvement in the efficiency of its marketing department, a two-thirds reduction in stockholding, a 30 per cent reduction in service labour costs, a ten percent increase in the productivity of distribution systems, and other major benefits.

Source: Bendell, T., Boulter, L., and Kelly, J., *Benchmarking for Competitive Advantage*, Pitman, 1993.

MEASURES OF COMPANY PERFORMANCE

3. Performance indicators

These may be results-orientated or effort-orientated. Examples of results-based performance measures are:

sales volumes and/or revenues;
rates of return on investments;
average stock levels held;
market share;
growth of assets.

Effort-based performance measures could involve:

- number of potential customers contacted (even if the contacts do not lead to sales);
- number of complaints processed,
- extents of relationships with suppliers;
- efforts applied to improving industrial relations;
- rates of absenteeism (high levels of absence often indicate low morale and lack of effort);

- the vigour with which debtors are pursued;
- frequency of reports submitted to higher management;
- research and development activity (which might not have led to any tangible results).

Normally results-based measures represent the 'bottom line', with effort-based yardsticks being scrutinised to identify the causes of above or below average levels of performance.

Certain performance indicators cannot easily be measured in quantitative terms (corporate social responsibility, ethical behaviour or employees' personal development for example).

4. Choice of performance indicators

The first issue is to determine what to measure in order to assess performance. This will depend on the firm's mission and objectives, the activities that are most critical to the firm and the size of the organisational unit (division, department, SBU or whatever) under consideration. Performance measures should be based on fair and logical criteria. They may be quantitative or qualitative (see 3) and might involve 'standards', i.e. minimum or maximum values of key variables. Examples of performance standards are:

- average sales revenue per salesperson per month;
- maximum proportions of daily production outputs that are defective;
- average output level per manufacturing worker;
- maximum processing times for various categories of document;
- average number of letters word-processed per hour.

5. Return on capital employed

This is the ratio of profit to capital employed in the business. Gross capital employed is defined as fixed assets plus current assets. Net capital employed comprises fixed assets plus current assets less current liabilities. Proprietors' capital employed means net capital employed less long-term loans owing by the firm. Problems arise in measuring asset values (cost or market valuations for example) and choosing which assets to include in computations. For instance, some firms regard cash and other idle assets as irrelevant when assessing performance, because idle assets are not involved in profit creation. And how should goodwill be treated? Note moreover how the ratio has little meaning in a high profit firm that has few fixed assets. Consider for example a commercial radio station that rents its premises, furniture and equipment and broadcasts its programmes via a transmitter owned by another organisation. Its balance sheet assets will be negligible, leading to a return on capital employed of many thousands per cent.

Further problems arise when defining profit. Earnings retained within the business for future investment may be thought of as a profit which has not been distributed; or alternatively as a working asset used to generate further revenues.

The return on capital employed is an overall measure of efficiency and as such is commonly used to compare firms and industries. Often, low risk firms in stable industries have lower-than-average values for this ratio.

6. Price earnings (P/E) ratio

'Earnings per share' is computed as annual after-tax profit divided by the total number of a certain category of the company's shares (usually ordinary shares). Division of the market price of a share by earnings per share gives the 'price-earnings ratio' which shows how many years it would take an investor to recoup his or her capital outlay if current earnings continue and all these earnings are paid out as dividends. The following should be noted when interpreting price-earnings ratios:

(a) Profitable fast-growing companies which plough back most of their earnings into new investment have low declared profits, but might be greatly valued by investors. Hence the share price and P/E ratio of such a company will be high.

(b) Declared profits can be affected by windfall income, sale of capital assets, etc., and thus give a misleading picture of the strength of the firm.

(c) A company's P/E ratio can change dramatically on rumours of a takeover bid, even though the firm's operational capacity has not altered.

7. Other performance indices

Excessive stockholding is revealed in the 'stock turnover ratio':

$$\frac{\text{Cost of sales}}{\text{Average stock}}$$

where cost of sales is the value of opening stock plus stock purchases during an accounting period less stock at close. This ratio shows the speed of inventory turnover. If, for instance, the accounting period is one year and the ratio has a value of two, then on average a unit of stock is held for six months. Values lower than two mean that stock is held longer than six months and vice versa. High values are appropriate for firms facing irregular market demand where sudden changes in taste can lead to heavy, unexpected sales.

Debt collecting
The ratio:

$$\frac{\text{Value of debtors}}{\text{Annual sales}} \times 12$$

shows the average period, in calendar months, required to collect debts.

Dividend yield
Proportionate dividend returns to an investor are shown by the ratio of dividend per share to that share's market price.

Dividend cover

The ratio of earnings per share to dividend per share shows the extent to which the firm is paying out its earnings to shareholders in the form of dividends, rather than retaining profits within the business.

Profit and cost ratios

The firm might compute ratios for net trading profit to sales; cost of goods to sales; and distribution, selling and administrative expenses to sales. Average values of such ratios over time can be used as performance targets, and are particularly useful if comparable data can be obtained on rival firms (provided the information is reliable and the other businesses are genuinely similar to the enterprise in question).

NETWORK METHODS

8. Network analysis

A network is a schematic description of all the activites involved in a project and all the interconnecting links between events. Its purpose is to determine how quickly the project can be completed and to assist in scheduling, co-ordinating and controlling work. The 'critical path' of a network is the sequence of key activities that cannot be held up without postponing the completion date of the entire project. Other activities have 'float' time associated with their durations. Float is the *extra* time that can be taken over an activity in addition to its expected duration without affecting the completion time of the project as a whole.

The usefulness of network planning can be illustrated by considering a large construction project such as building a house. Scores of activities are involved: a survey, soil testing, ordering supplies, hiring labour, laying foundations, inspection of work, etc. Many of these tasks will interact, some need to be completed before others can begin while some may be undertaken at any time. The builder must calculate the expected duration of each task, and sort tasks into the order in which they have to be completed. It is then possible to work out which activities can be performed alongside others, and which must be finished before others can begin. The critical path is the shortest time between the first activity and the last, given that some activities can be completed while others are in progress. Accordingly, crucially important activities are highlighted and it becomes possible to see how the project can be speeded up through reallocating labour and other resources from some tasks to others, and how strikes, holidays, staff illnesses, non-delivery of supplies, etc., might affect the project's estimated completion date.

9. Critical path analysis (CPA) and project evaluation review technique (PERT)

These are the two main approaches to network analysis. They were developed simultaneously but independently and in different locations. CPA began in 1957 with the work of James Kelly and Morgan Walker in a US chemical company; PERT was first used by the US Navy in 1958. Although conceptually similar, CPA and PERT differ in their assumptions: CPA regards individual activity times as predetermined and constant, whereas PERT uses three alternative durations for each activity – optimistic, pessimistic, and most likely.

CPA is said to be activity-orientated in that networks simply illustrate series of operations that must be performed one after the other, while PERT is event-orientated showing estimates of times needed to reach each stage in the project – having incorporated allowances for uncertainty. CPA assumes that activity times can, if necessary, be reduced provided costs are correspondingly increased (see **12** below). Thus, CPA derives the solution which incurs least cost from a choice of alternative project completion times assumed to be known with certainty. PERT, on the other hand, requires known (or guessed) probabilities of activity durations. Expected values must therefore be computed for each period.

10. An example of CPA

To illustrate, consider a project that requires six activities, indicated by letters A to F (Figure 16.1). Activity D must follow activity C, which itself must follow B; and B must follow A. Activity E starts at the same moment as A, but must be completed before activity C can begin. Likewise, F starts when A starts, and must be finished before D can commence. Activity A takes five weeks, B takes two weeks, C requires fifteen weeks; activities D, E and F need eight, fifteen and six weeks respectively.

The critical path is the sequence E – C – D requiring thirty-eight weeks in total. It is impossible to complete this project in less than 15 + 15 + 8 = 38 weeks. While completing E the firm can get on with A and B which, together, take seven weeks. Activity C cannot begin until E is finished, and E requires fifteen weeks; therefore the firm can take anything up to eight extra weeks in completing A and B without affecting the total project duration. Activity F is not critical because it needs only six weeks whereas thirty weeks are available for completion of this work: there is a twenty-four weeks float attached to activity F. By definition, the critical path (E – C – D) has no float whatsoever. Activity A has ten weeks float (fifteen minus five) and B has eight.

A PERT solution to this problem would require the estimation of most optimistic, most pessimistic, and most likely completion times for each activity.

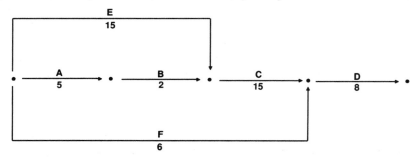

Figure 16.1 CPA network

Normally it is assumed that pessimistic predictions will be realised more often than optimistic predictions, as it seems there are many more causes of project delay than project acceleration. Then, probabilities of individual activity durations, and of the time to completion of the project as a whole, are computed.

11. Resource levelling

Resource constraints (limits on the numbers of available workers for example) must be incorporated into the project plan, since it might not be possible to have a team do several things simultaneously. For instance, activity A might require two weeks whereas activity B, which can begin at the same time as A, may require only one. Normally, therefore, the firm would want someone to be getting on with B while A is being completed. But suppose A and B each require two workers, so that four people in total are needed for one week, and that only two are available. In this case A and B cannot be done at the same time! In consequence, it is necessary to 'level resources', i.e. to assume that B must follow A (or vice versa). Hence the entire network and its associated critical path will change.

12. Crash-cost CPA

In CPA it is common to assume that activity times can be reduced provided the costs of operations increase. The time needed to paint a house might for example be one week if just a single worker is employed, or three days using two workers (and paying double wages). Thus, a number of alternative possible situations are simulated and the 'least cost' solution adopted depending on the various times and relative costs involved. Note that penalty or bonus clauses in contracts specifying various completion times can drastically alter the best way of scheduling a project: it might be better to accelerate activities at higher cost (overtime payments, etc.) in order to win a lucrative bonus for early completion. The absolute minimum time in which a project can be finished regardless of cost is called the 'crash' time, and the extra expense associated with this is known as the crash cost.

13. Uses and benefits of network analysis

CPA and PERT have applications in production, marketing, installation of new equipment and introduction of new products and processes; indeed anywhere a distinct final objective can be discerned. The technique has been successfully applied to design projects; ship, bridge and motorway construction; launching new products; installation of new plant and machinery; control of sub-contract work; and movement of factory premises. Network anaysis is not suitable for intellectual activities such as creative research, or for personnel or welfare work where time horizons are unclear and specific objectives usually difficult to describe.

Network analysis is a powerful technique of planning and control. Projects are broken down into logically ordered components, work schedules are precisely defined, progress is systematically monitored. The resources necessary for successful completion of each stage can be assessed. Crucially important tasks are identified, potential trouble spots predicted, and resources may perhaps be reallocated to hasten completion of the work. Further benefits include:

(a) forced preplanning of tasks; co-operation and co-ordination between departments;

(b) the requirement that specific targets be defined clearly and in depth;

(c) easier estimation of project completion dates and hence more accurate prediction of project costs;

(d) more effective budgetary control following detailed analysis of resource requirements;

(e) identification of inter-relations between activities;

(f) the ability to compare actual with predicted costs as the project develops. Sources of delay and exceptional costs may be quickly isolated.

OTHER PRACTICAL PLANNING METHODS

14. APACS

APACS – the 'adaptive planning and control sequence' – is a useful planning model that incorporates SWOT analysis. Eight steps are involved:

(a) statement of objectives;

(b) appraisal of internal strengths, weaknesses, and the external environment;

(c) specification of activities necessary to achieve objectives;

(d) evaluation of the consequences of alternative courses of action;

(e) prediction of results of actions chosen;

(f) the issue of orders to ensure implementation of plans;

(g) assessment of results;

(h) if necessary, modification of the plan.

15. POISE

A common and straightforward approach to plan formulation entails the firm asking itself appropriate questions, and planning its activities according to the replies. Examples of sets of relevant questions are as follows:

(a) What is the current rate of technical change in the industry? How might this alter? And what does the company need to do to beat its rivals in the technical field?

(b) How does the company's output differ from that of competitors, and what should it do to take full advantage of these differences when marketing its products?

(c) Is the company's access to raw materials and skilled labour assured, and if not what can be done to improve this (e.g. by offering higher wages or raw materials prices in order to secure continuing supply)?

POISE ('philosophy, organisation, information, strategy and efficiency') is an interrogative technique of this nature. It can be used for strategy formulation as well as planning *per se*. POISE begins from the specification of the company's mission statement, with plans being laid down depending on the firm's:

- *environmental circumstances* – problems and opportunities available in the outside world;
- *resources* – what it has and what it needs; and
- *competencies* – what it is good at; its strengths and weaknesses.

In drafting plans, management asks the following questions:

(a) Are the firm's management information systems, forecasting procedures, means of co-ordinating activity, and general administration capable of supporting the policies needed to implement plans; and if not, why not?

(b) How adequate are marketing and product research for the specified tasks?

(c) Does the firm possess a reliable materials procurement system?

(d) What measures exist for ascertaining when existing products have reached the ends of their life cycles?

(e) Has the firm an organisation development programme capable of effecting structural change, and if so how long will structural alterations take to implement?

(f) What mechanisms exist for controlling expenditures?

(g) How adequate are the company's human resources?

(h) What does the company need to do in order to beat its rivals in the technical field (e.g. initiate product and market research, establish a system for monitoring economic and other trends)?

(i) How does the company's output differ from that of competitors and what must it do to take full advantage of such differences?

(j) Are relations with suppliers and major customers satisfactory? What can be done to improve such relations?

QUANTITATIVE PLANNING MODELS

16. The quantitative approach

Numerous quantitative planning models have been developed, including:

(a) critical path and programme evaluation and review techniques (see **9**);

(b) transportation models, which purport to minimise the costs of sending goods from a number of supply points to various destinations;

(c) production planning models that aim to determine the mix of resources used to manufacture outputs;

(d) inventory control systems for minimising the firm's stockholdings while (hopefully) ensuring there is only a small chance of running out of stock;

(e) planned maintenance models for deciding when to replace equipment in order to maintain maximum efficiency, given certain relationships between the age of equipment and maintenance costs.

Quantitative planning models are said to bring objectivity, consistency and logical reasoning to the planning process. Advantages to the quantitative approach are that:

(a) complex problems are reduced to a handful of variables, which may be precisely stated using mathematical symbols that can be manipulated easily. Hence, peripheral issues are not considered. Rather, the *essence* of the problem is examined in depth;

(b) subjective value judgements, committees and other joint decision-making might not be required, conclusions can be drawn quickly and based on relevant information;

(c) managers are compelled to consider the basic assumptions behind their decisions;

(d) many hundreds of cross-relationships can be handled by even the simplest of contemporary computer software packages for business planning;

(e) application of quantitative models is financially inexpensive when compared to having all plans determined by committees.

Quantitative models are most appropriate, perhaps, for short-term, clearly defined and predictable situations where the costs of a mistake will not bankrupt the company. Also the outputs to quantitative models can be used as the *basis* of decisions (subject to qualitative alteration) rather than as 'tablets of stone' solutions.

Further problems with the application of quantitative planning techniques are that:

(a) many business situations are dominated by non-quantifiable factors;

(b) measurement errors are common and can be enormous;

(c) most quantitative models are only able to optimise one variable at a time, whereas in business it is typically necessary to optimise a large number of variables simultaneously.

UNCERTAINTY

17. Risk and uncertainty

A 'risky' situation is one in which the probabilities of various outcomes can be measured; an 'uncertain' situation is where they cannot. Risk is involved in most planning scenarios. The size of the risk must be compared with the expected benefits of a particular decision.

Low-risk high-return solutions are obviously preferable to high-risk low-return options. Typically, however, a compromise between risk and return has to be struck and the precise nature of the compromise will depend largely on the risk preferences of the person taking the decision. Some people enjoy assuming risk, others are highly averse to risky behaviour. Indeed, a few individuals find risk so exciting that they are prepared to forego satisfactory outcomes just to experience the exhilaration it provides. The adverse consequences of risk and uncertainty can be reduced through information gathering and careful planning; but risk can never be removed entirely as it is endemic to business situations.

18. Expected values and the minimax rule

The 'expected value' of an outcome is the probability of it occurring multiplied by the value of that outcome. For example, a production line organised in a certain way might generate 10,000 items per week with a probability of 0.4, or if organised differently might be expected to produce 9,000 items with a probability of 0.6. The expected value of the first option is 10,000 times 0.4, i.e. 4,000, while in the second case the value is $9,000 \times 0.6 = 5,400$ items. Normally, the firm should select the option that creates the highest expected value, although alternative decision rules exist. With the 'maximin' rule, for example, the firm will ascertain the maximum loss that can occur under each alternative course of action and choose the outcome which minimises the maximum loss, i.e. choose the best of the worst possible outcomes. Here the firm adopts a pessimistic view of likely events and seeks to minimise the damage. Note that the maximin rule is sometimes called the 'minimax cost' rule because minimising the maximum loss is exactly the same as maximising the minimum loss that might be incurred. The 'maximax' criterion on the other hand selects the 'best of the best'. It is assumed that the most favourable possibilities will actually materialise and the option that seemingly offers the maximum gain is chosen. A third approach is the pursuit of 'satisficing' outcomes whereby the firm specifies minimum criteria that any solution must satisfy, and then examines alternatives one after another, stopping at the first that satisfies all the minimal criteria. Satisficing behaviour is very common in management situations since, typically, constraints exist on the amounts of time that can be spent looking for solutions (especially to routine, relatively unimportant problems). Unfortunately, 'satisfactory' outcomes need not be optimal: better solutions might appear if the search is continued a little longer.

19. Dealing with uncertainty

Coping with situations where the probabilities of events cannot be meaningfully estimated typically involves the following:

(a) Creation of reserves, surplus capacity and extra inventories capable of accommodating the effects of unforseeable eventualities. This obviously increases costs, but provides a defence against possible stockouts, random cash flow deficits, receipt of exceptionally large orders, etc.

(b) Contingency planning (see **20**).

(c) Negotiating stand-by loans with the firm's bank.

(d) Purchasing appropriate insurance.

(e) Preparation of scenarios (see **4.9**).

(f) Substantial investment in information collection and environmental monitoring systems, in order to obtain early warnings of changes likely to damage the business.

(g) Diversification of activities over many fields.

Monte Carlo simulation is a common technique for predicting possible outcomes in uncertain situations. The idea is to replicate mathematically a real life business scenario as accurately as possible, showing all the cause and effect relationships but introducing chance via the variation of the values of key variables at random and observing their effects. Random number tables (or a computer program that throws out numbers at random) are used to generate changes in the variables concerned. Monte Carlo models are relatively simple to construct and apply, but suffer all the drawbacks associated with mathematical modelling as outlined in **16**. In business, moreover, causal relationships might not continue for very long.

20. Contingency planning

Contingency plans are necessary in situations where an event is known to be extremely likely, but its timing cannot be predicted. Examples of such scenarios include:

(*i*) the onset of the next economic recession (it is inevitable that a recession will occur eventually, although no-one can say precisely when);

(*ii*) major systems failure (the collapse of a firm's entire computer system for instance);

(*iii*) loss of an important customer;

(*iv*) entry to the company's main market of an aggressive new competitor;

(*v*) interruption of supplies;
(*vi*) effects of bad weather;
(*vii*) strikes by distributors.

Preparation of contingency plans enables the firm to react instantaneously to changes in future environments or circumstances, even though it is not known when they will occur. Contingency planning differs from other forms of planning in that it is (obviously) impossible to develop quantitative models to plan for various contingencies. Rather simulations, scenario building and 'what if' types of analysis are necessary. As it is impossible to plan for *all* eventualities, a systematic procedure for identifying the contingencies which have the most critical implications for the firm is required. This will cost money, so a cost-benefit analysis to weigh up the benefits of 'being prepared' against the financial costs of such preparation is also needed.

The process of contingency planning is as follows:

(*i*) Identification of key environmental factors likely to affect company performance in terms of their probability of happening and potential to damage the firm.
(*ii*) Drafting a plan based on the most probable assumptions.
(*iii*) Revision of the plan assuming that a variety of less probable events will occur.
(*iv*) Variation of the assumptions underlying the plan.

A major advantage of contingency planning is that reactions to chance events can be predetermined, and actions decided in a calm atmosphere when plenty of time is available to consider their consequences.

Problems with contingency planning are that:

(*i*) the number of possible contingencies might be enormous;
(*ii*) management might not know what the various options are;
(*iii*) considering the wide range of potential outcomes it might be better simply to wait and see what happens and then respond to events.

TOP-DOWN VERSUS BOTTOM-UP PLANNING

21. Top-down planning

Top-down planning involves tight supervision of the entire planning process by the top management of the organisation, and has two alternative forms:

1. Senior management determines and hands down plans to lower levels without the latter's participation in their formulation.

2. Top management expresses its initial expectations and issues broad guidelines to lower levels, which then translate these aspirations into concrete action plans.

Top-down planning facilitates co-ordination and control of activities, and decisions can be made quickly. Management takes the initiative in devising plans, defines problems and imposes solutions. Problems with the approach are that:

- it can result in the domination of the planning process by people who are ill-equipped for the task;
- managers preparing the plan might be remote from the realities of the organisation;
- lack of involvement in the formulation of plans by lower levels could lead to plans not being implemented.

22. Bottom-up planning

Here, departments generate their own plans for achieving broadly defined objectives. Hence the firm's overall corporate plan is built up from a series of components prepared by operating units. With bottom-up planning a central planning unit (e.g. a planning committee – see 15.11) devises a general format to be followed by operating units when initiating proposals, and then co-ordinates the suggestions that emerge. It will still be the case, however, that *some* key plans will have to be prepared by the central planning department in a bottom-up system, notably plans for new product introductions or organisational restructuring, joint ventures and other projects not assignable to individual departments or subsidiaries. Bottom-up planning is sometimes effected via the issue to departments of a planning manual outlining the steps to be followed through and the issues addressed when preparing a departmental or divisional plan. The manual might contain forms and pro-forma guides to be completed by department heads.

The central planning unit of a company that practises bottom-up planning is likely to be small, as most of the nitty-gritty work is done by operating units. Note how the discussions leading to statements of departmental, subsidiary or divisional goals can be extremely time consuming and generate a significant bureaucracy in a bottom-up system. Further problems are:

(a) Consolidation of departmental plans may amount to little more than adding them together, without any genuine integration or co-ordination of intended actions.

(b) Departmental planners might believe that their plans are creative and innovative, whereas in fact they are wholly unrealistic in the context of the strategic management of the entire organisation.

(c) Junior managerial employees may not have the expertise necessary to formulate sensible plans.

(d) Departmental executives might not be familiar with the work of other sections or with the firm's overall situation.

(e) Each department, division or other operating unit is likely to have its own set of aspirations.

(f) Unit plans will be accompanied by requests for resources for implementing the plans in the units concerned, and the total amount of resources requested might exceed the level available within the organisation. Hence resource requests will be reduced according to some formula determined by top management, possibly resulting in unsatisfactory resource allocations for many units.

(g) The aggregated corporate plan resulting from bottom-up planning may lack coherence.

(h) The need for confidentiality in planning procedures relating to certain matters (attempts to out-manoeuvre competitors for instance) might prevent operating units being given all the management information needed to formulate unit plans effectively.

(i) Bottom-up planning cannot survive in an organisation in which it represents the *only* form of lower-level participation in management decision making.

(j) It invariably generates a great deal of (costly) activity but does not necessarily lead to any major decisions.

(k) Critical strategic decisions might be made outside the procedure (because of the latter's protracted nature) leading to disillusion with the system.

Advantages to the bottom-up approach are that it:

(a) utilises the skills and experiences of the staff who will be responsible for implementing the plans;

(b) motivates individuals towards the achievement of the targets that emerge;

(c) should facilitate the development of a common purpose within the organisation;

(d) develops decision-making abilities among lower-level managers;

(e) encourages responsible and flexible attitudes among employees and positive responses to change;

(f) enables management to receive valuable feedback from employees about day-to-day operations;

(g) involves a greater number of people in taking decisions and hence a lower risk of important factors being overlooked.

Implementation

In practice a mixture of top-down and bottom-up approaches is likely to emerge, with regular interaction between senior management and operating units.

Implementation of a plan will involve:

- allocation of responsibility for completing various tasks;
- preparation of budgets;
- scheduling of activities;
- co-ordination of work;
- establishment of review points at which progress will be evaluated;

- determination of procedures for altering the plan as circumstances change.

23. Evaluating the planning process

The following questions need to be asked when appraising the value of a planning process:

(a) How much did it cost? A plan may help the company attain its mission, but only at a prohibitively high cost. If the same amount of resources had been devoted to other activities, organisational effectiveness might have been improved.

(b) How closely were plans followed and what are the explanations for divergences?

(c) Were the objectives specified by the plans attained within the permitted time period?

(d) How did the plans contribute to the implementation of strategies?

(e) In retrospect, were the resources allocated adequate for specified tasks?

(f) Were the key assumptions underlying the plan valid?

(g) Has the system generated meaningful information on the behaviour of competitors?

(h) Have internal communications and the co-ordination of activities improved since the system was introduced?

(i) Is the system compatible with the management style practised within the company?

(j) Is the system properly understood throughout the organisation?

(k) Do heads of functions and other line managers find the system useful? Are these individuals aware of the financial costs of planning exercises and, if so, do they regard these expenditures as representing good value for money?

(l) Has the system identified major business opportunities and/or revealed significant threats?

(m) How useful has the system been for developing long-term objectives, appraising internal strengths and weaknesses, clarifying priorities, and stimulating fresh ideas?

Major criteria for appraising the calibre of a planning system are as follows:

(a) The extent to which the system has assisted the organisation in fulfilling its mission.

(b) Whether the stated purposes of the system have been achieved.

(c) How well the system compares with 'state-of-the-art' methods used by comparable organisations elsewhere (particularly rival firms).

(d) Whether plans have coincided with reality (though note how major divergences can result from unforeseeable events, quite independent of the quality of the firm's planning system).

The essential problem is to disentangle the effectiveness of the company's planning *system* from the individual skills and competencies of the people who implement the plans.

24. Failure of planning processes

Common reasons for the failure of planning processes include:

(a) excessive concentration on short-term issues connected with the maximisation of present profits, at the expense of long run growth;

(b) hostility towards the planning department by managers in other fields. Note how the staff involved in planning are typically well educated with more 'academic' backgrounds and orientations than many other managerial employees – leading perhaps to distrust on the part of executives who have 'risen through the ranks';

(c) lack of support for the planning function from top management;

(d) not rewarding people and departments who prepare and execute excellent plans, and not taking action to deal with poor planning efforts;

(e) not monitoring, measuring and controlling the development of plans;

(f) 'marginalising' the planning function, i.e. not integrating it into the firm's total management system;

(g) confusion of planning with forecasting, i.e. treating simple statistical extrapolations as 'plans';

(h) not adopting a bird's-eye view of the planning process and placing too much emphasis on petty detail;

(i) use of incorrect information and/or not devoting sufficient attention to the collection of information;

(j) not involving departmental and divisional heads in reviewing long-range plans developed by senior management;

(k) adhering to plans as if they were blueprints to be followed rigorously and without deviation, even though circumstances have changed;

(l) conducting a planning exercise once a year and then forgetting about the conclusions during the intervening 12 month periods;

(m) using planning mechanisms to delay decision making;

(n) not adopting an orderly and systematic approach to planning the planning process itself;

(o) not reviewing plans at regular intervals;

(p) abandoning plans at the first sign of trouble;

(q) line managers perceiving the chief executive and other senior executives as being generally uninterested in the firm's corporate plan;

(r) a single person attempting to write the entire corporate plan single-handed;

(s) not appreciating the multi-dimensional nature of the planning process.

Another source of difficulties might be the delegation of responsibility for the control and co-ordination of plans to too low a level in the management hierarchy. Then, senior management devotes excessive amounts of its time to current problems rather than to longer-term issues. Managers are busy people with many things on their minds. Hence it is not uncommon for managers to devote *all* their attention to day-to-day operational matters and to forget to plan. This creates the wrong *organisational climate* for effective planning.

Plans will fail, moreover, if:

- they do not relate to definitive and coherent strategies;
- senior management takes arbitrary decisions at odds with previously determined plans;
- there is poor communication between and co-ordination of sections and departments;
- no standards and benchmarks are established for comparing planned and actual performance.

Progress test 16

1. What is gap analysis?

2. State the three types of bench-marking.

3. Define 'return on capital employed'.

4. What do the acronyms APACS and POISE stand for?

5. Explain the maximax decision criterion.

6. List the problems associated with top-down planning.

7. State six questions that need to be asked when appraising the value of a planning exercise.

17

OPERATIONAL PLANNING

1. Need for operational planning

There is little point in having corporate strategies and overall company plans without preparing detailed operating plans to accompany them. Operational planning is the force that drives the implementation of corporate plans. It is action orientated and necessarily involves line executives in plan formulation. This section examines the operating plans necessary for the four basic functional areas of business: production and operations management; marketing; human resources; and finance. Benefits derived from the preparation of operational plans are that:

- morale and commitment among the junior managers involved in their development should improve;
- day-to-day operational difficulties will be pinpointed;
- they provide a basis for control and employee/sectional appraisal;
- junior managers gain valuable experience that will eventually help them undertake more senior planning duties.

PRODUCTION AND OPERATIONS MANAGEMENT

The nature of operations management is discussed in 13.1. It is particularly associated with techniques of production, although many of the core concepts of operations management are equally applicable to service firms.

2. Production planning

Production planning involves first 'preproduction programming', which concerns (i) production specification, deciding the quantity and rate of production, and (ii) process engineering; choosing production methods, work study, design of tools and equipment. It further involves work planning, including determination of project completion dates, the drafting of networks, arrangement of tools, materials and equipment, and the scheduling of activities.

Activities relevant to production planning include: design; specification of dimensions, materials inputs and quality; ensuring the compatibility of one component with others; job description; issuing detailed instructions to supervisors; inspection; quality control; packaging, loading and despatch. Production plans are implemented by controllers responsible for minimising manufacturing delays by regulating flows of work. Effective production control depends on information about work priorities or constraints; available machinery, labour and materials; and about the existing workload. Employees known as progress chasers follow work all the way through the production process. Reasons for delays are investigated, bottlenecks are anticipated, interruptions in work flow are remedied. An effective progress chaser will know, at any moment in time:

what work is being done;
how it is done;
which machines are being used;
how much labour is available;
what raw materials and other inputs are currently in stock.

Interruptions may result from non or late delivery of materials, machine breakdowns, staff sickness, strikes, staff lateness due to public transport difficulties, computer malfunctions or stock shortages. Efficient communication between the shop floor and the controlling unit is essential. There has to be a continuous flow of information on workloads, raw materials availabilities, surplus capacities, breakdowns and maintenance activities. Scheduling is especially problematic when demand for output fluctuates suddenly. Often, it is cheaper to continue production during slack periods because of set-up costs and the problems of regaining skilled labour following temporary shut-downs.

Acceptance of large contracts

A major problem is deciding whether to accept major contracts from new customers or, if demand is increasing generally, the rate at which the firm should expand. Suppose for example that new production lines are established to supply a big order – resources are diverted from other areas, extra workers are hired, more raw materials are purchased. But then the order is cancelled, or the customer ceases to trade, after the supplying firm has already incurred all its set-up costs. Equally, higher output levels might create labour and materials shortages and cause bottlenecks within the firm: delivery dates lengthen, quality and reliability of production could diminish. Increases in demand can quickly be followed by demand reductions and, in consequence, excess capacity. Thus, firms often handle busy periods through increased overtime, extra shifts, or sub-contracting to avoid having to purchase additional plant. The overall issue of business expansion is discussed in Chapter 3.

3. Purpose of production planning

The purpose of production planning is to ensure that the right number of finished items are produced at the right level of quality at the right time. Specific reasons for undertaking production planning are to:

- smooth the flow of production;
- meet contracted delivery dates;
- utilise human resources to the best advantage;

- reduce stocks of raw materials and work-in-progress and hence minimise inventory holding costs;
- reduce idle time for machines and labour;
- minimise the use of (expensive) overtime working;
- improve the speed and quality of feedback;
- reduce scrap and material wastage;
- generate information on the whereabouts of materials and work-in-progress at any moment during the production process;
- make the best use of plant, equipment and premises;
- avoid bottlenecks in production;
- control production costs;
- co-ordinate production and marketing activities;
- avoid having to 'rob' one order to satisfy another;
- minimise hold-ups due to materials and parts shortages;
- cope with the technological complexity of modern production methods.

4. The production planning process

The main steps in the production planning process are as follows:

(a) Determination of the basic manufacturing methods to be applied to particular jobs and items.

(b) Gathering information on machine and labour options, input availabilities, extent of spare capacity, etc.

(c) Deciding on the materials to be used in production and scheduling the arrival of stock and work-in-progress in time with their utilisation.

(d) Scheduling the progress of batches of production through the system.

Contents of production plans

Production planning means deciding what is to be done, where, when, how and by whom. It involves *scheduling* the timing of processing, assembly and manufacture (i.e. determining start, completion and delivery times); *machine loading* (i.e. assignment of work to particular machines and equipment); *materials availability planning* (including the storage and handling of items); and arranging for *dispatch* to customers. Production plans need to consider:

- new equipment requirements;
- process layouts;
- machine capacities;
- materials handling and storage requirements;
- factory layout;
- delivery periods for inputs and new equipment;
- maintenance requirements and durations;
- the relationships between various operations and activities;
- the costs and time requirements of tasks.

Characteristics of typical production plans are that they:

(a) have short time horizons (usually a few weeks or months);

(b) are subject to frequent change as input and machine availabilities, etc., alter;

(c) are fully determined, with each job being carefully scheduled (as opposed to broad objectives being specified);

(d) are highly detailed;

(e) necessarily generate large amounts of feedback to the production planner;

(f) are quantitative rather than qualitative;

(g) production planning is necessarily extensive, covering all aspects of the manufacture of an item, from the procurement of raw materials through to final despatch.

5. Scheduling

A schedule is a programme of activities to determine the production of particular items by specific times, accompanied by a list of priorities and contingencies for when things do not work out as intended. The schedule will allocate start and finish times to each job and specify when materials components and work-in-progress are to be shifted between sections. All the jobs and operations needed to complete each order must be documented, and the order in which they should take place has to be outlined (via PERT for example – see 16.9). The purpose of scheduling is to organise work in such a way as to deliver orders on time, at the minimum production cost. Effective scheduling results in a smooth flow of work between each stage of production, with regular movements of work and all machine groups, etc., having an even workload. Establishing priorities for jobs might not be a straightforward matter. Various criteria can be used to determine which orders receive priority, including:

- the value of the job;
- the importance of the customer;
- giving priority to jobs that will take the longest time to complete;
- prioritising jobs with the shortest production times;
- dealing with orders strictly according to the sequence in which they are received.

Scheduling can only succeed if there is existing reliable information on existing work loads and future commitments, estimated processing times, stock delivery leadtimes, machine capacities and despatch requirements.

6. Capacity planning

This means relating the intensity of a firm's production operations to the forecast level of demand for its products. Capacity planning has two aspects: predicting future capacity requirements, and deciding how present capacity should be utilised. It purposes are to:

- relate the level of production to the level of sales;

- avoid bottlenecks in production;
- facilitate scheduling (see **5**);
- identify inadequacies in the capacities of various operational areas and hence provide a rational basis for future capital investment decisions.

Capacity depends on the number of machine hours available and output per machine. These are determined by the number of shifts worked, setting-up time, inspection and quality checking requirements, relaxation allowances for machine operatives, etc. Increased production capacity may be obtained through:

(a) more intense operation of existing plant and equipment (overtime working, speeding up production lines, etc.). Note the additional costs (higher wages and maintenance bills for example) that such measures involve;

(b) purchase of new plant and equipment for use within the present premises;

(c) acquiring or merging with other firms;

(d) contract manufacturing (see 13.**21**) and licensing arrangements.

Further capacity requirements will depend on the firm's overall corporate strategies (especially diversification strategies) and on market circumstances (rate of growth, bouyancy, seasonal factors, taste changes in consumer taste, etc.). Usage of current capacity will relate to the firm's decisions *vis-à-vis* various items, the relative importance of particular customers, and to the availability of skilled labour and other crucial resources. Other factors influencing capacity planning include:

(a) the firm's make or buy policies (see 13.**18**) and how it deals with fluctuations in demand (e.g. the extent to which it is prepared to produce for stock);

(b) sales forecasts;

(c) whether economies of scale are available from long production runs;

(d) how easily the level of output from a machine can be varied (via flexible manufacturing for instance – see 13.**7**);

(e) possibilities for sub-contracting.

Operating on a low level of capacity utilisation gives the firm the advantage of always being able to complete extra orders at short notice, but leaves expensive plant and equipment standing idle for long periods. A company that uses all its capacity all the time will need to sub-contract in the event of demand for its output suddenly increasing.

Capacity planning can be long term or short term. Long-term capacity planning seeks to provide the production capacity and resources that the firm will need over the next two or three years, as determined by the business's overall strategic plan and taking into account likely changes in markets and technical methods. The essential feature of long-term capacity planning is that it assumes that resources are flexible: that new machines and equipment may be purchased; and that surplus equipment can be discarded. Short-term capacity planning (where the total amount of capacity available is fixed) is sometimes referred to as 'aggregate planning'. Its aim is to create the appropriate amount of short-term spare capacity at each stage in the production process. Usually the planner will wish to minimise the degree of spare capacity carried (but see 7). Another goal is to reduce the inventory of work-in-progress to the lowest possible level. Short-term capacity planning involves decisions on producing for stock, the timing of machine maintenance, overtime working, labour lay-offs, engagement of temporary employees, transfer of labour between sections, and subcontracting.

Machine loading

Machine loading decisions concern which machines (or collections of machines) are to be used for which purposes and for what periods. To take such decisions it is necessary to prepare a detailed schedule of the output capacities of all the machines in the company and then relate work requirements to these capacities having regard to expected stoppages (for breakdowns, maintenance, tool adjustments, etc.), operator efficiency, and possibilities for overtime working. Efficient machine loading will reduce (i) waiting time for work-in-progress, (ii) machine idle-time and (iii) set-up costs. An even balance of work undertaken by various machine groups should be established.

7. Optimised production technology (OPT)

This is more of an overall approach to production management than a specific technique. It seeks to minimise work in progress by isolating and, where possible, removing bottlenecks in materials flows. Importantly, it does *not* assume that peak efficiency is attained by keeping every machine, worker and process fully employed all the time. The steps involves in installing an OPT system are as follows:

(a) Identify bottlenecks, e.g. the time taken to set up machines or to adjust tolerances, delivery holdups, stockouts, etc.

(b) Devise work schedules to guarantee that the equipment or processes associated with bottlenecks are fully supplied at all times – even if this means plant, equipment and labour standing idle further back in the chain of production.

(c) Integrate the entire system under a single coherent production plan.

8. Materials requirements planning (MRP)

This means scheduling the manufacture of dependent items (components, sub-assemblies and so on) that have varying lead times and inventory requirements, in order to satisfy customers' orders on time but with minimum holdings of work-in-progress stocks. MRP synchronises the ordering and delivery of manufacturing processes. It requires accurate forecasting of the demand for the final products and precise timetabling of activities. Sophisticated versions of such (computerised) systems are called 'manufacturing resource planning' methods. These integrate MRP with the total management information system of the firm.

9. Just-in-time (J-I-T) procedures

In a J-I-T production control system, work is planned so that each production unit delivers to the next unit precisely the input it requires in order to proceed with the next stage of manufacture (or processing) and delivers the input just in time for the work to begin. In consequence, few if any stocks of inputs are carried, and there is no bunching of production lines or queues anywhere in the system.

Production workers themselves are expected to operate the system, which – if it succeeds – will result in the need to carry much less work-in-progress than before (sometimes as much as four times less than previously). Each worker assumes personal responsibility for quality and production control. Workers are organised into 'cells' which organise their own work and are put in charge of the repair and maintenance of the equipment they use, of quality control, and the timing of movements of work from one cell to another. Hence they acquire much experience of operational decision making and routine production control.

The Japanese Toyota Motor Company was one of the first in the world to adopt a fully integrated just-in-time production system. Tasks completed by each worker are designed to take about the same time to complete and to involve similar paces of working. The aim is to have all jobs finished at the same instant, both upstream and downstream within the system. Anyone experiencing a difficulty may activate an alarm which triggers a bell and flashing yellow light on his or her workstation. Then employees from neighbouring units quickly down tools and move to help solve the problem. Periods lost through stoppages at various workstations are recorded automatically through the computerised production control system. The causes of difficulties are analysed on a daily basis, with specific problems being referred to the appropriate quality circle. Ninety-five per cent of all system improvements are proposed and implemented by the firm's own workers. Transporters continuously move up the assembly line carrying components for incorporation into part-finished vehicles. As soon as one transporter is empty another takes its place, removing the need for idle stocks of door panels, seats, windscreens, etc. Externally purchased inputs are obtained from suppliers (usually just one for each category of component) with which Toyota has long-term contractual agreements and which regularly contribute to discussions concerning the types of input required and the appropriate level of quality. Suppliers are given training and other assistance in relevant circumstances. Hence, supplies arrive in a reliable and predictable sequence so that no capital need be tied up in inventory.

Requirements of J-I-T systems

J-I-T requires precise scheduling of raw materials procurement, production processing and despatch. And there has to be a predictable daily demand throughout the entire sequence of manufacture, with minimal changeover time and extremely reliable equipment. Arguably, moreover, successful application of J-I-T methods implies the need to simplify products and rationalise product lines to avoid having to carry numerous different components and other input stocks. Further prerequisites for an effective J-I-T system include:

(a) high standards of equipment maintenance to prevent breakdowns, plus immediate attention to machine failures that do occur;

(b) flexible and well-trained operatives capable of undertaking work anywhere it is currently required;

(c) an efficient monitoring system for identifying problems as they arise.

10. Problems in production planning

Production of goods in batches is subject to complex movements of items between work units and operatives, and it is easy for batches mistakenly to be broken up. Machine loading (see 6) can also be complicated. Further difficulties are:

(a) It might not be possible to avoid particular batches lying around for long periods between operations.

(b) Extensive documentation of movements of batches around a factory may be required.

(c) Materials can fail to arrive at specific work points, preventing the processing of work-in-progress and causing great disruption to the entire system.

(d) Frequent movement of goods and materials creates the need for the storage of items in many places and at many times during the production process. Storage must be planned separately from production.

With continuous flow production, conversely, the problems are:

(a) ensuring the uninterrupted arrival at the firm's premises of large amounts of raw materials and/or input components;

(b) integrating the flow of production of finished output with the marketing activities necessary to promote and sell the goods;

(c) arranging the warehousing of the flow of output, especially when customer demand is low;

(d) coping with a breakdown in the system, which will cease to operate in its entirety following just a minor hold-up. Input materials will have to be put into storage while the stoppage is sorted out.

Planning for continuous flow production is perhaps easier than when batches of items are involved because less detailed scheduling (and associated paperwork) is required. There is a single flow of work through the system – changes to which are simple to implement. On the other hand, planning for continuous production is inflexible in that labour and other resources cannot readily be redeployed among different machine/equipment groups in the event of a breakdown (as is the case with batch production, where orders can be rerouted, temporarily held back or accelerated through part of the system).

FINANCIAL PLANNING

11. Nature of financial planning

Operational planning *vis-à-vis* finance involves budgeting (see 18.**12**), selection of sources of short-term funds (see 10.4), fund flow analysis (see below) and cash flow forecasting (see **12**), investment appraisal, and establishing targets for certain financial ratios (see 16.**4–7**). The goals of financial planning are to maintain the liquidity of the business (i.e. ensure it has enough short-term assets to settle current liabilities), have cash flowing into the firm at crucial moments, and be able to replace capital assets when necessary.

Fund flow analysis

Aggregate fund flow analysis is a key tool in financial planning. It might relate to the firm as a whole and/or to specific projects, and will seek to predict inflows and outflows of funds (e.g. inflows from money contributed by shareholders; outflows to purchase other businesses) and to assess the implications of various options for financing projects. Fund flow planning involves the following:

(a) Forecasting the magnitudes of the funds circulating within the business.

(b) Balancing inflows and outflows (via borrowing and/or new share issue if appropriate).

(c) Estimating the likely bad debt situation.

(d) Relating the timing of expenditures on materials, equipment, etc., to income from sales.

12. The cash flow forecast (CFF)

Aggregate planned income and expenditure for the year should be broken down into monthly totals showing expected receipts and payments for each month, with the closing cash balance of one month being carried forward to an opening balance for the next. The CFF is important because it takes into account the effects on monthly cash balances of credit sales and the *timing* of expenditures. Businesses frequently fail because – despite their being potentially solvent in aggregate terms – they do not realise that debtors can take extremely long periods to settle bills, whereas suppliers may have to be paid instantly and in cash. Certain quarterly payments might all fall due at the same time, possibly coinciding with other large expenditures.

Each month's figures should contain details of expected cash sales and a realistic estimate of revenue from credit sales, business expenses (telephone, heating, stationery, etc.), payments for capital equipment, wages, and drawings, loan repayments, and tax and national insurance obligations, including VAT. The methods used to calculate figures should be specified in notes appended to the document. For example, it might be assumed that one quarter of all invoices sent out during a month will be paid within that month, half during the next month, and two-thirds of the remainder in the month after that. Similarly, the CFF might assume that all materials and equipment purchases are paid for in the month following delivery.

HUMAN RESOURCE PLANNING

13. Nature of human resource planning (HRP)

HRP seeks to forecast the number and types of employee that the firm will require in the future and the extent to which this demand is likely to be met. It involves the comparison of an organisation's current human resources with likely future needs and, consequently, the establishment of programmes for hiring, training, redeploying and possibly discarding employees. Effective HRP should result in the right people doing the right things in the right place at precisely the right time.

Examples of outcomes to an HRP exercise include:

- rationalisation of the workforce (e.g. via redundancy or early retirement for some workers and the retraining and redeployment of others);
- changing the balance of skills and competencies within the workforce;
- alterations in the internal communication system, especially in relation to making employees aware of the firm's major objectives;
- changing the accountability structure within the enterprise;
- implementation of recruitment and training programmes.

Factors likely to influence a firm's human resource plan include:

(a) existing labour resources in terms of the competence, ages, motivation and training of currently employed workers;

(b) labour productivity in various sections of the company;

(c) the attitudes of senior management towards employment matters (recognition of trade unions, use of casual workers, commitment to the provision of continuous employment, etc.);

(d) the firm's competitive environment;

(e) the state of the labour market (external supply of labour, wage levels, workers' willingness to work overtime, and so on);

(f) forecasts of new technological developments;

(g) sales forecasts;

(h) the extent to which the firm is willing to produce for stock during slack periods;

(i) the company's overall plans *vis-à-vis* the introduction of new products, growth and diversification, etc.

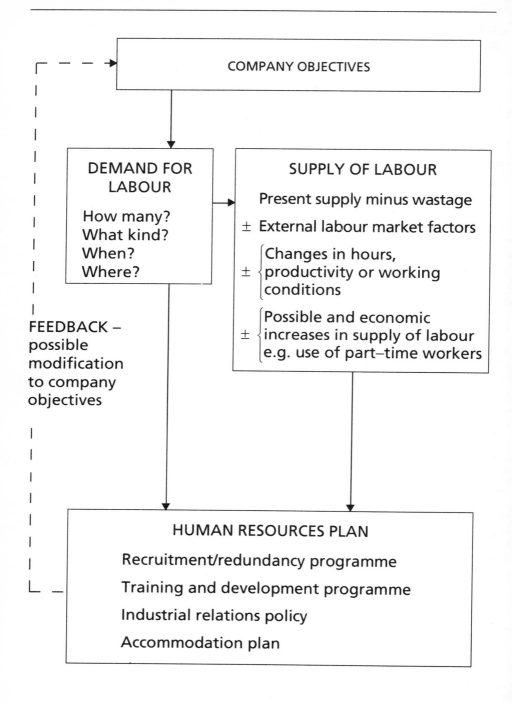

Figure 17.1 The HRP process

14. Need for human resource planning

The desirability of HRP is evident in the growing needs for companies to utilise the right sorts of skilled worker and to minimise recruitment and training expenditures. Further reasons for engaging in HRP include:

(a) the disruptions in production caused by the non-availability of labour;

(b) the high proportion of total cost attributable to wages and other labour expenditures in many industries;

(c) the bad effects on the morale of the workforce if compulsory redundancies become necessary;

(d) increasing organisational complexity which generates demands for a wider range of specialist competencies than previously;

(e) the long training and employee development periods necessary for certain types of occupation;

(f) employment protection legislation which requires that statutory procedures be followed to the letter when making workers redundant;

(g) the need to compete in fiercely competitive international markets against rival companies with low labour costs;

(h) firms' inabilities to expand their operations without having access to skilled labour;

(i) desires to provide employees with a career ladder and genuine prospects for promotion;

(j) the advent of new technologies (especially those involving robotics and computers – see 13.8) that have transformed the structure of employment and the skills, knowledge and attitudes required of workers;

(k) problems created by age imbalances within an organisation (i.e. having too many very young or old workers – the former lack experience while the latter might all retire at the same time).

15. Contents of the human resources plan

The HRP should indicate in detail, by function, occupation and location, how many employees it is practicable to employ at various stages in the future. The following should be included:

(a) jobs which will appear, disappear, or change;

(b) to what extent redeployment or retraining is possible;

(c) necessary changes at supervisory and management levels;

(d) training needs;

(e) recruitment, redundancy or retirement programmes;

(f) industrial relations implications;

(g) arrangements for feedback in case modifications in the plan or company objectives are necessary;

(h) details of arrangements for handling any human problems arising from labour deficits or surpluses (e.g. early retirement or other natural wastage procedures).

The advantages of HRP include the following:

(a) The organisation should be better equipped to cope with the human resourcing consequences of changed circumstances.

(b) Careful consideration of likely future human resource requirements could lead the firm to discover new and improved ways of managing human resources.

(c) Labour shortfalls and surpluses might be avoided.

(d) It helps the firm create and develop employee training and management succession programmes.

(e) Some of the problems of managing change may be foreseen and their consequences mitigated. Consultations with affected groups and individuals can occur at an early stage in the change process: decisions can be taken unhurriedly and by considering all relevant options, rather than being taken in crisis situations.

(f) Management is compelled to assess critically the strengths and weaknesses of its labour force and personnel policies.

(g) Duplication of effort among employees can be avoided, co-ordination and integration of workers' efforts is improved.

Problems with HRP include the following:

(a) It concerns human beings, and humans sometimes behave in seemingly irrational and unpredictable ways – making accurate forecasting of behaviour (resignation rates for instance) extremely difficult.

(b) Plans can become too complex for effective implementation.

(c) HRP exercises might lead to labour hoarding, as management may be reluctant to depart from carefully formulated plans following downturns in demand.

(d) Market environments may be so volatile that consequent requirements for labour could be virtually impossible to predict. Note the large number of external variables affecting the company's demand for labour (growth rate of the economy, inflation, levels of national unemployment, government taxation of consumers, etc.) that are beyond the firm's control.

(e) Employees might resist the changes suggested by the plan.

(f) The need to have very complete and accurate employee records, maintained for at least the last five years, which it is hoped can be used to detect trends in employee movements. These trends may, however, be very unreliable in times of high unemployment.

(g) The plan may indicate recruitment and training programmes which, although desirable, may be impossible to put into practice because the money to pay for them may not be currently available. Because of its financial position the company may find long-term plans useless.

MARKETING PLANS

16. The marketing audit

Marketing plans derive from marketing strategies. They quantify and precisely specify targets for each element in the company's marketing mix. Typically, the first step in the production of a marketing plan is the completion of a 'marketing audit', i.e. a comprehensive review of the effectiveness of the firm's current marketing activities. Audits should be completed periodically or whenever environments significantly change.

Internal audits cover such matters as the efficiency of the salesforce, the analysis of causes of differences in the performances of various marketing staff, the adequacy of existing products and the usefulness of current advertisements and other promotional techniques. Other topics for examination include:

- product knowledge of employees;
- effects of salespeoples' commission systems;
- desirability of product standardisation;
- possibilities for doing more things in-house rather than relying on outsiders (advertising agencies for example);
- training and staff development needs;
- adequacy of existing marketing budgets.

External audits investigate market trends, profitabilities of various markets, the strengths and weaknesses of competitors, and the impact the firm's corporate image presently creates. Distribution systems should also be analysed, especially possibilities for changing or removing intermediaries.

17. The marketing plan

The marketing plan is the device whereby all the company's marketing activities are integrated in order to implement a marketing strategy. Its purposes are to:

- co-ordinate marketing, production and distribution activities;
- identify profitable marketing opportunities;
- facilitate the development of new products;
- deploy marketing resources in the most efficient manner (including the sales force);
- maximise the firm's competitive advantages in various fields;
- ensure that the correct prices are charged for the firm's products.

Major inputs to the marketing plan comprise the sales forecast, results from marketing research exercises (see Figure 17.2), market and competitor analyses, and corporate plans in relation to new product development, market entry and distribution arrangements. Available resources have to be examined and any additional resources necessary to attain objectives determined.

The plan itself needs to contain sales targets, budgets, media advertising schedules and action plans for implementing marketing policies. Decisions are required in relation to:

- the market segments to be targeted;
- how, where and when ideas for new products are to be generated, screened and tested;
- the timing of new product introductions and the withdrawal of declining products;
- field sales operations and product distribution;
- distribution channels;
- market research activities;
- the market shares and profit margins required of various products.

Product planning

Product planning seeks to ensure that the firm always possesses a balanced portfolio of products (see 3.27). Thus it is necessary to monitor the demand for various product features and deploy resources to guarantee the availability of the skills and materials needed to supply appropriate items.

Sales planning

Targets are needed for sales volume, costs and profits per sale. This involves determining policies for discounts and credit allowable, sales training, and the deployment and appraisal of the salesforce (see **18**).

Media planning

This concerns planning the firm's advertising effort, setting budgets and evaluating advertising effectiveness in terms of cost, market penetration and coverage. This is discussed further in **19**.

Need for marketing planning

Much wasteful expenditure will occur if goods that are advertised and otherwise promoted in the market place are not in fact available for purchase (e.g. because of interruptions in production or problems with distribution channels). Also the timing of marketing activities is crucial to the success of a promotion: discounts must be made available at just the right moment; advertisements need to be scheduled to achieve maximum effort; salespeople should call on key customers when they are likely to be most receptive, etc.

18. Deployment of salespeople

Salespeople can be deployed by geographical area (thus minimising travelling times between home and office and customers) or be assigned to selling one

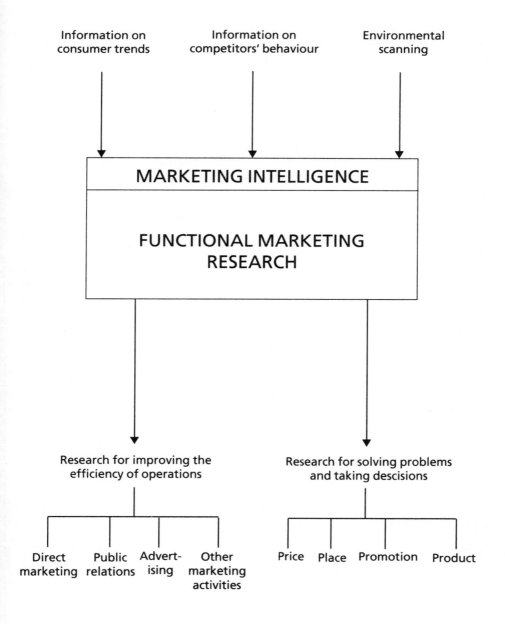

Figure 17.2 Marketing research

(usually technically complex) product to any customer in any location. Large companies taking large orders have advantages here, since small firms dealing in low quantities must pay their sales staff similar wages to bigger firms whose staff sell larger amounts.

Measuring a salesperson's performance solely on the basis of value of orders received is unsatisfactory because one or two really big orders will create impressions of efficiency that are not necessarily true. Hence, sales volume should be considered relative to other factors, such as the number of orders obtained; number of calls made; how many completely new customers are secured; size of territory covered and the amount of travelling needed to contact customers. Thus, good salespeople should outperform their colleagues regardless of the particular area covered.

19. Media planning

Media planning involves the determination of the best means for delivering, at the lowest available cost per thousand prospects, promotional messages to as wide an audience of target customers as possible and scheduling the appearance of advertisements so as to maximise consumer response and/or awareness. This necessitates matching carefully defined target market segments with media vehicles that possess audiences which closely parallel the characteristics of target consumer groups. The closer the match, the less money is wasted on communicating with individuals who are not remotely likely to purchase the advertised brand. Key elements in a media plan include statements of campaign objectives, how often advertisements will appear and the target number of people that will see them, a customer profile, how much is to be spent on advertising in each media category (radio, TV, newspapers, etc.), an execution schedule and a budget. Reasons for selecting particular media vehicles (i.e. individual magazine titles, television channels, *specific* radio channels, etc.) need to be outlined, and the methods and criteria to be used for evaluating the effectiveness of the campaign must be stated.

20. Advertising budgets

Budgeting and budget allocations generally are discussed in 18:12. Advertising budgets may be determined according to any of the methods there discussed, although in practice the most popular approach is the 'percentage of sales method' whereby the firm automatically allocates a fixed percentage of the value of its (say) quarterly sales of each of its products to advertising those products. It is assumed that increasing sales require additional advertising to sustain them. There are a number of advantages to the technique:

1. It guarantees that the firm only spends on advertising as much as it can afford.

2. Advertising effort becomes 'market led' in that resources are channelled primarily towards products that have genuine market appeal and which therefore are likely to do even better in future. The percentage of sales approach prevents 'good money being thrown after bad'. Each product is given the advertising it deserves.

3. Expanding markets are automatically developed as increased advertising within them will generate greater public awareness of the firm's output, hopefully generating even more sales.

4. Periods of exceptionally high sales create windfall income that can be used to experiment with new media, fresh creative strategies and high risk avant-garde approaches that otherwise could never be considered. A single successful experiment might lead to a promotional breakthrough with enormous long-term benefits for the advertising firm.

This method is particularly suitable for low-cost high-price (and hence relatively lower sales levels) items, since here there is a large margin available for advertising, which should of course boost sales.

The main disadvantage of the approach is that it ignores the possibility that extra spending on advertising may in fact be necessary when sales are declining, in order to reverse the trend. Other problems are that:

(a) the technique cannot be used to launch new products or to enter fresh markets;

(b) advertising costs can differ significantly from country to country, so that a greater level of expenditure may be needed to achieve a given level of performance in some markets than in others.

(c) the method's convenience and simplicity encourages management not to bother investigating the relationships between advertising and sales or to analyse critically the overall effectiveness of its advertising campaigns.

Progress test 17

1. What dangers are associated with the acceptance of large contracts?

2. List some of the reasons for production planning.

3. Define capacity planning.

4. What is meant by the term 'optimised production technology'.

5. What are the goals of financial planning?

6. Why is it essential for a firm to have a cash flow forecast?

7. List some of the possible outcomes to a human resources planning exercise.

8. What are the advantages of human resources planning?

9. Explain the purpose of a marketing audit.

10. What is media planning?

11. List the benefits of setting an advertising budget according to the percentage of sales method.

18

MANAGEMENT CONTROL

1. The control function

Control has three aspects: establishing standards and targets; monitoring activities and comparing actual with target performance; and implementing measures to remedy deficiencies. Control links inputs to outputs and provides feedback to those in command. The firm's corporate plan should represent a comprehensive statement of the intended activities and goals of a variety of functions and departments. Thus, mechanisms are needed to ensure that plans are implemented and the work of disparate sections effectively controlled. Further purposes of control are:

- to improve operational efficiency;
- to facilitate the management of change:
- to develop a common culture within the organisation;
- to assist the application of modern management methods such as just-in-time (see 17.9) and total quality management.

Control systems are needed for both strategic and operational purposes. Strategic control involves establishing benchmarks for determining whether current strategies should be altered and, if so, how and when. It requires information on key external events and environments, and the data collected has to far more wide-ranging than that necessary for operational control.

An effective control system will enable the rapid deployment of resources to their most efficient uses; disperse management expertise throughout the organisation; and generate comprehensive information on the activities of subsidiary units.

2. Control systems

Devices for effecting control include:

- organisation charts and manuals;
- delegation;
- PERT systems (see 16.9);
- ratio analysis (see 7);
- feedback and feedforward systems (see 6);
- management by objectives (MBO);
- exception reporting (see 5);

- employee appraisal systems;
- APACS (see 16.**14**);
- budgets.

In general, the less expensive the control process the better. Thus, automatic control systems that require minimal human intervention are normally more efficient than systems which require constant supervision. Control systems need to contain three major elements: information input, data evaluation, and feedback to the controlling authority. Rapid feedback is essential; otherwise problems could develop faster than the controller's capacity to correct them. Action should always be taken when targets are not achieved, since there is little point in installing a sophisticated control mechanism only to ignore the deficiencies it reveals.

The first stage in the control process is the careful description of all current activities. Achievements are compared with targets and, if necessary, corrective action is taken or targets are amended to more realistic levels. Problems inevitably occur. Among the more substantial are the possibilities that:

(a) Current activities may not be reported accurately, comprehensively, or in sufficient detail.

(b) Inappropriate criteria might be used when setting performance objectives, resulting in unattainable targets which render the entire system inoperable.

(c) Historical records of relevant activities could be inadequate;.

(d) Information retrieval systems may be faulty.

Control systems usually (and perhaps necessarily) involve some degree of bureaucracy, but should not be allowed to inhibit creativity and innovation within the firm. The system should follow from the determination of strategies and plans, and not itself influence how strategies are formulated.

3. Control procedures

'Procedures' are standard ways of doing things. The main advantages to having standard procedures are that unqualified and/or recently appointed employees can complete tasks without having to set up administrative frameworks or take decisions, and that duplication of effort may be avoided. Further benefits are that:

(a) There is no need for staff to exercise discretion when undertaking tasks.

(b) Written records of standard procedures can be kept in a manual.

(c) There is less scope for arguments between people and departments regarding how work should be completed.

Problems with the application of standard procedures arise when:

(a) they become out of date but are still utilised;

(b) personnel apply them without any thought and in inappropriate situations;

(c) procedures are regarded as convenient devices for solving problems that in fact require careful analysis and discussion;

(d) they become part of a rigid bureaucracy, stifling innovation and creativity.

Procedures should be reviewed periodically in order to assess their value and to determine which should be revised or discarded.

4. Principles of control

The more clearly specified are a company's mission, strategies and policies then the more obvious and consistent will be the plans it produces, and the more self-evident the types of control mechanism it needs to apply. The following general principles should be adopted when devising a control system.

(a) Controls should focus on the key variables that determine the success or failure of the business. Obviously the control of routine duties is important, but the consequences of inadequate control will be nowhere near as catastrophic for the organisation as a whole as neglecting to control success factors that are absolutely critical for the well-being of the firm.

(b) Reports submitted through the system should relate to issues rather than individual performance. Inaccurate information will be submitted if a report might reveal failure to meet standards, with consequent penalties for the person or section concerned.

(c) Early feedback on problems should be generated.

(d) The control system should itself be subject to control. Performance of the system should be regularly monitored, especially in relation to its ability to co-ordinate the work of various sections and departments.

(e) Control information needs to be presented to people in formats that appeal to them and which they fully understand.

(f) The system should be financially cost-effective.

(g) Control mechanisms need to be sufficiently flexible to operate effectively even if corporate plans have to be altered.

The information on which a control system is based needs to be accurate, comprehensive and directly relevant to the firm's activities. It should be as objective as possible, and preferably stated in quantitative terms. Note however that some information necessary for effective control will inevitably be subjective – assessments of staff morale or customer satisfaction for example.

5. Control by exception

A common approach to control is the application of the principle of 'management by exception' (MBE), i.e. the practice of employees submitting to their bosses only brief condensed reports on normal operations but extensive reports on deviations from past average performance or targets set by higher management. Once established, standards should be monitored by picking out significant deviations from predetermined norms. Exceptionally good or bad results are analysed in detail and explanations supplied, but the day-to-day functioning of the organisation within reasonable divergences from normal practice is not questioned.

MBE enables senior managers to devote their full attention to major policy issues and avoid becoming immersed in routine administration. However MBE does have disadvantages, as follows:

(a) Delays occur between the moment a problem arises, the moment it is noticed, and the time remedial action is implemented.

(b) Since 'acceptable deviations' from target performance are tolerated without investigation, it is possible for a particular activity to be perpetually above or below standard by a relatively small amount without the fact ever being reported.

(c) The administrative work involved in preparing summary statistics to ascertain whether operations are within acceptable limits can itself be extensive.

Note how the computerisation of business and manufacturing systems has removed the need for many management by exception procedures. MBE was popular in years past because of the enormous volume of information continuously generated within firms, and the physical impossibility of continuously monitoring actual activities. Thus, data was collected continuously but analysed periodically (weekly, monthly, quarterly, annually). With computers however, continuous monitoring of all activity within the firm becomes possible. Information on costs, outputs, revenues, and other relevant variables can be immediately analysed at the moment of collection, and existing summaries can be updated at once. Managers in control of a computerised system can requisition information at will and order its presentation in any one of a variety of alternative forms. Problems are highlighted instantly – they will be observed on the appropriate manager's visual display unit whenever he or she types into the system a command to update information on current activities. Production lines which begin to produce defectives; labour and materials costs which start to get out of hand; increasing overheads; falling sales, etc., can be identified as they happen so that remedial action can be applied at once. Functions such as stocktaking, collation of production figures or the preparation of management accounts can be undertaken on a continuous basis.

6. Feedforward and feedback

Performance indices such as return on capital employed or profit per unit of sales are necessarily retrospective. They are computed after events have taken place, and when the information arrives it may be too late to remedy malfunctions. For instance, in January, management might decide to alter its advertising strategy: new media are selected and different product images are formed. The revised approach is introduced in June and results are closely monitored. Salespeople submit reports on customer response, sales figures are collated, and opinion surveys conducted. But data will not begin to arrive until some time after the initial launch and, if mistakes have been made, their consequences might, by now, be extremely severe. Feedback does not anticipate future eventualities or evaluate what is happening here and now.

It may be preferable therefore for the control system to attempt to identify and measure variables likely to influence future performance. Likely problems are forecast in advance and measures implemented now in order to overcome them. Thus, whereas feedback systems concentrate on initiating remedial actions at the output stage, feedforward schemes are pre-emptive and centre on decision making in the input period. If inputs differ from activities necessary to overcome predicted difficulties, they are altered in appropriate ways. For example, management might predict today that future sales will fall because of increased marketing activity by a major competitor. Consequently, the firm alters its marketing policies, increases its advertising and public relations expenditure, and generally intensifies its selling efforts in order to counteract the forecast decline in sales.

Closed and open-loop feedback systems

With a closed-loop system, information on current performance automatically adjusts operations in an attempt to rectify divergences between planned and actual activity. For example, the speed of a production line might automatically and instantly adjust itself according to the number of defectives it produces, or inventories might be automatically replenished as stock usage rates increase. Open-loop systems, in contrast, require human intervention. They remain constant unless someone takes the initiative to implement an alteration.

7. Ratio analysis

Some of the key performance ratios that businesses need to monitor are outlined in 16:3. Analysis of such ratios permits the comparison of relative performance figures (rather than absolute amounts) over time. Each department must choose the ratios most relevant to its needs. A credit control department for instance will be interested in the ratio of bad debts to sales, while production managers will want to measure (among others) ratios of costs to outputs and average inventory to purchases. Normal values for key ratios may be predetermined, and acceptable deviations specified. Management by exception procedures (see 5) can then be applied.

Ratios should be relevant to the purpose for which they are intended, and should be computed consistently; data definitions should not be altered without good cause. If a change in the basis of computation is inevitable, ratios calculated using different criteria should not be compared.

8. Co-ordination

This means the unification of effort, i.e. ensuring that everyone within the enterprise is working towards a common goal. Effective co-ordination requires efficient control, which presupposes the existence within the firm of sound information gathering and reporting procedures, appraisal systems, and so on. The main techniques for co-ordinating organisations are as follows:

(a) Appointment of a full-time liaison manager whose main duty is the co-ordination of the work of several subsidiary units. The problem here is deciding to whom this person should report. If the co-ordinator outranks each of the heads of participating units, the status of these units might be lowered. If conversely, the liaison manager is accountable to the head of department (e.g. of an international division), then that department may be seen by others as occupying a special and undeservedly privileged position.

(b) Feedback systems involving frequent reports (possibly on a daily basis) to a central control. Normally, reports will be restricted to key data and to unexpected occurrences (including deviations from targets) since otherwise head office becomes overloaded with information.

(c) Regular face-to-face meetings of managers of the firm's operations in various areas. Note the costs and time involved, and the possibility that discussions at meetings may be trivial.

(d) Standardisation of administrative procedures in all the company's establishments at head office and in subsidiaries, divisions, etc.. Consequently a uniform and simplified set of policies can be applied and monitored 'across the board' to all the firm's operations.

9. Controlling subsidiary operations

The essential issue is whether to centralise decision taking at head office or allow local subsidiary units to control local operations. Factors affecting this decision might include the size and complexity of the business, ease of communications with local units, and the extent of the information on local market conditions available at head office. A two-tier control mechanism might be feasible with tight and centralised monitoring and control of some subsidiary units and the adoption of an arms-length approach elsewhere. Whichever method is adopted, head office needs to be well-informed of local activities, problems and prospects.

Appraising the performances of subsidiaries

Effective appraisal of a subsidiary relies critically on accurate measurement of its performance. Typically, head office will establish standards and measure and establish the reasons for deviations from these norms. Standards might be set for each particular subsidiary and performance assessed against these unique yardsticks, or an identical set of standards could be applied to all subsidiaries, so that the performance of each unit can be evaluated against the performance levels achieved by the others. The advantage to the latter method is that standardised record keeping and reporting procedures may be applied to all subsidiaries.

Foreign subsidiaries

Assessment of the efficiency of a foreign subsidiary and of individual managers who work for it is especially difficult because its profitability will be affected by many factors beyond the parent company's control. Returns in one country may be much lower than in others through taxes, laws, regulations, etc., specific to that country, not through inefficiency in the subsidiary. Also, decisions taken at head office will influence how various subsidiaries perform. Prices, for instance, might be centrally determined, or a subsidiary might be instructed not to sell its output in a market that head office has decided to leave for another subsidiary in another country.

10. Appraisal of foreign subsidiaries

To appraise the performances of its foreign subsidiaries a company needs a continuous flow of information, not only about the internal efficiency of subsidiaries but also about changes in the environments – political, social and economic – in which they operate. A number of difficulties arise in this respect, as follows:

(a) *Choice of currency for measuring profits*
Evaluation against hard quantitative criteria is obviously desirable, but comparisons of subsidiaries' achievements in monetary terms (levels of sales, costs, wage payments, etc.) may not be meaningful because rates of inflation vary enormously between countries. If values are measured in local currency terms, managers in countries with the highest rates of inflation will show the best performances. Why not, therefore, measure monetary variables in real terms expressed in local currency units? The difficulty here is that to compare one operation with others it is necessary to convert the real performance achieved in local currency into some other base currency. Suppose for instance a UK domiciled MNC has plants in Spain, Nigeria and Hong Kong and the profitabilities of these are to be compared. Spanish profits (albeit measured in real terms against some base year) are expressed in pesetas, Nigerian profits in naire, Hong Kong profits in Hong Kong dollars. Meaningful comparisons between the three are not possible unless monetary values are converted into a base currency, say sterling. But then the reported results will depend crucially on fluctuations in the rates of exchange between local currencies and the chosen base. Inflation in the home country will affect currency exchange rates with other countries depending on the extent of the home country's foreign trade with them.

(b) *Differing accounting conventions in host countries*
Accounting conventions vary throughout the world. In some countries assets are valued at cost, in others at market value. Methods of depreciation differ. There are different rules governing share issue, disclosure, debenture arrangements, etc., between nations. Such conventions may be so fundamental that the creation of an entirely separate set of books for the MNC's own auditing might be impossible, or at least extremely difficult.

(c) *Delays in reporting*
Despite vastly improved communications and the increasing availability of international computer linkages, long delays in the transmission of important data might occur. Subsidiaries might not realise the significance of a particular piece of information for the global strategy of the parent corporation, and thus report it late or exclude it altogether.

11. Appraising divisions

Problems similar to those encountered when appraising subsidiaries arise when evaluating the performances of divisions. These problems include:

(a) deciding whether divisions should manage their own idle cash balances or turn them over to a central treasury for investment outside the division (externally or elsewhere in the company);

(b) overhead allocations *vis-à-vis* shared common services (administrative premises for instances) and relating these to estimates for divisional rates of return on capital employed;

(c) assessing the effects of company policies on the profits made by a particular division (e.g. the effects of artificially low input prices from other divisions);

(d) choice of criteria for measuring profitability (absolute money values, rates of return on capital employed, etc);

(e) deciding whether each division is to be regarded as a cost centre in its own right ('buying in' materials and services from other divisions).

BUDGETING

12. Nature of budgets

Budgeting is perhaps the most widely used of all control methods. Budgets are at one and the same time a device for allocating resources, an aid to planning, a forecast of future events, and a set of instructions to departments and individual managers. Budgets compare actual costs and achievements with planned achievements and expenditures. Upper spending limits (or minimum performance standards – sales or production levels for instance) are specified for each of a number of functions (purchase of supplies, secretarial assistance, office equipment, etc.) over a predetermined period (usually 12 months). The amounts given to departments are then broken down into subsidiary budgets relating to specific tasks. Hence, for example, the marketing department's budget might be split into components for advertising, marketing research, distribution, sales promotions and so on.

Budgets and plans

Budgets outline the financial implications of corporate plans and the resources necessary to implement them. Also they provide a convenient device for monitoring progress towards the attainment of the firm's operational goals. Plans specify objectives, identify strategic issues, and outline the anticipated consequences of intended actions. Budgets relate to plans in that they are explicit policy statements, indicating the organisation's concrete intentions regarding resource allocation, departmental responsibilities for various activities, and timetables for the completion of projects. They are quantitative statements (whereas plans might contain qualitative elements) and highly detailed. Hopefully, plans and budgets will coincide as activities develop, although budgets are normally less flexible than plans.

13. Purposes of budgeting

Budgets provide a quantitative statement of the firm's targets and plans. The basic purposes of budgeting are:

(a) to facilitate co-ordination and control. There needs to exist a budget that correlates with each major aspect of the company's operations, hence allowing the delegation of authority without significant loss of control;

(b) to enable senior management to take a bird's-eye view of the spending patterns of the entire organisation;

(c) to constrain expenditure;

(d) to provide a basis for performance appraisal and management by objectives;

(e) to facilitate delegation;

(f) to highlight problems as quickly as possible.

Advantages of budgeting

In preparing budgets, management is compelled to relate resource requirements to corporate objectives; and the meetings, discussions, joint decision making and general co-ordination of activities necessitated by budget planning encourage co-operation and common approaches to achieving company aims. Budgets impose financial discipline on those responsible for their administration. Spendthrift departments are identified and can be penalised by reductions in future allocations, while cost increases which cause rapid exhaustion of existing budgets can be isolated and their effects on the organisation as a whole assessed. Further advantages to budgetary control include the following:

(a) The firm's existing accounting systems are utilised.

(b) A common denominator (money) is used to compare disparate activities.

(c) Attainment of budgeting targets is directly and identifiably related to the company's profits.

(d) Observed deviations of actual from budgeted figures may be quickly detected and investigated.

(e) Excessive costs can be traced back to those responsible for them and unacceptably expensive activities can be curtailed.

14. Problems with budgeting

A number of difficulties attach to the budgeting process, as follows:

(a) Managers sometimes deliberately overspend in order to strengthen their arguments for increased allocations in future periods.

(b) Attempts to keep within budget limits may cause managers to cut costs excessively, thus depriving the firm of essential investments in new equipment, machines and administrative facilities.

(c) Budgeting might act as a surrogate for more general corporate planning. A budgetary system should be an outcome to the planning process, not a stand-alone process.

(d) Heads of department often ask for larger budgets than are actually necessary, in anticipation of having their budgets cut. The determination of sensible budgets becomes haphazard in these circumstances.

(e) Some budgets are overspent, others do not use all the funds available. Thus, a mechanism (referred to as 'virement') is necessary for transferring unused balances to areas which require extra funds. So why bother with budgets in the first instance? Note that the preparation of detailed budgets is time consuming and expensive.

(f) It is difficult to distinguish between a budget which has been exceeded because of genuine additional spending requirements and one exceeded through administrative incompetence.

(g) Budgets can hide inefficiencies. Naturally, managers will seek to spend all the money they receive even if the expenditure is not objectively necessary.

(h) If a budget remains unspent towards the end of a financial year, departmental managers might indulge in wasteful spending simply to exhaust the outstanding balance.

(i) Budgeting can become a complex, bureaucratic and ritualistic exercise so cumbersome that it generates meaningless results.

(j) The process may come to be seen by departmental managers as a punitive device intended to curtail their innovatory potential.

(k) Certain managers might possess superior political and negotiating skills relative to colleagues and use these to obtain budget allocations they do not really need.

Conditions for success

If they are to succeed, budgeting systems require:

(a) the full and committed support of top management;

(b) the backing of a sound management information system;

(c) policies consistent with the attainment of budgetary objectives;

(d) honesty and a sense of responsibility among the people who bid for budget allocations;

(e) the active participation in the budgetary process of those who will be responsible for implementing the system. This is referred to as 'bottom-up' budgeting, as opposed to 'top-down' budgeting whereby senior management simply imposes budgetary constraints on lower levels. The value of a bottom-up approach lies in the fact that departmental and/or functional managers are more likely to be able to assess accurately their own needs, provided they approach the task honestly. See 16.21 for further information on top-down planning.

Further requirements are that budgets be set for each major area of activity/ responsibility within the firm and that performance standards necessary to attain them be specified. Comparisons between actual and budget outcomes must be made on a regular basis and all significant differences quickly investigated. Budgets should be reasonable, attainable and directly relevant to departmental needs.

15. The budgeting process

Most budgetary control systems begin by considering carefully the sales forecasts embodied in a firm's marketing plan. These indicate anticipated revenues from the sale of target numbers of units of output at certain prices allowing for the effects of bulk order discounts and/or special promotions (money-off coupons, etc.) and associated costs. The expected costs of creating the level of input envisaged in the sales forecasts will be set out in the firm's production, overheads and capital expenditure budgets. Figure 18.1 illustrates the process.

Major budgets within a system might include the following.

The production budget

This specifies the expected cost of creating a certain volume of output, allowing for the cost of overtime working, for warehousing and other inventory costs and for raw materials and finished component purchases. Usually, separate sub-budgets are established for the acquisition of significant inputs. For example, a raw materials budget might be established to plan the purchase and delivery of raw materials and to ensure that storage facilities are available when they arrive.

The labour utilisation budget

The purpose of this budget is to itemise the costs of employing and deploying labour, including training costs, recruitment expenses, overtime costs, plus estimated losses caused by employee sickness and other sources of absenteeism.

Plant utilisation budgets

These state the planned costs of operating various categories of plant and equipment. (The technical difference between 'plant' and 'equipment' is that plant is fixed in location, whereas equipment can be moved around.) Maintenance costs are usually included here.

Overheads budget

For budgeting purposes overhead items are broken down into categories for production, marketing and administration, and for generic items such as rent. Often, research and development expenditures are classed as a general overhead and thus incorporated into this budget rather than treated as an operating expense.

The capital expenditure budget

Acquisitions of major items of capital plant and equipment benefit the firm for several years (or more). Thus, even though capital assets might be paid for in a

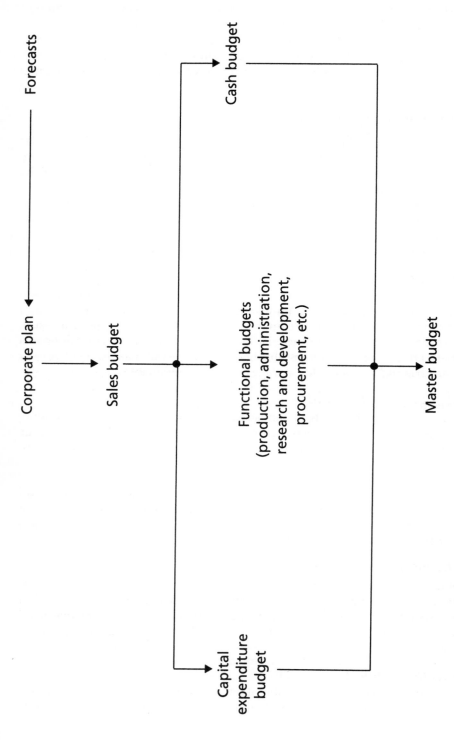

Figure 18.1 The budgeting process

lump sum, only a proportion of their total cost should be set against the capital expenditure budget for a particular period.

Additional budgets may be prepared for administrative costs such as general management, legal services, audit fees, etc., and for whichever particular functions (personnel, packaging, distribution, special production processes) are relevant to the firm.

All budgets which are measured in monetary units are drawn together in a master budget showing all anticipated operating and capital expenditures grouped together under appropriate headings. Thereafter, differences between actual and budget figures must be measured periodically (e.g. weekly, monthly or quarterly) and incorporated into budget reports.

16. Allocation methods

Longer-term budgets may be variable or fixed. Variable budgets relate the amounts allocated to appropriate performance indices. Marketing budgets, for example, are frequently determined by the volume of sales achieved – it is assumed that increasing sales will require additional marketing resources in order to sustain and continue expansion. This approach ignores the possibility that extra expenditure on marketing functions – advertising, sales promotions, new product development, etc. – could actually cause initial increases in sales. Another technique of variable budgeting is the simultaneous specification of not one but several different budgets for the same department or activity. The actual budget applied will depend on the particular circumstances prevailing at the moment of implementation. Here, the firm recognises the impossibility of foreseeing all future circumstances and so makes allowance for a range of contingencies. Several other approaches to budget allocation are possible, as follows:

(a) The responsibility (operational) approach. Individuals are asked how much they need in order to achieve predetermined objectives. Resources are then distributed for administering the resulting budgets.

(b) Rolling budgets. The budget allocated for the next 12 months is set equal to actual expenditures during the previous 12 months, updated on a month by month basis.

(c) Competitive parity. The firm estimates and copies the budgets allocated to various functions by major competitors.

(d) The profit level approach. Departmental budgets are automatically increased when profits are high and vice versa.

(e) The zero-base approach. This attempts to overcome the problem of managers deliberately overspending in order to increase future allocations. There is no presumption whatsoever that the amount given during one budgetary period will be repeated. Indeed, each departmental budget is initially set at zero, assuming thereby that no funds at all will be made available in the future. Hence, heads of department must argue for a new allocation at the start of each and every period. Intended activities have to be respecified and their expected costs re-estimated. Managers are forced to review periodically their plans and working methods, thus encouraging the identification of high cost activities. The draw-back to zero-base budgeting is the enormous amounts of time managers must devote to periodic assessments of costs and to the repeated presentation of budget proposals.

17. Limiting factors

These are the major constraints which limit an organisation's activities (and hence its ability to spend). Usually the dominant constraint is expected sales revenue since this determines how much money will (or should) be available to purchase the inputs needed to produce the goods. Other possible limiting factors (sometimes called 'principal budget factors') are shortages of labour, scarcities of raw materials, or restricted machine capacities. Budget systems normally proceed by first preparing those budgets most critically affected by the principal limiting factors. Thus, for example, a business that faces acute shortages of skilled labour will draft its labour utilization budget before considering anything else.

18. Budget reports

These should be clear, precise and easily understood by recipients. They must highlight problems and, wherever possible, indicate the measures necessary for their solution. Note how report formats that appeal to accountants might utterly confuse other managers. The following rules should be applied to budgetary reporting procedures:

(a) Figures quoted in reports should be directly comparable between one period and the next. Data definitions and the time intervals to which information refers should be stated.

(b) Reporting procedures should be regularly reviewed to avoid duplication of information.

(c) Problems should be reported to the managers who are empowered and in a position to take corrective action.

(d) Statements of the causes of divergences and the measures needed to rectify them should, whenever possible, be included with reports. Guidelines regarding appropriate remedial action should be available so that a large divergence of actual from budget performance will automatically trigger relevant follow-up action.

Progress test 18

1. Control has three aspects. What are they?

2. List six devices for effecting control.

3. What is a 'procedure'?

4. Explain the difference between feedforward and feedback control systems.

5. List four techniques for co-ordinating the activities of a large organisation.

6. What are the special problems attatched to the appraisal of foreign subsidiaries?

7. How do budgets relate to plans?

8. List some of the problems associated with budgeting.

APPENDIX I

REFERENCES AND BIBLIOGRAPHY

Ansoff, H.I., 'Strategies for Diversification'. *Harvard Business Review*, Sept–Oct, 1957

Ansoff, H.I., *Implementing Strategic Management*, Prentice-Hall, 1984

Argyris, C., 'Double Loop Learning in Organisations', *Harvard Business Review*, Sept/Oct 1977

Bennis, W., *Organisation Development: Its Nature, Origins and Prospects*, Addison-Wesley, 1969

Borden, N.H., 'The Concept of the Marketing Mix', in *Science in Marketing*, G.Schwartz (ed.), Wiley, 1965

Buckley, P.J., Pass, C., and Prescott, K., 'Measures of International Competitiveness: A Critical Survey'. in *Journal of Marketing Management*, 4(2), 1989

Burns, T., and Stalker, G.M., *The Management of Innovation*, Tavistock Publications, 1961

Carnal, C.A., *Managing Change*, Routledge, 1990

Chandler, A.D., *Strategy and Structure*, MIT Press, Cambridge, Mass., 1962.

Chandler, A.D., *The Visible Hand: The Managerial Revolution in American Business*, Harvard University Press, 1977.

Child, J., *Organisation: A Guide to Problems and Practice*, Harper and Row, 1977.

Collingridge, O., *The Social Control of Technology*, Open University Press, 1980.

Day. G., 'Diagnosing the Product Portfolio', *Journal of Marketing*, April 1977.

Drucker, P.F., *Concept of the Corporation*, John Day, New York, 1946.

Drucker, P.F., *Managing in Turbulent Times*, Harper and Row, 1980.

Fayol, H., *General and Industrial Management*, Dunod, Paris, 1916.

Freeman, R.E., *Strategic Management*, Pitman, 1984.

Goold, M., and Campbell, A.L, *Strategies and Styles*, Blackwell, 1987.

Greenley, G.E., 'Does Strategic Planning Improve Performance?', *Long Range Planning*, Vol. 19(2), 1986.

Handy. C., *Understanding Organisations*, Penguin, 1976.

Harrigan, K.R., *Strategies for Declining Businesses*, Lexington Books, 1980.

Hax, A.C., and Majluf, N.S., 'The Use of Growth-Share Matrix in Strategic Planning'. *Interfaces*, 13(1), February 1983.

Hayes, R., Clark, K.B., and Wheelwright, S., *Dynamic Manufacturing*, Free Press, New York, 1988.

Hurst, D.K., 'Why Strategic Management is Bankrupt', *Organisational Dynamics*, Autumn 1986.

Kanter, R.M., *The Change Masters*, Simon and Schuster, New York, 1983.

Kotter, J.P., and Schlesinger, L.A., 'Choosing Strategies for Change', *Harvard Business Review*. March-April 1979.

Lawrence, P.R., and Lorsch, J.W., *Organisation and Environment*, Harvard University Press, 1967.

Lewin, K., *A Dynamic Theory of Personality*, McGraw-Hill, New York, 1935.

Lewin, K., 'Frontiers in Group Dynamics', *Human Relations* 1, No.1, 1947.

McCarthy, E.J., *Basic Marketing: A Managerial Approach*, Irwin, 1981.

Mintzberg, H., *The Rise and Fall of Strategic Management*, Prentice-Hall, 1994.

Perrow, C., *Organisational Analysis: A Sociological View*, Tavistock Publications, 1970.

Peters, T.J., and Waterman, R.H., *In Search of Excellence*, Harper and Row, 1982.

Porter,M., *Competitive Strategy*, The Free Press, New York, 1980.

Porter, M., *Competitive Advantage*, The Free Press, New York , 1985.

Porter, M., *The Competitive Advantage of Nations*, MacMillan, 1990.

Quin, J.B., *Strategy for Change: Logical Incrementalism*, Irwin , 1980.

Senge, P.M., *The fifth discipline: The art and practice of the learning organisation*, Century Business, London, 1990.

Simon, H.A., *Administrative Behaviour*, MacMillan, 1960.

Skinner, W., 'The Focused Factory', *Harvard Business Review*, Issue 3, 1974.

Sloan, A.P., *My Years with General Motors*, Doubleday, New York, 1954.

Stacey, R., *Strategic Management and Organisational Dynamics*, Pitman, 1992.

Ulrich, D., and Lake, D., *Organisational Capability*, Wiley, 1990.

Urwick, L., *Scientific Principles of Organisation*, American Management Association, New York, 1938.

Wilson, R.M.S., 'Corporate Strategy and Management Control', in Hussey, D.E. (ed) *International Review of Strategic Management*, Wiley, 1991.

Zaleznik, A., 'Power and Politics in Organisational Life', *Harvard Business Review*, May–June 1970.

APPENDIX 2

EXAMINATION TECHNIQUE

1. Before the examination. There is no substitute for sound preparation prior to sitting an examination in strategic management. Students need to have read through their notes several times, and to possess an adequate grasp of relevant theories, principles and applications.

Practice in writing essays is essential, especially for students who have not written essays for a considerable time. Examiners recognise that essays written in examination conditions – hurriedly and under stress – will not be grammatically perfect, but they do demand certain minimum standards and will penalise students whose written presentation is not up to scratch. Accordingly, the student should avoid using vague, meaningless statements; try to spell correctly, and seek to cultivate a direct and forthright style using short clear sentences.

2. Past examination papers. Analysis of past examination papers provides a valuable insight into how the examiners feel about the subject. Often, the same questions reappear year after year, albeit written slightly differently. While it is obviously useful to predict questions, students should always remember that no question can ever be guaranteed to come up. Also, syllabuses and examiners change, and each examiner has personal preferences regarding the content and style of questions that need to be asked.

3. Inside the examination room. Students must read questions carefully and ensure they fully understand what each question is asking. It is a good idea to underline key words and to break the question down into separate component parts.

A question might ask the student to describe things (questions beginning 'What do you understand by ...?', or 'List and explain ...' are usually of this type), or it could require the student to 'compare and contrast' various techniques or concepts. In the latter case, simple description is not sufficient. Rather, the student must highlight the similarities and differences between the items discussed.

For questions starting with the words 'Explain' or 'Examine', description of a topic should be supplemented with examples, counter-examples, alternatives (where appropriate), and a list of advantages and disadvantages. Similarly, questions involving quotations followed by the word 'Discuss' invite candidates to identify crucial issues and to interpret and comment on various aspects of the topic.

4. Planning time. The first few minutes of the time allocated to each answer should be used for jotting down the main points of the answer in an essay plan. Thereafter the following rules should be observed:

(a) The time allowed for each answer (a three hour paper demanding five answers permits 36 minutes per question) must be adhered to rigidly. As soon as the period is up the student should move on to the next question.

(b) Students should leave a space at the end of the question in order to be able to come back to the question if he or she has any spare time at the end of the examination.

(c) Easy questions should be answered first. This increases the student's confidence, assists concentration and establishes rhythm for tackling the rest of the paper. However, students should not spend too much time on easy questions. Each answer needs to be of approximately equal length.

It is a well-established fact that the bulk of a candidate's marks obtained on a specific question are achieved in the first ten or fifteen minutes of writing; extra marks then become progressively harder to obtain. By spending too long on a question the student only gets a fraction of the marks available for the first couple of paragraphs of the next answer.

5. Essay plans. These should include not only the major points to be emphasised, but also particular topics. Preparation of a good essay plan saves time in the long run and the examiner can see at once how much the student knows about the subject. Examiners usually want to mark scripts in the shortest possible time, and are pleased to give marks to candidates who openly exhibit their knowledge in a rough essay plan. The plan guides the student (and the examiner) through the essay. Supplementary information can be added and chosen themes expanded as the essay is developed.

6. Situation-based questions and mini-cases. To answer questions of this type the student should proceed as follows.

(*i*) State the essential nature of the issues and problems raised by the case.
(*ii*) Analyse the circumstances of the case using a technique (e.g. SWOTs or the Seven-S system), appropriate for the particular situation. Environmental factors must be considered.
(*iii*) Define the objectives which the people or organisations mentioned in the case need to achieve in order to improve their position.
(*iv*) List the difficulties involved in attaining objectives, plus alternative options and their implications.

It is most unwise to leave an examination before the end, as there is nearly always something useful that can be added to answers. The script should be re-read and extra points inserted – on separate sheets for subsequent insertion in the answer book if necessary – though irrelevant statements and useless repetition of points must be avoided.

APPENDIX 3

SAMPLE EXAMINATION QUESTIONS

The following questions are reproduced with the kind permission of the professional bodies listed below.

Chartered Institute of Management Accountants (CIMA)
Institute of Administrative Management (IAM)
Chartered Insurance Institute (CII)
Chartered Institute of Bankers (CIOB)
Institute of Management Services (IMS)
Chartered Association of Certified Accountants (ACCA)
Institute of Chartered Secretaries and Administrators (ICSA)
Communication, Advertising and Marketing Foundation (CAM)
London Chamber of Commerce and Industry (LCCI)
Chartered Institute of Marketing (CIM)

1. (*a*) Define 'strategic management'
   (*b*) Define the major factors that influence the effectiveness of strategic management.
   (LCCI)

2. What is corporate planning, and why is it carried out? Describe and show the relationships between its different components at strategic, tactical and operational levels.
   (ACCA)

3. State six steps that are essential for the implementation of a strategic plan.   (CII)

4. Summarise the role of the board of directors of a company.   (CII)

5. How is planning related to other managerial processes?   (CIOB)

6. What is meant by 'control' as a management function? What are the essential requirements for a manager to exercise effective control?   (CII)

7. Describe and compare critical path analysis (CPA) and programme evaluation review technique (PERT). What are some of the advantages and disadvantages of these techniques as management tools?   (ACCA)

8. Amongst the key activities of a manager within a 'business as usual' environment are:
   (*a*) forecasting
   (*b*) planning
   (*c*) organising and
   (*d*) monitoring and controlling.

Briefly describe each of these activities. (CIOB)

9. (a) How should long-term organisational objectives be set?
   (b) Discuss the possible conflict between long-term and short-term objectives, indicating how you would resolve this conflict and achieve a reconciliation of these aims. (IAM)

10. Why is it necessary for companies to establish and periodically review their objectives? What objectives should a business aim to achieve? (CIM)

11. The senior management of your organisation has expressed the opinion that 'social responsibility' should be exercised by the firm's managers.
    (a) What do you understand by 'social responsibility'?
    (b) How would you envisage this being implemented by management? (IAM)

12. Social responsibility may be defined as the obligations which an organisation has towards society and the broad environment in which the organisation operates. Management, therefore, should concern itself with the way in which the organisation interacts with its environment.

   Explain how and to what extent should management recognise social responsibility extending beyond the boundaries of the organisation. (ICSA)

13. You are required:
    (a) to list five aspects of the environment that affect organisations
    (b) for each of these aspects, to describe the environmental trends likely to affect an international company during the next ten years. (CIMA)

14. A UK company manufactures marine instrumentation which it sells throughout the world. The board of directors has asked you as management services manager to propose mechanisms by which it can monitor response to the social and political changes expected over the next five years. Describe appropriate monitoring policies and procedures for the company. (IMS)

15. Identify the various groups who have a stake in the performance of a public limited company. What are the responsibilities of management towards each group and what are the possible conflicts arising from the exercise of these responsibilities? (CIOB)

16. Among the 'stakeholders' in a large financial organisation are:

    (i) the community, and
    (ii) the state.

List the organisation's main responsibilities to each of the stakeholders mentioned above. (CIOB)

17. Describe some of the major advantages and disadvantages of decentralising decision making in organisations. (IAM)

18. (a) Discuss the essential elements in the design of a well balanced and effective organisation.
    (b) Indicate the possible effects on the organisation of any deficient elements. (IAM)

19. (a) Organisation structures may be 'tall' or 'flat'. Explain this statement.

(b) State and comment in each case on four advantages of:

(i) 'tall' structures

(ii) 'flat' structures. (IAM)

20. Discuss the research work of Lawrence and Lorsch into organisation structure, and comment on their conclusions. (CIMA)

21. What is the organisational purpose of divisionalisation? Comment on the advantages and disadvantages to a business organisation of pursuing a policy of divisionalisation. (ACCA)

22. Describe the line and staff system of organisation. Give two examples of staff manager and the general nature of the duties they perform to line staff. (CIMA)

23. You are required to describe the structure of an organisation of your choice, and to explain the advantages this structure has over others which might have been used. Relate your answer to the concepts of organisation theory. Include an organisation chart. (CIMA)

24. Functional departments tend to have priorities which conflict with those of other functional departments. You are required to explain briefly

(a) three conflicting priorities which occur between marketing departments and operations departments

(b) two conflicting priorities which occur between marketing departments and research and development departments. (CIMA)

25. The focus of much marketing activity is to place before the customer, the right product, at the right time and at the right price. Examine how the marketing function of an organisation seeks to achieve these aims. (IAM)

26. 'Product pricing is the essence of effective marketing'. Discuss. (LCCI)

27. Is there such a thing as global marketing, or does the marketing strategy have to be planned differently for each country? (LCCI)

28. How can computer-based information systems influence organisational structures? (ICSA)

29. Some time ago an organisation decided to automate one of its business functions. A number of personnel were recruited to form an information technology department. The various knowledge areas required in the department's work were identified, and the department was structured accordingly. Completion of the first project took much longer than expected because the demarcation between disciplines caused disputes, during which some tasks were not carried out.

As there was a growing need for automation, it was decided to restructure the department so that each project has its own team to complete the work. There is now seen to be a waste of resources due to overlapping and therefore duplication of effort.

You are required to:

(a) analyse and explain the development of this service department so far

(b) propose an alternative structure which might avoid the problems experienced and identify other problems which might occur with your proposed structure. (CIMA)

30. Decision making at the strategic level in organisations needs to be supported by information systems that are flexible and responsive. How important is this statement given the present climate of change? (ICSA)

31. When developing a strategic plan it is essential to consider the organisation's operating environment. Discuss. (CII)

32. Explain and comment on the objectives, techniques and management of quality control in manufacturing or service enterprises. Illustrate your answer using examples with which you are familiar. (ACCA)

33. Describe and comment on the role of the research and development (R&D) function in a business enterprise? What are some of the problems associated with the management of R&D? (ACCA)

34. What factors should affect the decision of the size of batches to put into production? (CIMA)

35. (a) 'The distinction between policy and strategy is not clear'. Explain this statement, with particular reference to personnel policy and strategy.
(b) Indicate, with relevant examples, the procedures you would use in devising personnel policies. (IAM)

36. It has been argued that human resources management, properly conceived and executed, is worthwhile only for organisations with more than 1,000 employees. How far would you agree? (ICSA)

37. State six objectives of financial planning in the development of a business plan. (CII)

38. (a) What is the relationship of the Corporate Plan of an organisation to the development of departmental budgets?
(b) Explain how budgets, expressed in monetary terms, can be used to achieve the objectives of the Corporate Plan when these objectives are not capable of being exactly quantified. (IAM)

39. A publicly quoted consumer advertising agency group wishing to expand into public relations is considering buying a privately owned consultancy specialising in consumer and financial public relations. What broad strategic and financial issues and alternatives might the board of the agency consider in deciding whether or not it should acquire the consultancy? Specifically, what financial considerations and fund raising options are available to the agency? What information sources might help their decision making? (CAM)

INDEX